The PICK Operating System

A PRACTICAL GUIDE

The PICK Operating System

A PRACTICAL GUIDE

Roger J. Bourdon
Aston Technology Ltd

ADDISON-WESLEY PUBLISHING COMPANY

Wokingham, England · Reading, Massachusetts · Menlo Park, California
New York · Don Mills, Ontario · Amsterdam · Bonn
Sydney · Singapore · Tokyo · Madrid · San Juan

The programs in this book have been included for their instructional value. They have been tested with care but are not guaranteed for any particular purpose. The publisher does not offer any warranties or representations, nor does it accept any liabilities with respect to the programs.

The PICK Operating System is a proprietary software product of Pick Systems, Irvine, California. This publication contains material whose use is restricted to authorized users of the Pick System. Any other use of the descriptions and information contained herein is improper.

Cover design by Ken Arlotte.
Typeset by Columns, Reading.
Printed in Great Britain by T J Press (Padstow) Ltd, Cornwall.

First printed 1987. Reprinted 1987, 1988, 1989 and 1990

British Library Cataloguing in Publication Data

Bourdon, Roger J.
The PICK operating system : a practical guide.
1. Pick (Computer operating system)
I. Title
005.4′3 QA76.76.063

ISBN 0–201–18055–3

Library of Congress Cataloging in Publication Data

Bourdon, Roger J. (Roger James), 1947–
The PICK operating system.

Includes index.
1. PICK (Computer operating system) I. Title.
QA76.76.063B65 1987 005.4′46 86–17330
ISBN 0–201–18055–3 (pbk.)

To Alf and Ivy

Foreword

The PICK system is the computing environment choice among software developers and companies that depend on computers to control all phases of their business. PICK has played this role over the last ten years and its acceptance continues to grow, particularly with the recent introduction of PICK on microcomputers. The popularity of the PICK system has created an increasing need for more off-the-shelf books on its benefits and internal workings. This book by Roger Bourdon is admirably suited to meet this need. It is detailed in its explanations of the technical aspects of PICK but does it in simple terms. It also includes numerous examples – many of which are taken directly from computer screens. The book will be useful both as a reference manual for the seasoned professional and to expose new people to the benefits of PICK. It may also serve well as a text book for university students both in the computer sciences and in business schools.

PICK Systems is very grateful to Roger Bourdon for his effort in writing this book. We feel it will help in the effort to expose the business computing community to this easily-used and powerful operating system environment.

Phil Earl
Director of Product Management, PICK Systems

It is a tribute to the interests of PICK users that this publication, *The PICK Operating System: A Practical Guide*, is written. The interest has spread from a small group of dedicated users to a worldwide following. The heart of the PICK system is a 'Data Model' that can closely store information in real world relationships. It was designed for business and can totally automate the working environment. Once a user or programmer experiences PICK, there is a dedication and enthusiasm not seen in other data processing circles. Today, PICK is a Business Solution Standard. Other software strives for PICK functionality. This book will provide a strong influence for stimulating future awareness about the PICK operating system.

Paul Anderson
Formerly Director of Education, PICK Systems

Preface

Until three years ago, I had working experience of many operating systems, but none of PICK. As soon as I was involved with PICK I became one of its loyal fans and advocates. I had to learn the hard way, as at that time there were no publications or training courses available. This book contains the information I have acquired during the past few years, explained in detail and illustrated richly with examples.

In recent years much greater importance has been placed on the capability of the operating system and on the issue of software portability. In this respect the PICK operating system has been seen to emerge as a recent finding. In fact, the PICK operating system is a well established and proven operating system and is now seen to be a prime contender in the race to find an 'industry standard' operating system for multi-user computers.

PICK is an extremely sophisticated, yet easy to use, operating system which, by virtue of its structure, is best suited for commercial and business applications. This book, lavish with examples, provides a practical approach in its detailed and comprehensive description of the PICK operating system, and is described in terms that are both simple and easy to understand. It fully describes those aspects of PICK essential to anyone responsible for the management of a PICK-based computer system. Whilst aimed at those using or considering PICK for the first time, it equally provides a comprehensive and valuable reference for the more experienced user.

This book covers each of the major features of the PICK operating system in a completely practical and fully illustrated manner. It starts, therefore, with how the system is powered up and continues its step-by-step description of each facet of PICK until the reader is able to produce his own management information and manage and control the entire system.

It contains a detailed description of the data structure, which is what sets PICK apart from other operating systems, and subsequent chapters describe the other major elements of PICK such as the use of printers, the editor, the programming language (PICK BASIC), the procedure processor (PROC) and the powerful enquiry language (ACCESS). The book illustrates methods for ensuring the security and integrity of the system and advice on carrying out day-to-day management tasks. Finally, it devotes a complete chapter to the PICK implementation on the IBM PC and compatibles, discusses the implication of fourth-generation application generators and concludes by looking at PICK's position as an operating system and its future in the commercial world.

Acknowledgements

I would like to thank Kim Jones for her support and encouragement during the many, many hours taken to write this book and John Taylor, BSc(Hons), MIAP, AMBCS, and Marcus van Raaltè for their assistance with its preparation.

Whilst every effort has been made to ensure the accuracy of this book, the author cannot guarantee that the book is error-free or accurate, nor can he accept responsibility for any problems associated with its use. It should be noted that there are differences of implementation on a number of manufacturers' computer systems which frequently result in minor differences of operation.

PICK is the registered trademark of PICK Systems, Irvine, California.

Roger Bourdon
Birmingham, 1986

Contents

Foreword vii

Preface ix

Chapter 1 Introduction 1

1.1 An overview of PICK 1
1.2 How the operating system developed 4

Chapter 2 The PICK Database Structure 7

Chapter 3 Getting Started 11

3.1 Powering up and powering down 11
3.1.1 Powering up 11
3.1.2 Powering down 14
3.2 Logging on and logging off 14
3.2.1 Logging on 14
3.2.2 Logging off 14
3.3 Looking around your system 16

Chapter 4 The Handling of Data 21

4.1 The handling of accounts 21
4.1.1 Creating an account 21
4.1.2 Removing an account 22
4.2 File handling 23
4.2.1 Creating a file 23
4.2.2 Creating multiple files with a common dictionary 24
4.2.3 Removing a file 25
4.2.4 Clearing a file 25
4.3 Data handling 26
4.3.1 Creating data items 26
4.3.2 Removing data items 26
4.3.3 Copying items 26

4.3.4 Changing item-ids 29

Chapter 5 The PICK Database Structure in Detail 31

5.1 The PICK database structure explained 31
5.1.1 Data file structure 34
5.1.2 The dictionaries 36
5.1.3 Dictionary item types 39
5.2 File allocation and information retrieval 40
5.2.1 Disk map 41
5.2.2 Frame allocation 41
5.2.3 The storage and retrieval of items in a file 46
5.2.4 Frame and group formats 46
5.2.5 How to size files correctly 46
5.3 Checking item distribution and optimizing file size 49
5.4 File sizing and resizing 52

Chapter 6 Q-Pointers 54

6.1 Reasons for use of Q-pointers 54
6.2 User identification (user-id) 55
6.3 Q-pointers to files 56
6.4 Temporary Q-pointers 58

Chapter 7 Using the Editor 60

7.1 An introduction to the editor 60
7.2 Editor concepts 60
7.3 A summary of the editor commands 62
7.4 Using the editor 65
7.4.1 Adding new items with the editor 65
7.4.2 Changing the details of an item 66
7.4.3 The principles of replacing data 68
7.4.4 Merging data with the editor 70
7.4.5 Using the search facility 71
7.4.6 Using the wildcard facility 71
7.4.7 The use of prestored commands 73

Chapter 8 Printer Control 77

8.1 An introduction to the spooler 77
8.1.1 Spooler options 80
8.1.2 LISTPTR, LISTPEQS, SP-STATUS and LISTABS 80
8.2 Adding and removing printers 84
8.2.1 The STARTPTR command 84
8.2.2 The STOPPTR command 85
8.2.3 The SP-KILL command 87
8.3 Directing printer output with SP-ASSIGN 90
8.4 Manipulating the spooler with SP-EDIT 91

8.4.1 SP-EDIT options 93
8.4.2 The interactive session of SP-EDIT 94
8.4.3 Removing reports using SP-EDIT 95
8.4.4 Redirecting reports with SP-EDIT 95
8.4.5 Restarting reports with SP-EDIT 96
8.5 How to handle spooler and printer problems 96
8.6 Control of the printer via PROC 98

Chapter 9 Information Retrieval Using ACCESS 99

9.1 An introduction to ACCESS 99
9.2 The principles of file dictionaries 101
9.2.1 The structure of file dictionary records 102
9.3 The ACCESS enquiry language 127
9.3.1 Producing unsequenced reports 131
9.3.2 Producing reports in sorted sequence 137
9.3.3 Specifying the data to be output 138
9.3.4 Modifiers and options 139
9.3.5 Accessing individual values of multi-values 142
9.3.6 The use of throwaway connectives 143
9.3.7 Selection criteria 144
9.3.8 The use of breaks and totals 145
9.3.9 Headings and footings 150
9.3.10 Producing output in label format 150
9.3.11 Miscellaneous ACCESS verbs 153
9.3.12 The principles and uses of 'lists' 154
9.3.13 The SELECT and SSELECT verbs 156
9.3.14 Saving and manipulating saved lists 158
9.4 Summary 159

Chapter 10 Programming in PICK BASIC 160

10.1 An introduction to PICK BASIC 160
10.2 Creating, compiling and running BASIC programs 161
10.3 PICK BASIC conventions 167
10.4 The control of terminals in BASIC 169
10.4.1 Terminal input 169
10.4.2 Terminal output 171
10.4.3 Special screen control functions 172
10.4.4 Format masks 173
10.4.5 Limiting the data printed 174
10.4.6 Sounding the bell 176
10.5 The control of printers in BASIC 176
10.5.1 Headings, footings and page throws 177
10.6 File control in PICK BASIC 180
10.6.1 The OPEN statement 180
10.6.2 The READ statement 181
10.6.3 The WRITE statement 183
10.6.4 The DELETE statement 185

10.7 Handling arrays in BASIC 186
10.8 The handling of variables in BASIC 188
10.9 Multi-user aspects of file control 189
10.10 Handling dynamic arrays in BASIC 191
10.10.1 The INSERT and REPLACE statements 192
10.10.2 The DELETE and EXTRACT statements 192
10.10.3 The LOCATE statement 194
10.10.4 The COUNT and DCOUNT statements 197
10.11 Structured programming 198
10.11.1 Internal subroutines 199
10.11.2 The IF statement 200
10.11.3 The CASE statement 200
10.11.4 Various methods of programming 202
10.11.5 The handling of external routines 204
10.12 Other program statements 213
10.12.1 The date and time 214
10.12.2 The SYSTEM statement 216
10.12.3 Other string functions 217
10.13 Batch processing 218
10.13.1 The PROCREAD and PROCWRITE statements 221
10.14 The interactive debugger 224
10.15 BASIC optimization techniques 229

Chapter 11 The Procedure Language – PROC 233

11.1 An introduction to PROC 233
11.2 A simple PROC using the C,H,P and STOFF commands 235
11.3 The use of the STACK 238
11.4 Screen formatting and cursor control 240
11.5 Moving parameters with the A command 242
11.6 Conditional operations with IF and GO 244
11.6.1 Further forms of the IF statement 244
11.7 Linking to other PROCs 246
11.7.1 Transferring control to another PROC 246
11.7.2 Using another PROC as a subroutine 246
11.8 Printer control under PROC 249

Chapter 12 RUNOFF – the Text Processor 252

12.1 An introduction to RUNOFF 252
12.2 RUNOFF command summary 252
12.3 Special control characters in RUNOFF 255
12.4 Using RUNOFF 256
12.5 Some useful tips 258
12.5.1 The BOX command 258
12.5.2 The PARAGRAPH command 258
12.5.3 The TEST PAGE command 260
12.5.4 The FILL, NOFILL and JUSTIFY commands 260
12.5.5 Mailmerge techniques using READNEXT and CHAIN 261

12.5.6 The HEADING and FOOTING commands 262
12.5.7 Producing an index 264

Chapter 13 Security and Integrity 265

13.1 An introduction to security 265
13.1.1 Password protection 266
13.1.2 System privilege levels 266
13.1.3 Update (L/UPD) and retrieval (L/RET) lock codes 267
13.1.4 Restricting TCL access 268
13.1.5 Restricting use of TCL verbs 268
13.1.6 The System Accounting History file ACC 268
13.2 An introduction to integrity 273
13.2.1 Tape and floppy disk handling 274
13.2.2 System generation backup and restore processes 276
13.2.3 The FILE-SAVE backup and restore processes 276
13.2.4 Checking the data secured 278
13.2.5 The ACCOUNT-SAVE backup processes 278
13.2.6 The ACCOUNT-RESTORE process 280
13.2.7 The file backup process using T-DUMP 281
13.2.8 The file restore process using T-LOAD 282
13.2.9 Selective restores 283
13.2.10 Controlled shutdown 283

Chapter 14 Managing Your System 284

14.1 The role of the System Administrator 284
14.2 System start up and close down 284
14.3 Logging on and logging off 285
14.4 Setting the date and time 285
14.5 Control of printers 286
14.6 Control of terminals 286
14.7 Sending messages 289
14.8 Handling disk usage 289
14.9 Optimizing response time 292
14.10 Handling system hangs and system errors 293
14.11 Backup procedures 296
14.12 Other useful commands 296

Chapter 15 PICK and Application Generators 297

15.1 An introduction to application generators 297
15.2 How the PICK 4GL products work 298
15.3 The case for fourth-generation languages 305
15.3.1 Advantages of fourth-generation languages 305
15.3.2 Disadvantages of fourth-generation languages 305
15.4 Summary 306

Chapter 16 PICK on the IBM PC and Compatibles 307

16.1 An introduction to PC PICK 307
16.2 PC-specific software features 308
16.2.1 COLOR and MONO verbs 308
16.2.2 The PRINT @ functions 308
16.2.3 Defining the keyboard functions 311
16.2.4 Setting baud rates 313
16.2.5 Use of storage media 314
16.2.6 Setting the date format 314
16.2.7 Moving data between PICK and DOS 315
16.2.8 Powering off and rebooting 317
16.3 Making PICK run on a compatible 318
16.4 The IBM PC-AT 321
16.4.1 PC-AT serial I/O ports 322
16.4.2 Installing parallel printers 330
16.4.3 Installing serial printers 332
16.4.4 Slave printers 333
16.4.5 Installing modems 334
16.4.6 Hard disk installation 334
16.4.7 Installing tape backup 337
16.4.8 Hardware-related error messages 338

Chapter 17 PICK: Its Place as an Operating System 341

17.1 Other major operating systems 341
17.2 A brief overview of UNIX 342
17.3 How PICK and UNIX compare 344
17.4 PICK's weaknesses 347

Chapter 18 PICK in the Commercial World 349

18.1 The problems besetting the businessman 349
18.2 The problems besetting the computing industry 351
18.3 What PICK and 4GL products provide 351
18.4 PICK the right approach? 352
18.5 The future of the PICK operating system 354

Appendices 355

Appendix A Error Messages 357

Appendix B Table of Prime Numbers 369

Appendix C TCL Verbs and General Commands 374

Appendix D BASIC Functions 388

Appendix E Formatting Program 396

Appendix F PROCs for JET and RUNOFF 399

Appendix G Table of ASCII Codes 417

Appendix H List of PICK Frames 425

Appendix I PICK Licensees 432

Glossary of Terms 434

Index 441

1 Introduction

1.1 An overview of PICK

If you have just taken delivery of your PICK-based computer system you are to be congratulated for choosing one of the most powerful, yet easy-to-use multi-user operating systems available. If you are still trying to decide whether PICK is for you, then read on.

The PICK operating system is possibly the longest running project in the history of computers. It started in 1965 under Richard Pick and it still has the same project leader! PICK is an operating system that provides the means to store, process and retrieve information whilst automatically taking care of the use of printers, terminals and the other hardware of a computer system such as memory, disks and magnetic tapes.

What makes PICK special is that it incorporates, as part of the operating system, features that are found only as add-ons in other systems. At the heart of PICK is a database system, truly integrated into the operating system, which handles variable-length records. Around this is implemented virtual memory management, a system which enables the hard disk to be used as an extension of the computer's real memory or RAM (Random Access Memory). This advanced facility removes the restriction found in most systems, that the number of tasks which can be undertaken at any one time is a function of physical memory. For the technical amongst you, PICK makes available up to 8 Gbytes (8000 million characters) of memory, dependent on the amount of disk space available. It also allows for a true multi-user environment in as little as 256 Kbytes (256 thousand characters) of physical memory. Indeed, in most implementations the maximum amount of physical memory supported is 2 Mbytes (2 million characters). More important to the user, PICK includes an English-like non-procedural enquiry language known as ACCESS. Since all data is stored in one common format, then ACCESS can be used on *any* file in the system regardless of whether it contains programs, user or system data; similarly only one editor is needed. Other facilities combine with these to make PICK one of the most comprehensive and easy-to-use operating systems available today.

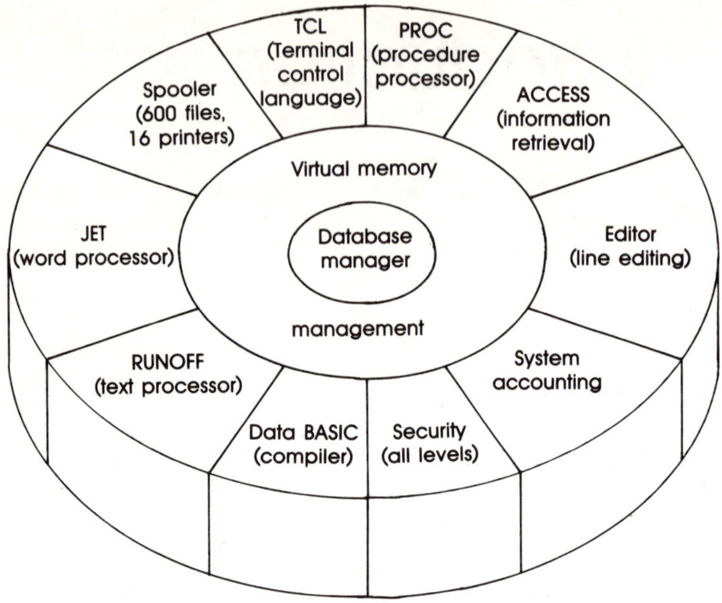

Figure 1.1 The facilities of PICK centre around a database system and virtual memory management.

PICK features the following as standard:

- **Terminal Control Language (TCL)** This forms the main interface between the user and the computer system. There are currently over 200 system utilities and procedures that can be invoked from the TCL environment as well as an unlimited number of user-defined procedures. It is from TCL that all other processes, such as the EDITOR, ACCESS or BASIC are invoked. It is a feature of PICK that these commands can be removed or renamed (possibly in a foreign language) providing a tailored environment for each user. The TCL processor is automatically entered at 'logon' and normally whenever other processes are completed. The normal TCL prompt is '>' although some implementations use '**:**'. The '>' will be used throughout this book when TCL commands are explained.
- The **EDITOR**, which provides for interactive online modification of the database. It can access *any* element of data within any file in the system and create, modify or delete it. The editor works on the current line for making these changes and incorporates a facility for handling prestored commands for repetitive tasks. In addition data can be 'merged' from other files.
- The **PROC** processor, which allows a sequence of operations to be executed by use of a single-word command. Any sequence of operations that can be executed from a terminal can also be prestored

using PROC, thus simplifying the day-to-day use of the system. PROC is effectively a job-control language with one or two enhancements. It can control input and output from a user's terminal with validation, branching, field manipulation and links to subroutines.

- A programming language called **BASIC** (Beginners All-purpose Symbolic Instruction Code); this is an extension of Dartmouth BASIC and provides a popular and easy-to-use compiler that caters for the unique PICK data structure. It is easier to use than standard BASIC, removing many of its irritating constraints. It permits the use of meaningful variable names, a capability usually only found in high-level languages such as COBOL, Pascal or C, and permits variables to be of any length and type. BASIC features a high-level interface with the database manager and consequently can access most of the functions provided by ACCESS, including selection, sorting and print formatting. The compiler provides a number of useful options including the ability to output a program listing with opcodes and 'pseudo' assembly code. The generation of variable and statement maps lets the programmer accurately monitor the execution of the program to improve performance in critical areas.
- **ACCESS**, one of the most useful and powerful features of PICK. It is a non-procedural English-like enquiry language where the user is in control and can enquire on any information in the database. Database enquiries can be made using a relatively free format language, closely related to normal English. This makes it easy to learn and simple to use, quickly inspiring confidence in the user, making him feel that the computer system is working for him. By using PICK's data dictionaries to define interrelationships, ACCESS enables information from several files to be sorted (ascending or descending), counted or totalled. Information is selected using logical operators such as equal, not equal, less than or greater than together with the connectives AND and OR. By use of such vocabulary, people with very little training soon feel comfortable with the system and can produce their own enquiries and reports.
- An **Output Management System** or **Spooler** capable of handling a wide variety of devices, including 16 serial printers and four parallel printers, is an integral part of the operating system. At any one time, 600 print files (reports) may be retained and controlled. A comprehensive set of utilities are provided which allow for changes to be made to the print queue, for the examination of individual reports (including a search for a specified string of characters), and for the set up of specific printers for specified terminals. It also controls and monitors the backup processes.
- **System Accounting**, a means of monitoring the use of the system. The accounting history file (`ACC`) maintains a complete audit log for the

system showing such details as the duration of time a user was logged on, the amount of CPU (Central Processor Unit) time used and the number of pages spooled to the printer. Users also have the option of charging specified portions of their system usage to nominated sub-accounts which permits true project costing. Various reports are available which, amongst others, show the system loading by port, the average connect time per type of user and the average number of 'sessions' per user. The information so produced can also be used to produce invoices for computer usage.

- A **security** system protects sensitive information from unauthorized access. Initial system entry can be password-protected and the user's 'logon' profile determines his read and write capabilities on other files. Individual command files can be set up to control the entire user session from the time users log on to the time they log off and such a command file can also include automatic logging of system usage.
- A text processor called **RUNOFF** which facilitates the preparation of documents such as memos, reports and manuals. RUNOFF uses commands embedded in the text to handle such things as justification, indenting, headings, footings and page numbering. For complex and lengthy documents it can also automatically produce the index and table of contents.

1.2 How the operating system developed

Following his MBA at Berkeley University, Richard Pick started his career in data processing as a programmer with Mattel Toys. It was his interest in finding better, more efficient ways to develop applications that was to bring about the PICK operating system. It started in 1965 when he joined the giant US military contractor TRW and, in conjunction with Don Nelson, was involved on a system specification that was to develop an English-based enquiry language. This system, called GIRLS (Generalized Information Retrieval Language System), was developed on an IBM 360 and enabled remote terminals to locate parts for rocket engines which might have been anywhere in the TRW organization.

Eventually the US army took an interest in the project and decided to fund a data management system to support the tracking of the Cheyenne helicopter project. This public funding had a significance later on, because in the USA the results of a project funded publicly tend to become freely available in the public domain.

By 1972 Richard Pick and Don Nelson had produced the first commercial implementation of PICK known as the Reality operating system on the Microdata 1600. In this implementation PICK put much of the operating system into firmware (microcode). This means that tasks such as managing the virtual memory system and handling the terminal I/O could be carried out at very high speed.

In 1974 Microdata (now McDonnell Douglas Information Systems) made its first major thrust into the end user market with 'Reality' and went on to create a national dealer network with what was undoubtedly a revolutionary product. In as little as 32 Kbytes of real memory, 10 or more users could work satisfactorily online using variable length data in a true multi-user environment. Many of these features we now take for granted of course, but in those days they were truly remarkable.

Pick's natural interest in putting his product on other machines ultimately caused a breakdown of the relationship with Microdata and in 1977 a lawsuit started. This produced a counter lawsuit and it was some four years later before a settlement took place during which time both continued their developments independently. The outcome of the legal wranglings resulted in both companies having the rights to the product.

During this four-year period, Pick, who had set up his own company, Pick and Associates, announced the Evolution computer system, based on the Intertechnique processor built in France and also ported his system on the Honeywell Level 6. The Ultimate Corporation marketed the Level 6 product and this marked a major milestone in the history of PICK, being the first well known computer to run the operating system. It could also run more terminals and cope with larger applications than before and hence proved to be a highly successful venture. It is likely to have been instrumental in encouraging other hardware manufacturers to offer PICK on their own systems. It is also worth noting that during this same period, in 1978, the Devcom Corporation began an emulation of PICK which they called 'Information', designed to run on Prime computers.

The first implementation on IBM equipment started in 1981 on the Series 1 and shortly after Pick and Associates adopted the name for which they are known today, that of PICK Systems. From this point on implementations flowed fast and furious. The year 1982 saw the start of six new ports on equipment from Altos, ADDS, Systems Management Inc. (SMI) on the IBM 4300, Datamedia, General Automation and the Pertec Computer Corporation.

There are now many more implementations with manufacturers queuing at Pick's door for their port of his operating system. Undoubtedly the most significant port which greatly increased the credibility of PICK is that released in 1984 for the IBM PC-XT. The PC-XT version, the first to be marketed by PICK Systems directly, is a full implementation of PICK for around £495, which turns the PC into a multiuser micro able to support three users plus parallel printer. In addition to standard PICK facilities, the PC-XT implementation supports the IBM bit-mapped screen and colour, as well as providing an interface to MS-DOS. In October 1985, PICK Systems launched the PC-AT implementation, with two versions, one to support 1–3 users, the other for 1–6 users. Like the PC-XT implementation, the PC-AT version was R83-based (the version first released in 1983 and subsequently enhanced) and not as was first planned, Open Architecture (Open Architecture is the latest version of PICK first announced in 1984). These PC implementations mean the operating system is now available on equipment ranging from the personal computer right through to the large mainframes, such as IBM 4300 and 30XX products (where the number of users is in the hundreds).

When you consider the number of systems now running PICK it may seem strange that the system is not more widely known. In the early days, of course, it was being offered as Reality, Ultimate or Evolution and, unlike many other operating system suppliers, Richard Pick kept close control over the implementations. We are now seeing the emergence of PICK as an industry standard operating system, and one that offers true portability of application software. PICK's data handling and enquiry language are the best available for the business and commercial marketplace for which they were designed. For those in the scientific and engineering industries PICK is not for you and operating systems such as UNIX or its derivates will be best suited, offering a variety of languages, in particular C and Fortran.

In 1984 Pick announced Release 84 or R84 as it became to be known. This project was to set the long-term development of the operating system in a way that would make the operating system more efficient, powerful and far easier to link to other systems. During the course of 1984 it was renamed 'Open Architecture' to denote the major advancement and philosophy of the system structure. The first implementation of Open Architecture was on the TDI Pinnacle and was not released until the IDBMA Spectrum show in London in October 1985.

With over thirty direct or related PICK licensees, the related licensees being COSMOS with Revelation under MS-DOS, PRIME with INFORMATION under PRIMOS and VMARK with UNIVERSE under UNIX, there are in excess of 70 000 PICK installations and 650 000 users worldwide. PICK Systems' objective is to ensure that the knowledge of the virtues of their product continues to be spread around the world so that the issue is no longer whether or not to use PICK, but which piece of hardware should be chosen to run it and which is the most suitable application package!

Whilst a number of existing licensees have expressed only a passing interest in Open Architecture, the implementation by PICK Systems on the PC-AT released early in 1987 has set the standard the industry is expected to follow.

The examples in the rest of this book are illustrated using the following conventions:

slanted text	characters must appear exactly as shown;
{ }	optional parameters;
[CR]	carriage return;
CTRL/C	depress both keys together (in this case the control key and c).

2 The PICK Database Structure

Before we look at using a PICK system, it is essential to look at the way in which data is stored and handled. Much of PICK's strength is by virtue of the power and flexibility gained from its unique database structure. All information in the system is stored in files. There are two main types of file, data and dictionary, and these files are organized in a hierarchy with four distinct levels, system dictionary (SYSTEM), master dictionary (MD), file dictionary (DICT) and data files. Figure 2.1 shows a pictorial representation of this data hierarchy.

PICK controls data in a logical way which can be readily compared to the way in which any business handles its information. Figure 2.2 demonstrates the way in which a company can be represented, with the managing director in control of a number of departments each controlling their own data files, some of which may be shared with others. PICK controls information in a similar fashion. As with a company which has files of information stored within individual departments, PICK groups together logical files of information which it calls **accounts**.

In order to keep control of these accounts, PICK has a **system dictionary** which is at the top of the PICK data structure hierarchy. In our company analogy of course, this position is held by the managing director!

From this point on, a company is broken down into divisions each controlled by a single director. In PICK the system is divided into a series of accounts, each controlled by a single **master dictionary**.

Each director has a number of managers controlling specific departments, each of which has its own data files stored in drawers, filing cabinets and so on. In PICK each account can have a number of **data dictionaries**, each controlling a number of **data files**.

To look at the details of a particular stock record in a manual stock system it would be necessary to go to the stock file containing a number of records and locate the appropriate record by means of its stock code, a *unique* code used to identify the product.

PICK controls information in its files in a similar way, except that it calls records **items** and requires that each has a unique key which in PICK

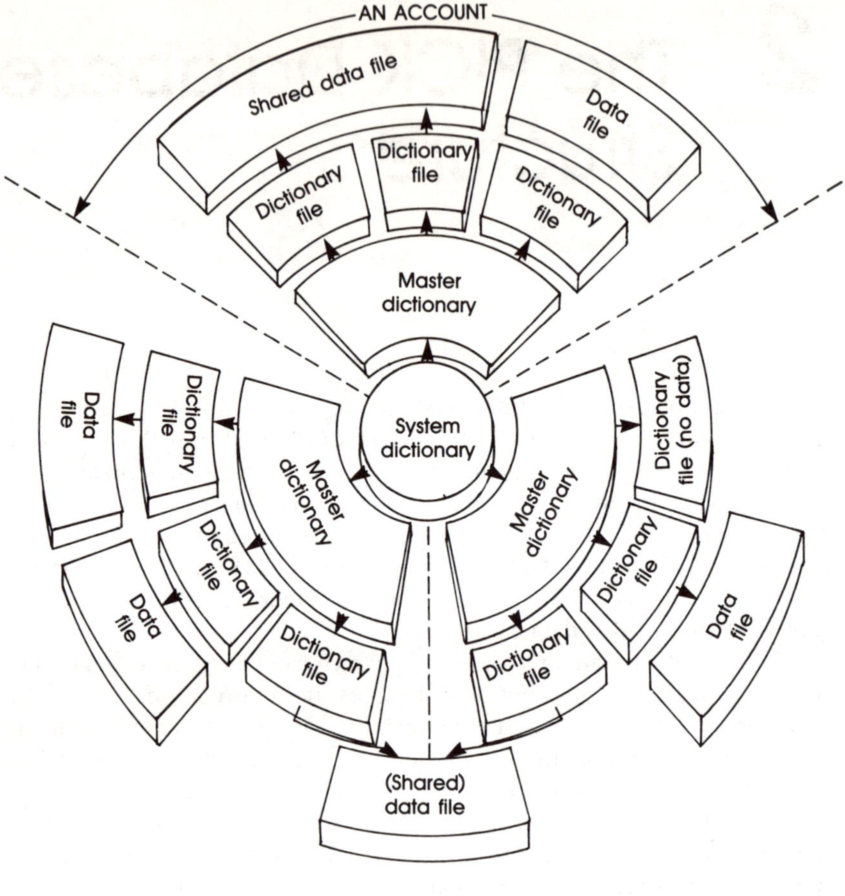

Figure 2.1 The PICK data structure.

terminology is referred to as the **item-id** (item identifier).

In any office the records kept by one department are usually different both in content and format to those of another. Quite frequently the information held is clarified by having headings on the record card, which define the nature of the information held in a specific part of the record. Indeed, many parts of a record may contain a code which, whilst not always known to outside departments, are applied by known rules within the department in which the records are kept. In PICK this sort of information, the structure of the data, is held in a **file dictionary** referenced as **DICT**, which defines the format and shape of the data itself. These 'parts' of a record are frequently referred to as 'fields' in data processing, but within PICK are called **attributes**. Figure 2.3 represents the way in which files are broken down into items, each of which contains attributes with the first of these being the item-id. In this example the

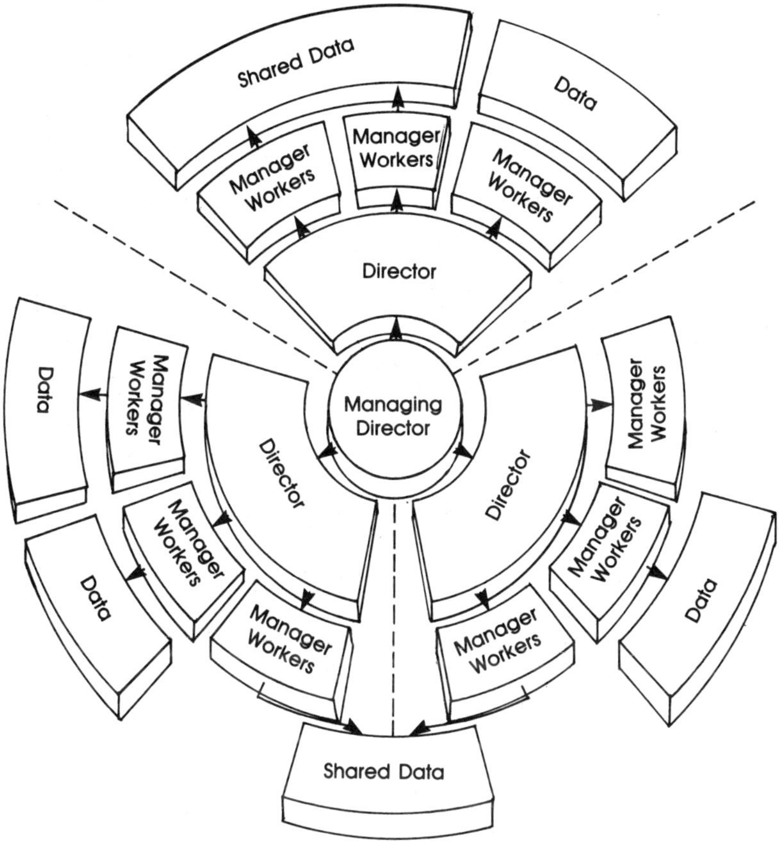

Figure 2.2 The company structure.

filing cabinet represents the file, a particular stock record card, an item, the unique stock code used to identify the stock record card, the item-id and the elements of data on the stock records card, the attributes.

In the same way that a departmental head is responsible for the control and security of the information in his department, PICK mirrors this by assigning one **master dictionary** to each account.

Each account, therefore, has a master dictionary and a series of data dictionaries each controlling respective data files. Logging on to a PICK system consists of logging to one of these accounts (an environment), rather than to the system in general. Without setting pointers to information held outside the account, the only information available to you is that held within the account you are logged to. The use of these pointers, known as **Q-pointers**, is fundamental to the workings of any PICK system and is described in detail in Chapter 6.

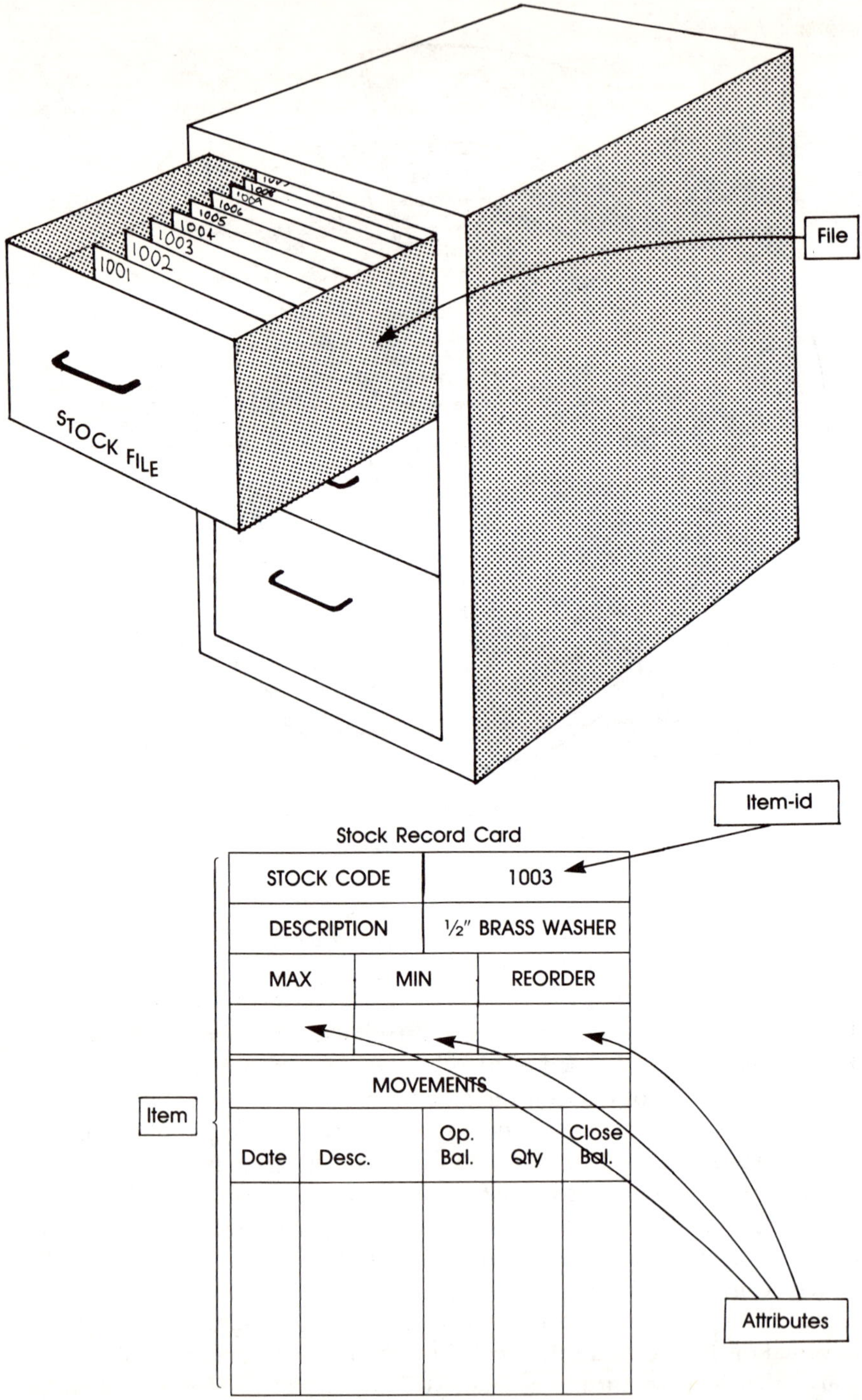

Figure 2.3 PICK terminology explained.

3 Getting Started

TCL verbs and general commands covered in this chapter

COUNT	CT	FLUSH	LIST	LISTFILES	LISTVERBS
LOGOFF		LOGON	LOGTO	OFF	SORT

3.1 Powering up and powering down

3.1.1 Powering up

PICK was designed as a multi-user operating system and requires at least one hard disk. The system will also have a backup device for the hard disk such as floppy disk, ¼-inch cartridge tape and ½-inch reel-to-reel tape. Attached to the computer will be a number of peripherals such as terminals (VDUs) and printers. None of these are usable until the PICK operating system has been loaded and is operational, assuming of course that PICK is the only operating system the computer supports!

The day-by-day process of loading the PICK operating system for use is called 'booting' the system. This can be handled in one of two ways, by invoking the **cold-start** or **warm-start** procedures.

Cold-start procedures vary from machine to machine and you should refer to your manual for the one specific to your system; however the tasks undertaken are very much the same. The cold-start procedure is a list of instructions that have to be performed each time a machine is powered up (without a prior 'warm save', discussed later) to set up the working environment of the system. It consists of PICK checking the number of ABS frames, and checking the availability of ports, memory, disk space, and the physical devices such as printers and tape drives. Following this the monitor, which controls all input, output and process scheduling, is loaded into memory and the spooler is started. The start-up options are then displayed. These are usually:

X – for eXecute, when workspace is relinked, following which the cold-start PROC (procedure) is executed.

F – for File restore, which acts as with X but also restores the entire data area and reorganizes the disk from a tape or diskette backup.

Whilst you should refer to your manual for the actual procedure to follow, a typical cold-start session is shown in Figure 3.1. If no cold-start procedure exists in the main system management account (SYSPROG) on your system, PICK will try to log to an account called COLDSTART (the password is usually CS), to run the cold-start procedure. If this account is missing it will display the error message USER-ID? and take you straight to the logon prompt.

```
LOADER VERSION 4.0.0
R204    DD/MM/YY

512KB  RAM
OPTIONS (X,F) = X[CR]

SPOOLER STARTED
LINKING WORKSPACE FOR LINE 0
```

Figure 3.1 The cold-start process.

After the linking workspace message, a banner may appear followed by a LOGON prompt. This initial logon request should be ignored as the operating system is still loading and will display a further LOGON prompt once loading is complete. Figure 3.2 shows the continuation of the cold-start process from Figure 3.1.

The cold-start procedure (PROC) usually prompts for date and time, and the port the printer is attached to. These ports start at zero, so if the printer is in the third physical port you should advise PICK that the printer is 'attached' to port two. The XXXXXX in the LOGON message normally refers to the make of equipment you are using and is usually customized by your supplier.

Some manufacturers provide a controlled shutdown procedure which enables a copy of the memory of the system to be written to disk when the system is powered off and written back into memory when the machine is powered up again. The system effectively starts from where it left off, in which case the options X or F may not be presented, nor may a cold-start procedure be required as the working environment is already

```
*******************************************************************************
*                                                                             *
*                                                                             *
*******************************************************************************
LOGON TO XXXXXX AT 10:42:56 :

*******************************************************************************
<<<                                                                         >>>
<<<                                                                         >>>
<<<                                                                         >>>
*******************************************************************************

THIS IS THE SYSTEM SETUP PROCEDURE
  ================================

Now setting the default terminal type for this system

The computer's clock currently shows 10:43:03   12 MAY 1985

Enter the correct time (press RETURN if it is correct)
   (Example 13:01 sets the clock to one minute after 1PM) = [CR]

Enter the correct date (press RETURN if it is correct)
  (Example 15MAY84 for MAY 15th 1984) = [CR]

What port is your printer plugged into?
                    (RETURN for no printer) = [CR]

*******************************************************************************
*                                                                             *
*                                                                             *
*******************************************************************************
LOGON TO XXXXXX AT 10:43:55 :
```

Figure 3.2 The cold-start session to completion.

defined. This booting facility is called a 'warm boot' of the operating system.

Once the start-up processes are complete a logon prompt will be given. This is another area where PICK systems differ, since invariably this screen will have been customized by your supplier. The message displayed at logon is held in a file called **SYSTEM** under the name **LOGON**. After you have logged on, the message **LOGON** from the file **ERRMSG** is displayed followed by another **ERRMSG** item called **335**. The item **335**, displayed each time anyone logs on, is usually used to contain day-to-day messages and forms a useful control mechanism for System Administrators.

3.1.2 Powering down

This is the procedure of closing down the system and switching off the power. There may be a controlled procedure supplied by your manufacturer, in which case it should be followed implicitly. If not, then you should ensure that everyone else is logged off the system and should wait until *all* disk activity has stopped, normally about half a minute, before turning off the system. This ensures that any data held in memory is written to disk. In some implementations you will find the command FLUSH implemented, which will carry out the same task. In this case when everyone has logged off, type in the command FLUSH, wait for the TCL command prompt to reappear, ensure all disk activity has stopped, then power off the system.

If the system is not shut down in one of these controlled ways it is possible that valuable information will be lost, and the integrity of files affected. This is because of the workings of the memory management system which holds data in memory for long periods of time without needing to update records held on disk.

3.2 Logging on and logging off

3.2.1 Logging on

Once the equipment is powered up, logging on consists of logging to an account (a group of logically related files), by either giving an account name or user identity. The raw PICK system comes with just one specialized user account, SYSPROG, the System Programming account, which can be logged to by typing in the word SYSPROG at the logon prompt followed by any requested password. Since there is no common password for the account SYSPROG, if you need one you will have to see your System Administrator. It is worth noting at this point that a raw PICK system has several other accounts, but none of them can be logged to, to do anything useful.

```
LOGON PLEASE : SYSPROG{,.password}[CR]
```

If you are at the TCL prompt and wish to log to a particular account, then you can use the LOGTO command.

```
>LOGTO SYSPROG{,.password}[CR]
```

3.2.2 Logging off

Logging off consists of typing OFF at the TCL prompt. If you need to log off another terminal, other than the one you are using, the TCL command is LOGOFF. The form of this command is:

LOGOFF {U}[CR] (remember that braces indicate options)

If no option is taken you will be asked for the channel (otherwise known as port line, or process) of the terminal you want to log off:

CHANNEL:

By entering '1' the terminal on port 1 will be logged off, assuming it exists and is in use. The U unconditionally logs off any terminal on the system. If the line specified does not exist, an error message is displayed:

[535] ILLEGAL LINE NUMBER

This is just one of many messages within PICK that use the word 'illegal'. It sounds a little daunting, but all it really means is that you got it wrong! The number 535 in square brackets is the reference number of the error message. All error messages are held in the file ERRMSG which we will review later. For a full list of these messages refer to Appendix A. It is more likely that you will get the channel number correct, in which case, after logging off the requested line, a confirmation message is displayed.

[534] LOGOFF SUCCESSFUL

In this case, the ERRMSG file is used to display confirmation of the action taken, so it is difficult to describe the ERRMSG file as an error message file, which is what its name suggests. Two other possibilities exist. Firstly, that the terminal is already logged off, in which case you are told so:

[536] ALREADY LOGGED OFF

It may be however that the terminal is not switched on, in which case the terminal being used to log off the others will 'hang', until the terminal on the appropriate line is switched on. On the occasions when the terminal cannot be switched on, it is possible to break out of the process by using the BREAK key if your terminal has one, failing that by depressing CTRL (control) and C together or another combination of keys as advised by your System Administrator. By doing so you are entering into what is called DEBUG and an exclamation mark or asterisk is displayed. Any process can be terminated in this way, although use of this facility in novice hands can be exceedingly dangerous. For this reason users are frequently prevented from being able to BREAK a process in this way and enter the debugger. Figure 3.3 shows a typical debug display.

The cursor will wait by the '!' for information to be typed in. Debug is one of the areas of PICK where considerable damage can be done by the inexperienced user, so frequently the ablity to break into the system is restricted. If it can be used then there are three safe entries to make at this point: END which takes you to TCL, OFF which will log you off the system or G which will resume the process broken into, displaying the system accounting information and the logon prompt, as shown in Figure 3.4.

```
I a.b
!
```

In this example a.b refers to the operating system frame a (the term frame is explained later; it is basically an area of the disk containing 512 characters) and b the position within it (shown in hexadecimal), at the time of the BREAK. Typically this would look like:

```
I 278.41C
!
```

Figure 3.3 A typical display when using the BREAK key.

```
I 278.41C
!OFF[CR]
<CONNECT TIME = 3 MINS.; CPU = 20 UNITS;LPTR PAGES = 0                      >
<LOGGED OFF AT 12:23:14          ON 7 DEC 1985                              >

*****************************************************************************
*                                                                           *
*                                                                           *
*****************************************************************************
LOGON TO XXXXXX AT HH:MM:SS  :
```

Figure 3.4 A typical display when logging off.

3.3 Looking around your system

Assuming you have logged to SYSPROG and are now at the TCL prompt, the '>' sign, or that you are able to select TCL as one of your SYSPROG menu options, we can look at some simple TCL commands. At TCL we can now look at the original files supplied with your system. The list of available files is produced by using the command LISTFILES and is illustrated in Figure 3.5. It should be pointed out that the display you get from the command could be quite different to that shown in Figure 3.5 and if it is please don't be alarmed.

This report lists the files within the SYSPROG account, explains their file type (see Section 5.1.3) under the heading CODE and gives information about the location and size of each file under the remaining three headings.

BP The conventional name for the BASIC program file, where both source and object programs reside. Notice that the file type is DC. It is

```
>LISTFILES[CR]

PAGE   1 *** MD *** FILE DEFINING ITEMS   20 JAN 1985

NAME................ CODE F/BASE....... F/MOD...... F/SEP.

BP                   DC            3214           1     1
NEWAC                D             3201           1     1
POINTER-FILE         DC            2878          27     1
STAT-FILE            D             3016           7     1
SYSPROG-PL           DC            2905           1     1
ACC                  Q              ACC         ACC
BLOCK-CONVERT        Q    BLOCK-CONVERT
ERRMSG               Q           SYSTEM      ERRMSG
M/DICT               Q
MD                   Q
PROCLIB              Q          PROCLIB     PROCLIB
SYSTEM               Q           SYSTEM
12 ITEMS COUNTED
```

Figure 3.5 The output from LISTFILES.

only possible to hold object programs in a file if the type is DC. In these files the source code is held as data, the object code is held in the dictionary part of the file.

NEWAC Contains the standard master dictionary items copied to each new account created.

POINTER-FILE Contains pointers to selected lists of items. Whilst it is one file held in SYSPROG in many implementations, in some it is an account, whilst in others it will be a file in each account.

STAT-FILE Contains statistical information about data files and is updated when a FILE-SAVE command is processed.

SYSPROG-PL Contains the procedures used for system maintenance.

ACC This account contains accounting history data and keeps track of the people (users) logged in to the system.

BLOCK-CONVERT This account contains items that define the format of characters displayed by the command BLOCK-PRINT. It also contains a list of opcodes and their symbolic names; used when compiling a BASIC program with the A option which generates a list of the assembled source code.

ERRMSG Contains the messages used by PICK and each account created must have a 'pointer' to this file. This pointer is just one of the many master dictionary (MD) items to be found in NEWAC.

M/DICT and **MD** These are the master dictionaries and are shown with reflexive Q-pointers pointing to themselves, and you will notice that there are no file names under the headings **F/BASE** and **F/MOD**

PROCLIB Contains all commonly used procedures (**PROCS**).

SYSTEM This entry is a pointer to the system dictionary, going up one level in the file hierarchy.

Having looked at the files available, we can establish a list of available commands using **LISTVERBS**. Figure 3.6 shows the typical output from this command.

```
>LISTVERBS[CR]

PAGE   1                                  11:02:22 27 APR 1985
M/DICT.......... *A1....... *A2....... *A3........ *A4......

:ABSLOAD        |  P        D7
:FILELOAD       |  P        20D7
:STARTSPOOLER   |  P        500A      60B6       10AF
      :         } item-ids
      :         |
      :         |
WHO             |  P        10BB
XTD             |  P        20A0

179 ITEMS LISTED   ← Count of number of items in the file
```

Figure 3.6 The output from LISTVERBS.

The items listed are verbs found in the master dictionary, and alongside each is shown the contents of their first four attributes (fields). You will notice that at the end of both of the lists we have produced so far is a count of the number of items. To establish the number of items in a file without listing them all out, we can use the command **COUNT** and Figure 3.7 demonstrates the use of this command on the file **PROCLIB**.

```
>COUNT PROCLIB[CR]

 32 ITEMS COUNTED
```

Figure 3.7 Output from COUNT.

The command LIST lists the items in a file, in the sequence in which they are stored, whilst using the command SORT the same list of items can be produced in a given sequence. Try the commands:

```
>LIST PROCLIB[CR]

>SORT PROCLIB[CR]
```

You will notice in both cases that, in addition to the item-id (key) being listed, a lot of other information relating to the item is also printed. In a large file where you are only interested in knowing which items exist in a file, this can be not only annoying and confusing, but also time wasting. If you wish to limit the information displayed to show *only* the item-id, then include the word ONLY in your command:

```
>LIST ONLY PROCLIB[CR]

>SORT ONLY PROCLIB[CR]
```

LIST and SORT are two of the main information retrieval commands covered in Chapter 9 on ACCESS. Having listed the items in PROCLIB, you can look at the contents of any individual item by the command CT

```
>CT PROCLIB LISTFILES[CR]

    LISTFILES
PQ
C This PROC lists the files in an account
IF #A2 IH MD
IF A2 # LPTR IF A2,2 # ((P) G 10
IH MD
S3
IH LPTR
10 H SORT
A2
H WITH D/CODE "D]" WITH D/CODE "Q" F/NAME D/CODE F/BASE
    F/MOD F/SEP
H HEADING "PAGE'P'  *** 'F' *** FILE DEFINING ITEMS
'DL' "
H BY D/CODE1 BY F/NAME
IF A3 = LPTR   H LPTR
IF A3,2 = ((P) H LPTR
H ID-SUPP
P
```

Figure 3.8 The contents of the item LISTFILES.

(Copy to Terminal). In fact, the CT verb is just a PROC using a verb COPY whose workings are explained later on. Figure 3.8 shows how to display the contents of the item LISTFILES in the file PROCLIB. Do not concern yourself with the contents of the item LISTFILES as this is the procedure language, PROC, and has not yet been discussed.

What has been displayed on the terminal in Figure 3.8 is the procedure for displaying the files of an account, a procedure used earlier and shown in Figure 3.5. The procedure language enables a series of TCL and ACCESS commands to be stored and executed by typing in a single command and is described fully in Chapter 11.

4 The Handling of Data

TCL verbs and general commands covered in this chapter

CLEAR-FILE	COPY	CREATE-ACCOUNT	CREATE-FILE	DELETE
DELETE-ACCOUNT		DELETE-FILE	EXCHANGE	

4.1 The handling of accounts

4.1.1 Creating an account

An account is created by the command CREATE-ACCOUNT. This invokes a PROC (procedure), restricted to the SYSPROG account, which prompts for the information it requires. When creating an account it is possible to set up security codes to prevent unauthorized access. These codes are known as retrieval locks (L/RET) and update locks (L/UPD). Further it is possible to determine the initial amount of space to allocate to the account by assigning values to the 'modulo' and 'separation'. The larger the values set, the larger the amount of initial space allocated and vice versa.

Space is allocated in units of 512 characters each, known as frames. The separation is the number of these frames that make up a single block, whilst the modulo is the number of these blocks to be used. The next chapter explains, in detail, the way in which this works.

Figure 4.1 shows an example of creating an account called TEST using the CREATE-ACCOUNT command. This command is handled by a procedure (PROC) which varies between implementations, so don't be surprised if yours is not exactly the same as Figure 4.1.

Figure 4.1 shows how an account called TEST can be created. It has no retrieval lock codes (L/RET), no update lock codes (L/UPD) and is protected by the password PICKTEST. The account carries the highest security level or privileges (SYS2) and uses a default modulo and separation of 29 and 1. The use of L/RET and L/UPD are covered in full in Section 13.3.

```
>CREATE-ACCOUNT[CR]
ACCOUNT NAME?TEST[CR]
L/RET CODE(S)?[CR]
L/UPD CODE(S)?[CR]
PASSWORD?PICKTEST[CR]
PRIVILEGES?SYS2[CR]
MOD, SEP?[CR]

FILE 'TEST'      CREATED; BASE 22588 MODULO= 29 SEPAR= 1

256 ITEMS COPIED
'TEST' UPDATED
'TEST' COPIED
```

Figure 4.1 The creation of a new account.

For those of you who like to know a little more about what goes on internally, having allocated the required amount of space to the account, in this case 29 blocks (known as groups in PICK terminology), PICK copies the contents of the NEWAC file into the MD of the newly formed account. It also adds a file synonym (Q-pointer) to the new account in the MD of the SYSPROG account and a file definition item or D-item in the system dictionary file to point to the MD of the new account.

A group of users can use the same account, and are given access to the account by a series of user codes known as user-ids. Each user can be given differing security levels and file-access privileges, although it should be noted that no user can be given higher privileges than those assigned to the account as a whole. Section 13.1 covers the way in which this is handled.

4.1.2 Removing an account

DELETE-ACCOUNT is another PROC and can only be run from SYSPROG; again this PROC will vary from implementation to implementation. It is recommended that all users be logged off from the account before running this command, since PICK removes the D-item from the system dictionary during this process not only for the account but for any user-ids that refer to the account.

As a protection against removing the wrong account, a list of files within the account is displayed and final confirmation requested before the account is finally deleted. Figure 4.2 shows the typical dialogue in using the DELETE-ACCOUNT command.

With the account deleted, PICK returns you to the TCL prompt to await the next command. You will notice in Figure 4.2 two references to

```
>DELETE-ACCOUNT[CR]
ACCOUNT NAME?DEMO[CR]

FILES TO BE DELETED IN ACCOUNT DEMO      12 MAY 85     PAGE 1

FILE              BASE     MOD      SEP

MD                25890    29       1
DEMOFILES         34352    11       1
DEMOFILES         35688    101      1
    :
    :

DO YOU STILL WANT TO DELETE THE ACCOUNT?YES[CR]

>
```

Figure 4.2 Deleting an account.

the file DEMOFILES. The reason for this is that there are two files with that name in the account, one containing the dictionary information for the file and the other containing its data.

4.2 File handling

4.2.1 Creating a file

The CREATE-FILE command is used to generate new dictionary and data files. These can be generated independently by the commands CREATE-FILE DICT and CREATE-FILE DATA, though more usually they are created together by the command CREATE-FILE which contains the modulo and separation parameters that relate to the initial sizing of the file, for both the dictionary and data portions. Do not worry too much about the terms modulo and separation here, since they are explained fully in the next chapter.

PICK does not allow a data file to be created without having a dictionary level file pointing to it. Hence the dictionary part of the file must exist and this is why the dictionary modulo/separation parameters come before those for the data file in the CREATE-FILE command. In most implementations the CREATE-FILE command will default to a separation of 1 unless told otherwise. So the creation of a file is normally as shown in Figure 4.3 with both the dictionary and data files being created at the same time, each with a default separation of 1.

Once again reference is made to the ERRMSG file, using message number 417 to confirm the file parameters. The command in Figure 4.3

```
>CREATE-FILE DEMO 1 11[CR]

[417] FILE 'DEMO' CREATED; BASE= 24046, MODULO= 1, SEPAR= 1.
[417] FILE 'DEMO' CREATED; BASE= 24292, MODULO=11, SEPAR= 1.
```

Figure 4.3 Creating a file.

has created a file called **DEMO** in the account you are logged to, with a dictionary size of 1 frame and a data area of 11 frames. Exactly the same could have been achieved by two separate commands, one to create the dictionary (DICT) file and the other to create the data (DATA) file; Figure 4.4 gives an example of this. Remember though, the dictionary file must be created first!

```
>CREATE-FILE DICT DEMO 1[CR]

[417] FILE 'DEMO' CREATED; BASE=24046, MODULO= 1, SEPAR= 1.

>CREATE-FILE DATA DEMO 11[CR]

[417] FILE 'DEMO' CREATED; BASE= 24292, MODULO=11, SEPAR= 1.
```

Figure 4.4 Creating a file by creating dictionary and data files separately.

To create dictionary or data files with a separation other than 1, follow the modulo size, of either or both, with a comma and the separation size. Hence to provide a separation of 2 for the data file, leaving the dictionary file as a separation of 1, use the command

```
>CREATE-FILE DEMO 1 11,2[CR]
```

4.2.2 Creating multiple files with a common dictionary

Whilst every data file must have a dictionary file relating to it, it does not have to have its *own unique* dictionary file. There are some instances where it is helpful to split data across several data files but, since each has the same format, to let them all share one dictionary file.

These multiple data files are created, and subsequently referred to, by following an existing data file name with a comma and the new data file name. Taking the example of Figure 4.4 a stage further, let's assume we wish to create the data file **DEMO1** to use the existing dictionary, defined for the file **DEMO**. This process is explained in the example of Figure 4.5.

From this point on, all references to the file **DEMO1** must be made in

```
>CREATE-FILE DATA DEMO,DEMO1 7[CR]

[417] FILE 'DEMO1' CREATED; BASE= 24303, MODULO= 7, SEPAR= 1.
```

Figure 4.5 Creating a data file to use an existing dictionary file.

conjunction with its linked dictionary file **DEMO** by using the words **DEMO,DEMO1**. It is possible to edit items in the file, use ACCESS to enquire on the file and use any of the other PICK commands on this file. It is, and can be treated, just like any other file provided you refer to it by its full name **DEMO,DEMO1**.

4.2.3 Removing a file

In the same way that a file's dictionary and data portions can be created separately or together, they can be removed in the same way. Again, since the dictionary must exist before the data file, it is not possible to delete the dictionary and leave the data file.

To delete both dictionary and data you should use the following command:

```
>DELETE-FILE DEMO[CR]
```

This command releases back to the free space manager, the **OVERFLOW** manager, all the frames used by the file **DEMO** which are immediately made available to all applications. There are occasions when you may wish to remove the dictionary or data files independently, in which case you should use the commands shown in Figure 4.6.

```
>DELETE-FILE DATA DEMO[CR]

>DELETE-FILE DICT DEMO[CR]
```

Figure 4.6 Deleting the data and dictionary portions of a file.

4.2.4 Clearing a file

PICK provides the means to clear the contents of a file, be it dictionary or data, with the command **CLEAR-FILE**. This leaves the file empty, releases any frames that were linked to the primary file area, but leaves unaffected all references and pointers to the file. It is not possible to clear both the dictionary and data portions of a file with a single command. The commands to use are shown in Figure 4.7.

```
>CLEAR-FILE DICT DEMO[CR]

>CLEAR-FILE DATA DEMO[CR]
```

Figure 4.7 Clearing the dictionary and data portions of a file.

4.3 Data handling

4.3.1 Creating data items

There is no need for a special command to create items in PICK since as soon as you refer to a new item it is created for you. Items are created in a number of ways; either through the editor (refer to Chapter 7), via an application program written in BASIC (refer to Chapter 10) by using TCL commands like COPY to copy items from one file to another or through reformatting commands in ACCESS (refer to Section 9.3.11).

4.3.2 Removing data items

As well as the editor and application programs, it is possible to delete items from a file with a TCL command. The command is DELETE where in addition to the file name, the item names are also given. Some implementations offer a far more convenient means of deleting several items. Instead of listing the item-ids alongside the file name, it is possible to press the RETURN key immediately after inputting the file name, and be prompted for each of the item-ids or record keys one after the other. The process is terminated by pressing the RETURN key in response to NEXT ITEM. Figure 4.8 shows both methods in action where two items with item-ids (keys) of 1001 and 1005 are removed from the file DEMO.

4.3.3 Copying items

The COPY command is extremely powerful and is used to copy items to another file or to make duplicate copies of items within the original file. As discussed later, it can be used in resizing the contents of a file.

The COPY command can also be used to copy items to a terminal or printer and hence there are a number of different options that can be applied. It is also possible to use the copy command on the dictionary file, so the general format of the command is:

```
>COPY {DICT} filename item-list {(options)}[CR]
TO:{(}/{DICT} filename{)} {itemlist}[CR]
```

```
>DELETE DEMO 1001 1005[CR]
'1001' DELETED
'1005' DELETED

>

>DELETE DEMO[CR]
NEXT ITEM1001[CR]
'1001' DELETED
NEXT ITEM1005[CR]
'1005' DELETED
NEXT ITEM[CR]

>
```

Figure 4.8 Deleting items from a file.

The options at the end of the command, if used, must be enclosed in parentheses with multiple options being typed together or separated by a comma or space. If data is copied to another file then the destination file name is enclosed in parentheses in response to the TO prompt.

Figure 4.9 shows how to copy an existing item (1001) to a new item (1005). This duplicates the data record in the same file, but with a different key (item-id).

```
>COPY DEMO 1001[CR]
TO:1005[CR]

1 1001 TO 1005

1 ITEMS COPIED
```

Figure 4.9 Copying an item within the same file.

Figure 4.10 shows how to copy the contents of an entire DEMO file (which contains five records) to a new file called TEMP. This assumes that the file TEMP already exists. If it doesn't the copying process will fail so the file must be created first (see Section 4.2.1). Once the file exists, the entire contents of another file can be copied to it using a wildcard facility designated by an asterisk. If the item-id of an item on the original file already exists on the destination file, PICK will display error message 415 to that effect and the item will not be copied over, unless the overwrite option O is chosen (see Figure 4.12 for a full list of options).

```
>COPY DEMO *[CR]
TO:(TEMP[CR]

1  1001
2  1002
3  1003
4  1004
5  1005

5 ITEMS COPIED
```

Figure 4.10 Copying items to a different file.

Notice in Figure 4.10 the use of parentheses following the 'TO' prompt, which denotes the items are being copied to a different file. In most implementations you will find that only the first bracket, the (is required, the second being superfluous. Figure 4.11 shows how to copy an item to a different file, in this case TEMP, and how to give it a different item-id (1022). Once again the parentheses are needed.

```
>COPY DEMO 1003[CR]
TO:(TEMP 1022[CR]

1  1003 TO 1022

1 ITEMS COPIED
```

Figure 4.11 Copying an item to a different item in a different file.

The copy facility is very useful and one that you will use regularly. There are many different options that you can use, for example, the T option, which copies the items to the terminal, although this can equally be achieved by pressing the RETURN key in response to the TO prompt.

Like many of the TCL commands, including the majority we have used already, there is an option to direct the output of the command to the printer, the P option. As mentioned above, all options used need to be in parentheses with multiple options separated by a comma. Figure 4.12 shows an example of the copy command using several options and then lists all available options and gives their meaning. In the case of the example shown in Figure 4.12 the contents of items 1002 and 1003 are to be listed on the printer with their contents being shown in hexadecimal format. For those of you who have not come across the word hexadecimal before, do not be concerned – you will probably never need to use it. It is

```
>COPY DEMO 1002 1003 (P,X[CR]

 ENTRY # 1
```

The available options following the open bracket are:

n – a number specifying the number of items to copy
D – deletes the original item when the copy is complete
F – denotes a form-feed is required between each item. (Only valid for terminal or printer output)
I – suppresses the list of item-ids being shown on the screen
M – items will only be copied to the destination file where an item with the same name exists. The new item overwrites the old
N – if used in conjunction with printer or terminal output, inhibits the automatic pause at the end of each page
O – overwrites existing items when duplicates are found
P – sends output to the printer
S – suppresses error messages which warn of items not copied
S – if used in conjunction with printer or terminal output, suppresses the line numbers
T – directs the output to the terminal
X – displays the informations in hexadecimal form

Figure 4.12 The COPY options.

a method of representing numbers to the base of 16, and is only used by technicians!

The COPY options, as with those on a number of TCL verbs, include some that are mutually exclusive. For example, the items copied can either be copied to a file, to the printer or to the screen. They cannot be directed to more than one device in one command. You will have to experiment with the above options to gain an understanding of which combinations are possible and which are not. Since all are fairly straightforward this should not represent any major difficulties to you.

4.3.4 Changing item-ids

Some implementations of PICK contain a useful PROC called EXCHANGE. This enables the contents of two *existing* items to be exchanged and is achieved by copying the contents of the first item into a temporary area, copying the second item to the first, and then copying the temporary area to the second item. If that sounded confusing, Figure 4.13 shows how simply it is achieved.

After the exchange operation the data contained in item 1002 has been transferred to item 1007 and vice versa. The temporary item %TEMP% used

```
>EXCHANGE DEMO 1002 1005[CR]
1   1002 TO %TEMP%
2   1005 TO 1002
3   %TEMP% TO 1007

3 ITEMS COPIED
```

Figure 4.13 Output from EXCHANGE.

in the process is deleted automatically. If your system does not contain this PROC, you can create it using the editor (see Chapter 7) by typing in the following details:

```
     EXCHANGE
PQ
C A PROC TO EXCHANGE THE ITEM-IDs OF TWO ITEMS IN A FILE.
C
IF A2 = DICT F
IF A F
IF A F
IF #A X
HCOPY
A2
IF A2 = DICT G 10
S3
G 11
10 A3
11 C
A
A
H%TEMP% (O,D)
STON
H%TEMP%
S2
IF A = DICT F
F
A
H
A
H<
P
```

5 The PICK Database Structure in Detail

5.1 The PICK database structure explained

In earlier chapters we have used terms like frame, modulo and separation – all of which are important elements of the PICK database structure and all of which are explained in detail in this chapter.

In Chapter 2 we looked at the general philosophy of the PICK database and drew an analogy to the way an organization is structured. Figure 5.1 is a copy of the PICK data structure we referred to in that chapter.

- The **System Dictionary**, referred to as `SYSTEM`, is the highest level dictionary in the PICK hierarchy. As its name suggests it controls 'the system' and hence there is only ever one per copy of the PICK operating system. It contains all the information about the authorized users, their passwords and any update or retrieval locks associated with them which is held in the master dictionary for each account.
- The **Master Dictionary**, referred to as `MD` or `M/DICT`, is where information specific to the account is stored. Whilst there is no limit to the number of accounts on a system, other than the restriction of physical disk space, there can only be one master dictionary per account. The master dictionary holds definitions of the files within the account, pointers to their file dictionary together with their locking codes, the TCL and ACCESS verbs available to the account as well as its `PROC`s (procedures) and BASIC programs. It also stores pointers to files outside the account.
- The **File Dictionary**, referred to as `DICT`, describes the structure and format of data held within the respective file and stores the pointer to it. There is generally only one file dictionary for each data file. Although the concept of more than one data file per file dictionary is possible and is explained in Section 4.2.2, it is not widely used.
- The dictionary file contains a record defining each **Attribute** (or field). Hence, for a personnel file, the dictionary could readily contain a record to describe the format of the employee name,

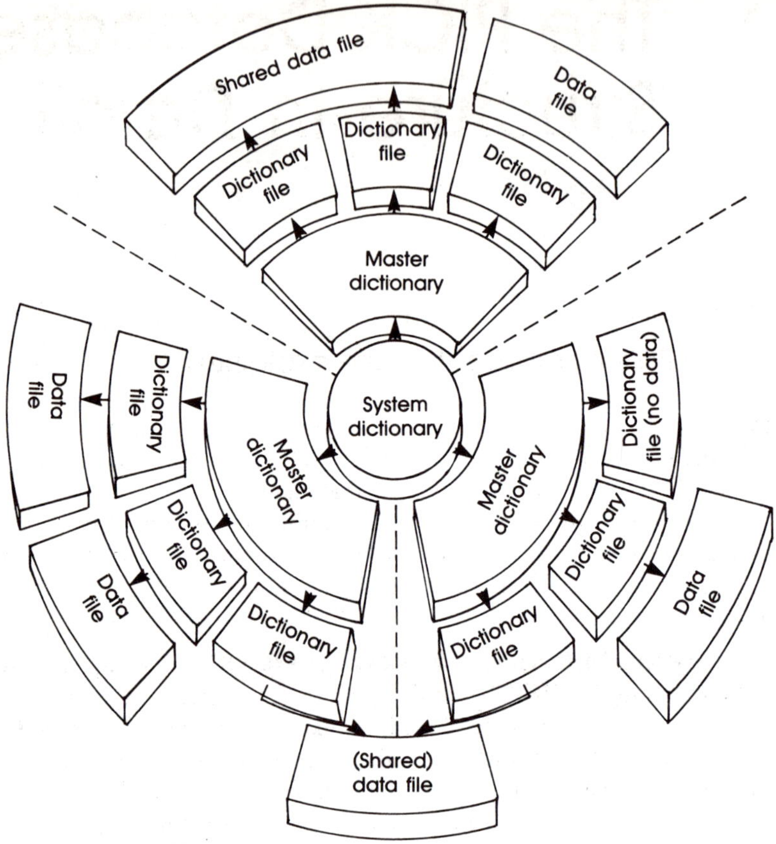

Figure 5.1 The PICK database structure.

another dictionary record would define the employee department, another would define the employee salary and so on.

- The **Data File** is where the actual data held in variable length format is stored. Hence, using the personnel file as an example again, the data file contains the physical data defined by the dictionary file. The data file would contain, therefore, actual names, actual departments and actual salaries of actual employees! Figure 5.2 illustrates this hierarchical relationship. Although not obvious from Figure 5.2, *all* elements of the database are variable length whether they reside in the system dictionary, master dictionary, the file dictionaries or data files. Hence *all* files on the PICK system are variable length.

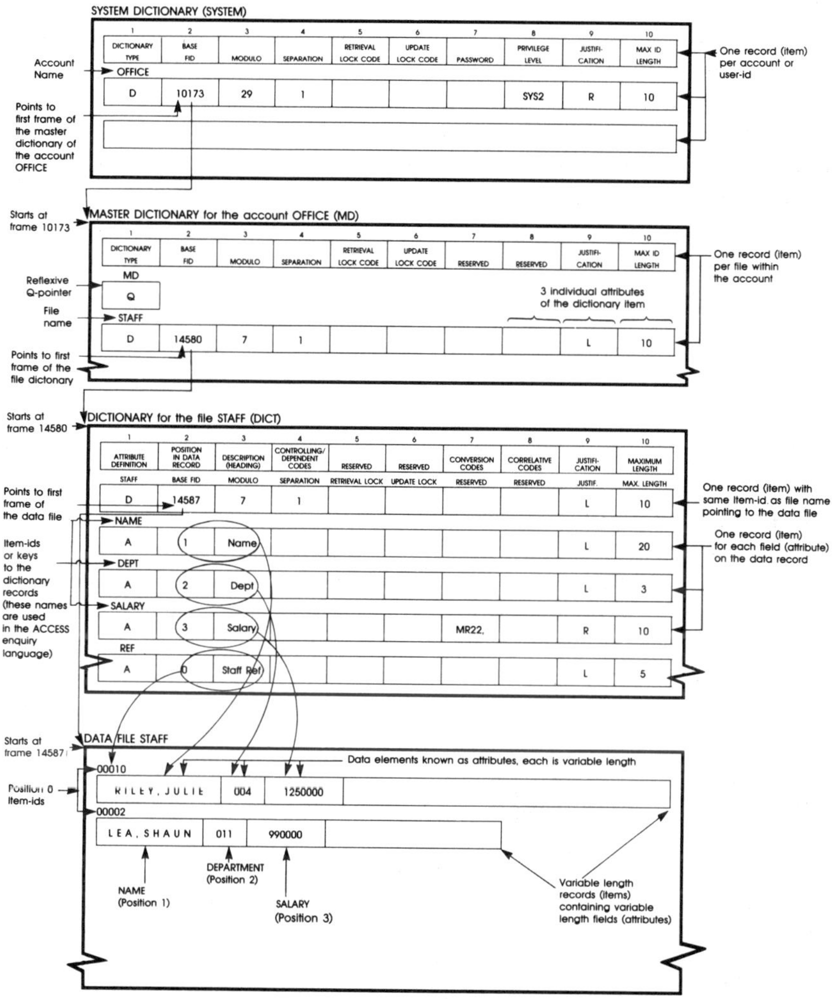

Figure 5.2 The workings of the PICK database.

5.1.1 Data file structure

All data held on the database is held in files; some of these files are dictionary files (system dictionary, master dictionary and file dictionaries) whilst others hold data (data files). A file is a collection of logically related information which can be of any size, subject to the amount of free disk space available. Whilst the initial creation of a file requires the assigning of an amount of disk space known as the primary area, the file can grow or shrink during use without any further intervention. Note, however, that it will not shrink below the original (primary) amount of space allocated to it, so it is not sensible to define file space much larger than that expected to be used.

A file is made up of a number of **items**, the equivalent of the term 'record' in ordinary data processing. If you look at Figure 5.2 carefully you will see that each file in the hierarchy contains a series of items. Within most implementations of PICK the largest item (record) size permitted is 32 268 bytes (characters). Since the number of records in a file is unlimited, restricted only by the amount of physical disk space available, the record size limit is rarely a problem. In any case, the record size limitation has been completely removed in Open Architecture, in which items can be of any size.

An item can be subdivided into a number of **attributes**; again, to use conventional terminology, these are the equivalent of fields. The key field, known as the **item-id**, is mandatory and is at the beginning of the item in attribute 0. The maximum length of the item-id is often 50 characters. From this point on, however, the parallel to conventional systems stops and the power of the PICK data structure comes into its own.

Attributes may be divided into multiple **values**, which in turn may be further divided into **subvalues**. Within the limitation of item size (and for those who thought the number 32 268 looked familiar it is 32K less 500), any attribute, any value or subvalue within it, can be of any length.

A typical application of this structure might be a personnel system where, amongst other information, it is required to monitor all the salary changes of employees. In a conventional system using COBOL you have to define the largest, expected, number of occurrences – and that isn't always easy to determine – and then reserve that fixed amount of space for each person. In PICK, the built-in mechanism for defining data means that no fixed number of multivalues need be determined since these values (in this case salary changes) can be added and deleted dynamically. The amount of space used directly relates to the amount of data stored. Figure 5.3 shows the difference in these two methods of data storage.

PICK's data structure enables values to be broken down further into subvalues, each of which is held as variable length. This means that the multivalues of salary can themselves contain multiple entries, perhaps to

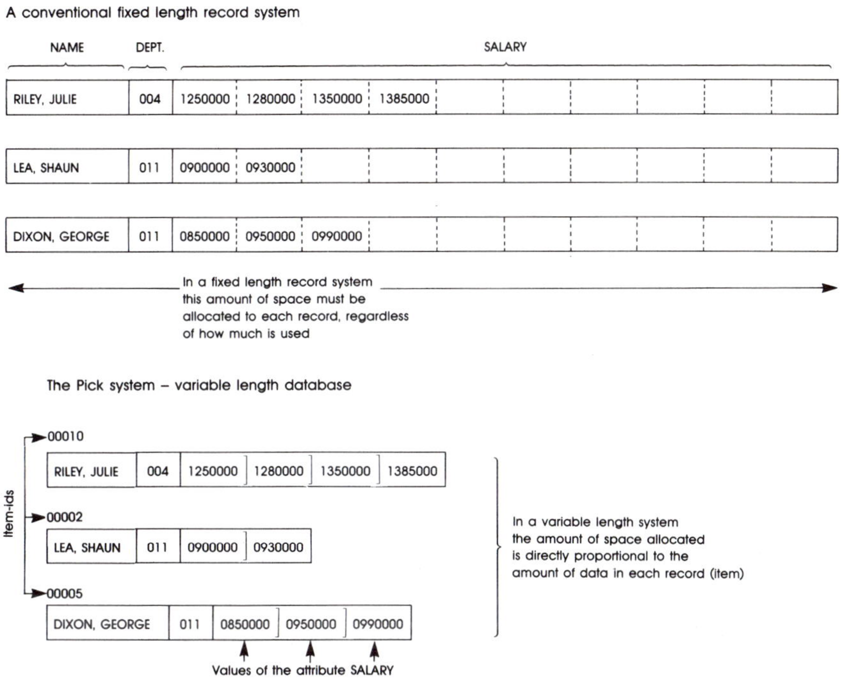

Figure 5.3 The difference between PICK and fixed length record systems.

show the constituent parts of salary such as tax, NHI, pension and so on. This effectively gives a three-dimensional aspect to the data, as illustrated in Figure 5.4.

The strength of PICK lies in the ease with which such a complex data structure can be changed to incorporate the requirements of a business, such as adding bonus pay as an element of salary. Once incorporated, bonus pay becomes another element of salary, whilst those earlier salary values prior to the bonus scheme being introduced are unaffected; they

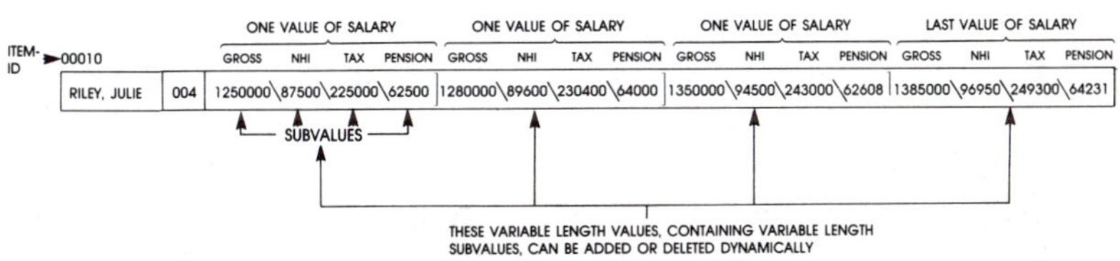

Figure 5.4 The subvalue concept.

effectively contain a null bonus pay amount. Hence it is possible to make modifications to the data structure even when the system is 'live', without affecting the existing data. Figure 5.5 illustrates how bonus pay is introduced on the last two salary values.

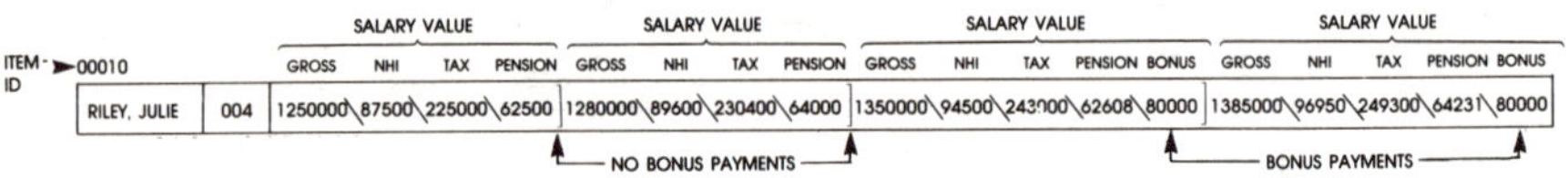

Figure 5.5 Changing the subvalue data structure.

The data structure defined by the dictionaries is extremely flexible, allowing existing attribute definitions to be changed in seconds, merely by editing the attribute definition item in the dictionary file. Previously defined attributes, even the key of the file known as the item-id, can be changed without affecting existing data, thus removing the restrictions imposed by conventional systems.

It is quite feasible, having implemented such a personnel system, to change the key of the file, i.e. personnel code, from its original five digits to seven digits, just by making a simple change to the dictionary. This merely requires changing the last attribute (attribute 10) of the dictionary item REF in the file dictionary (see Figure 5.2) from 5 to 7. No more than a few seconds' effort in total! From this point on, *every* reference to the personnel code can be up to seven digits in length, i.e. for every data entry screen, every printed report, every pre-printed form, every transaction process using the personnel code. The reason for this is that before PICK accesses the data it accesses the dictionary to determine the format of the data. Hence, from the time the change is made to the dictionary, it knows that the maximum length of the reference number is seven digits.

In any conventional system not using a database such a change, so simple to implement in PICK, is a nightmare and could involve hours if not days of work editing and recompiling programs.

5.1.2 The dictionaries

For those of you more familiar with conventional data processing, let me remind you that in PICK terminology records are called items and fields are called attributes.

Since the dictionary is itself a file, it contains items in the same way as any data file. In this instance, however, each item defines the structure of an individual element of data contained in the files held at the next level in the hierarchy.

We have discussed the hierarchy of dictionaries in the PICK system, which start at the top level with the system dictionary with 'pointers' to the master dictionary which in turn has 'pointers' to the file dictionaries. These 'pointers' are produced automatically by PICK when accounts or files are created, and consist of an entry in the respective dictionary. Hence, when an account is created, an entry is placed in the system dictionary with the name of the account created. When a file is created within an account, the name of the file is an entry in the account's master dictionary. Figure 5.2 illustrates how this works.

In the case of data files, the 'pointer' in the master dictionary is to the file's file dictionary. Within this file dictionary is an entry, with the same name as the file, 'pointing' to the start of the data.

The file dictionary, sometimes known as the data dictionary, and referred to as `DICT`, is used to define the format of the data contained in the data file. Thus a data file has two parts, one containing the data itself, the other, the file dictionary, defining the structure of the data.

In a personnel system for example, the main file of personnel records might be called `STAFF` and would contain a number of items (records) each of which would contain a number of attributes (fields). For the purpose of this example let's assume each item comprises the following attributes:

1. Staff reference;
2. Name;
3. Department;
4. Salary;
5. Address;
6. Age;
7. Date of birth.

The purpose of the file dictionary is to define the structure of the item, i.e. the sequence of the attributes in the item, and the format of each attribute. Having pulled in a data record PICK needs to know which part of it contains salary information, which contains the name and so on. To do this the file dictionary contains an item for each attribute of the data record which defines its format giving such information as its length, its position in the data record, how it is to be displayed and so on. In other words, for each of the above seven components of the personnel record there is an item (a record) in the dictionary file. This dictionary item defines an attribute of the record. Figure 5.2 shows just four of these and there are just seven listed above, but in real life a dictionary would contain very many more entries.

In building the dictionary item (record), a meaningful abbreviated name is given to it. This is the item-id of the dictionary item. This 'shorthand tag' is what is used from this point on within PICK to refer to the data held on the data record.

Description	Abbreviated name (DICT name – item-id)
1. Staff reference	REF
2. Name	NAME
3. Department	DEPT
4. Salary	SALARY
5. Address	ADDR
6. Age	AGE
7. Date of birth	DOB

Hence, if you want to list the departments and salaries of all people on the database you would type in the enquiry LIST STAFF DEPT SALARY where STAFF is the name of the file being enquired on and DEPT and SALARY are items in the dictionary referred to by their item-ids, which define where in the data record the required data is held. Having located the file, the ACCESS processor picks up the two file dictionary items from their item-ids (keys), which it interprets to find whereabouts on the data record the department and salary are held, and reads each record on the STAFF file displaying the contents of attribute (field) 1 and attribute 3.

The data dictionary, therefore, will contain an item (record) for each of the above attributes (fields) with an item-id (key) of the abbreviated, dictionary name. Hence, using the above example, the dictionary (DICT) portion of the data file contains the following items (records):

```
REF
NAME
DEPT
SALARY
ADDR
AGE
DOB
```

Each of these dictionary entries serves to define the format of one attribute of the data file, STAFF, and contains such information as the description of the attribute, its maximum length, the attribute number (or the position of the data in the item) and the way the information is to be displayed, i.e. left or right justification, the number of decimal places, and so on. The key (item-id) to each data record is the 'Staff Ref' and *must* come ahead of any data on the record. In PICK the item-id is attribute 0 and all other attributes tend to be numbered sequentially thereafter (see Table 5.1). Just to complete the story, however, you should note that PICK will not complain if an attribute number is missing; it will consider the attribute to have a null value.

Table 5.1 A typical dictionary format.

Position of data in record (attribute number)	*DICT name*	*Description (heading)*	*Length (in chars)*
0	REF	Staff reference	5
1	NAME	Name	20
2	DEPT	Dept	3
3	SALARY	Salary	10
4	ADDR	Address	30
5	AGE	Age	2
6	DOB	Date of birth	8

If you were to look at all the dictionary entries of the file you would notice one extra item (record). This item has an item-id of the same name as that given to the file itself, i.e. STAFF. This entry, illustrated in Figure 5.2, is produced automatically by PICK when the file is created and serves to define the file itself, with such information as its location on disk and its retrieval and update codes.

5.1.3 Dictionary item types

There are various types of dictionary item which are defined by the contents of attribute 1 of the item defining the file. The system dictionary defines the master dictionaries, whilst the master dictionaries define the data files.

- **File Definition Item – or D-item**, where D is held in attribute 1. If this record is in the system dictionary it defines the pointer to the master dictionary or account. In the master dictionary, the D-item defines a file dictionary and in a file dictionary it defines a data file.
  - Files holding the compiled form of BASIC programs should contain DC in this attribute.
  - Files not to be saved when a Filesave command is executed should contain DX in attribute 1 in the item in the file dictionary (DICT) which defines the data file. In the example shown in Figure 5.2, this is the item in the file DICT with the item-id STAFF. This can be a very useful means of reducing backup time, especially for files that are not frequently updated. It is not without its dangers however. Beware when restoring from a filesave tape which does not contain all the files of your system. The filesave tape overwrites the *entire* file system, so if a file is DX'd and not backed up, it will not be restored either and valuable data could be lost forever! It is therefore essential when restoring from a filesave tape that either it

contains copies of **all** files on the system or those not on the tape are held on others.

- Files containing a `DY` in the first attribute will not be saved on a filesave tape either. In this case, however, when the file restore is carried out, the file will be recreated empty, i.e. containing no records. An example of the use of this type of file would be temporary transaction files.

- **File Synonym Definition Item – or Q-item**, where Q is held in attribute 1. If these occur in the system dictionary they 'point' to an account that a user logs on to and this is the way in which user-ids are established, giving each user a unique logon name and password. In the master dictionary the Q-pointer is used to enable access to files held in another user's account. In the file dictionary the Q-pointer redefines attribute names, either to make them shorter and easier to refer to, or to give them an alternative name to enable various departments of a company to refer to the same data by names they are familiar with. This concept of Q-pointers is fundamental to the PICK system and the next chapter is completely devoted to it.
- **Attribute Definition Item – or A-item**, where A is held in attribute 1. This is mostly found in file dictionaries and is used, amongst others, to define the way in which data is to be formatted when output. It is important to bear in mind that ACCESS, the enquiry language, will use these A-items. For example, dates are held on the database as the number of days since 31 December 1967, with prior dates being held as negative numbers. The date can be displayed in various ways, dependent on the code held in the A-item. For instance, with the code `D` the date for 17 December 1986 will be displayed as 17 DEC 1986, but with the code as `D2/` the date will be displayed as 17/12/86. Regardless of the 'output' format the date will be held on the database as a number, which for 17 December 1986 would be 6926, i.e. 6926 days subsequent to 31 December 1967!
- **PROCS** are generally stored as items in the master dictionary and represented with 'PQ' in attribute 1. Chapter 11 describes the procedure language in detail.

5.2 File allocation and information retrieval

Before we start to use and manipulate data extensively within PICK accounts and files we need to know a little about the way in which data space is allocated and information stored and retrieved within it.

5.2.1 Disk map

PICK divides the entire hard disk into a series of blocks called frames, each of which is numbered consecutively from one up to the maximum FID (frame-ID) that the computer system can support. Figure 5.6 shows how the entire disk is divided into units called frames. These frames fall into four main sections:

- **ABS frames** are reserved for the operating system and normally reside between frame 1 and frame 1023. These frames are normally 2048 bytes each. All other frames are normally 512 bytes. The word 'normally' has been used here, since this is an area where implementations may differ.
- **PCB frames** where Program Control Blocks are stored for each of the physical, external ports on the system, i.e. the maximum possible number of users of the system, plus an additional PCB for the Spooler. Each PCB is 32 frames long.
- **WSX frames** (Workspace Extension) where frames are once again allocated to each external port and the spooler for extra workspace. Each WSX is 381 (3 × 127) frames long.
- **Data/overflow frames** begin immediately after the workspace area and finish at the maximum FID. Those frames not containing data are maintained as a pool of spare frames known as overflow.

Figure 5.6 illustrates how the disk map would look for a computer system with four physical ports.

As can be seen from Figure 5.6, the way in which the disk is laid out is dependent on the number of *physical* ports on the system. It is worth noting here, therefore, that if the number of ports on your system is increased at any time by the addition of new hardware, it will necessitate the reloading of the complete operating system and data files from a 'system generation' tape or diskettes. This will cause PICK to reorganize the disk and increase the number of PCB and Workspace areas and start the system files at a new and higher frame number or FID.This is because PICK is able to detect the number of ports a system has and organizes the hard disk accordingly.

5.2.2 Frame allocation

Information as we know is stored in a series of frames, each of 512 bytes (characters). PICK uses the first 12 bytes of each frame for control information, leaving 500 bytes for user data. In creating a file it is necessary to define the initial number of frames it requires (its primary area), and that number of contiguous or adjoining frames are then

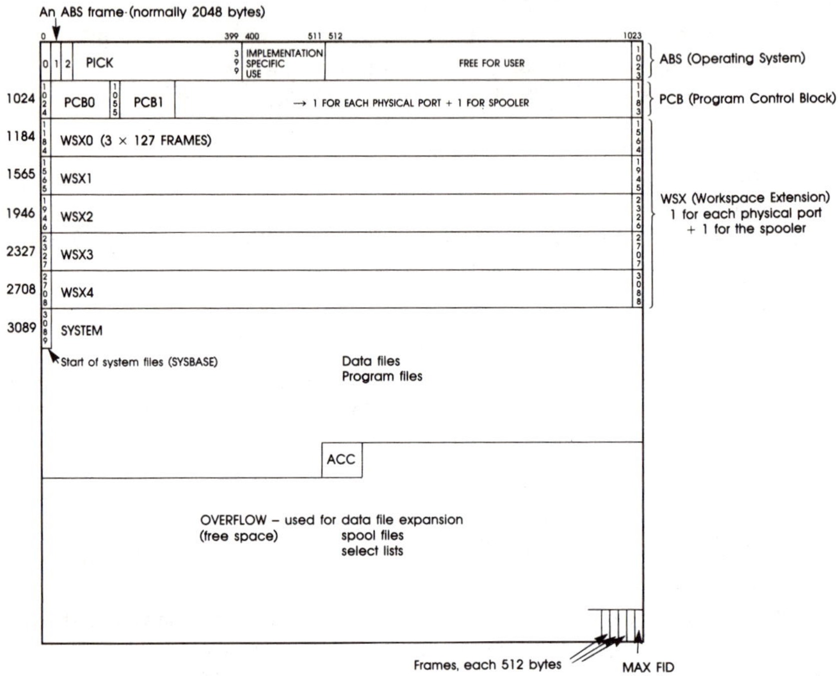

Figure 5.6 The disk map.

allocated. Bear in mind, however, that whilst the initial amount of disk space can grow or shrink during its use, it will not shrink below that of the initial space allocated. This presents the dilemma of sizing your file sensibly (discussed in detail later in this chapter). If the initial space is too big, valuable disk space will be wasted. If however the initial space is too small, PICK will have to make many disk accesses to find the data, thereby lengthening response times.

If the disk is very badly fragmented and the number of frames you need initially are scattered about the disk rather than available as one contiguous area, the file cannot be created and PICK will tell you so. Whilst this rarely happens it is worth being aware of, especially if you intend using large files.

When frames are linked together to form a file, they are no longer referred to as frames, but as groups. This is because other frames can be linked into them as the storage requirements for the file increase. If we create a file containing seven frames initially, those frames will be

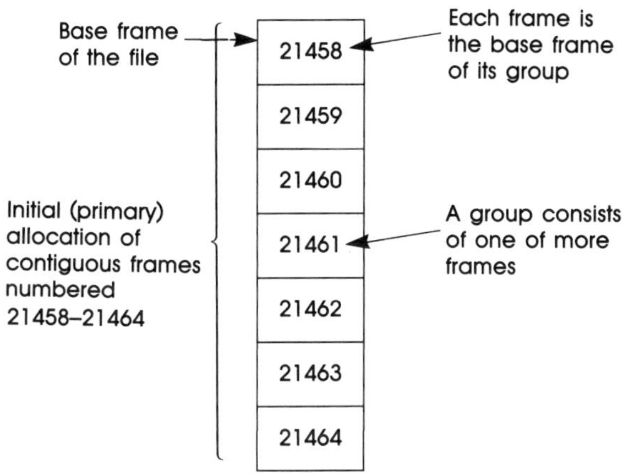

Figure 5.7 Initial allocation of frames to a file.

adjoining and each now becomes the base frame of its group. The very first frame used is known as the base frame of the file. Figure 5.7 shows such a file using frames 21458 to 21464.

The number of groups a file contains is known as its **modulo**. Hence the file created in Figure 5.7 has a modulo of 7 (or primary space of seven frames). If, as data is stored in the file, the initial allocation of frames is insufficient, PICK will link in others. These are not tagged onto the end of the existing file, but linked into the existing group requiring the space. Using the example of Figure 5.7, this means that the additional frames are linked into the existing frames, 21458–21464, rather than extending the original number of base frames by adding from 21465 onwards. This is illustrated by Figure 5.8 where two linked frames have been added to group 21459 and a single linked frame added to groups 21462 and 21463.

The idea in creating a file is to optimize the time taken to read and write data to it. As is apparent from Figure 5.8, the frames subsequently linked into a group bear no relation to the original ones. They may be higher or lower and are linked in on the basis of being the 'next available' in the list of unused frames. This means that after coming to the end of one frame, to get to the next PICK will have to 'jump' to it generating what is known as a 'frame fault'. This is nowhere near as drastic as it sounds. It just means that PICK has to issue a command for the appropriate frame to be read from disk. Obviously a certain amount of time will be wasted in doing so, since the location of the frame has to be determined and a disk read initiated.

Since there are only 500 bytes (characters) that can contain data in each frame, any file containing records regularly over 500 bytes will

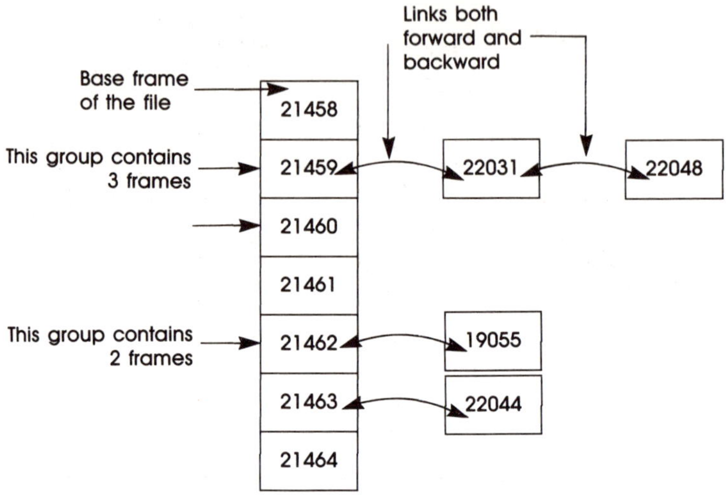

Figure 5.8 The linking of frames to a file.

frequently generate frame faults, which in turn will obviously have an effect on response times. To minimize this effect it is possible to specify the number of frames to be allocated to each contiguous group. This number is known as the **separation** of the file. In the example of Figure 5.7, since no special steps were taken, the number of frames in each group was one and new frames linked in were linked in one at a time. Its separation, therefore, is 1.

For files containing large records, the separation can be increased to 2 or more. In doing so, the number of initial frames allocated to the file (its primary space) will be its modulo (the number of groups it contains) multiplied by its separation (the number of contiguous frames in a group). Once again the *entire* number of initial frames a file needs must be available in one contiguous area. Figure 5.9 shows how initial space is allocated to a file whose modulo is 7 and whose separation is 2. A total of 14 consecutive frames are used, 21458–21471.

Additional frames as needed are linked to the existing groups as before, except that they are linked in, in multiples of the separation. Hence if the separation is 3, three adjoining frames at a time are linked in; if the separation is 2, then two adjoining frames at a time are linked in and so on. Figure 5.10 shows how two batches of frames have been linked to group 21460, whilst groups 21466 and 21468 contain just one additional link of two frames.

Care should be exercised when increasing the separation above 1, since it could readily result in considerable wasted disk space. If the

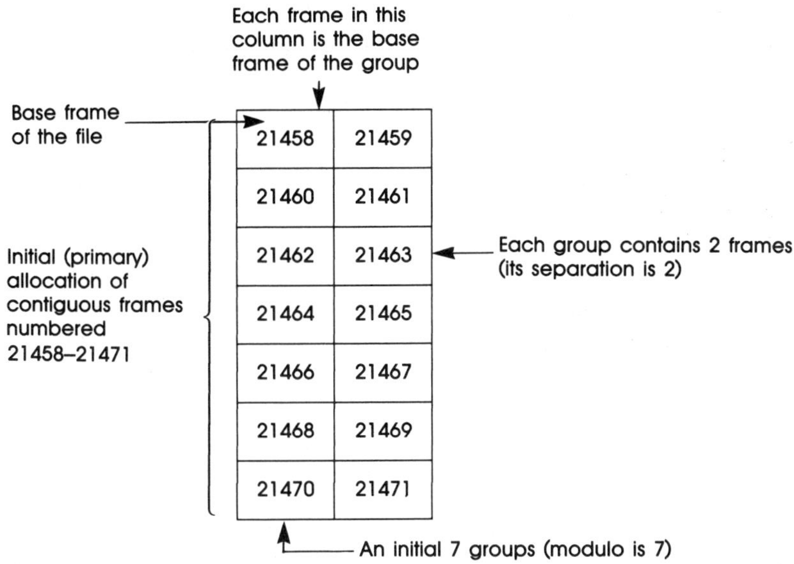

Figure 5.9 Initial allocation of frames to a file whose modulo is 7 and whose separation is 2.

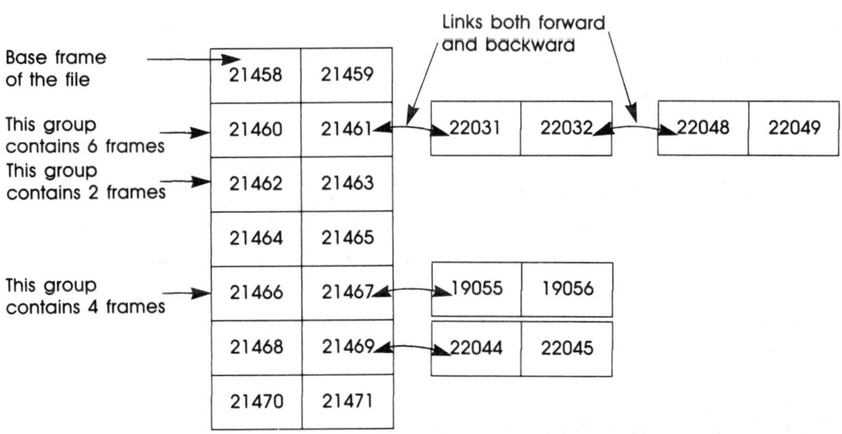

Figure 5.10 Linking additional frames to a file with a separation of 2.

average record requires 550 bytes, to allocate two frames as the separation would mean that on average 450 bytes ((2 × 500) − 550) would be wasted in each group! It may well be better to leave the separation at 1 and incur the frame faults. This is the dilemma to be faced when creating a file: a balance has to be struck between the speed of data access and wasted disk space.

It is important to note that in a multi-user environment the separation is usually set to 1. This is because by the time PICK has determined that the data it is looking for is not in the frame searched and generates a 'frame fault', another user has sought information from the disk causing the disk heads to be moved elsewhere. It is therefore of limited value to have the frames located together with a separation greater than 1, other than in a single-user or low-activity multi-user environment.

5.2.3 The storage and retrieval of items in a file

PICK uses a hashing technique to store and locate a specific item in a file. It uses a mathematical formula on the item-id and the file modulo and separation to compute a 'remainder' that it adds to the file base to give the starting FID (frame number) of the exact group to contain the item. Whilst PICK does not know where in the group the item is, it normally takes very little time to search through the group's frames. In a correctly sized file the hashing algorithm gives almost instant access to information, regardless of the number of records stored, and cuts out the overhead of searching through indices or B-tree structures which is how many other database systems structure their data.

Items are stored sequentially within their group, each being separated by a special character called a **delimiter**. New items that are added to a group are added to the end of the existing chain of items within it. So as you can see there is no order *at all* to the sequence of items held in a group.

Items that get changed during processing are treated as if they were a new item. They are first removed from their original position in the group with the rest of the items in the group being shuffled up to close the gap. After processing, the 'new' item is added to the end of all the other items of the group. When the initial allocation of frames in the group has been used up, other frames are linked into the group by a series of pointers and data continues into them.

5.2.4 Frame and group formats

A frame consists of 512 bytes, the first 12 of which are used by PICK to link forwards and backwards to other frames. The layout of these 12 bytes is shown in Figure 5.11.

1	2	3	4	5	6	7	8	9	10	11	12
*	NNCF	← Forward Link →				← Backward Link →				NPCF	*

* – Reserved

NNCF –The count of the number of contiguous frames linked forward from this one (the Number of Next Contiguous Frames)

Forward Link –The FID of the frame linked forward from this one

Backward Link –The FID of the frame linked previous to this one

NPCF –The count of the number of contiguous frames linked backward to this one (the Number of Previous Contiguous Frames)

NNCF and NPCF are usually zero, except in data files whose separation is greater than 1

Figure 5.11 Frame format – the first 12 bytes.

The remainder of the frame (500 bytes) is used for the data. At the start of each item are 4 bytes specifying the item size. Directly following this is the item-id (attribute 0) followed by an attribute mark, followed by attribute 1 and an attribute mark and so on. Between each attribute of the item is the attribute delimiter '^' (ASCII value 254). Should the attribute contain multivalues, the value mark ']' appears at the end of each value. The segment mark '_' is placed at the end of the item and a

```
>DUMP 21458[CR]

FID:  21458 : 0     0  0  0  (53D2: 0  0   0   0)

  1:01F30001^This is the first attribute^This is the s:
 51:econd attribute^This attribute has MULTI-VALUES]Ne :
101:xt multi-value]Third multi-value]and a final multi :
151:-value^This is the final attribute^_01A10012^The n:
201:ext item starts here and continues until the next  :
251:item is reached and so on. At the end of the group :
301:are two segment markers^ _ _                       :
351:                                                   :
401:                                                   :
451:                                                   :
```

Figure 5.12 The typical output from dumping a frame.

second segment mark follows it if the item is the last in its group. So to look at a frame by dumping its contents would show not only the data, but all the delimiter characters too. A typical frame format is shown in Figure 5.12.

When more than one frame is linked together in the group it is possible to see the entire contents of the group by typing the letter **G** (group) after the frame number. In Figure 5.13 the output from dumping a group of two linked frames is shown. This follows the links forward.

```
>DUMP 21458 (G[CR]

FID:   21458 :  0  20295    0   0   (53D2: 0  4F47  0   0)

   1:01F30001^This is the first attribute^This is the s:
  51:econd attribute^This attribute has MULTI-VALUES]Ne:
 101:xt multi-value]Third multi-value]and a final multi :
 151:-value^This is the final attribute^_01A10012^The n:
 201:ext item starts here and continues until the next  :
 251:item is reached and so on. At the end of the item t:
 301:here is a segment marker^_02A20012^This is the sec :
 351:ond item in the group^It too contains multi-values :
 401:]and other multi-values]and others but because of  :
 451:the length of its data finally is too long for the :

FID: 20295 :  0       021458   0  (4F47: 00      53D2      0)

   1:first frame and flows into the linked one^This ite:
  51:m then becomes the last in the group and is therefo:
 101:re ended by TWO segment markers^ _ _              :
 151:                                                  :
 201:                                                  :
 251:                                                  :
 301:                                                  :
 351:                                                  :
 401:                                                  :
 451:                                                  :
```

Figure 5.13 Typical output from dumping a group of frames.

5.2.5 How to size files correctly

Having talked about the way in which items are stored in files, it is apparent that it is very important to select the correct modulo and separation for a file in order to minimize the number of frame faults when accessing data and to minimize the amount of wasted space. As we have seen there is a fine balance to be taken between the two. Further, to assist in optimizing retrieval time, it is important to spread the data *evenly* throughout the file.

The number of disk reads, which increases dramatically as the number of frames per group increases, is the factor that will contribute most to the degradation of your system. Even so, it is not wise initially to allocate the maximum number of frames you think a file will use, because the original, contiguous number of frames assigned will not be reduced and a lot of space, not frequently used, will be wasted. You should aim, therefore, to allocate an initial area which takes the average file size into account, since PICK will link extra frames into a group as it needs to, and will release those frames when they are no longer needed. These 'available' frames are taken from, and returned to, a central pool called 'overflow'.

In normal practice the modulo and separation of a file can be calculated as follows:

1. Determine the total file size by multiplying the average record length by the average number of records.
2. Determine the separation (maximum 127). Ensure that any frame above 1 is more than 50% utilized.
3. Divide file size, from (1), by 450 and divide the result by the separation. This will give the modulo.
4. Take the result from (3), and convert it to the next highest prime number in the table shown in Appendix B. The modulo of a file should be a prime number to achieve the optimum distribution of items in a file. It should NEVER be a multiple of 2 or 5.

There are many who will never increase the separation above 1 in the firm belief that by virtue of PICK offering a multi-user environment the disk head will almost definitely have moved between the request for the first and subsequent frames of a group, making the importance of having these frames adjacent only marginal. Whilst this is often true, certain computers can take advantage of having the data adjacent, in which case the use of a separation greater than 1, where appropriate, would improve response times.

5.3 Checking item distribution and optimizing file size

Having stressed the importance of sizing files correctly, you will be pleased to know that PICK gives you the means not only to check the distribution of items within a file using its current modulo, but to test the impact on the distribution of the items of an alternative modulo, a 'what if' process. The verb to check out the existing file modulo is `ISTAT`. This provides a histogram of the items held within each group and, at the end of the list, produces statistics which assist in deciding whether the current modulo size is correct. We can try this out on the system dictionary and Figure 5.14 shows a typical output.

It can be seen from Figure 5.14 that there is no problem with the file modulo of the system dictionary. Items are distributed fairly evenly with, on average, just under two items per group. There are few empty groups

```
>ISTAT SYSTEM[CR]

FILE= SYSTEM  MODULO=  11  SEPAR=   1
FRAMES BYTES  ITMS
    1     93    2 *>>
    3   1384    3 *>>>
    1     40    1 *>
    1      0    0 *
    1    152    4 *>>>>
    1     46    1 *>
    1    180    4 *>>>>
    1    133    3 *>>>
    1      0    0 *
    1     36    1 *>
    1     28    1 *>
   13

ITEM COUNT =            20, BYTE COUNT=  2092, AVG. BYTES/ITEM= 104.6
AVG. ITEMS/GROUP=  1.8, STD DEVIATION=   1.4, AVG BYTES/GROUP= 190.1
```

Figure 5.14 Output from ISTAT on the system dictionary.

```
>HASH-TEST SYSTEM[CR]

TEST MODULO:3[CR]

FILE= SYSTEM  MODULO=   3  SEPAR=   1
FRAMES BYTES  ITMS
    1    292    7 *>>>>>>>
    1    290    7 *>>>>>>>
    4   1510    6 *>>>>>>
    6

ITEM COUNT =          20, BYTE COUNT=     2092, AVG. BYTES/ITEM= 104.6
AVG. ITEMS/GROUP= 6.6, STD DEVIATION=     .5, AVG BYTES/GROUP= 697.3
```

Figure 5.15 Output from HASH-TEST testing modulo of 3 on system dictionary.

and an acceptable average number of bytes per group. The verb HASH-TEST is used to test out alternatives. It enables a 'what if' test to be done, without affecting the existing file. Figure 5.15 shows HASH-TEST being used on the system dictionary, with a test modulo of 3 frames.

At first glance the results shown in Figure 5.15 seem to provide a better, more even, distribution. However the average bytes per group now exceeds one frame. We could try a further alternative and Figure 5.16 shows the use of a test modulo of 21. This modulo would provide too many empty frames and is not currently the best option. Since the number of accounts of the system will undoubtedly increase, the default modulo size of 11 for the system dictionary is best left unchanged.

```
>HASH-TEST SYSTEM[CR]

TEST MODULO:21[CR]

FILE= SYSTEM  MODULO=  11  SEPAR=   1
FRAMES BYTES  ITMS
     1    47    1 *>
     1    55    1 *>
     1     0    0 *
     1     0    0 *
     1    84    2 *>>
     1    85    2 *>>
     1    83    2 *>>
     1    40    1 *>
     1    51    1 *>
     1    74    2 *>>
     1    36    1 *>
     1     0    0 *
     1    88    2 *>>
     1    28    1 *>
     1     0    0 *
     1     0    0 *
     1     0    0 *
     3  1297    1 *>
     1     0    0 *
     1    47    1 *>
     1    77    2 *>>
    23

ITEM COUNT =         20, BYTE COUNT=    2092, AVG. BYTES/ITEM= 104.6
AVG. ITEMS/GROUP=   .9, STD DEVIATION=   .8, AVG BYTES/GROUP= 99.6
```

Figure 5.16 Output from HASH-TEST testing modulo of 21 on system dictionary.

Where the average bytes per item is below 250 characters you should aim to provide a modulo that keeps all groups in the file between one and two frames, minimizing those which are empty. When the average item size is much larger the aim is to provide a modulo that keeps group sizes as small as possible whilst keeping the number of empty frames to a minimum. Do give careful consideration to the growth of files before spending time trimming down file sizes and regularly check files to see if they need resizing. The file statistics report from a `FILE-SAVE` will be very valuable for this purpose (see Section 13.2.3).

5.4 File sizing and resizing

The `FILE-SAVE` command, explained further in Chapter 13, produces a valuable statistics report which assists in locating files that need resizing. If a file stats report is not to hand, one can be produced by the command `LIST-FILE-STATS`.

Having decided a file needs resizing and armed with the new modulo and separation for it, there are a couple of ways in which you can carry out the resizing exercise. The second is by far the most usual in practice:

1. Create a temporary file (`CREATE-FILE`) and copy (`COPY`) into it the contents of the file to be resized. Delete the original file (`DELETE-FILE`) and recreate it with the new modulo. Then copy back all the items from the temporary file and delete the temporary file.
2. Using the editor (`ED`) place the new modulo and separation in attribute 13 of the file definition item in the form (n,m), where n is the new file modulo and m is the new file separation. The next time the file or account containing the file is saved and restored, either as part of a full file save (`FILE-SAVE`) or selective account restore (`ACCOUNT-RESTORE`), the file will be restored with its new modulo and separation.

   a) **Resizing the data file**. Modify the file definition item held in the DICT (File Dictionary). For example, for the file `TEST`

   ```
   >ED DICT TEST TEST
   .P
   001 D
   002 57494
   003 101
   004 1
   005
   006
   007
   008
   009 L
   ```

```
010 10
011
012
013 (203,7) ← resize to MODULO      203
                        SEPARATION   7
```

b) **Resizing the dictionary**. Modify the file definition item held in the MD (Master Dictionary). For example, for the file TEST

```
>ED MD TEST
.P
001 D
002 57900
003 7
004 1
005
006
007
008
009 L
010 10
011
012
013 (11,1) ← resize to MODULO      11
                       SEPARATION   1
```

6 Q-Pointers

TCL verbs and general commands covered in this chapter

```
ED   PASSWORD   SET-FILE
```

6.1 Reasons for use of Q-pointers

No discussion of the PICK operating system would be complete without detailed reference to one of its fundamental features, the Q-pointer. We have already seen that logging on in PICK is handled by logging to an account, rather than the system as a whole. An account, an environment containing a logical grouping of files, is analogous to a company department. Whilst people working within a department are primarily using the information held within their department, there are many occasions when they need information held elsewhere.

Within PICK, unless a Q-pointer is used, the only data available to the user is that held within the account to which he is logged. In operation, however, it is usually necessary to be able to access information held in other accounts. A typical example of this is where a number of accounts use the same program file. Rather than duplicate the program file and hold it within each account, a Q-pointer can be set up to 'point' to the account that holds the program file. The Q-pointer can also be used to give an alternative or shorter name to a file, often referred to as a synonym.

In the same way as different people within a department need to work with differing parts of their departmental files, some of which may be highly confidential, PICK, by using Q-pointers, provides the same facility. The Q-pointer provides alternative means to log to an account, enabling different users access to the same account, but with different security levels and passwords. Effectively, therefore, this gives the user a user code or user-id to the PICK system which tells PICK the facilities and files the user can freely access, the account the user has access to and the user's password.

6.2 User identification (user-id)

Before generating user-ids make sure that the accounts they use exist and, if not, create them. User-ids are created with the editor in the SYSPROG account by editing entries into the system dictionary.

The item-id created in the system dictionary becomes the user-id and the other attributes define the user's profile. The format of a system dictionary Q-pointer whose only content in the first attribute is a Q, is shown in Table 6.1.

Table 6.1 The format of a Q-pointer in the system dictionary to set up a user-id.

Item-id attribute	*User name*
1	Q
2	Account name to which the user will have access
3	Null value
4	Null value
5	Retrieval locking code
6	Update locking code
7	Password
8	Privilege level code
9	Justification code and to show whether the system accounting file is to be updated – value of 'L' 'R' or 'U'
10	Length

An example of creating the user-id MIKE to access the account SYSPROG at logon is shown in Figure 6.1.

Figure 6.1 shows the creation of another user who accesses the SYSPROG account with SYS1 privileges (see Chapter 13 for information on privilege levels). The user was created using the editor, described in detail in Chapter 7. Since it is not usual to directly edit null into an item, the attributes that are to be set to null are first set to a nominated character, in this case a full stop, which is then replaced by null. Notice too that the password is not set through the editor, but from the TCL command PASSWORD, which encrypts the password MJBUI so that anyone looking through the system dictionary cannot readily interpret the passwords.

Chapter 13 explains the way to control your system and covers, in detail, locking codes and privilege level codes whilst the use of system accounting is discussed in Chapter 14.

```
ED SYSTEM MIKE[CR] <------------- Create a new item in SYSTEM
NEW ITEM                          Called MIKE
TOP
.I[CR] <------------------------- Insert
001  Q[CR] <--------------------- Start entering the data
002  SYSPROG[CR]
003  .[CR] <--------------------- Use a '.' for attributes that
004  .[CR]                        should contain a null value
005  .[CR]
006  .[CR]
007  .[CR]
008  SYS1[CR]
009  L[CR]
010  10[CR]
011  [CR]
TOP
.F[CR] <------------------------- Flip buffers
TOP
.RU10/.//[CR] <------------------ Replace all '.' with a null
003
004
005
006
007
EOI  10
.FI[CR] <------------------------ File the item MIKE
'MIKE' FILED

>PASSWORD[CR] <------------------ Set a password for MIKE
ENTER ACCOUNT NAME?MIKE[CR]

ENTER NEW PASSWORD?MJBUI[CR] <--- Enter password

>
```

Figure 6.1 Creating a new user and password.

6.3 Q-pointers to files

File Q-pointers either point to files held in other accounts or are used to provide alternative and often shorter names to files in any account. Q-pointers are edited into the master dictionary of the account that uses them. It is worth noting here that anyone with the use of the editor can readily point to *any* file in the system, and hence access to the editor

Item-id (attribute 0)	Alternative name by which the item being referenced by the Q-pointer may be called
Attribute 1	Q
Attribute 2	The account name in which the file being referenced is to be found
Attribute 3	The name of the file being referenced
Attribute 4	Null
Attribute 5	Retrieval locking code
Attribute 6	Update locking code
Attribute 7	Conversion code
Attribute 8	Correlative code
Attribute 9	Justification
Attribute 10	Length

Figure 6.2 The format of Q-pointers.

needs to carefully controlled. All aspects of security are discussed further in Chapter 13. The format of a Q-pointer is shown in Figure 6.2.

Whilst a Q-pointer can have all ten attributes as shown in Figure 6.2 and can be used just like any other item within ACCESS (see Section 9.2.1), when used to point to files it rarely contains more than the first three. Figure 6.3 shows the format of a Q-pointer that points to a file called `CUSTOMER` in an account called `ACCOUNTS`. The Q-pointer is called `CUST`. As soon as the Q-pointer is created, any action taken on `CUST` like listing customers, or printing details of specific customers, will actually be referring to the data held in the `CUSTOMER` file in the account `ACCOUNTS`. Every part of the file is available to the account containing the Q-pointer just as though the file itself was resident in that account.

The Q-pointer `CUST` would be created by using the editor and is illustrated in Figure 6.4. The Q-pointer is edited into the master

Item-id	`CUST`
Attribute 1	`Q`
Attribute 2	`ACCOUNTS`
Attribute 3	`CUSTOMER`

Figure 6.3 A Q-pointer example.

```
>ED MD CUST
NEW ITEM
TOP
.I[CR]
001  Q[CR]
002  ACCOUNTS[CR]
003  CUSTOMER[CR]
004  [CR]
TOP
.FI
'CUST' FILED
```

Figure 6.4 Using the editor to create a Q-pointer.

dictionary with its first attribute as Q and the remaining attributes defining the account and file to which the Q-pointer relates.

There are several permissible variations. Firstly, what is known as the reflexive form, is where the Q-pointer references the file in which it is stored. This is to be found for the entry `MD` in the master dictionary of any account and dictionary-only files. If you refer back to Figure 5.2 you will see such an entry in the file `MD`. In this case attribute 1 contains the Q and attributes 2 and 3 are empty (see Figure 6.5). This is a technical, but essential, requirement which is automatically taken care of by the PICK operating system and which enables PICK to access the master dictionary, which it is unable to do if it is not present.

Item-id	`MD`
Attribute 1	`Q`
Attribute 2	
Attribute 3	

Figure 6.5 The content of the MD Q-pointer in the master dictionary.

6.4 Temporary Q-pointers

The above examples leave permanent entries in either the system or master dictionaries. There are many instances where a temporary pointer is needed. This is handled by the command `SET-FILE`, which updates the item `QFILE` in the master dictionary. Each time the command `SET-FILE` is used, the item `QFILE` is updated. Since there is only one item in the MD called QFILE, it is obviously not possible to have more than one temporary Q-pointer in any one account at any one time.

The SET-FILE facility is often used where it is necessary to make a change to a file in another account or where a file from another account is to be copied into your own account and where reference to that file is unlikely to be needed again.

Once the Q-pointer is set up, the file being pointed to is referenced by the name QFILE. Figure 6.6 shows how a temporary Q-pointer is set up to the CUSTOMER file in the account ACCOUNTS and how a list of the item-ids within the CUSTOMER file can be produced by reference to the temporary Q-pointer QFILE.

```
>SET-FILE[CR]
ACCOUNT NAME ?ACCOUNTS[CR]
FILE NAME ?CUSTOMER[CR]
'QFILE' UPDATED

>SORT ONLY QFILE[CR]

PAGE 1                                         17:58:00   7 JUN 1985
QFILE...........

A01
B01
B02
B03
D02
S01
T01
W01
W02

9 ITEMS LISTED
```

Figure 6.6 The use of the temporary Q-pointer, Q-FILE.

The example given by Figure 6.6 shows the typical use of a temporary Q-pointer. It is important to realize that the temporary Q-pointer exists as the item QFILE in *each* master dictionary. As such, anyone with access to the account and the command SET-FILE can change the file it points to. PICK will not stop two people using the command SET-FILE in the same account at the same time. Hence the last person to update the Q-pointer QFILE by the command SET-FILE will determine its contents and for this reason the temporary pointer should be seen as such and treated with care.

7 Using the Editor

TCL verbs and general commands covered in this chapter

```
ED   EDIT
```

7.1 An introduction to the editor

An editor is an essential ingredient of any operating system, and whilst the PICK editor is a line rather than full screen editor, it provides a powerful tool to access and modify any piece of information within the database. As we have seen PICK comprises a series of files of just one format and hence only one editor is required.

Whilst the editor can freely make changes throughout the database, it is not the common form of file updating which is routinely handled by application programs written in BASIC. The editor is most frequently used to make entries in dictionaries, to set up Q-pointers and to create or modify PROCS and BASIC programs. It is the ability to access and change *anything* within the PICK database that makes the editor so powerful and obviously a security hazard! The aspects of security are discussed fully in Chapter 13, but obviously one aspect to the management of any PICK system is controlled access to the editor.

The editor works on what is called the current line concept, which means that at any given time there is a current line which is addressed and against which information is added, changed, deleted or displayed. Once the simple editor concept is understood, all that is required to make full use of the editor, is access to its list of commands.

7.2 Editor concepts

The editor works with a temporary version of the data which it manipulates in two variable length work buffers. The original and

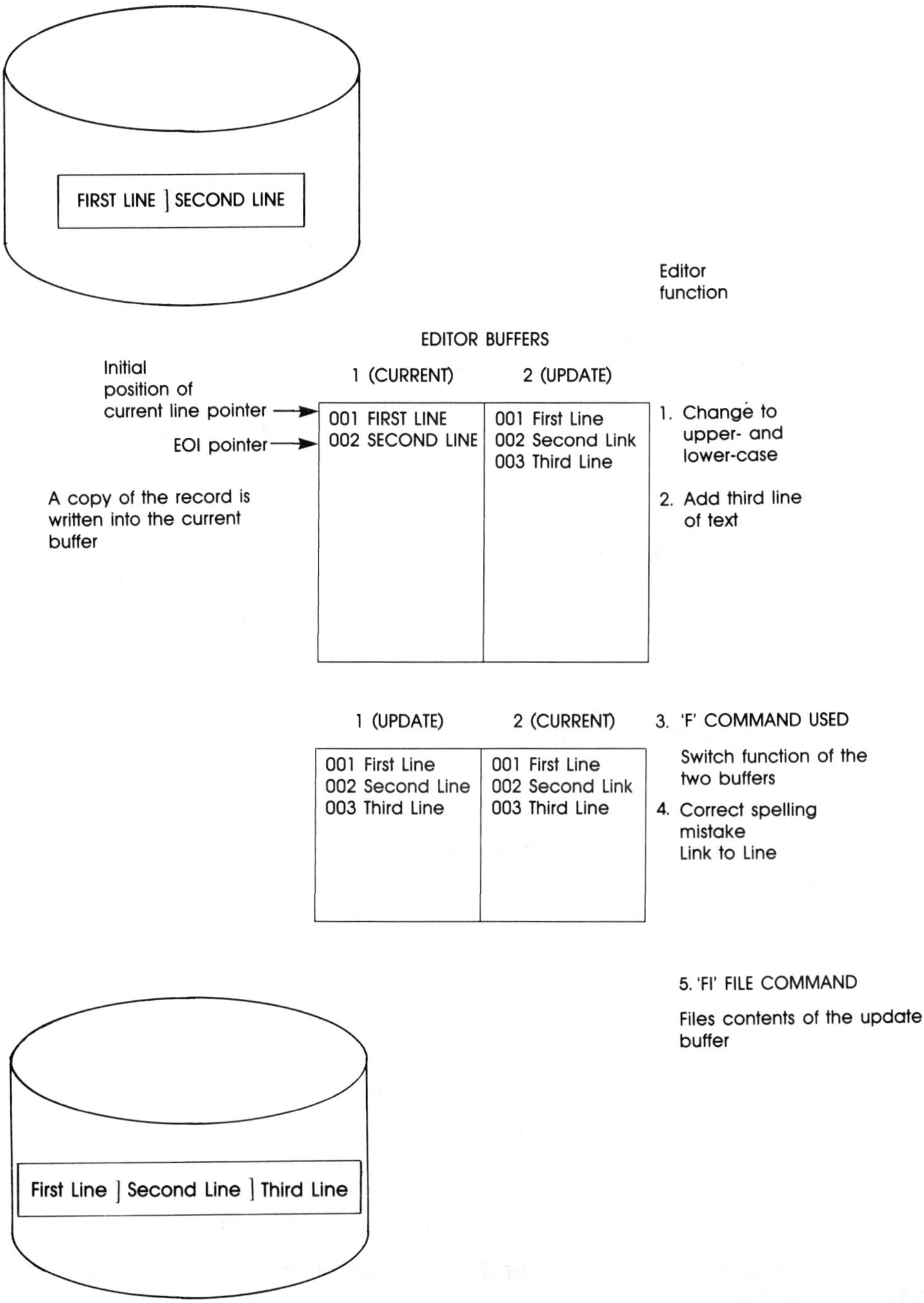

Figure 7.1 The editor concept.

permanent version held on disk is *only* altered when the changes made with the editor are filed away. When the editor is invoked, a copy of the record is read into buffer 1. Each attribute of the item is assigned a sequential number starting at 1, with the current line pointer pointing to the current line, initially the top of the item and an End-of-Item (EOI) pointer pointing to the last line of the item.

As changes are made in buffer 1 (Current Buffer), a new version is built up in buffer 2 (Update Buffer) and hence, for fairly obvious reasons, updating can only continue in ascending line number sequence. To view the 'current' state of the edited item, the contents of buffer 2, the update buffer, have to be made available. This is handled by an F (Flip buffer) command which resequences the attributes within the update buffer and switches the functions of the buffers. From this point on, until another F command is executed, changes are made to the contents of buffer 2, now the Current Buffer, which are written away in buffer 1, the update buffer. This process of toggling the buffers can continue indefinitely until the item is filed away or the edit abandoned.

Figure 7.1 provides a pictorial representation of the editor, showing a typical editing session. It explains how a two-line item on disk is updated to a three-line item. The original record is first copied to the current buffer. The text of the record in the current buffer is changed to upper and lower case and a third line added. However a spelling mistake is made in line two, which can only be corrected by flipping the buffers, making buffer 2 current. The spelling correction is then made and the record filed back on disk.

7.3 A summary of the editor commands

The editor commands and their functions are as follows:

Options	*Description*
[CR]	Next line
^	Toggle 'wildcard' function
?	Status – displays filename, item-id and current line number
n	Go to line n
A	Again – repeats last locate or search command
AS	Toggles display of data in assembly format
B	Go to the bottom of the item
C	Display column numbers

Options	*Description*
DE	Delete current line
DEn	Delete n lines starting at current line
DEn/X	Delete lines containing string X in the next n lines starting at the current line
EX	Exit, do not change the existing record. It is the equivalent of ABORT
EXK	As with EX, but return immediately to TCL. Useful if you want to abandon the list of edits being processed
FD	Delete the item being edited from the file
FDK	As with FD, but return immediately to TCL
FI	File item, including changes made
FI n	File item, including changes, with the item-id n
FIK	File current item, including changes made and return immediately to TCL
FI (f i	File the item in file f with an item-id i

Note Any of the above FI options can include the K option to return immediately to TCL, an O option to overwrite any item found with the same item-id or L which converts files to list format

FS	File current state of edited item on disk, but continue with the edit session. A useful way of saving current work when processing a large item
FS n	As with FS, but save to item n
FS (f i	As with FS, but save on file 'f' as item 'i'

Note Any of the above 'FS' options can include the 'O' option to overwrite an existing item with the same item-id or 'L', which converts the item to list format

Gn	Go to line 'n'
I	Insert after current line
Ln	List 'n' lines from current line
L/X	Locate string 'X' from current position in current line
Ln/X	Locate string 'X' in 'n' lines starting at current line
Ln/X/a-b	Locate string 'X' in 'n' lines starting at current line and occurring between columns 'a' and 'b'
L:X	Locate string 'X' which starts in column 1

Options	Description
M	Toggle macro expansion
MEn//	Merge 'n' lines from current item from line 1
MEn//m	Merge 'n' lines from current item from line 'm'
MEn/i/	Merge 'n' lines from item 'i' in current file starting at line 1
MEn/i/m	Merge 'n' lines from item 'i' in current file starting at line 'm'
MEn (f i	Merge 'n' lines from file 'f' item 'i' starting from line 1
MEn (f i)p	Merge 'n' lines from file 'f' item 'i' starting from line 'p'
N	Redisplays current line
Nn	Moves down 'n' lines
P	Execute prestored command 0
Pn	Execute prestored command n
Pn X[Y[Z	Set prestore command 'n' to perform task 'X' followed by task 'Y' followed by task 'Z'. The ESC key delimits each command
PD	Display contents of all prestored commands
R	Replace contents of current line
Rn	Replace contents of next 'n' lines from current line
R/X/Y	Replace string 'X' with string 'Y'
R/X//	Replace string 'X' with null
R//X	Insert string 'X' at the beginning of current line
Rn/X/Y	Replace the first occurrence of string 'X' in the next 'n' lines with the string 'Y'
Rn/X/Y/a-b	Replace the first occurrence of string 'X' in the columns 'a' to 'b' in the next 'n' lines with the string 'Y'
RU...	Used in place of 'R' to indicate that every, rather than just the first, occurrence of a string in a line, is to be replaced
S	Toggles suppression of line numbers
S?	Displays the size of the item in bytes – only accurate if the buffer has been flipped
T	Go to the top of the item
TB n,m...	Sets tab stops at position 'n', 'm' and so on
Un	Go up 'n' lines

Options	Description
`X`	Cancels effect of last insert, replace or delete commands
`XF`	Cancels the effect of all commands since the last 'F' command
`Z a-b`	Set zone between columns 'a' and 'b' and only display data within these columns

7.4 Using the editor

The editor is invoked by the TCL command **EDIT**, normally abbreviated to **ED**. Either of these commands will call up the editor which then needs to be told the file and item in the file to be edited. The format of the command is:

```
>EDIT {DICT} filename itemlist
```

or

```
>ED {DICT} filename itemlist
```

The editor can either edit an existing item, or create a new one. The editor is simple and easy to use. Once you have grasped the concept of the way it works, i.e. the use of its buffers, the rest is plain sailing and just a case of learning the commands. Probably the easiest way of learning the editor is to spend time in a test file creating and amending items, merging data from other items and trying out all the other options.

By way of an introduction and to show the features of the editor we will create and then modify a list of the names of the months of the year in an item called **MONTHS** in a file called **DEMO**. The editor will not create the file as well as the item, so if the file does not exist it should first be created with the **CREATE-FILE** command (see Section 4.2.1).

7.4.1 Adding new items with the editor

To explain in detail the workings of the editor we will first create the item **MONTHS** in the file **DEMO** with just the first six months in it. Figure 7.2 shows how this is achieved.

The final command in Figure 7.2 files away the item **MONTHS** in the file **DEMO**. You can see that each line entered is given a unique number by the editor so that it can be referred to at any time. As you may have noticed in Figure 7.2, the item is only half complete and one of the months is

```
>ED DEMO MONTHS[CR]
NEW ITEM <-------------- Shows that the item does not
TOP                      already exist
 .I[CR]<---------------- Editor prompt is '.', the I
 001+JANUARY[CR]         is the insert command
 002+FEBRUARY[CR]
 003+MARCH[CR]
 004+APIL[CR]
 005+MAY[CR]
 006+JUNE[CR]
 007+[CR]
 TOP
.FI <------------------- The 'file away' command
'MONTHS' FILED.
```

Figure 7.2 Creating a new item with the editor

spelt incorrectly. The next section shows how to use the editor to add the rest of the months and to correct the spelling mistake.

7.4.2 Changing the details of an item

Editing changes into an existing item is handled by adding new lines (attributes), replacing all or part of an existing line or by deleting lines. All of these functions are shown in Figure 7.3.

```
>ED DEMO MONTHS[CR]
TOP
.L20[CR]<--------------- List 20 lines
001 JANUARY  ]
002 FEBRUARY ]
003 MARCH    ]
004 APIL     }<--------- Current buffer contents
005 MAY      ]
006 JUNE     ]
EOI 006<---------------- End of item pointer, line 6
.G4[CR]<---------------- Go to line 4
004 APIL<--------------- The editor displays current contents
.R[CR]<----------------- Replace the line
004 APRIL[CR] <--------- Type in new contents
.B <-------------------- Go to bottom
EOI 006
```

```
.I ◄──────────────── Insert command
006+JULY[CR]
006+JULY[CR]
006+AUGUST[CR]
006+SEPTEMBER[CR] ◄── New details added into
006+OCTOBER[CR]       update buffer
006+NOVEMBER[CR]
006+DECEMBER[CR]
006+[CR]
E01 006
.T[CR ◄───────────── Go to top of item
TOP
.L20[CR] ◄────────── List 20 lines
001 JANUARY
002 FEBRUARY
003 MARCH
004 APRIL ◄───────── Current buffer contents
005 MAY
006 JUNE
EOI 006
.F[CR] ◄──────────── We must 'flip' buffers to view
TOP                  changes made
.L20[CR] ◄────────── List 20 lines
001 JANUARY   ┐
002 FEBRUARY  │
003 MARCH     │
004 APRIL     │
005 MAY       │
006 JUNE      │
007 JULY      ├ ◄─── Current buffer contents
008 JULY      │
009 AUGUST    │
010 SEPTEMBER │
011 OCTOBER   │
012 NOVEMBER  │
013 DECEMBER  ┘
EOI 013
.8[CR] ◄──────────── Go to line 8
008 JULY
.DE[CR] ◄─────────── Delete line
.FI[CR] ◄─────────── File item away
'MONTHS' FILED
```

Figure 7.3 An editor session on an existing item.

Figure 7.3 demonstrates a number of editor functions and shows the way in which you can readily move around the item: T for top, B for bottom, n or Gn for line n and so on. In addition changes had to be made in ascending sequence, hence the contents of line 4 are replaced *before* other lines are added at the bottom. If we tried to do it the other way round the editor would have complained with the error message SEQN?, which is always a signal to flip the buffers using the F command and to look at the contents of the item before going further.

The other commands used, as with a number of others, can be applied to more than one line by including the number of lines with the command, such as L for list which on its own lists just one line, whereas L20 lists 20 lines. In the same way DE deletes the current line, but DE5 will delete five lines starting at the current line.

Hopefully the principles are now clear. Changes are applied in ascending line number sequence by moving the current line pointer to the appropriate line and then applying the required command. Once a change is needed to be made to an earlier line or to new lines added, the F command must be used to flip the buffers and make the current state of the item available for editing.

7.4.3 The principles of replacing data

In the last example we saw one way in which information can be replaced. By completely re-inputting the line – the word APIL was replaced by APRIL. This is not too difficult when the amount of information to type in is small, but on a long line this is not only time-wasting but prone to error. Hence the editor provides a way of replacing part of a line. This is done by identifying a sequence or string of characters in the original line to be replaced by a different string. The general format is shown in Figure 7.4.

Hence, to correct the spelling of APIL in Figure 7.3 we could have used:

```
>R/PI/PRI/[CR]
```

or, by using an asterisk as the delimiter, as explained in Figure 7.4,

```
>R*I*RI*[CR]
```

Replacing strings becomes a lot more difficult when the text string occurs several times in the line. Take the following example:

```
003 sdfsdfsdfsdfsdfsdfsdfsdfsdfsdfsdfsdfsdf
```

where we want to replace the sixth occurrence of sdf with xxx. Without typing in the full 18 characters it would seem impossible to point at the specific part of the line to be replaced. However there is a way in which you can replace the first occurrence of a string from a particular column

```
R{U}{n}/Current string/Update string/{c{-d}}
```

where:

- R stands for the replace command
- U means universal or every occurrence in a line
- n means that the string replacement is made in the next n lines from the current line. Unless the U option is taken, only the *first* occurrence of the current string is replaced with the update string in each of these lines
- / known as the 'delimiter' and used to separate the two character strings. Whilst the / is the usual delimiter, any character not contained in either character string, can be used
- c starting column position
- d ending column position

The start and end column positions are used to restrict the location of the data to be replaced.

Figure 7.4 The format of the editor replace command.

```
>ED DEMO DUMMY
TOP
.3[CR]
003 sdfsdfsdfsdfsdfsdfsdfsdfsdfsdfsdfsdfsdf
.C
          1         2         3         4         5
   1234568901234567890123456789012345678901234567890123456
.R/sdf/xxx/16    ←  Replace first occurrence from column 16
.FI              ←  It is not necessary to flip buffers
                    before filing if you are certain of
                    your actions
'DUMMY' FILED
```

The data string now looks like this:

```
sdfsdfsdfsdfsdfxxxsdfsdfsdfsdfsdfsdfsdf
```

Figure 7.5 Replacing a character string with the editor.

position and to make life easier the C command will produce a column ruler. Let's see this in action in Figure 7.5 to replace the string sdf in column 16 with the string xxx.

The replacement command is of particular value in reproducing the null character, quite frequently needed when defining dictionary items. In these cases a special character not used elsewhere is placed on these lines and then the special character is replaced with the null value. In Figure 7.6 a user-id called MIKE is set up in the system dictionary. Those lines needing null values are first given a value of '.' which is replaced by a null value.

Another way of editing in a null value is by pressing the control key and up-arrow key simultaneously.

7.4.4 Merging data with the editor

The command ME will allow data from the existing or a totally different PICK file to be included in the item being edited. The data merged is not removed from the originating file, but copied from it and hence the original file remains intact. The line number of the information held in

```
ED SYSTEM MIKE[CR]
NEW ITEM
TOP
.I[CR]<------------- Create a new item in the system dictionary
001 Q[CR]
002 SYSPROG[CR]
003 .[CR] ]
004 .[CR] |
005 .[CR] }<-------- Assign the value '.' to
006 .[CR] |          all items requiring a
007 .[CR] ]          null value
008 SYS1[CR]
009 L[CR]
010 10[CR]
011 [CR]
TOP
.F[CR]<------------- Flip buffers
.RU99/.//[CR]<------ Replace up to 99 occurrences of a
003 ]                '.' with a null value
004 |
005 }<-------------- Editor responds with the line
006 |                number of those changed
007 ]
EOI 10
.FI[CR]<------------ File away the item in its current state
'MIKE' FILED
```

Figure 7.6 Creating a user-id with the editor.

```
ME{n}itemid/{m}
```

where the item is in the file being edited, or

```
ME{n}({DICT} filename itemid){m}
```

another file altogether, where:

- n represents the number of lines to be merged
- m represents the starting line number; when omitted line 1 is assumed

To merge lines from the item being edited, use null as the item-id. This is usually represented by two '/', although any character not in the character string can be used as the delimiter.

```
ME{n}//{m}
```

Figure 7.7 The format of the editor merge command.

the originating file is used to determine what is to be merged. The general format of this command is shown in Figure 7.7.

Take care to ensure you have flipped the buffers and have studied the current state of the item before carrying out the merge command, particularly where you are merging lines from the item itself. Having merged the data the editor responds with its prompt '.', so you should flip the buffers after a merge to ensure the correct data has been merged.

Figure 7.8 shows how an item containing a list of the months of the year is changed using the merge command. Firstly lines 3 and 4 of the item are merged within itself at line 6, and then one line is merged from another item, DUMMY in the same file (DEMO) as the item being edited. Finally three lines are taken from a completely different file and item and merged in.

7.4.5 Using the search facility

Looking for a particular string of characters in an item is handled by the locate command L. Having found the string the editor displays the line it was found on. The A command will carry out the search again.

Like the replace command, the search command can look for the first n occurrences of the string and can limit its search to a range of specified columns, giving the general format of the command as shown in Figure 7.9. If however the search requires that the string start in column 1, then the format of the command is L:String.

7.4.6 Using the wildcard facility

The up-arrow input on the command line toggles the wildcard facility allowing future use of the '^' (up arrow) to indicate a wildcard character,

```
>ED DEMO MONTHS[CR]
TOP
.6[CR]
006 JUNE
.ME2" "3[CR]          ← Merge two lines from this item
.F[CR]                  starting at line 3
TOP
.L10[CR]
001 JANUARY
002 FEBRUARY
003 MARCH
004 APRIL
005 MAY
006 JUNE
007 MARCH
008 APRIL
009 JULY
010 AUGUST
.ME1/DUMMY/3[CR]      ← Merge one line from item DUMMY
.F[CR]                  held in this file, i.e. DEMO starting at line 3
TOP
.7[CR]
007 MARCH
.ME3(TEST TEST1)      ← Merge three lines from item TEST1
.F[CR]                  from the file TEST starting at
.6[CR]                  line 1
.L10[CR]
007 MARCH
008 FIRST LINE FROM TEST1
009 SECOND LINE FROM TEST1
010 THIRD LINE FROM TEST1
011 APRIL
012 JULY
013 AUGUST
014 sdfsdfsdfsdfsdfsdfsdfsdfsdf
015 SEPTEMBER
016 OCTOBER
.FI[CR]
'MONTHS' FILED
```

Figure 7.8 Examples of the editor merge command.

```
L{n}"String"{c{d}}
```

where:

- n means that the string search is made in the next n lines from the current line.
- " Known as the 'delimiter' and used to separate the character string. Whilst the " is the usual delimiter, any character not contained in the character string can be used
- c starting column position
- d ending column position

Figure 7.9 The editor locate command.

```
.ED DEMO TEST[CR]
TOP
.L20[CR]
001 MY NAME IS TOM
002 I HAVE A FRIEND CALLED TIM
003 TIM HAS A VERY BAD TEMPER
EOI 003
.^[CR]
/X^/ ON
.T[CR]
TOP
.RU99/T^M/XXX/[CR]
001 MY NAME IS XXX
002 I HAVE A FRIEND CALLED XXX
003 XXX HAS A VERY BAD XXXPER
EOI 003
.FI[CR]
'TEST' FILED
```

Figure 7.10 The use of the wildcard facility.

i.e. any character. This enables you to determine the same course of action for strings of characters which are similar, but not the same. Figure 7.10 shows how this is used.

7.4.7 The use of prestored commands

The editor has the means to store one or a number of editor commands in one of ten command buffers numbered from 0 to 9. The commands held within them are executed by requesting use of the prestored command facility, denoted by the letter P followed by the appropriate command buffer number. Hence by typing in P0 the editor would execute the commands found in prestored buffer 0; likewise P1 would perform the commands found in prestored buffer 1.

On entering the editor you will find that the prestored command P0, usually referenced simply as P, is set to L22 automatically. Hence by typing P at the editor prompt, the next 22 lines will be displayed.

The contents of the prestored commands are listed by the command PD (display prestored commands), at the editor prompt. It should be noted however that all command buffers other than P0, i.e. P1 to P9, are cleared as soon as the edit session has been terminated. The prestored command buffers are temporary and only apply to the edit session in progress.

These buffers need first to be given the appropriate command sequences, which is handled by entering the prestored command number followed by the string of commands. The general format for this is shown in Figure 7.11.

```
Pn Command 1 [ Command 2 [ Command 3 .....
```

where:

n	represents the prestored command buffer number
Command	is the editor command that would be typed in manually
[	is the special character that separates the commands. This is achieved by pressing the ESC key. Note that whilst this prints as a left square bracket, it is not one and the [key will not achieve the correct result.

Figure 7.11 The format of editor prestored commands.

The prestored command facility is of particular value when you need to make a change within a number of records in a file, for example to correct spelling. In Figure 7.12 all records in an address file which have the name DERBY spelt as DERBBY are corrected.

In Figure 7.12 an entire file, albeit of five records, was searched looking for a misspelt word. The spelling mistake was found in two records, requiring a total of three corrections to be made. After the corrections were made control was returned to the TCL prompt. Another common use of this editor feature is to search through the master dictionary to change Q-pointers that point to one account and to change them to point to another. This would typically occur when new programs need to be tested. In this case a copy of the live account would be

```
ED ADDRESS *[CR]                  ← Edit all records in the file
10012                             ← Item-id of first record found
TOP
.P2 R99/DERBBY/DERBY/[FI[P2[CR    ← Replace occurrences
                                    of DERBBY with DERBY, file the item
                                    and re-execute command P2
.P2[CR]                           ← Execute the commands held in the
                                    prestore command buffer number 2
EOI 016
'10012' FILED.                    ← No change made to this record
10160
TOP
EOI 017
'10160' FILED                     ← No change made to this record
10101
TOP
012 DERBY                         ← Line 12 of this record changed
018 County of DERBY               ← Line 18 of this record changed
EOI 020
'10101' FILED.
10114
TOP
011 DERBY                         ← Line 11 of this record changed
EOI 015
'10114' FILED.
10115
TOP
EOI 016
'10115' FILED.                    ← No change made to this record
```

Figure 7.12 The use of editor prestored commands.

restored to a test account and the Q-pointers within the test account changed to point at the account containing the programs for testing. This is illustrated in Figure 7.13, using exactly the same principles as described in Figure 7.12.

In operation this command is so quick that it is impossible to read what is displayed on the screen. If you wish to temporarily stop the screen display press CTRL/S. Once you are ready for the operation to proceed, type CTRL/Q. These commands can be used to stop and restart any screen output which displays too fast to read.

```
EMD MD *[CR]                          ← Edit all records in master dictionary
MEHELP                                ← Item-id of first record found
TOP
.P1 R999/LIVE/TEST/[FI[P1[CR]         - Replace occurrences
                                        of LIVE with TEST,
                                        file the item and
                                        re-execute command P1
.P1[CR]                               ← Execute the commands held in the
                                        prestore command buffer number 1
EOI 010
'MEHELP' FILED.                       ← No change made to this record
T-REW
TOP
EOI 003
'T-REW' FILED.                        ← No change made to this record
DM13
TOP
002 TEST                              ← Line 2 of this record changed
EOI 003
'DM13' FILED.
DM15
TOP
002 TEST                              ← Line 2 of this record changed
EOI 003
'DM15' FILED.
    :
    :
    :
```

Figure 7.13 The use of editor prestored commands to change Q-pointers in the master dictionary.

8 Printer Control

TCL verbs and general commands covered in this chapter

:STARTSPOOLER	LISTABS	LISTPEQS	LISTPTR	SP-ASSIGN
SP-CLOSE	SP-EDIT	SP-KILL	SP-OPEN	SP-STATUS
STARTPTR	STOPPTR			

8.1 An introduction to the spooler

The spooler controls two classes of peripheral device:

1. A save device, such as the floppy disk or tape unit;
2. One or more printers.

The spooler, therefore, controls the backup procedures (described in Chapter 13), as well as the printers (to which this chapter is devoted).

One of the important considerations of any multi-user system is the control of printing, where one or more printers is to be shared amongst a number of users. No user wishes to be constrained by what is being printed at the time he is ready to produce a report, nor does he want to wait until his report has finished printing before being able to use his terminal again.

The PICK spooler provides a powerful and extensive facility for controlling all printed reports. Once a report has been generated, from whatever process, it is stored on disk and PICK creates a control record which refers to it. The spooler then takes over and fully controls the printing process. By producing reports in this way the user is held up for only the time required to prepare a copy of the report on disk and is able to produce reports freely regardless of whether or not a printer is available for immediate use. Thereafter, whilst the report is printing or awaiting its turn in the queue, the user's terminal is free to carry out any other task.

The spooler runs as a separate process in the system although it is called a 'phantom' process since it is treated as the last and non-physical port on the system. Hence if a system has 12 physical ports, the spooler is port 13 and, as discussed in Section 5.2.1, Program Control Blocks (PCB) and Workspace Extensions (WSX) are allocated to the spooler as though it were a user of the system. The spooler is normally started automatically as an option in the `FILE-RESTORE` or `COLD-START` processes and can be restarted at any time at TCL with the `:STARTSPOOLER` command. This command should only be used as a last resort, since it causes all spooled reports to be lost. The spooler can control up to 16 serial and four parallel printers at any one time, with up to 600 print files scattered amongst them. The key features of the spooler are shown in Figure 8.1.

Each printer used is assigned a number, with printer number 0 (zero) normally being used as the default or system printer. To make use of a printer other than printer 0, the user will need to assign another printer to himself. This assignment is, as may be expected, only effective for

- Up to 600 print files may be retained and controlled.
- Up to 60 print files may be produced simultaneously.
- Up to 125 output queues may be defined. (An output queue is a queue – for example, to which a report is sent to be printed and can therefore be considered as a particular printer loaded with a particular type of stationery.)
- Up to 125 copies of a report can be requested at a time.
- Up to 16 serial printers can be defined.
- Up to 4 parallel printers can be defined.
- Print files can be transferred to and from storage media such as tape, floppy or hard disk.

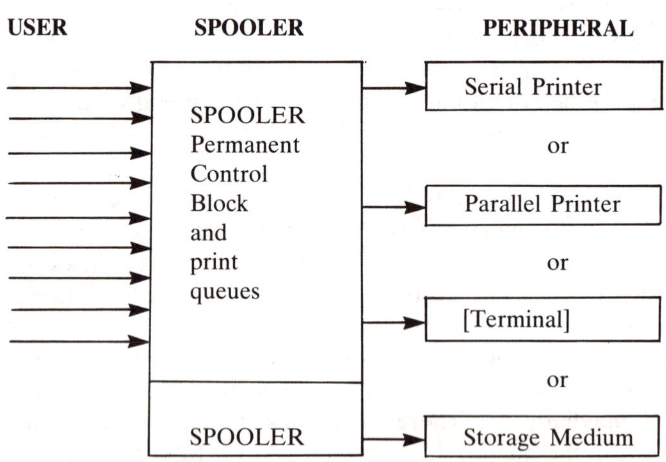

Figure 8.1 Features of the spooler.

output from the terminal that originated the assignment. What is not made generally clear, however, is that this assignment is lost as soon as the user logs to another account and, unless a further printer assignment is made, all subsequent reports will then, by default, be produced on the system printer!

Each printer must have a form queue number assigned to it, which represents a specific printer with specific stationery. Where a system has a number of the same printers each using the same stationery then all printers can be given the same form queue number, i.e. zero. In this case the spooler will take each report in the spool queue and direct it to the first available printer. It is rarely that simple, however, since most companies have a mixture of printers, some letter-quality, some matrix, and will also have a number of different types of stationery.

If some printers are letter-quality printers working at 50 cps and others are fast dot-matrix printers at 200 cps or more, then you would want to ensure that outside correspondence was produced on the letter-quality printer and lengthy draft reports on the matrix printer. In this situation you need assign different form queues to each printer, for example form queue 0 for the matrix printer (the system printer and nominated as printer 0) and form queue 1 for the letter-quality printer (printer 1). In this example each printer on the system is given the same number as its form queue number, form queue 0 to printer 0, form queue 1 to printer 1 and so on. This situation is preferable since many of the spooler commands refer to the form number rather than printer number and it is far easier to know what response to give if you know they are both the same!

To enable the use of special stationery, however, each printer can be allocated up to three different queue numbers. This means that for any printer you can send reports to one of up to three different print queues, each of which will be printed by the same printer. For instance one queue might handle normal reports using plain stationery, the second, invoices on pre-printed invoice stationery, whilst the third may require that reports be printed on four-part plain stationery. Unless you have a dedicated printer for each of these different requirements, an existing printer will have to be used for them all.

To handle a situation that requires the use of special stationery (for *special* read *different*) for a printer that is being used for other work you will need to undertake the following steps:

1. Assign a unique form queue number in the range 0–125 for the special stationery. Use the command `STARTPTR` described in Section 8.2.1. If preprinted stationery is used, the `A` (alignment) option should be used with the `STARTPTR` command.
2. Before running the program that uses special stationery, assign the form queue number using the hold options `HS`. Use the command

SP-ASSIGN described in Section 8.3 to achieve this.

3. Once the program has finished, the output will be held on the spool queue under a spool queue number. Once the printer has been loaded with the special stationery, release the output from the spool queue by use of the SP-EDIT command described in Section 8.4.

8.1.1 Spooler options

Many of the verbs used to control the spooler share a common options handler and are therefore treated in the same manner. The verbs affected are:

```
:STARTSPOOLER  SP-EDIT      T-ATT    T-RDLBL
DUMP           SP-KILL      T-BCK    WHAT
LISTABS        SP-STATUS    T-DET    WHERE
LISTPEQS       SP-TAPEOUT   T-FWD    WHO
LISTPTR        STOPPTR      T-READ
```

You should refer to your manual under the section 'Spooler Verb Options Handler' for details of its workings.

8.1.2 LISTPTR, LISTPEQS, SP-STATUS and LISTABS

Before we take any action at all, we need to find out what printers are known by the system and what state they are in. There are a number of useful commands that explain which printers are already configured and available to the system and give information about the state of the spooler. Firstly LISTPTR lists the printers available, their type and the line to which they are attached. The LISTPEQS command produces a list of all the entries on the spooler and gives information on each, whilst the SP-STATUS command provides useful status information on all spooler-controlled devices. Another helpful command is LISTABS, which provides a list of the form queue associated with each physical line on the computer.

```
>LISTPTR[CR]

PRINTER ASSIGNMENTS                          10:15:22

PRINTER        OUTPUT QUEUES   PAGE  DEV OR  STATUS
TYPE    NUMBER                 SKIP  LINE #

SERIAL       0  0                 0       2  INACTIVE
SERIAL       1  1                 0       3  ACTIVE
```

Figure 8.2 Output from LISTPTR.

Figure 8.2 shows a typical display from the LISTPTR command. It shows there are two serial printers attached to the system, but only one, printer number 1 on line 3, currently in use. The LISTPTR verb, like most spooler commands, has a number of options which follow the verb. These are:

- n{–m} A range of printers from number n to m
- B Reports on the 20 possible printers regardless of whether they are in use or not
- N The NOPAGE option, displaying in continuous mode on the terminal
- P Produces the output on the printer rather than the terminal

Hence, the command LISTPTR 1 would produce a report of printer status and queue allocation information for printer number 1 only, whilst LISTPTR 1P would send the same report to the printer.

The LISTPEQS command illustrated in Figure 8.3, has even more options:

- n{–m} A range of print file numbers from number n to m
- A Outputs the status of all reports generated on the account to which you are logged
- C Outputs a count of the number of spooled reports and the amount of storage space they are using
- E Displays the frame location of the spooled entries
- F Displays the entries on the spooler in form queue order (0–125)
- L Displays reports that have been deleted, in addition to the current ones
- P Causes the output from the command to be sent to the printer rather than terminal
- ACC Displays the status of all reports produced from the account ACC

The first example of Figure 8.3 shows that two reports have been spooled from the SYSPROG account which have been given the spooler references (entry numbers) 1 and 2. These numbers can be used within the command SP-EDIT to manage the spool queue. The status codes show that the first entry on the spooler is being printed on form queue 0, and in each case just one copy of the report has been requested. The status codes that may be encountered are:

- A Indicates that the control block is available for use. These are shown when the L option is used. This will occur when several reports have been spooled and an earlier one printed. The earlier control blocks will be reused before additional ones are allocated
- C Indicates the print file is closed. If this code is not shown it means

```
>LISTPEQS[CR]

SPOOLER ENTRIES                    29 JUL 1985  16:21:28
# STAT LK LN STATUSES      CP FO FRMS  DATE    TIME   ACCT
1 48A5     0 P C SO L      1  0   1 28/07/85 15:53:19 SYSPROG
2 48C1     0 P  L          1  0   1 28/07/85 15:58:42 SYSPROG

2 QUEUE ELEMENTS LISTED.         2 FRAMES IN USE.

LISTPEQS L[CR]

SPOOLER ENTRIES                    06 APR 1986  14:18:04

# STAT LK LN STATUSES      CP FO FRMS   DATE    TIME   ACCT
1 8880     0 H C           1  0   3 12/04/86 14:07:16 SYSPROG
2 88C1     0 A (H C  L)    1  0   2 12/04/86 14:18:04 SYSPROG
3 8880     1 H C           1  0   2 12/04/86 14:14:41 STOCK
4 8880     0 H C           1  0   2 12/04/86 14:14:46 SYSPROG
5 8880     2 H C           1  0   2 12/04/86 14:15:44 STOCK

5 QUEUE ELEMENTS LISTED.         9 FRAMES IN USE.

>LISTPEQS E[CR]

PRINTER LIST ELEMENTS              06 APR 1986  14:15:44

STAT LK LN      CURPOS    BEGFID CP FO FRMS DATE   TIME    ACCT

8880    1 000100003D57 00003D57 1 0  3   12/04/86 14:07:16 MTC
8880    0 00010000349B 0000349B 1 0  2   12/04/86 14:13:57 SYS
8880    0 00010000349D 0000349D 1 0  2   12/04/86 14:14:41 SYS
8880    0 00010000349F 0000349F 1 0  2   12/04/86 14:14:46 SYS

4 QUEUE ELEMENTS LISTED.           9 FRAMES IN USE.
```

Figure 8.3 Output from LISTPEQS.

that the report is being generated or that an SP-OPEN condition exists

- G Indicates the control record references a phantom print file being the alignment segment of another print file which was aligned
- H Specifies the entry to be a hold file by virtue of the SP-ASSIGNment under which it was created or because it was dequeued by SP-KILL Fn (where n is the entry number) or due to the occurrence of a cold start
- I Specifies that immediate printing of the report was requested by virtue of the SP-ASSIGN I option being taken
- L Indicates the record is locked and cannot be SP-EDITed. It is

locked when it is available, open, spooled, being output or while it is being SP-EDITed

N Indicates that the print file was generated under an SP-OPEN condition

O The report is being output

P Indicates the output is to go to the printer

R Indicates the entry has been SP-EDITed and sent to the printer

S Indicates the report has been spooled using SP-EDIT

T Indicates that the report has been sent to the storage medium (tape, floppy, etc.)

X Indicates the report was aborted using SP-KILL

```
>SP-STATUS[CR]

THE SPOOLER IS INACTIVE

PRINTER # 0 IS SERIAL, INACTIVE, AND ON LINE.
THE PRINTER IS RUNNING ON LINE 2.
ASSIGNED OUTPUT QUEUES: 0.
THE NUMBER OF INTER-JOB PAGES TO EJECT IS 0.

PRINTER # 1 IS SERIAL, ACTIVE, AND ON LINE.
THE PRINTER IS RUNNING ON LINE 3.
PRINT FILE BEING OUTPUT IS ELEMENT 1, A CLOSED FILE FOR LINE # 0
   GENERATED ON ACCOUNT SYSPROG, WHICH IS 58 FRAMES LONG.
ASSIGNED OUTPUT QUEUES: 1.
THE NUMBER OF INTER-JOB PAGES TO EJECT IS 0.
```

Figure 8.4 Output from SP-STATUS

Figure 8.4 shows the output from the SP-STATUS command which gives a self-explanatory status report of the up-to-date position on each printer. This general overview first indicates whether or not the spooler is active. It then shows the number of frames taken up by any spooled report, the form queues assigned to each printer and the physical line to which each printer is attached.

Figure 8.5 shows the typical output from the LISTABS command, a very useful command when things start to go wrong. If reports are being printed on the wrong printer, or do not start printing at all, this command helps you to find out why since it shows the print queues assigned to each port. Using this information with that of SP-STATUS the printers associated with each user can readily be established.

Figure 8.5 shows that lines 0, 1 and 5 are using form queue 0, whilst lines 4, 6 and 7 are using queue number 1. Lines 2 and 3 are the printers

```
>LISTABS[CR]

LINE  STATUS COP  FORM
  #          IES    #

  0  P        1    0
  1  H        1    0
  2           0    0
  3           0    0
  4  P        1    1
  5  P        1    0
  6  P        1    1
  7  P        1    1
```

Figure 8.5 Output from `LISTABS`.

themselves, since they have no form queue number next to them. The status codes which may be encountered with this command are:

- `C` Choke the creating process to printer speed
- `H` Create and keep a copy on hold
- `I` Immediate output
- `O` Keep the print file open at completion
- `P` Output to the printer
- `T` Output to the tape

These status codes are based on options taken when the printer is assigned using the `SP-ASSIGN` command. Refer to Table 8.1 on page 91 for a detailed explanation of these codes.

8.2 Adding and removing printers

8.2.1 The `STARTPTR` command

The PICK system allows printers to be added and removed from a system configuration with very little effort. The command `STARTPTR` is used to add a printer to the system. The same command is used to assign a further form queue to an existing printer or restart an existing printer that has been stopped with the `STOPPTR` command. The general format of the command is shown in Figure 8.6.

The first example in Figure 8.7 shows the addition of a new printer to the system. The serial printer, number 1 attached to line 4, is given the form queue number 3 with two pages being specified to be thrown between each report printed.

>STARTPTR n,F,P,TN,A {(O}

where

- n is the actual printer number (0 is system printer); this can be a number between 0 and 19
- F the form queue number in the range 0 to 125. It is possible to assign up to three form queues per printer. If more than one is assigned, these are separated by commas and enclosed in parentheses, i.e. (0,2,3) assigns form queues 0, 2 and 3
- P the number of blank pages to eject automatically between reports
- T the printer type, where S = serial and P = parallel
- N the line number of the printer
- A the alignment option for preprinted stationery. Causes the prompt LINES?, asking for the number of lines for each alignment test. After each trial the prompt AGAIN(Y/T/N) will be displayed. In response Y continues the alignment trials, N stops them and T stops the alignment and the printer
- O Other options, such as S to suppress first form feed on serial printers X followed by a number to specify the lines per page for serial printers.

Figure 8.6 The general format of STARTPTR.

The second example in Figure 8.7 shows the same printer being added to the system, but this time the form queue numbers 2 and 3 are assigned to it.

On the final example in Figure 8.7 the same printer is restarted after it had previously been stopped by the STOPPTR command. The STOPPTR command is explained in Section 8.2.2. Since the printer has only been stopped from printing and its other details (such as line number and form queue numbers) are known, it only requires a start instruction followed by the printer number.

8.2.2 The STOPPTR command

The STOPPTR command does not remove a printer from the configuration, but stops the printer after it has finished the report it is currently printing. Neither does STOPPTR stop the spooler, it only stops a particular printer, and only when the report in progress has been completed. As with most PICK commands there are a number of options that can be used and these are explained in Figure 8.8. However, the user of this command must have the highest system privileges, SYS2. For further information on privilege levels see Section 13.1.2.

Allocate printer 1 with the following options
Assign form queue 3 to the printer
Eject two pages between each report
Printer is serial attached to line 4
Set the alignment option

```
>STARTPTR 1,3,2,S4,A[CR]
```

Set two form queues for printer 1

```
>STARTPTR 1,(2,3),2,S4[CR]
```

A simple 'restart' command after use of the STOPPTR command

```
>STARTPTR 1[CR]
```

PICK will respond with either:

```
The printer control block has been initialized,
and the printer has been started.
```

or

```
The printer control block has been initialized
hopefully, the correct paper is in the printer,
and the correct LPI is set.
```

Figure 8.7 Examples of the use of STARTPTR.

```
>STOPPTR {(options)}
```

where

n{–m}	are valid printer numbers in the range 0–19
B	will stop all printers
W	will cause the spooler to finish printing the reports on the spool queue, but stop the printer immediately they are complete. The terminal that carries out this command is returned to TCL after printing is complete

Figure 8.8 General format of STOPPTR.

Examples of the use of this command are shown in Figure 8.9.

Having used the W option, all subsequently produced reports will hold on the spool queue until released by a STARTPTR command (see Figure 8.8). The W option is of particular importance when handling the

>*STOPPTR 1*	Stops printer number 1
>*STOPPTR 1–3*	Stops printers in the range 1 to 3
>*STOPPTR B*	Stops all printers
>*STOPPTR 1W*	Stops printer 1 and waits until printer 1 is inactive before returning terminal to TCL

Figure 8.9 Examples of STOPPTR.

spooler within a PROC. The STARTPTR command will not work if the printer is still active, hence within a PROC the STOPPTR command should always contain the W option.

8.2.3 The SP-KILL command

The command SP-KILL performs three separate functions. It:

1. Immediately terminates a report that is being printed
2. Removes a printer from the spooler system
3. Removes entries from the spooler queue.

Terminating reports

The SP-KILL verb will 'immediately' stop a report from printing. The word immediately is enclosed in quotes because the spooler stops sending data to the printer immediately, but the printer buffers have to empty before the printer stops. In most cases this will take several seconds. Usually the user can only kill in this way the jobs generated on the account he is actually logged on to. Only the highest privilege level (SYS2) allows printing to be stopped on any printer (even if the job being output belongs to another account).

The verb requires that the logical printer number printing the report be quoted and will cause ABORT! to be printed one line after the point where the text of the report was terminated. This indicates that the report was abandoned part way through. The abort message can be suppressed if the N option is used.

The report will be released from the spooler unless action is taken to convert it to a hold file (see the next section). The printer will start printing the next report from its assigned queues unless a STOPPER has been executed.

Removing a printer from the spooler system

The SP-KILL with the D option and followed by the printer number is used to delete a printer from the spooler system. Carrying out the command whilst the printer is still working can cause all sorts of problems, so it is wise to ensure that the printer is stopped in a controlled manner (use STOPPTR followed by SP-KILL n where the report is a lengthy one – n being the printer number). Only then is it safe to remove the printer from the system configuration.

If the printer is a parallel printer it will just become inactive. If, however, the printer is a serial printer the port the printer is attached to is sent to logon, enabling a terminal to be connected to the port.

Removing entries from the spooler queue

Printed reports which are to be removed from the spooler queue are accessed by their entry number, the number displayed on the screen at the time the report was produced. If these have been forgotten, a full list of spooler entries can be gained using the command LISTPEQS (Section 8.1.2).

Only those with the highest privilege level (SYS2) are permitted to dequeue any report whilst others can only remove the reports they generated from the account they are logged on to.

Either way, reports are removed from the spool queue by using the SP-KILL with the F option followed by the entry number. When used successfully, this will convert the report to a 'hold' file which is then available to be SP-EDITed. One of the options of SP-EDIT (see Section 8.4) is to delete the report entirely.

If the report is currently being output and you require to keep the report, then SP-KILL n where n is the printer number will lose the report and SP-KILL Fn where n is the entry number will not work. In this case it will be necessary to include an O with the F option. Hence the command becomes SP-KILL FOn where n is the entry number, and the report is converted to a hold file which can be manipulated with the command SP-EDIT (see Section 8.4).

SP-KILL – its format and examples of its use

Figure 8.10 shows the general format of the SP-KILL command whilst Figure 8.11 gives examples of its use.

The SP-KILL command is used in many situations but naturally, as its name suggests, it needs to be used wisely and carefully. If a report has taken considerable time to send to the spooler, you won't want to make a mistake in controlling it that requires it to be respooled. Figure 8.11 gives some examples of the SP-KILL command in use.

If after having spooled a report to a printer, you realize it was sent to the wrong printer or wrong form queue, you can use the SP-KILL command to take two courses of corrective action. If the report is being printed you can kill the printer, thereby removing all reference to it on the spooler. This will require the report to be respooled.

Otherwise if the report is lengthy an alternative to deleting it from

>SP-KILL {(options)}

where

n{–m}	are valid printer numbers in the range 0–19. This kills the spool queue entry for the report being produced on logical printer number n, and optionally through to printer number m
A	kills reports produced on the account onto which the user is logged
B	kills all possible spooler entries. If you have SYS2 privileges this kills everything; if not it kills all reports on all printers created on the account to which you are logged
Dn{–m}	deletes printer(s) n–m from the system and treats line as a logon port, if the printer is a serial printer
Fx{–y}	changes status of any entry in the range 0–600 in the spool queue, not being printed, to a hold file
N	suppresses the ABORT! message
O	removes from spooler queue the report currently being printed and converts it to a hold file

Figure 8.10 The general format of SP-KILL.

>SP-KILL 1[CR]	immediately stops the report being printed on printer number 1
>SP-KILL 1–3[CR]	Immediately stops the reports being printed on printers number 1, 2 and 3.
>SP-KILL B[CR]	stops printing immediately on all printers on the system
>SP-KILL 1N[CR]	immediately stops the report being printed on printer number 1 and suppresses the abort message.
>SP-KILL D1	will remove printer 1 from the system configuration, and will treat the line as a logon port, i.e. for use by a terminal
>SP-KILL BD[CR]	removes all printers from the system configuration, and leaves their lines ready for use by terminals
>SP-KILL F4[CR]	changes spooler queue entry number 4, not currently being output, into a hold file
>SP-KILL FO4[CR]	changes spooler queue entry number 4, currently being output, into a hold file

Figure 8.11 Examples of SP-KILL.

the spool queue and respooling it for output to a different printer, is to use the F option to convert it to a hold file. Once in this state it can be manipulated by the command SP-EDIT (covered in Section 8.4). SP-EDIT enables you to direct 'held' reports to other printers, take extra copies of reports and even convert them back into a data file on disk. Another use of the F command is to take entries in the spool queue which are queued to a busy printer and reassign them to one that's free, which evens out the printing load and cuts down waiting time. The way to do this is covered in Section 8.4.4.

8.3 Directing printer output with SP-ASSIGN

Reports are produced on the printer by taking the appropriate menu option within an application package or by adding LPTR or (P to the end of an ACCESS command or (P to the end of a TCL command. Unless some previous action has been taken, reports, by default, will be produced on the printer looking after form queue 0 and referred to as the 'system' printer.

Each user can modify his device assignment by use of the SP-ASSIGN verb. On its own, without any options, it will assign the system printer, but reports can be sent to any printer on the system and may also be spooled to magnetic tape or diskette. The SP-ASSIGNment is made to a specific form queue, which is again why form queue numbers tend to be the same as the printer numbers. The format of the command is SP-ASSIGN Fn where n is the form number.

Before taking any action we need to know whether the printer assigned to us is the one we want to use and whether the correct number of copies will be produced. As we saw, LISTABS gave the form queue assignments for all users and provided you know which port you are using (the command WHO will give you this if you are unsure), then you can establish which form queue your report will go to. Another way to find out details of your printer assignment is to use SP-ASSIGN ?, which gives this information for the terminal at which the command was entered.

As with so many PICK commands, there are numerous options which can be applied to SP-ASSIGN and these are represented in Table 8.1.

Examples of the various ways in which the SP-ASSIGN command can be used are given in Figure 8.12. It is important to become familiar with these, particularly when your system has more than one printer.

Any item on the spool queue with a hold status can be accessed by a very useful command SP-EDIT, enabling the manipulation of these reports on the spooler.

Table 8.1 The SP-ASSIGN options.

Option	*Meaning*
C	Choke the printing process to printer speed. This *must* be used with an I option, and can *not* be used with the H option. This ensures that the spooler does not use much space on the disk and is useful for the production of large reports on small disks. The maximum number of frames in use at any time is 20. The number of copies to be printed cannot exceed 1 with this option
Fn	Directs all future output to the form queue number, given by the number n. The default is 0, the maximum number is 125. The form number must immediately follow the F without spaces
H	Causes the output to be retained as a hold file
I	There are two enqueuing times, at the end of the job and immediate. This option specifies immediate enqueuing and must be used when the C option is taken
O	Keep the print file open at completion of this report. This is useful where a number of reports are to be kept together and prevents anyone else printing until an SP-CLOSE command is used. It does not prevent others spooling reports, only printing them. This option has the same effect as using SP-OPEN
Rn	Used in conjunction with the PRINT ON n statement in BASIC, where the BASIC program is sending reports to a number of printers
S	Suppress the printing. Used when the report is required to be printed later, and is used in conjunction with the H option
T	Send the report to tape or diskette as well as printing it
?	Display current spooler assignments
n	Produce n copies (between 1 and 125) of all future reports produced by this account

8.4 Manipulating the spooler with SP-EDIT

The SP-EDIT verb provides all the facilities needed for the System Manager to take complete control of spooled reports. Once entered on the spool queue as a 'held' report, the print file can:

- be produced on another printer;
- have as many further copies produced as are required;
- be reprinted from any point;
- be removed from the spool queue altogether;
- be spooled to tape or diskette;
- be converted into a data file.

>SP-ASSIGN ?[CR]	← What are the current spooler assignments?
LINE STATUS COP FORM # IES #	
0 P 1 0	← The user is on line 0, with output going to the printer. One copy of each report will be produced on form queue 0
>SP-ASSIGN H[CR]	← Print the report, but also produce a hold file on disk containing this report
>SP-ASSIGN HS[CR]	← Produce the hold file, but do not print the report
>SP-ASSIGN F1[CR]	← Print all future reports on form queue 1
>SP-ASSIGN 3 F1[CR]	← Print 3 copies of all future reports on form queue 1
>SP-ASSIGN CIF1 2[CR]	← Print 2 copies of all future reports on printer 1, start printing immediately, but constrain the spooler to printing at the speed of the printer using no more than 20 frames on disk
>SP-ASSIGN HSR1[CR]	← Causes the print file generated by a PRINT ON 1 statement in a succeeding BASIC program to be made into a hold file, without any output being produced

Figure 8.12 Examples of SP-ASSIGN.

It is important to realize that only reports produced as 'held' reports can be manipulated in this way. It is the SP-ASSIGN command which not only assigns a particular printer to a user but also determines whether or not the reports are to be given hold status. Any report on the spool queue can be converted to a hold file using SP-KILL (see Section 8.2.3).

The SP-EDIT command is very powerful and has options too numerous to discuss in great detail. All of these will be found in your manual, and provided you understand the principles of the SP-EDIT command these options will present you with no difficulty. The most common uses of this command are to remove reports from the print queue, to redirect the report to a different printer and to restart the report at a specific point.

There are two parts to SP-EDIT: firstly, the selection and manipulation options which form part of the command line and, secondly, the interactive session to determine the action to be taken on the reports selected.

8.4.1 SP-EDIT options

Using the command without any options will allow the manipulation of all the hold files which have been produced on the account to which the user is logged and are not being output. Anyone with SYS2 privileges can use the U (Universal) option to access all hold files or can follow the command by an account name, enclosed in single quotes, which will allow

Table 8.2 SP-EDIT options.

Option	*Meaning*
Selection	
'Account Name'	Selects reports generated from the specified account. SYS2 privileges required
Fn or Fn-m	Selects reports on specified form queue(s)
n or n-m	Selects report number n or reports n to m on the spool queue
U	Accesses all reports on the spooler. SYS2 privileges required
Manipulation	
D	Deletes each report selected
H	Suppresses the label when the report is output to diskette or tape. This requires the T option on SP-EDIT or SP-ASSIGN to be effective
L	Looks at the contents of the reports on the spooler. The first 500 characters are displayed. If you require to look at more use the T option
MD	Allows multiple reports to be deleted without intervention at each prompt. This is dangerous in inexperienced hands since all held reports will be deleted without the opportunity for a second chance as with the D option
MS	Allows multiple reports to be spooled without intervention at each prompt. All held reports will be printed
N	Only effective with output to terminals. This causes the display to run continuously, ignoring page breaks
O	Used in conjunction with the L option to look at reports being printed
P	Directs the report to the currently assigned printer
R	Changes the original output parameters (form queue and number of copies) to those of the current SP-ASSIGN.
TW	Directs the output to diskette or tape and waits for the device to be ready, if it is not already. Whilst the W (wait) here is strictly optional, it makes great sense to use the two together
V	Converts the held report to a data file without removing trailing blanks or blank lines

access to all print jobs produced by that account:

```
>SP-EDIT[CR]
>SP-EDIT U[CR]
>SP-EDIT 'SYSPROG'[CR]
```

The SP-EDIT options are shown in Table 8.2.

8.4.2 The interactive session of SP-EDIT

Once the SP-EDIT command has been entered, the user can decide which of the hold files to access and manipulate. The same interactive session, as shown in Figure 8.13, will apply to all selected reports.

Meaning of options

ENTRY # NNN

DISPLAY (Y/N/S/D/X/(CR))?–

	Y	Display
	N	Skip to STRING question
	S	Skip to SPOOL question
	D	Skip to DELETE question
	X	Terminate SP-EDIT
	[CR]	Skip to next print file

Any other response will skip to the STRING question

STRING:–

	text	Scan report for first occurrence of text
	[CR]	Skip to SPOOL question

SPOOL (Y/N=CR/T/TN/F)?–

	Y	Spool the report
	N	Skip to DELETE question
	[CR]	Skip to DELETE question
	T	Output the report on the terminal a page at a time
	TN	Output the report on the terminal without stopping at the end of each page
	F	Convert the report into a data file

DELETE (Y/N=CR)?–

	Y	Remove the report from the Spool queue
	N	Do not delete the report and move onto the next selected report

Figure 8.13 The interactive session of SP-EDIT.

8.4.3 Removing reports using SP-EDIT

Provided the report is already on the spool queue as a hold file, removing it is a simple job. Figure 8.14 shows how to remove print file number 4 from the spool queue.

```
>SP-EDIT 4[CR]

ENTRY # 4
DISPLAY (Y/N/S/D/X/(CR))?-D[CR]

DELETE (Y/N=CR)?-Y[CR]

END OF REQUESTED PRINT FILES.
```

Figure 8.14 Removing a spooled 'hold' report.

A slightly more complicated series of commands is required if the report to be removed is on the spool queue but not as a hold file. Figure 8.15 shows how the report is first converted to hold status, using SP-KILL, and then removed using SP-EDIT.

```
>SP-KILL F4[CR]

PRINT FILE #4 WAS UNLINKED AND IS AVAILABLE AS A HOLD FILE

>SP-EDIT 4[CR]

ENTRY # 4
DISPLAY (Y/N/S/D/X/(CR))?-D[CR]

DELETE (Y/N=CR)?-Y[CR]

END OF REQUESTED PRINT FILES.
```

Figure 8.15 Removing a 'non-hold' file from the spooler.

8.4.4 Redirecting reports with SP-EDIT

Sending reports to a different printer than the one it was first assigned to is a two-stage process. First, assign the printer on which the report is now required using SP-ASSIGN. Secondly, use SP-EDIT to spool the report to the new printer. Figure 8.16 shows this in operation where report number 4, originally spooled to form queue 0, is redirected to form queue 1.

```
>SP-ASSIGN F1[CR]

>SP-EDIT R4[CR]

ENTRY # 4
DISPLAY (Y/N/S/D/X/(CR))?-S[CR]

SPOOL (Y/N=CR/T/TN/F)?-Y[CR]

END OF REQUESTED PRINT FILES.
```

Figure 8.16 Spooling report to a different printer.

8.4.5 Restarting reports with SP-EDIT

Within the interactive session of **SP-EDIT** it is possible to restart a held report at any point by locating a specific string of characters. The report can be spooled to the printer from the point at which the string of characters is located.

Before restarting the report make sure that your printer assignment (**SP-ASSIGN**) has no hold status otherwise an error message will be displayed and the report will not be spooled. Figure 8.17 shows such an error occurring and it being corrected by an **SP-ASSIGN** command, after which the report is spooled correctly.

Note from Figure 8.17 that the exact string of characters entered must exist in the spooled report before you can progress further. You should also be aware that **SP-EDIT** locates the first occurrence of the specified string within the report. It is therefore important that the string of characters entered be long enough to uniquely identify the point at which the report is to be restarted. Since the report has 'hold' status, once the reprinting is finished, the report will remain on the spool queue.

8.5 How to handle spooler and printer problems

If problems appear to occur with the spooler there are a number of checks that should be made before re-initializing the spooler:

- Make sure the printer is switched on in a 'ready' state.
- Make sure the printer cable is properly attached.
- Make sure you have defined the correct printer type, i.e. serial or parallel.
- Check that the baud rate of the printer matches that of the speed of the line. Refer to your printer manual for the baud rate for the

```
>SP-EDIT 4[CR]

ENTRY # 4
DISPLAY (Y/N/S/D/X/(CR))?-N[CR]
              ┌── Typing error 'IF' instead of 'If'
              ↓
STRING:-  IF this fails to work[CR]

STRING NOT FOUND

STRING:-  If this fails to work[CR]

SPOOL (Y/N=CR/T/TN/F)?-Y[CR]

YOUR OUTPUT SPECIFICATION IS NO OUTPUT
REASSIGN YOUR LINE IF YOU WISH OUTPUT A HOLDFILE

>SP-ASSIGN F1
>SP-EDIT 4[CR]

ENTRY # 4
DISPLAY (Y/N/S/D/X/(CR))?-N[CR]

STRING:-  If this fails to work[CR]

          SPOOL (Y/N=CR/T/TN/F)?-Y[CR]

          END OF REQUESTED PRINT FILES
```

Figure 8.17 Restarting printing from a specific point.

printer. Unless the SET-BAUD command is used (see Section 14.5), the speed of the line should be 9600 baud.

- Make sure the printer is known to the system by using the LISTPTR command. If not, use STARTPTR.
- Make sure the printer is connected to the port as shown by the SP-STATUS command. If not, either connect the printer to the correct physical port or change the system configuration with the commands SP-KILL and STARTPTR.
- Make sure the report has been sent to the spool queue by using the LISTPEQS command.
- Create a 'hold' report and try manipulating it with SP-EDIT. If problems still occur re-initialize the spooler.

The :STARTSPOOLER command will re-initialize the spooler at the TCL prompt without going through the normal coldstart procedures. Using the command without any options will re-initialize certain spooler controls, leaving it for use in the normal way. If this fails to work, the next option is to use the C option to clear all control blocks with the exception of the permanent master control record. Finally, if all else fails, the I option should be used:

```
>:STARTSPOOLER[CR]
>:STARTSPOOLER C[CR]
>:STARTSPOOLER I[CR]
```

In each case the message SPOOLER STARTED will be displayed. Using the command with either the C or I option will lose the printer assignments for all terminals and will remove all printers from the system configuration. Using the I option will also clear out all reports from the spooler.

8.6 Control of the printer via PROC

Chapter 11 is devoted to PROC, a procedure language which allows the user to prestore a complex series of operations that can be invoked by a single command. It also explains how the spooler can be manipulated within a PROC.

9 Information Retrieval Using ACCESS

TCL verbs and general commands covered in this chapter

COPY	COPY-LIST	COUNT	CT	DELETE-LIST
ED	EDIT-LIST	GET-LIST	HASH-TEST	ISTAT
LIST	LIST-ITEM	LIST-LABEL	QSELECT	REFORMAT
SAVE-LIST	SELECT	SORT	SORT-ITEM	SORT-LABEL
SREFORMAT	SSELECT	STAT	SUM	S-DUMP
T-DUMP	T-LOAD			

9.1 An introduction to ACCESS

It is within ACCESS that users start to recognize the power, the flexibility and virtue of buying a PICK system and, for those of you *still* unsure whether PICK is for you, I am sure this section will finally convince you!

ACCESS is a general-purpose information retrieval language and typically consists of a relatively free format sentence containing the name of the file to be enquired on, the selection criteria and the information to be printed and its format. It is known by other names within some PICK implementations, e.g. ENGLISH, INFORM or RECALL, to name just a few, but they all relate to the same facility.

Whilst it is an exaggeration to say you will never need to write a report program it is not far from the truth. The bulk of both the regular and *ad hoc* reports any business uses can be produced using ACCESS. ACCESS provides the means to selectively or conditionally retrieve information from the database and to report on it. Output reports can be produced on the printer or terminal and may be formatted and sequenced in a variety of ways. ACCESS features:

- relatively free form of input of the ACCESS sentence;
- generalized selection of information using logical and arithmetal relationships;

- the means to sort information in ascending or descending sequence;
- the creation and retention of lists of selected items for use in subsequent TCL processes or BASIC programs;
- the ability to search, select, sort, total, to break on a change of like items and to output based on items defined in the dictionary;
- the ability to produce automatic reports from a file, or user-defined reports with their own optional headings and footings, in columnar or non-columnar form;
- the generation of statistical information relating to files.

The general steps of the ACCESS processor are shown in Figure 9.1.

The ACCESS statement typed in at the TCL prompt

↓

1. Look up file name in master dictionary
2. Look up all modifiers and relational operators in master dictionary
3. Look up data definition items in file dictionary
4. Look up any unfound data definition items in master dictionary
5. Process correlatives

↓

INTERMEDIATE DATA used in
- selections
- sorts
- totals
- control breaks

↓

6. Process conversions

↓

OUTPUT DATA FORMAT

Figure 9.1 The steps of the ACCESS processor.

ACCESS is a dictionary-driven language in that the dictionary contains the names of the data elements to be used in the enquiry language and defines the way in which that data is to be presented. It also contains the vocabulary of the ACCESS enquiry language, such as `COUNT`, `LIST`, `SORT`, `TOTAL` and so on. Much of PICK's strength, and what sets it aside from the traditional databases, comes from the capability of its dictionaries. Do bear in mind, as you read on, that what we are discussing is a functional part of the PICK operating system.

ACCESS, therefore, is not a database management system 'bolted onto' the operating system, but a functional and extremely important part of it. Other operating systems do not offer these facilities and it is incumbent on the user to locate, purchase and 'bolt on' to his operating system a database of his own choice. Such is the importance of the dictionaries to the ACCESS language that the first part of this chapter is devoted to their structure and facilities.

9.2 The principles of file dictionaries

The dictionary is a file in its own right that contains records in the same way as any data file. (For further information on dictionaries and their types refer to Sections 5.1.2 and 5.1.3.) The dictionary records of a file dictionary define an individual element of data. In PICK terminology, therefore, each item in a file dictionary defines an attribute of the data item. Dictionary items are created using the editor or any piece of software provided by your supplier for the purpose. All application generators, for example, contain routines for building dictionaries. In the absence of such software it is a simple enough task with the editor. Assuming the dictionary for the file STAFF has already been created, to create the dictionary items SNAME and FNAME you would type in, at the TCL prompt:

```
>ED DICT STAFF SNAME FNAME[CR]
```

The editor would create two new items in the dictionary file of the file STAFF called SNAME and FNAME for which you would then need to define, for each, 10 attributes.

One of the important features of the dictionaries is the ability to redefine the same attribute by different names. This enables different departments of a company to refer to the data in terms they understand. Hence the Sales department could refer to models, the Production department to products and the Service department to parts each using names they are familiar with but each referring to the *same* data. These synonyms are created by copying one dictionary definition item to another, and then changing part of the attribute within the newly created item containing the headings displayed by ACCESS. It is necessary to change the headings to reflect the name the item is referred to, but it is only the headings that have to be changed because everything else remains the same. Figure 9.2 shows this with the existing dictionary item, MODEL, the term in current use on the STOCK file, being copied to new dictionary items PROD and PART, with the respective headings of these new dictionary items being changed.

```
>COPY DICT STOCK MODEL[CR]
TO:PROD[CR]

1 items copied.

>COPY DICT STOCK MODEL[CR]
TO:PART[CR]

1 items copied.

>ED DICT STOCK PROD PART[CR]
PROD
TOP
.3[CR]
003 Model No
.R[CR]
003 Product[CR]
.FI[CR]
'PROD' filed.
PART
TOP
.3[CR]
003 Model No
.R[CR]
003 Part No[CR]
.FI[CR]
'PART' FILED
```

Figure 9.2 Creating dictionary synonyms.

9.2.1 The structure of file dictionary records

The dictionary record consists of 10 separate attributes to define each element of data in a data file. Table 9.1 shows the format of a dictionary item and explains the function of each of its 10 attributes. In some implementations the number of attributes used for each dictionary item is greater than 10 to incorporate advanced features like updating within ACCESS. Some application generators also extend the number of attributes above 10. You are unlikely to need to use more than 10 attributes and should avoid doing so unless you are sure of what you are about.

Attribute 1 – attribute definition

Attribute 1 defines the type of item. Where the item provides the main

Table 9.1 The attributes of a dictionary record

No.	*Name*	*Description*
1	"A"	Attribute definition. This contains A or S
2	AMC	The position of the attribute within the item. It is referred to as the AMC – the attribute mark count. (For the item-id this is always 0)
3	TAG	The text to be used as a heading for the attribute
4	STRUCT	Specifies the attribute controlling and dependent relationships
5		Not used
6		Not used
7	CONV	Conversion code. A code which is used to convert data between formats for displaying/printing and those held internally on the database
8	CORR	Correlatives. A preprocessing code to denote a special function to be carried out on data. It is 'derived' data
9	TYPE	Defines the justification required. Valid options are L, R, T or U
10	MAX	Maximum number of characters in the attribute

definition, this attribute contains A. Where the item is a redefinition or synonym of the main definition this attribute contains an S.

Attribute 2 – location definition

This attribute defines the position of the dictionary item in the record of the file it's defining. Hence, if in a personnel system, a record has as the item-id a personnel code, which is followed by the surname, then the first name and so on. The item-id is located in position 0 (the key field), the surname in position 1, the first name in position 2 and so on. Hence, in this example, attributes would contain 0, 1, or 2, respectively.

There are two special location definitions which are useful. If attribute 2 of a dictionary item contains 9999 it will provide the size of the selected item in bytes. If it contains 9998 it will produce a sequential item count of the items selected.

Attribute 3 – heading definition

This attribute contains the text for the heading to be used in the ACCESS report. If this attribute contains a null value, the item-id of the attribute is used as the heading. If this attribute contains a backslash (\), no heading text is shown. In all cases if the heading text is less than the maximum number of characters as defined in attribute 10, the heading text is padded out with full stops. If the text of the heading is greater than the maximum number of characters, the full heading is displayed.

It is possible to have multiple line headings, achieved by placing value marks (CTRL/]) at the end of each line of text. In this instance each heading line follows the previous one. If the second or subsequent lines of the heading are greater than the first, the first line will be padded out with full stops to the length of the longest heading. The multiline heading only works where the headings appear above columns of data.

Figure 9.3 gives examples of these for the dictionary item SNAME which defines the surname in a personnel system.

It should be noted that data will only be output in columns providing the total length of each data line is less than 132 characters. Where the length exceeds 132 characters the report is produced down the page with each element of each item of data appearing on a separate line.

Attr. 10 *(Size)*	Attribute 3 *(Description)*	OUTPUT REPORT *(Output)*
5	Surname	Surname
10	Surname	Surname...
5	Surname]of]Staff member	Surname... Of Staff member
5	\	.....
5		SNAME

Figure 9.3 The heading definition attribute.

Attribute 4 – controlling and dependent

The fourth attribute of a dictionary definition item defines the controlling and dependent relationship. For example, in an order-processing system each line of an order contains information dependent on each other, the product code, unit price, quantity ordered and so on. Whilst each of these is dependent on each other in that each line of the order requires all these elements to be present, they are controlled and hence will only be present where a new line of the order is completed. In this situation the order line number controls the other elements of data which are dependent on it.

Attribute 4 is where this kind of relationship is defined. The controlling dictionary item contains a C in this attribute, followed by ;nn for each data element it controls, where nn defines the location of the dependent element in the record. A dependent element contains a D in this attribute followed by a single ;nn, where nn defines the location of

```
DICT      --Dictionary Attributes--
Name       1 2 3              4
- - - - - - - - - - - - - - - - - - - - - - - - -
ORDNO     A 0 Order Number
LINENO    A 1 Line Number       C;2;3;4;5
PRODNO    A 2 Product Number    D;1
LISTP     A 3 List Price        D;1
QTY       A 4 Quantity Ordered  D;1
LINEVAL   A 5 Line Value        D;1
```

Figure 9.4 The controlling and dependent attribute.

the controlling attribute. Figure 9.4 shows how this works for an order-processing system containing a number of data elements used for each order line.

Attributes 7 and 8 – conversions and correlatives

As was shown in Table 9.1, conversion codes appear in attribute 7 whilst correlatives appear in attribute 8. Both of these, however, are preprocessing codes to the ACCESS report, which can appear either in attribute 7 or attribute 8. Conceptually, however, the conversion code is used to reformat data and a correlative is a 'ghost' field – a field which does not exist and therefore does not use space on the file being interrogated, but is 'computed' and derived at run time.

The important difference in using these preprocessing codes is the way in which ACCESS itself works. During the execution of an ACCESS statement, data is taken from the database in its raw form and any correlative code applied to it. This provides an intermediate format which is used whenever:

1. The attribute name is part of a sort key.
2. The data is *compared* in a selection criterion.
3. The data is used in producing totals.
4. The data produces a control break.
5. The data is printed, *except* on break lines.

Once any of the above steps have been taken, the conversion code is applied to produce an output format of the data. This reformats the data into the format provided in the ACCESS report, which can either be shown on the screen or produced on the printer. A summary of the possible conversion and correlative codes is shown in Table 9.2.

Table 9.2 Summary of conversion and correlative codes.

Code	*Description*
A	**Arithmetic** computes mathematical expressions and is converted to an 'F' code at runtime
C	**Concatenate** concatenates attributes together
D	**Date** converts dates to external format
F	**Function** computes mathematical and relational operations on attributes
G	**Group** extracts data elements from a group of elements by specifying a delimiter that separates them
L	**Length** specifies output length constraints
MC	**Mask character** has various options to convert strings to upper and lower case or to extract numeric or alphabetic characters from strings
MD and MR	**Mask decimal** performs output conversions, literal insertions and currency formatting on numeric fields held in internal format
ML	**Masked decimal** As MD but with left justification
MT	**Mask time** converts time of day into external format
MX	**Mask hexadecimal** converts ASCII strings to hexadecimal format
MY	**Mask hexadecimal** converts hexadecimal strings to ASCII format
P	**Pattern match** limits items selected to those of a specific pattern of characters (including literals)
R	**Range** restricts items selected to those that fall within a particular range of values
S	**Substitution** allows other data to be substituted where a zero or null value is found
T	**Text extraction** extracts any number of characters from any position in the attribute
Tfile	**File translation** enables a file look-up facility based on the value held in the attribute
U	**User-defined** A means to invoke user routines written in assembly to perform special conversions or correlatives

The A *code (Arithmetic) correlative*

This correlative is used to carry out arithmetic calculations and, whilst all its functions can be performed using an F correlative, the syntax of the A correlative is simpler and hence easier to understand and maintain. The A correlative is generally placed in attribute 8 of the dictionary definition item. The A correlative can use dictionary names, dictionary positions or literals in its calculations and has the general format:

```
A;(expression)
```

Where dictionary names are used, the name is enclosed in

parentheses and preceded by the letter N. Dictionary positions are defined by specifying their position number and literals are enclosed in single or double quotes. Care must be taken in deciding whether to use names or attribute positions in these correlatives since they are handled differently. If the position is used, the value used is that as stored in the appropriate position on the disk. If, however, the name is used, the ACCESS processor will look this up in the file dictionary and will apply any conversions or correlatives associated with it. In some cases this would cause significantly different results.

The 'A' correlatives are dummy fields and as such are mostly given dummy attribute positions. Usually these are given as attribute zero, the position of the item-id, although there are occasions where these are given the same position as the attribute they redefine.

The operators for addition, subtraction, multiplication and division, respectively +, −, * and /, can be used in calculations although it should be noted that the result of a division will always return an integer result. Hence "5"/"2" will return a result of 2 and not 2.5. If you require the decimal positions you will need to carry out a multiplication in the formula to factor the result. Thus to produce two decimal places in the result, the formula of ("5"*"100")/"2" that produces the answer 250 will require a conversion code of MR2 applied to it to give the output result 2.50. In order to define the precedence of operations up to 20 levels of parentheses can be used.

Some simple examples of A correlatives are shown in Table 9.3 including one that will accumulate the contents of all the multi-values of an attribute. This could be used where a customer's aged balances are held as multiple values in a single attribute, and you wish to know the total balance outstanding. The last example of Table 9.3 shows how the remainder from a calculation can be collected.

The arithmetic correlative can also use the relational operators, greater than, less than, equal to, not equal to, greater than or equal to, less than or equal to, respectively >, <, =, #, >= and <=. Where these are used, each operator takes two expressions as operands and the result evaluates to 1 if the relationship is true and 0 if the relationship is false. Table 9.4 gives an example of the use of relational operators. In this example, a bonus payment is to be paid only to staff earning less than £10 000.

There are some extremely useful operands which provide access to certain control values. These can be used in arithmetic correlatives and are shown in Table 9.5.

The ND function for example can be used to produce averages for specified attributes. In this case, the A code is used as a conversion and placed in attribute 7 of the dictionary definition item. Table 9.6 shows how this is defined and how an average can be produced for the contents of a multivalued attribute.

Table 9.3 The A correlative.

Attribute type	*Attribute number*	*Value*	*Function of correlative*
POSITION	2	0	
CORRELATIVE	8	A;6+7+"35"	Adds attributes 6 and 7 together and adds 35 to the result
POSITION	2	0	
CORRELATIVE	8	A;N(GROSS)−N(TAX)	Subtracts the value of the field TAX from the value of the field GROSS
POSITION	2	0	
CORRELATIVE	8	A;S(9)	Sums together *all* the values of the multi-values of attribute 9
POSITION	2	0	
CORRELATIVE	8	A;R(3/"4")	Provides the remainder from dividing attribute 3 by the literal 4

Table 9.4 Using relational operators in A correlatives.

Attribute type	*Attribute number*	*Value*
POSITION	2	0
CORRELATIVE	8	A;N(BONUS)*(N(GROSS)<"10000")

If GROSS is less than £10,000 then the last part of the correlative will equate to one and the bonus payment will be equal to the contents of the attribute 'BONUS' otherwise it will equate to zero and the bonus payment will be nil.

Table 9.5 Special operands for the `A` correlative.

Operand	*Description*
`D`	The system date in internal format
`LPV`	Load previous value
`NB`	The break-level counter; it is zero at detail time and increases by one for each break level encountered. It is 255 for the grand total. Use in attribute 7 only
`ND`	The detail line counter; it is 1 at detail time and is only valid at break time. Use in attribute 7 only
`NI`	The item counter; it is zero during select time and only active during the output stage. Can be used in attribute 7 or 8
`NS`	The secondary value counter; it is equal to 1 for the total line. Use in attribute 8 only
`NV`	The value counter; it is equal to 1 for the total line. Use in attribute 8 only
`T`	The system time in internal format

Table 9.6 Producing averages with the `A` code.

Example 1 Producing the average of the contents of attribute 3

Attribute type	*Attribute number*	*Value*	*Function of conversion*
POSITION	2	3	†Notice this is now 3 not 0
CONVERSION	7	`A;3/ND`	Divide the contents of attribute 3 by the number of detail lines since the last break

†Notice that the attribute number used throughout (i.e. 3) is the number of the attribute containing the data to be averaged. Further the `A` code is used as a conversion and hence placed in position 7 (not 8) of the dictionary definition item. Since `ND` only has a meaning at the total line, this dictionary item can only be used in conjunction with the `BREAK-ON` and `DET-SUPP` modifiers which must be included in the ACCESS statement.

Example 2 Producing the average of the contents of the multivalues contained in attribute 4

Attribute type	*Attribute number*	*Value*	*Function of correlative*
POSITION	2	0	
CORRELATIVE	8	`A;S(4)/S(4=4)`	Sums the number of multivalues and divides this into the sum of its contents

It is also possible to specify conversions to be applied to the full or partial results of an `A` correlative. This is achieved by placing the conversion code at the end of the section of the `A` code to be converted. Table 9.7 shows how this works, by taking the examples contained in Table 9.6 and changing them to produce their results to two decimal places. The `MR2` conversion code converts the result to two places of decimals and inserts the decimal point.

Table 9.7 Producing averages using `A` correlatives.

Example 1 Producing the average of the contents of attribute 3

Attribute type	*Attribute number*	*Value*
POSITION	2	3
CONVERSION	7	`A;((3*"100")/ND)(MR2)`

Example 2 Producing the average of the contents of the multivalues contained in attribute 4

Attribute type	*Attribute number*	*Value*	*Function of correlative*
POSITION	2	0	
CORRELATIVE	8	`A;(S(4*"100")/S(4=4))(MR2)`	

The `C` code (Concatenate) correlative

The `C` code provides the means to concatenate attributes and literals together. It is a simple correlative to use and has the format:

```
C;exp1 x exp2 x exp3 ...
```

where

exp1 is the first of the attributes or literals in the concatenated string, exp2 is the second and so on. In this correlative you cannot specify attributes by name, *only* by their position.

x is the character to be inserted between the attributes or literals. The reserved character is a semicolon which means no separation character is to be used.

Table 9.8 gives examples of the use of this correlative.

Table 9.8 The C correlative.

Assume attribute 6 contains '01'
attribute 7 contains '440 0906'

Attribute type	*Attribute number*	*Value*	*Function of correlative*
POSITION	2	0	
CORRELATIVE	8	C;6;7	Concatenates the contents of attribute 6 with the contents of attribute 7
Result 01440 0906			
POSITION	2	0	
CORRELATIVE	8	C;6–7	Concatenates the contents of attribute 6 with the contents of attribute 7
Result 01–440 0906			
POSITION	2	0	
CORRELATIVE	8	C;"BARNET ";6–7	Concatenates the literal BARNET with attributes 6 and 7
Result BARNET 01–440 0906			

The D *conversion code for Dates*

The date conversion code provides the means of converting the date, held on the disk in internal format, to a variety of output formats. Dates are stored on the disk in internal format, this being the number of days since 31 December 1967. If the date being stored is earlier than this date, it is held as a negative number. This compact way of storing dates not only saves space but enables arithmetic and sorting on any date field. The general format of the D conversion code is:

D{b}{xm}{o}

where

- n is the number of digits in the year (0, 2 or 4)
- x any single non-numeric character specifying the delimiter between fields for group extraction
- m specifies the number of fields to skip for group extraction
- o either the special single non-numeric character separates the day, month and year on output, or a special code being one of the following:
  - D for day
  - M for month
  - Q for quarter
  - Y for year

The topic of group extraction is covered below under 'The G correlative' and will not be discussed further in this section. Examples of date conversions for an internal date format of 6551 are shown in Table 9.9.

Table 9.9 The 'D' conversion code for dates.

Conversion	*Format displayed*	*Comments*
D	07 DEC 1985	
D/	07/12/1985	
D–	07-12-85	
DO	07 DEC	
DO/	07/12	Useful with US date format
D2/	07/12/85	
D2+	07+12+85	Any character can be delimiter
DD	07	The day
DM	12	The month
DY	1985	Four-digit year
D2Y	85	Two-digit year
DQ	4	The quarter

The F code (Function) correlative

The F correlative is a very powerful correlative, which enables arithmetic functions to be performed. It encompasses all of the features of the A correlative and offers a great deal more. All its operations are performed on the last two entries in a push-down stack and it is access to this stack that expands its power over the A correlative.

To its disadvantage calculations must be specified in Reverse Polish notation, a notation not too many people are familiar with! This makes it far more difficult to understand, to apply and to maintain and for this reason the `A` correlative was introduced. Another disadvantage of the `F` correlative is that it cannot use dictionary names.

In Reverse Polish notation, as an attribute number, constant or character string are encountered they are pushed onto the top of the stack, pushing all the other values on the stack down by one. When an operator is encountered, the specified operation is performed on the top one or two entries on the stack dependent on the operation being performed. When all the operations have been performed, the result is what is at the top of the stack.

Figure 9.5 shows how the `F` correlative is used to multiply the sum of 4 and 5 by 3. In this example the letter `C` preceding the number denotes that what follows it is a constant.

The 'F' code correlative : `F;C3;C4;C5;+;*`

	Stages				
	1	2	3	4	5
	C3	C4	C5	+	*
Stack 1	3	4	5	9	27
Stack 2		3	4	3	
Stack 3			3		
Stack 4					
. . .					
. . .					

The result is 27

Figure 9.5 The `F` code correlative.

The full facilities of this correlative are beyond the scope of this book. For those of you who have fully grasped the workings of the `A` correlative and require additional capability I refer you to your ACCESS manual for the detailed workings of the `F` correlative!

The `G` *correlative for Group extraction*

Group extraction enables the extraction of parts of a character string containing delimiters. The delimiter used in the group extraction syntax can be any character, including space, provided it is not a minus sign or one of the reserved special characters used to define the attribute mark, the value mark or subvalue mark.

In this context therefore it is possible to extract one or a number of words from a sentence, in which case the delimiter is obviously a space. The general format of the `G` correlative is:

```
G{n}xm
```

where

- `n` is the number of fields to skip. If omitted zero is assumed
- `x` any single non-numeric character defining the delimiter, provided it is not a minus sign nor a reserved character
- `m` a number signifying the number of contiguous fields to be extracted

Table 9.10 shows how a group extraction could be used to extract the first name and surname from a file whose names are held in attribute 6 in the format 'surname, first name', where the delimiter is a comma.

Table 9.10 The group extract function.

Attribute type	*Attribute number*	*Value*	
ITEM-ID	0	NAME	← The original definition of the name attribute
POSITION	2	6	

Attribute type	*Attribute number*	*Value*	*Function of correlative*
ITEM-ID	0	FIRSTNAME	
POSITION	2	6	
CORRELATIVE	8	G1,1	Extract one field after the comma, having skipped one field, i.e. select the second field
ITEM-ID	0	SURNAME	
POSITION	2	6	
CORRELATIVE	8	G,1	Extract one field, using a comma as the delimiter, skipping no fields, i.e. select the first field

Assuming the data held on file for NAME was:

```
DIXON,GEORGE
LEA,MARTIN
PIKE,JOHN
HARLOW,MARTIN
```

Then defining the dictionary items FIRSTNAME and SURNAME as shown in Table 9.10 would enable the data to be listed showing the first name and surname separately.

The list of first names by listing FIRSTNAME would give:

```
GEORGE
MARTIN
JOHN
MARTIN
```

The list of surnames by listing **SURNAME** would give:

```
DIXON
LEA
PIKE
HARLOW
```

Having done this it may be useful to be able to concatenate these two dictionary items together. In order to concatenate the surname onto the first name, we need to concatenate the dictionary items **FIRSTNAME** and **SURNAME** which can only be done by specifying them by name. This ensures that any conversion or correlative, in this case the **G** correlative, is applied before the data is retrieved from disk. Since it is not possible to use dictionary names with **C** correlatives it is necessary to concatenate them together within the **A** correlative. This is achieved by defining a new dictionary item, a further redefinition of the name attribute and hence in position 6, containing the following arithmetic correlative in attribute 8:

```
A;N(FIRSTNAME):" ":N(SURNAME)
```

This defines the concatenation of the two newly defined attributes, **FIRSTNAME** and **SURNAME**, separated by a space. Listing the full name would therefore produce:

```
GEORGE DIXON
MARTIN LEA
JOHN PIKE
MICHAEL HARLOW
```

It is worth reflecting for a moment what has been achieved in doing all this. The most important thing to understand is that the data has been stored once only in the format 'Surname, First name'. Through the group extraction using the **G** correlative we have been able to extract at will the first names and surnames and have been able to concatenate them together. This concatenation, using the arithmetic correlative, enables us to refer to the names in the usual form, with the surname appearing after the first name. All of these new dictionary definitions were defined as synonyms to the original dictionary definition item, being given, as their attribute position, that allocated to the original attribute, i.e. position 6. All of which I am sure you will agree is really clever. It demonstrates the power and flexibility provided by this unique operating system and further explains why people once exposed to the PICK operating system become won over by it!

The L *code (Length) correlative*

The L code correlative is used to restrict the output to data which is of a specified length. If it is longer or shorter a null value is output to the ACCESS processor. This has the effect of blanking out the data on the report, although it should be made clear that it will not prevent reference to the item appearing on the report. Hence, by adding L4 to attribute 8 of the dictionary definition item SURNAME used in Table 9.10 a list of first names and surnames would produce:

First Name	*Surname*
GEORGE	
MARTIN	
JOHN	PIKE
MARTIN	

As you can see, it only lists the surname where the length is four characters. Adding the L4 to the G code correlative already present in attribute 8 of the dictionary definition item SURNAME is handled through the editor. Multiple correlatives and conversion codes appear on the same line separated by a value mark, edited in using CTRL/]. This means attribute 8 of SURNAME would contain G,1]L4 to carry out both the group extraction and length test.

A length code of Ln,m will test a range of lengths between n and m and provided that the data falls within this range it will be output. Hence L4,9 will output all data whose length is between 4 and 9 characters inclusive.

The special conversion code L0 will return the length of the data itself. Hence changing the L4 correlative to L0 on SURNAME would produce the following list:

First Name	*Surname*
GEORGE	5
MARTIN	3
JOHN	4
MARTIN	6

The MC *(Mask Character) conversion code*

There are a variety of character conversion codes that can be applied to convert physically held data to an output form which shows it in upper, lower or upper and lower case. Some of the conversion codes will remove the numbers from an alphanumeric string of characters, others will remove the alphabetic characters. All of these 'masks' are applied to the physical data on output only. They do *not* affect or change what is held

Table 9.11 The MC conversion codes.

Code	*Description*
MCU	Converts all alphabetic characters to upper-case
MCL	Converts all alphabetic characters to lower-case
MCA	Prints only alphabetic characters in the string
MCN	Prints only numeric characters in the string
MC/A	Same as MCA
MC/N	Same as MCN
MCDX	Converts decimal values to hexadecimal
MCXD	Converts hexadecimal values to decimal
MCP	Converts unprintable characters to a full stop
MCT	Converts to upper- and lower-case, by making the first character in each word upper-case, with the rest of the word in lower-case

Table 9.12 Use of MC conversion codes.

Data on disk	*Code*	*Output displayed*
John Pike is 36	MCU	JOHN PIKE IS 36
JOHN PIKE IS 36	MCL	john pike is 36
John Pike is 36	MCA	JohnPikeis
John PIKE iS 36	MCN	36
JOHN PikE	MCT	John Pike

on disk. The conversion codes as shown in Table 9.11 should be edited into attribute 7 of the dictionary definition item.

Table 9.12 gives examples of the use of these codes. As can be seen the conversion code of MCT is extremely valuable for displaying names and addresses for mailing, when no consistent form of input has been used. It only has one drawback in that it will not print the Scottish 'Mc. . .' properly, so 'McBride' comes out as 'Mcbride'. The only way to overcome this is to put a space between 'Mc' and 'Bride' when keying in data.

The MD ML *and* MR *(Mask Decimal) conversion codes*

The two conversion codes MD and MR are identical and carry out conversions of numbers to decimal numbers with right justification of the result. The ML conversion code also carries out decimal conversion but with left justification. Numbers are stored on the database as numbers without any decimal point or indication of scaling. The MD, ML and MR codes indicate not only the scaling and justification to be applied, but also enable commas to be placed to represent thousands, millions and so on.

Table 9.13 Examples of **MD**, **ML** and **MR** mask codes.

Data on disk		*Conversion code applied*	*Result*	
123456		MR2	1234.56	
123456		MD2	1234.56	
123456		MR26	0.12 ←	rounded
123456		MR24	12.35 ←	
123456		MR2,	1,234.56	
−123456		MR2,E	<1,234.56>	
−123456		MR46,C$	$12.3456CR	
123456		MR2(%8)	01234.56 ←	notice decimal point part of the 8 chars
123456		MR2(*9)	**1234.56 ←	
123456		MR(###-##-##-#)		
	or	MR(3#-2#-2#-#)	1-23-45-6	
123456		ML(###-##-##-#)	123-45-6 -	

These codes also allow other editing characters to be included, such as **CR** and **DR**.

The general format of the conversion code, which is placed in attribute 7 of the dictionary definition item, is:

```
M(D/R/L){m}{n}{Z}{,}{C/D/E/M}{$}{(format string)}
```

where

- `D/R/L` represent the justification. **MD** and **MR** are the same
- `m` is the number of decimal places (0–9)
- `n` is the scaling factor to be applied. To descale by 10 set to 1; to descale by 100 this should be set to 2; and so on. Numbers are rounded up
- `Z` suppresses leading zeros
- `,` inserts comma in every thousands position
- `C/D/E/M/N` are further editing symbols:
  - `C` means follow negative numbers by **CR**
  - `D` means follow positive numbers by **DR**
  - `E` causes negative numbers to be enclosed in pointed brackets
  - `M` causes a minus sign to follow a negative number
  - `N` causes the minus sign to be suppressed
- `$` causes a **$** sign to be appended to the start of the number. Some implementations also support the pound sign.

In format string:

#n	displays data in a field of n spaces
%n	displays data in a field of n zeroes
mn	displays data in a field of n character ms. The fill character can be any character.

Numbers are handled through this conversion code in exactly the same way as they are handled in BASIC (see Section 10.4.4). Table 9.13 gives examples of these conversion codes which should be placed in attribute 7 of the dictionary definition item.

The MT *(Mask Time) conversion code*

The time of day is held on the system as a number of seconds since midnight. The MT conversion code converts this number to a time of day, optionally displaying this using the 24-hour clock system. The general format is:

MT{H}{S}

where

MT	is the mask time code
H	if present, specifies use of the 12-hour clock
S	if present, specifies that the number of seconds is to be displayed

Examples of this conversion code are given in Table 9.14.

Table 9.14 The MT time conversion code.

Value on disk	*Conversion code*	*Result*
53600	MTHS	02:53:20PM
53600	MTH	02:53PM
53630	MTHS	02:53:50PM
53630	MTH	02:53PM
53600	MT	14:53
53600	MTS	14:53:20

The MX *and* MY *(Hexadecimal) conversion codes*

The MX code enables character strings to be converted to hexadecimal characters and the MY code for reversing the process. Although not greatly used, it can be helpful for specialized work, and for finding the non-printable characters in a data string. It is simply represented by placing the code MX in attribute 7 of the dictionary definition item.

The P *code (Pattern) matching correlative*

The P code correlative enables data to be restricted to that which matches a specific pattern of characters. The characters that can be tested for are:

A for alphabetic
N for numeric
X for alphanumeric
a literal string

All of these, except the literal string, can have a number placed before them to indicate the number of characters. Hence 2N equates to two numeric characters and 4A to four alphabetic characters. Combinations of alphabetic, numeric, alphanumeric and literals can be mixed together in the pattern code. Pattern codes are enclosed in parentheses with multiple tests separated by a semicolon.

Hence P(2N–3N–4N) tests for a string of two numbers, followed by a hyphen, followed by three numbers, followed by a hyphen, followed by four numbers. Using this pattern test 01–387–9233 would pass and 061–334 8798 would fail the test, so 01–387–9233 would be printed and blanks would be output for the other.

To allow combination testing a semicolon is used. Hence to allow either the pattern of numbers 2N–3N–4N or 6A6N, i.e. nine numbers broken into three groups separated with a comma, or six alphabetic characters followed by six numbers, use the notation P(2N–3N–4N);(6A6N).

The R *code (Range) correlative*

The R correlative enables data that is displayed to be restricted to that which falls within a specific range of values. Multiple ranges can be specified each of which is separated with a semicolon. Hence R10,50 will test the data to be in the range 10 to 50 inclusive. A range code of R10,50;100,150 will print data which is in the range 10 to 50 inclusive or 100 to 150 inclusive. Any data found outside these ranges will have a null value sent to the ACCESS processor and hence will be shown as blank.

The S *code (Substitution) correlative*

The substitution correlative enables data to be substituted if a null or zero value is found. Two substitution parameters are used, one for when a null or zero is encountered, and one for when it is not. For example S;2;'NIL PAID' will print the words NIL PAID if the data encountered is null or zero, otherwise it will print the contents of attribute 2. If it is required to print the original data if no null or zero is found, then the first parameter should be an asterisk.

The `T` *code (Text extraction) correlative*

This is used to extract a specified number of characters from a string. The format is a `T` followed by a number denoting the starting position, a comma and a number denoting the number of characters to extract. Hence `T3,4` always takes the first four characters after the first three starting at the leftmost character in the string. If this were applied to the string `ABC1234` it would extract `1234`.

If the first parameter denoting start position is omitted, then extraction starts from the first character of the string, either from the right or left hand end dependent on the justification in attribute 9 of this dictionary definition item. If attribute 9 is `L`, counting starts from the left. If it is `R`, counting starts from the right.

The `Tfile` *code (Translation) correlative*

This correlative enables powerful look-up facilities, minimizing the duplication of data. For example, in a personnel system we would hold details of our staff and the departments they work in. Rather than have the description of the department held on each staff record, it is far better to put a department code on the record and to look up the description from a separately maintained file. In such a situation if a department changes its title only the department file is affected. If the department name were held on *every* individual staff record, it would be necessary to identify and change that department description on all affected staff records!

The format of this command is:

```
T{DICT}file;sc{n};i-amc;o-amc{;b-amc}
```

where

- `DICT` is when the dictionary file is used as the look-up file
- `file` is the name of the look-up file
- `sc` is a subcode denoting the action to be taken if the record being looked up does not exist:
  - `C` returns the item-id (the look-up key)
  - `I` input verify only
  - `O` output verify only
  - `V` it must exist, otherwise abort
  - `X` returns a null value
- `n` optional value mark count. If this is `N` it returns the value mark count in the target, an `*` takes the same value mark count as the source
- `I-amc` the attribute number for input conversion. It is not used by ACCESS and may be null or the same as the `o-amc`
- `o-amc` the attribute number whose value is to be passed as the translated value

b–amc the attribute number whose value is to be used in break-on and total lines in place of o–amc

To demonstrate the use of this correlative, we will assume that there are three files which are linked together: the STAFF file, which contains details of all personnel, the DEPT file which contains information about departments and the CC file which contains details of cost centres. The format of these files is as given in Table 9.15.

Table 9.15 File layouts showing linked files.

	File names		
Attribute number	STAFF	DEPT	CC
0	Staff no.	Dept. code	Cost centre code
1	Name	Dept. descr.	Cost centre descr.
2	Address	Annual budget	Annual budget
3	Tel. no.	Cost centre code	
4	Dept. code		

As can be seen from Table 9.15, the department code held on each staff record is what can be used to find the correct department record on the department file. The department file contains a cost centre code which can be used to look up the correct cost centre record. These file translations are performed by creating a dictionary synonym of the attribute containing the data that will be used for the file translation. It is important to note that the attribute position of the synonym *must* be the same as that of the look-up data and the synonym will contain the T-file code. So, to be able to refer to the department description on the STAFF file, we would create a synonym on the STAFF file with the same attribute position as the department code, i.e. 4, and to be able to reference the cost centre description on the CC file, we would create a synonym on the DEPT file whose attribute position (AMC) would be 3. Each of these synonyms would contain a Tfile correlative code. This would provide the situation illustrated in Table 9.16.

In both cases in Table 9.16 the correlative would use the contents of the appropriate attribute of each record as the key to access the file name contained in the Tfile correlative. If the record was found, it would return the contents of attribute 1 from the target file, i.e. the description. If the record was not found it would return a null value.

In Table 9.16 two separate correlatives were established. The first from the staff file to the department file, the second from the department file to the cost centre file. It is possible to set up a correlative on the staff

Table 9.16 The Tfile correlative.

Attribute number	STAFF	DEPT	CC
0	Staff no.	Dept. code	Cost centre code
1	Name	→ Dept. descr.	→ Cost centre descr.
2	Address	Annual budget	Annual budget
3	Tel. no.	Cost centre	
3		Cost centre descr.	
4	Dept.		
4	Dept. descr.		

The synonyms set up would be as follows:

File name	*Attribute type*	*Attribute number*	*Contents*	*Function*
STAFF	POSITION	2	4	
	CORRELATIVE	8	TDEPT;X;;1	Look up the contents of attribute 1 of the DEPT file using what is contained in this attribute as the key
CC	POSITION	2	3	As above but using the file CC
	CORRELATIVE	8	TCC;X;;1	

file to carry out both operations, thereby making the cost centre description accessible from the staff file. In this case the department code on the staff record is used to access the department record from which the cost centre code is used to access the cost centre file for its description. In this case the synonym, which again takes the same attribute position as the department code, contains a multiple Tfile correlative separated by a value mark (CTRL/]). This is shown in Table 9.17.

Sample data files are shown in Figure 9.6 as the basis for the examples shown in Figure 9.7.

In order to demonstrate the use of the Tfile correlatives, the output from a simple ACCESS report is shown in Figure 9.7. This uses the data in Figure 9.6 with the correlatives given in Table 9.17.

The U *(User defined code) conversion code*

The U conversion code specifies an entry point into a user-written piece of software. It is only for experienced PICK users and should not be used

Table 9.17 The use of multiple `Tfile` correlatives.

Attribute number	STAFF	DEPT	CC
0	Staff no.	Dept. code	Cost centre code
1	Name	→ Dept. descr.	→ Cost centre descr.
2	Address	Annual budget	Annual budget
3	Tel. no.	→ Cost centre	
4	Dept.		
4	Dept. descr.		
4	Cost centre descr.		

Notice that all the `Tfile` correlatives that use the department code to look up values on other files have the same AMC position in the dictionary.

The synonyms set up would be as follows:

File name	*Attribute type*	*Attribute number*	*Contents*	*Correlative*
STAFF	POSITION	2	4	
	CORRELATIVE	8	TDEPT;X;;1	DEPTDESC

The contents of the department code are used to locate the correct record and its description extracted.

File name	*Attribute type*	*Attribute number*	*Contents*	*Correlative*
			Value Mark CTRL/] (↓ points to the] in the contents below)	
STAFF	POSITION	2	4	
	CORRELATIVE	8	TDEPT;X;;3]TCC;C;;1	CCDESC

The content of the department code on the staff file is used to look up the cost centre code held as attribute 3 on the department record. The cost centre code on the department record is then used to extract the department description (attribute 1) from the cost centre file. If the department record is not present a null value will be returned. If however the cost centre record is not found, the cost centre code from the department record will be displayed instead – this being the purpose of the `C` option in the correlative, used in place of the `X` in previous examples.

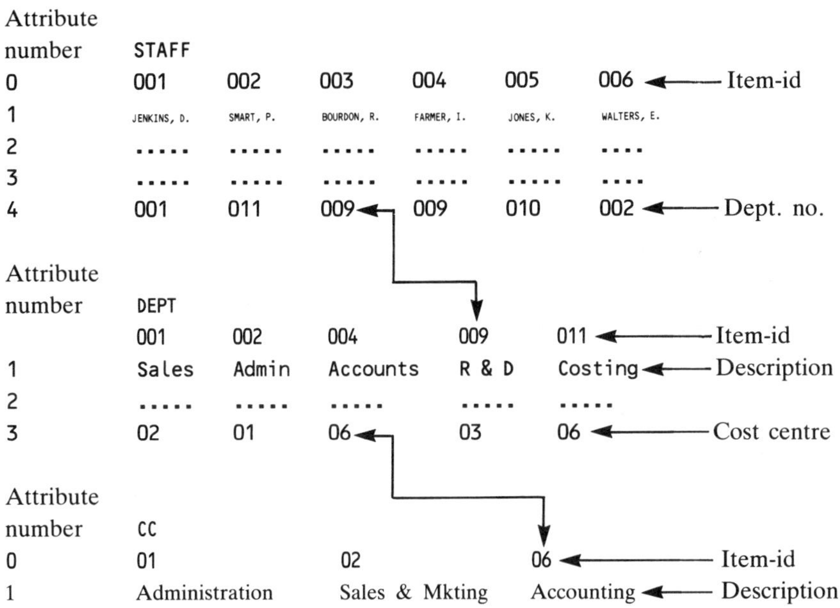

Figure 9.6 Sample data used in Figure 9.7.

unless you are fully conversant with its effects. Those who need to use it will find adequate instructions in the user manual.

Multiple correlatives

Whilst we only looked at one specific instance in `Tfile` correlatives, where multiple correlatives were used, it is possible to have multiple correlatives using any of the correlatives we have discussed. This is achieved by separating them with a value mark (`CTRL/]`), an example of which is shown in Table 9.17.

Attribute 9 – justification

Attribute 9 of a dictionary definition item determines the justification required. There are four options available.

- `R` right-justified
- `L` left-justified. Where data exceeds the maximum length specified in attribute 10, the data is folded, at the first character after the maximum, onto the next line.
- `T` left-justified, but where the data exceeds the maximum length specified in attribute 10, the data is folded into multiple lines, starting at a space

The correlatives

File name	*Attribute type*	*Attribute number*	*Contents*	*Correlative*
STAFF	POSITION	2	4	
	CORRELATIVE	8	TDEPT;X;;1	Dept.descr.
STAFF	POSITION	2	4	
	CORRELATIVE	8	TDEPT;X;;3]TCC;C;;1	Cost centre descr.

If record not found:
 Return null value (X)
 Return item-id (C)

A typical ACCESS enquiry

```
LIST STAFF NAME DEPTCODE DEPTDESC CCDESC
```

This requests a list from the STAFF file showing staff names, their department codes, department names and cost centre names.

The output

```
PAGE    1                               10:20:11 10 NOV 1985

STAFF..... Name......... Dept Dept Name CC Name.........

001        JENKINS, D    002  Admin     Administration
003        BOURDON, R    009  R & D     03
006        WALTERS, E    002  Admin     Administration
005        JONES, K      010
002        SMART, P      011  Costing   Accounting
004        FARMER, L     009  R & D     03
```

The effect of a correlative returning a null value when the look-up record is not found (JONES, K)

The effect of a correlative returning the item-id when the look-up record is not found (BOURDON, R)

Figure 9.7 Examples of output from Tfile correlatives.

U left-justified (no data is folded onto new lines)

These codes are also used when sorting takes place. Right-justified data is sorted into numeric sequence, whilst left-justified text is sorted into alphabetical sequence. Figure 9.8 demonstrates the effect of these codes.

Assume the following department descriptions

```
SALES
SW SUPPORT
MARKETING AND PR
```

The effect of a justification code defining a maximum column width of six characters for displaying the department descriptions is as follows:

```
         -- R --   -- L --   -- T --   -- U--
         Dept..    Dept..    Dept..    Dept..

          SALES    SALES     SALES     SALES
     SW SUPPORT    SW SUP    SW        SW SUPPORT
MARKETING & PR     PORT      SUPPOR    MARKETING AND PR
                   MARKET    T
                   ING AN    MARKET
                   D PR      ING
```

Figure 9.8 Justification using attribute 9.

Attribute 10 – maximum data length

This attribute specifies the maximum number of characters to be used when data is displayed. This maximum can be overridden as can be seen from Figure 9.8, if the current data stored is longer than the maximum number of characters. Remember too that attribute 2 of a dictionary definition item contains the text for the column heading. If this contains a heading which is less than the maximum number of characters as defined by attribute 10, the heading text is padded out with full stops. This padding only applies to the heading and does not affect the data listed.

9.3 The ACCESS enquiry language

As we have already discussed, ACCESS is a dictionary-driven language in that it is the dictionary that contains the names of the data elements to be used in the enquiry language and defines the way in which data is to be presented. It is the master dictionary (MD) in each account that contains the vocabulary of the ACCESS enquiry language, such as `COUNT`, `LIST`, `SORT`, `TOTAL` and so on.

In the earlier sections of this chapter we discussed the various ways in which the dictionary definition items could be manipulated to reduce the amount of data stored and to enable data to be presented in a suitable form. In the following sections we will see how to use the ACCESS processor to retrieve information from the database.

In developing ACCESS reports be careful not to fall into the trap of wasting a considerable amount of time trying to get ACCESS to produce a report it is incapable of doing – it is quicker to write a program! There are a few simple rules to follow which will ensure your success. These are:

1. ACCESS enquiries must be entered either at TCL or within the Primary Input Buffer of a `PROC` (see Section 11.2).
2. The first word of the ACCESS statement must be one of the ACCESS verbs contained in the master dictionary.
3. The statement must be terminated by a carriage return.
4. Multiple line statements can be entered by typing `CTRL/SHIFT/O` together followed by a carriage return at the end of each line. A `:` will be prompted by the ACCESS processor.
5. Only one file name can be used within an ACCESS sentence. To report on data held in more than one file, it will be necessary to set up correlatives.
6. The word `DICT` can precede the file name to enable ACCESS enquiries on dictionary files.
7. Any number of attribute names can be used in an ACCESS statement. If the amount of data to be displayed exceeds the printer width, the report will be printed down the page, one attribute to a line.
8. Any number of modifiers and relational operators, which are defined in the MD, may be used.
9. ACCESS verbs, file names, attribute names, modifiers and relational operators are separated by either blanks, quotes (" or ') or backslashes (\). It is rare to use anything other than a blank.
10. Specific items to be listed are enclosed in backslashes (\) or quotes (" or ') and *must* appear immediately following the file name.
11. Specific values are enclosed in double quotes ('') or backslashes (\) and apply to the previous attribute name.

There are two useful ways to abort the ACCESS processor. The first is `CTRL/X`, the pressing of the `CTRL` key together with the `X` key. This will terminate the display of the ACCESS report on the screen at the current page and saves you having to wade through masses of unnecessary information after you have found what you were looking for.

If you are just wanting to stop the display from scrolling up the screen, rather than terminate it completely, use `CTRL/S`. This will hold the display on the screen until a `CTRL/Q` is entered, after which time the output will recontinue and the report will scroll up the screen.

Another way is by use of the `BREAK` key or `CTRL/C`. This will terminate the ACCESS processor whilst it is compiling its report and is useful when an incorrect statement has been entered. Use of this function can be dangerous since it gives access to the system debugger and an exclamation mark is displayed to denote this. At this point the *only* command that should be entered is `END` to return to the TCL prompt. In extreme cases where the system does not respond to `END`, type `OFF` to log off the system.

The remainder of this chapter will reference data held on the files `STAFF` and `DEPT`. The contents of both the dictionary and data portions of these files are described below for reference.

Staff file dictionary

Item-id →	KEY	NAME	FNAME	SNAME
Attribute				
001	A	A	A	A
002	0	1	1	1
003	Ref	Name	First Name	Surname
004				
005				
006				
007				
008			G1,1	G,1
009	R	L	L	L
010	3	20	20	20

Item-id →	FULL	ADDRESS	TEL
Attribute			
001	A	A	A
002	1	2	3
003	Full Name	Address	Tel
004			
005			
006			
007			
008	A;N(FNAME):" ":N(SNAME)		
009	L	L	L
010	20	30	15

Item-id →	DEPT	DEPTDESC	INTERESTS	SALARY
Attribute				
001	A	S	A	A
002	4	4	5	6
003	Dept	Description	Interests	Salary
004				
005				
006				
007				MR22,
008	S;*;'NO'	TDEPT;C;;1		

009	L	L	L	R
010	3	20	20	10

Staff file data

Item-id	001
Name	DIXON, GEORGE
Address	21 GROVE LANE, CRAYTHORNE, LEICS
Tel No	0533 30303
Department	02
Interests	SQUASH BADMINTON BRIDGE
Salary	£12,500

Item-id	002
Name	LEA, SHAUN
Address	55 LYNDON WAY, LONDON NW1 7SZ
Tel No	01 346 2456
Department	11
Interests	SAILING SWIMMING READING
Salary	£10,250

Item-id	003
Name	PIKE, JOHN
Address	74 WASHWOOD HEATH ROAD, BIRMINGHAM B7 7RR
Tel No	021 359 6009
Department	13
Interests	BRIDGE SQUASH CHESS
Salary	£8,350

Item-id	004
Name	HARLOW, MICHAEL
Address	58 FOUNTAIN LANE, BILLERICAY, ESSEX
Tel No	0474 344255
Department	11
Interests	SQUASH MUSIC
Salary	£9,900

Item-id	005
Name	MORRIS, JIM
Address	33 MILL LANE, REIGATE, SURREY
Tel No	01 345 5454
Department	13
Interests	SQUASH BRIDGE RALLYING
Salary	£12,500

Item-id	006
Name	BRIGHT, IAN
Address	121 JOINERS LANE, WELWYN, HERTS WD1 1DD
Tel No	0244 99933
Department	02
Interests	KARATE MARTIAL ARTS
Salary	£12,400

Item-id	010
Name	RILEY, JULIE
Address	52 HIGHMEAD, SUTTON COLDFIELD, BIRMINGHAM B12 1TT
Tel No	021 355 6060
Department	11
Interests	SWIMMING SAILING
Salary	£11,550

Dept. file dictionary

Item-id →	KEY	DESC
Attribute		
001	A	A
002	0	1
003	Code	Description
004		
005		
006		
007		
008		
009	L	L
010	3	20

Dept. file data

Item-id (Attribute 0)	*Description (Attribute 1)*
01	ACCOUNTS
02	ADMINISTRATION
06	MAINTENANCE
11	SALES
13	SW SUPPORT

9.3.1 Producing unsequenced reports

LIST is one of the prime ACCESS verbs. It can be used with just a file name to produce a simple enquiry, or can additionally include selection criteria, output format specifications, item lists and other options to produce a more complex enquiry. In its basic form LIST will list the contents of a file or file dictionary as is illustrated in Figure 9.9.

```
>LIST STAFF[CR]

PAGE   1                                          09:34:54  31 DEC 1985

STAFF.....

006
001
002
010
003
004
005

7 Items listed.

>LIST DICT STAFF[CR]
Page   1                                          09:35:07  31 DEC 1985

STAFF : STAFF
1   D
AMC   13110
S/NAME   7
STRUCT   1
TYP   L
MAX   10

STAFF : SALARY
1   A
AMC    6
S/NAME   Salary
CONVERSION   MR22,
TYP   R
MAX   10

STAFF : ADDRESS
1   A
AMC   1
S/NAME   Address
TYP   L
MAX   30

STAFF : INTERESTS
1   A
```

```
AMC   5
S/NAME   Interests
TYP   L
MAX   20

STAFF : NAME
1   A
AMC   1
S/NAME   Name
TYP   L
MAX   30

STAFF : DEPT
1   A
AMC   4
S/NAME   Dept
CORRELATIVE   S;*;'NO'
TYP   L
MAX   3

STAFF : DEPTDESC
1   A
AMC   4
S/NAME   Description
CORRELATIVE   TDEPT;C;;1
TYP   L
MAX   20

STAFF : TEL
1   A
AMC   3
S/NAME   Tel
TYP   L
MAX   20

STAFF : KEY
1   A
AMC   0
S/NAME   Ref
TYP   R
MAX   3

9 items listed.
```

Figure 9.9 Simple enquiries using `LIST`.

You will notice from Figure 9.9 that, although in both cases we used the simple LIST command, in the case of the data we were only shown the item-ids whilst for the dictionary we were shown a great deal more information. In a large file where you are only interested in finding out which items exist in a file, this extra information is not only annoying and confusing, but also time-wasting. If you wish to limit the information displayed to show only the item-id, then the word ONLY should be included in the statement immediately after the LIST verb as shown in Figure 9.10.

```
>LIST ONLY DICT STAFF[CR]

PAGE    1                                      10:06:25  31 DEC 1985

STAFF.....

STAFF
SALARY
ADDRESS
INTERESTS
NAME
DEPT
DEPTDESC
TEL
KEY

9 items listed.
```

Figure 9.10 Listing item-ids using LIST ONLY.

Whilst we have now restricted the information for the dictionary items to that originally given by listing the data (the item-id only), it does not explain why the two lists shown in Figure 9.9 differed so greatly in the amount of information displayed. The reason is not obvious, but as you might have guessed is associated with the dictionaries controlling these files. By now you should be familiar with the PICK file hierarchy and know that the master dictionary controls the file dictionary, whilst the file dictionary controls the data. Normally, within the master dictionary are dictionary definition items with the item-ids 1, 2, 3, . . . , 10. This sequential set of ten item-ids will be referenced where no specific output specifications are quoted. The ACCESS processor will include any number of sequential item-ids starting at 1 as default output specifications where no others are given.

Since there are no similar dictionary items in the file dictionary of STAFF, no default output was produced from the simple LIST command. If, for example, we felt it would be useful to see the name and telephone number listed as defaults each time a simple LIST enquiry was processed, we could create two new entries, 1 and 2, in the dictionary of the file STAFF by copying the dictionary items NAME and TEL into them. The LIST command would then reflect their presence as is shown in Figure 9.11.

```
>COPY DICT STAFF NAME TEL[CR]
TO :1 2[CR]
    1 NAME TO 1
    2 TEL TO 2

2 items copied.

>LIST STAFF[CR]

PAGE    1                                              10:35:42  31 DEC 1985

STAFF ..... Name ................ Tel ............

006         BRIGHT, IAN           0244 99933
001         DIXON, GEORGE         0533 30303
002         LEA, SHAUN            01 346 2456
010         RILEY, JULIE          021 355 6060
003         PIKE, JOHN            021 359 6009
004         HARLOW, MICHAEL       0474 344255
005         MORRIS, JIM           01 345 5454

7 items listed.
```

Figure 9.11 Creating default reports using LIST.

There is another useful list verb called LIST-ITEM which combines the action of the COPY or CT verbs with the selection capability of ACCESS. A typical LIST-ITEM report is shown in Figure 9.12.

```
PAGE    1                                              10:40:24  31 DEC 1985

   006
001 BRIGHT, IAN
002 121 JOINERS LANE]WELWYN]HERTS WD1 1DD
003 244 99933
004 02
005 KARATE]MARTIAL ARTS
006 1240000

   001
001 DIXON, GEORGE
002 21 GROVE LANE]CRAYTHORNE]LEICS
```

continued over

continued

```
003 0533 30303
004 02
005 SQUASH]BADMINTON]BRIDGE
006 1250000

    002
001 LEA, SHAUN
002 55 LYNDON WAY]LONDON NW1 7SZ
003 01 346 2456
004 11
005 SAILING]SWIMMING]READING
006 1025000

    010
001 RILEY, JULIE
002 52 HIGHMEAD]SUTTON COLDFIELD]BIRMINGHAM B12 1TT
003 021 355 6060
004 11
005 SWIMMING]SAILING
006 1155000

    003
001 PIKE, JOHN
002 74 WASHWOOD HEATH ROAD]BIRMINGHAM B7 7RR
003 021 359 6009
004 13
005 BRIDGE]SQUASH]CHESS
006 835000

    004
001 HARLOW, MICHAEL
002 58 FOUNTAIN LANE]BILLERICAY]ESSEX
003 0474 344255
004 11
005 SQUASH]MUSIC
006 990000

    005
001 MORRIS, JIM
002 33 MILL LANE]REIGATE]SURREY
003 01 345 5454
004 13
005 SQUASH]BRIDGE]RALLYING
006 1250000
```

Figure 9.12 The output from LIST-ITEM.

9.3.2 Producing reports in sorted sequence

The reports we have produced so far have been in random sequence and are in the order that they are stored within the file. Whilst this is acceptable for small reports, it is far from satisfactory for management reports and reports that are used as reference documents, for example where you need to look up a telephone number. If today's telephone directories were not in alphabetical sequence we would never be able to use them. Sorting is another major ACCESS function and is handled by the verb `SORT`. Using `SORT` as we did `LIST`, without any further qualification, will produce a report in ascending sequence of item-ids as is shown in Figure 9.13.

```
SORT STAFF[CR]

PAGE   1                                10:52:22  31 DEC 1985
```

Remember dictionary items '1' and '2' have now been defined

```
STAFF      Name ...............  Tel ...........

001        DIXON, GEORGE         0533 30303
002        LEA, SHAUN            01 346 2456
003        PIKE, JOHN            021 359 6009
004        HARLOW, MICHAEL       0474 344255
005        MORRIS, JIM           01 345 5454
006        BRIGHT, IAN           0244 99933
010        RILEY, JULIE          021 355 6060

7 items listed.
```

Figure 9.13 Using an unqualified `SORT` verb.

The data can be sorted in any other sequence by adding the dictionary name of the attribute to sort on preceded by the word `BY`. To sort in descending sequence use `BY-DSND`. Examples of these two functions are given in Figure 9.14. Additionally there is a `SORT-ITEM` verb to perform a sorted `LIST-ITEM` function.

Sorting need not be limited to one attribute, since PICK is capable of sorting by up to 16 keys. Hence it would be possible to produce a report giving an alphabetical list of people broken down by departments using the command `SORT STAFF BY DEPT BY NAME`. Notice that the primary sort key is specified first and each attribute to be sorted on is preceded with the

```
>SORT STAFF BY NAME[CR]

PAGE   1                                          11:07:09  31 DEC 1985

STAFF ..... Name ................ Tel ...........

006         BRIGHT, IAN           0244 99933
001         DIXON, GEORGE         0533 30303
004         HARLOW, MICHAEL       0474 344255
002         LEA, SHAUN            01 346 2456
005         MORRIS, JIM           01 345 5454
003         PIKE, JOHN            021 359 6009
010         RILEY, JULIE          021 355 6060

7 items listed.

>SORT STAFF BY-DSND NAME[CR]

PAGE   1                                          11:07:09  31 DEC 1985

STAFF ..... Name ................ Tel ...........

010         RILEY, JULIE          021 355 6060
003         PIKE, JOHN            021 359 6009
005         MORRIS, JIM           01 345 5454
002         LEA, SHAUN            01 346 2456
004         HARLOW, MICHAEL       0474 344255
001         DIXON, GEORGE         0533 30303
006         BRIGHT, IAN           0244 99933

7 items listed.
```

Figure 9.14 Using the SORT verb.

word BY. Using the command as shown, however, will not list the department number as it is not one of the defaults listed in the dictionary. (Remember 1 defines the name and 2 the telephone number.) In order to list specific attributes it is necessary to switch off the defaults, and this is achieved by requesting specific attributes by name, even one of the defaults.

9.3.3 Specifying the data to be output

Specifying the data to be output switches off the default options and is achieved by including the dictionary names of the attributes in the

```
>SORT STAFF BY DEPT BY NAME DEPT DEPTDESC NAME[CR]
```

The sort keys (BY DEPT, BY NAME)
The data to be displayed (DEPT, DEPTDESC, NAME)

```
PAGE   1                                           11:45:06  31 DEC 1985

STAFF ..... Dept  Description ......... Name ...............

006         02    ADMINISTRATION        BRIGHT, IAN
001         02    ADMINISTRATION        DIXON, GEORGE
004         11    SALES                 HARLOW, MICHAEL
002         11    SALES                 LEA, SHAUN
010         11    SALES                 RILEY, JULIE
005         13    SW SUPPORT            MORRIS, JIM
003         13    SW SUPPORT            PIKE, JOHN

7 items listed.
```

Figure 9.15 Selecting the data to be output.

ACCESS statement following the LIST or SORT verbs as shown above. Figure 9.15 shows how this is used to produce a sorted report showing the department, its description and the name of the staff member in the department.

So far, the data we have listed has not been multivalued. If we were to list people's interests instead of the department name we would convert the report to look like the illustration in Figure 9.16.

As you can see from Figure 9.16, multivalues are listed underneath each other with a line being devoted to each value. In the case of this report, it would be easier to read if it were double spaced, with a blank line following the last interest shown. This facility is just one of a number of options available.

9.3.4 Modifiers and options

Modifiers and options can be used to further enhance the ACCESS statement. A modifier is included in the statement as part of the statement, whilst the options (most of which have an equivalent modifier) are included at the end of the statement enclosed in parentheses. The modifiers and options available are shown in Table 9.18.

```
>SORT STAFF BY DEPT BY NAME DEPT NAME INTERESTS[CR]

PAGE   1                                          11:57:54  31 DEC 1985

STAFF ..... Dept Name ................ Interests

006         02   BRIGHT, IAN           KARATE
                                       MARTIAL ARTS
001         02   DIXON, GEORGE         SQUASH
                                       BADMINTON
                                       BRIDGE
004         11   HARLOW, MICHAEL       SQUASH
                                       MUSIC
002         11   LEA, SHAUN            SAILING
                                       SWIMMING
                                       READING
010         11   RILEY, JULIE          SWIMMING
                                       SAILING
005         13   MORRIS, JIM           SQUASH
                                       BRIDGE
                                       RALLYING
003         13   PIKE, JOHN            BRIDGE
                                       SQUASH
                                       CHESS

7 items listed.
```

Figure 9.16 A report containing multivalues.

Table 9.18 Modifiers and options.

Modifier	*Option*	*Description*
BREAK-ON		Specifies a break will occur when the value of a specified attribute changes
BY		Designates the attribute immediately following as a sort key
BY-DSND		Specifies sorting by the attribute immediately following to be in descending sequence
BY-EXP		Sorts by exploding multivalued attributes in ascending sequence

Table 9.18 continued

Modifier	*Option*	*Description*
BY-EXP-DSND		Sorts by exploding multivalued attributes in descending sequence
COL-HDR-SUPP	C	Suppresses the output of the time/date heading, the column headings and the end-of-list message
DBL-SPC		Double spacing
DET-SUPP	D	Suppresses the detail lines when used with TOTAL or BREAK-ON
DICT		Specifies interrogation of the dictionary
EVERY or EACH		Modifies a selection criterion requiring *every* value of an attribute to meet the specified condition for the criterion to be true for the item. It must immediately follow the modifier WITH
FOOTING		Specifies the text string to appear at the bottom of each page output
	F	Specifies that a new page is to be started for each item when using the LIST-ITEM, COPY and SORT-ITEM verbs. Note, there is no equivalent modifier
GRAND-TOTAL		Specifies the text to be printed alongside the grand total
HEADING		Specifies the text to appear at the top of each page output
HDR-SUPP or SUPP	H	Suppresses the output of the time/date heading and the end-of-list message
ID-SUPP	I	Suppresses the list of item-ids for LIST and SORT functions
LPTR	P	Sends output to the spooler for printing
ONLY		Suppresses default report attributes. It must precede the file name
NOPAGE	N	Stops display halting at the end of each page, when report being displayed on the terminal
TAPE		Sends report to tape in T-DUMP format
TOTAL		Produces totals for the attributes following this modifier
USING		Causes the attributes to be obtained from a file other than the dictionary-level file
WITH or IF		Specifies the attribute name immediately following is part of a selection criterion
WITHOUT		A synonym for WITH NOT or WITH NO
WITHIN		Specifies a special form of processing in which items may contain additional item-ids relating to the primary item-id

We have already used some of the modifiers shown in Table 9.18 and can see the effect of some others in Figure 9.17, which is a modification of the report shown in Figure 9.16.

```
>SORT STAFF BY DEPT BY NAME DEPT NAME INTERESTS DBL-SPC
 COL-HDR-SUPP (I[CR]

02   BRIGHT, IAN          KARATE
                          MARTIAL ARTS

02   DIXON, GEORGE        SQUASH
                          BADMINTON
                          BRIDGE

11   HARLOW, MICHAEL      SQUASH
                          MUSIC

11   LEA, SHAUN           SAILING
                          SWIMMING
                          READING

11   RILEY, JULIE         SWIMMING
                          SAILING

13   MORRIS, JIM          SQUASH
                          BRIDGE
                          RALLYING

13   PIKE, JOHN           BRIDGE
                          SQUASH
                          CHESS
```

Figure 9.17 The use of modifiers and options.

9.3.5 Accessing individual values of multi-values

ACCESS has a powerful feature enabling multivalues to be 'exploded' to effectively become items in their own right. This is handled by the **BY-EXP** verb and enables the sorting of the multi-valued 'interests' attribute in ascending (**BY-EXP**) or descending (**BY-EXP-DSND**) sequence. Figure 9.18 gives an example of this facility.

```
>SORT STAFF BY-EXP INTERESTS INTERESTS NAME TEL (I[CR]

PAGE  1                                            14:01:14  31 DEC 1985

Interests           Name ............... Tel ............

BADMINTON           DIXON, GEORGE        0533 30303
BRIDGE              DIXON, GEORGE        0533 30303
BRIDGE              PIKE, JOHN           021 359 6009
BRIDGE              MORRIS, JIM          01 345 5454
CHESS               PIKE, JOHN           021 359 6009
KARATE              BRIGHT, IAN          0244 99933
MARTIAL ARTS        BRIGHT, IAN          0244 99933
MUSIC               HARLOW, MICHAEL      0474 344255
RALLYING            MORRIS, JIM          01 345 5454
READING             LEA, SHAUN           01 346 2456
SAILING             LEA, SHAUN           01 346 2456
SAILING             RILEY, JULIE         021 355 6060
SQUASH              DIXON, GEORGE        0533 30303
SQUASH              PIKE, JOHN           021 359 6009
SQUASH              HARLOW, MICHAEL      0474 344255
SQUASH              MORRIS, JIM          01 345 5454
SWIMMING            LEA, SHAUN           01 346 2456
SWIMMING            RILEY, JULIE         021 355 6060

18 items listed.
```

Figure 9.18 The use of BY-EXP.

9.3.6 The use of throwaway connectives

Throwaway connectives are used to add clarity and naturalness to the ACCESS statement. In the examples used so far, where we have specified the data to be output, we have just included the dictionary names to be output. To some people ACCESS may be easier to use if it were possible to include the word DISPLAY or SHOW in the statement. These additional words are known as throwaway connectives; whilst they aid the clarity, they add no functionality. Some are already provided by PICK, these being

```
A     ANY    IN     OR
AN    FILE   ITEMS  THE
ARE   FOR    OF
```

Others can readily be created by copying any of the above entries in the master dictionary to the new throwaway connective required. Figure 9.19 shows this working by creating the new throwaway `DISPLAY`, which is used in a subsequent ACCESS enquiry.

```
>COPY MD A[CR]
TO:DISPLAY
1 A TO DISPLAY

1 items copied.

>SORT STAFF FILE BY DEPT BY NAME DISPLAY DEPT NAME
 TEL (I[CR]

PAGE   1                                    14:20:40  31 DEC 1985

Dept Name ............... Tel ...........

02   BRIGHT, IAN          0244 99933
02   DIXON, GEORGE        0533 30303
11   HARLOW, MICHAEL      0474 344255
11   LEA, SHAUN           01 346 2456
11   RILEY, JULIE         021 355 6060
13   MORRIS, JIM          01 345 5454
13   PIKE, JOHN           021 359 6009

7 items listed.
```

Figure 9.19 Using throwaway connectives.

9.3.7 Selection criteria

In all the examples so far we have reported on all items in the files being interrogated. Whilst this is helpful in many instances, equally it is necessary to be able to extract part of the database that meets specific criteria. ACCESS provides the means to do this with the relational operators and logical connectives shown in Figure 9.20.

Within these selection criteria, it is possible to carry out string searches. These are handled in one of four ways:

"[xxx" A left square bracket means ignore what is to the left of the string being searched, but look for those ending in the character string xxx.

"yyy]" A right square bracket means ignore what is to the right of the string being searched, but look for those beginning with the character string yyy.

"[zzz]" Square brackets surrounding a text string means look for

Operator	*Description*
= or EQ	Equal to
> or GT or AFTER	Greater than
< or LT or BEFORE	Less than
>= or GE	Greater than or equal to
<= or LE	Less than or equal to
≠ or NE or NOT or NO	Not equal to or null value

Note: if a relational operator is not used, EQ is assumed

Connective	*Description*
AND	Both parts linked by the AND must be true
OR	Either or both parts linked by the OR must be true

Note: if a connective is not used, OR is assumed

Figure 9.20 Relational operators and logical connectives.

that text string somewhere within the character string being searched.

An up-arrow means ignore the character in this character position in the string – a wildcard feature.

These features combine to provide a powerful and flexible interrogation facility. It enables the majority of *ad hoc* as well as regular reports to be produced using ACCESS. Figure 9.21 shows how this would be used to select all staff with an interest in squash in order to set up a squash ladder and how it would be used to select those people living in the London or Birmingham telephone areas with a view to setting up a social club. The next example combines the selection criteria of both previous examples. The last example in Figure 9.21 shows how the wildcard facility can be used to select all those working in departments from 10 through to 19.

9.3.8 The use of breaks and totals

Reports can be divided into sections by means of the BREAK-ON verb. This will cause a break to be established in a report as soon as the value in the attribute following the BREAK-ON verb changes. In fact it is not the entire value which is compared for a change, but the first 24 characters only and the check is made by working from left to the right in the string.

```
>SORT STAFF BY DEPT BY NAME WITH INTERESTS = "[SQUASH]"
 DEPT NAME TEL INTERESTS (I[CR]

PAGE  1                                           15:06:38  31 DEC 1985

Dept Name ................ Tel ............Interests

02   DIXON, GEORGE         0533 30303       SQUASH
                                            BADMINTON
                                            BRIDGE
11   HARLOW, MICHAEL       0474 344255      SQUASH
                                            MUSIC
13   MORRIS, JIM           01 345 5454      SQUASH
                                            BRIDGE
                                            RALLYING
13   PIKE, JOHN            021 359 6009     BRIDGE
                                            SQUASH
                                            CHESS

4 items listed.
```

```
>SORT STAFF BY TEL WITH TEL = "01]" OR "021]" NAME ADDRESS
 TEL DBL-SPC (I[CR]

PAGE   1                                          15:11:47  31 DEC 1985

Name ................ Address                 Tel ............

LEA, SHAUN            55 LYNDON WAY           01 346 2456
                      LONDON NW1 7SZ

MORRIS, JIM           33 MILL LANE            01 345 5454
                      REIGATE
                      SURREY

PIKE, JOHN            74 WASHWOOD HEATH ROAD  021 359 6009
                      BIRMINGHAM B7 7RR

RILEY, JULIE          52 HIGHMEAD             021 355 6060
                      SUTTON COLDFIELD
                      BIRMINGHAM B12 1TT

4 items listed.
```

```
>SORT STAFF BY TEL BY NAME WITH TEL = "01]" OR "021]" AND
 WITH INTERESTS = "[SQUASH]" NAME TEL INTERESTS (I[CR]

PAGE   1                                          15:27:33  31 DEC 1985
```

```
Name ............... Tel ...........Interests

MORRIS, JIM          01 345 5454     SQUASH
                                     BRIDGE
                                     RALLYING
PIKE, JOHN           021 359 6009    BRIDGE
                                     SQUASH
                                     CHESS

2 items listed.

>SORT STAFF BY DEPT BY NAME WITH DEPT = "1^" NAME ADDRESS
 TEL (I[CR]

PAGE   1                                           15:41:49:  31 DEC 1985

Dept Name ............... Tel ...........

11   HARLOW, MICHAEL      0474 344255
11   LEA, SHAUN           01 346 2456
11   RILEY, JULIE         021 355 6060
13   MORRIS, JIM          01 345 5454
13   PIKE, JOHN           021 359 6009

5 items listed.
```

Figure 9.21 The use of selection criteria.

When a control break occurs, ACCESS will automatically print '***' underneath the attribute causing the change, unless told otherwise. Further, a maximum of 15 control breaks can be specified, the highest level being the first one to be specified in the ACCESS statement. When a control break occurs numeric attributes can be totalled using the `TOTAL` verb. Any attribute specified as a control break or a total field will automatically be listed in the report so should not be specified separately as an attribute to be displayed.

Figure 9.22 illustrates the use of both the `BREAK-ON` and `TOTAL` verbs.

It is possible to replace the three asterisks by meaningful text by including the text to be printed in double quotes immediately following the `BREAK-ON attribute name`. This text can include the following options, enclosed in single quotes, to enhance it further:

- `B` Specifies that this control break attribute name is to be used in place of the `HEADING B` option (see next section). It is not meaningful to specify this option within more than one control break specification.

```
>SORT STAFF BY DEPT BY NAME BREAK-ON DEPT DEPTDESC NAME
 TOTAL SALARY (I[CR]

PAGE   1                                         16:00:17  31 DEC 1985

Dept Description ........ Name ............... Salary ....

02   ADMINISTRATION       BRIGHT, IAN             12,400.00
02   ADMINISTRATION       DIXON, GEORGE           12,500.00

***                                               24,900.00

11   SALES                HARLOW, MICHAEL          9,900.00
11   SALES                LEA, SHAUN              10,250.00
11   SALES                RILEY, JULIE            11,550.00

***                                               31,700.00

13   SW SUPPORT           MORRIS, JIM             12,500.00
13   SW SUPPORT           PIKE, JOHN               8,350.00

***                                               20,850.00

                                                  77,450.00

7 items listed.
```

Figure 9.22 The output using BREAK-ON and TOTAL.

- D Suppresses the break data line if only one detail exists since the last break.
- L Suppresses the blank line preceding the break data line and is ignored when the U option is used.
- N Resets the page numbering to 1 on a break.
- P Starts a new page after a control break.
- R Inhibits page rollover, thus forcing all data associated with a break to be on one page.
- U Underlines all total fields on a control break.
- V Inserts the value of the control break into the text.

Similarly, text can be added against the grand total line which may include any of the options U (underline), L (line suppress) and P (page eject). The underline will produce underlining as a row of equal signs whilst the page eject option is extremely useful where the final total is meaningless. It means that the final total will be produced on a separate page which can then be thrown away! Figure 9.23 demonstrates the use of these options.

The DET-SUPP modifier enables the detail lines of the report to be suppressed, giving a totals only report. In this situation a correlative will not be evaluated unless it is the control break attribute. This leads to a summary report as shown in Figure 9.24.

```
>SORT STAFF BY DEPTDESC BY NAME BREAK-ON DEPTDESC
 " 'VLU' Total" NAME TOTAL SALARY GRAND-TOTAL "TOTAL
 SALARIES FOR THE COMPANY"[CR]

PAGE   1                                        16:49:56  31 DEC 1985

STAFF ..... Description ......... Name ............... Salary ....

006         ADMINISTRATION        BRIGHT, IAN            12,400.00
001         ADMINISTRATION        DIXON, GEORGE          12,500.00
                                                         ---------
            ADMINISTRATION Total                         24,900.00

004         SALES                 HARLOW, MICHAEL         9,900.00
002         SALES                 LEA, SHAUN             10,250.00
010         SALES                 RILEY, JULIE           11,550.00
                                                         ---------
            SALES Total                                  31,700.00

005         SW SUPPORT            MORRIS, JIM            12,500.00
003         SW SUPPORT            PIKE, JOHN              8,350.00
                                                         ---------
            SW SUPPORT Total                             20,850.00

TOTAL SALARIES FOR THE COMPANY                           77,450.00

7 items listed.
```

Figure 9.23 Inclusion of text on control breaks.

```
>SORT STAFF BY DEPTDESC BREAK-ON DEPTDESC TOTAL SALARY
 DET-SUPP (I[CR]

PAGE   1                                        16:13:24  31 DEC 1985

Description ......... Salary ....

ADMINISTRATION          24,900.00

SALES                   31,700.00

SW SUPPORT              20,850.00
                        77,450.00

7 items listed.
```

Figure 9.24 A summary report using DET-SUPP.

9.3.9 Headings and footings

Text to be printed at the top or bottom of each page can be defined with the modifiers `HEADING` and `FOOTING`, each of which must be followed by text enclosed in double quotes. Within the text of these a number of options can be included, which if used must be enclosed in single quotes. These are:

- B Inserts the current break value provided the `B` option has been specified along with the control break field.
- C Centres the text on the current line.
- D Inserts the date in the form `DD MMM YYYY`.
- F Inserts the name of the file being interrogated.
- Fn Causes the file name to be included, left-justified in a field of `n` blanks, where `n` is a decimal number.
- L Specifies the start of a new line, allowing for multiple line headings and footings.
- P Inserts current page number right-justified in a field of four blanks.
- Pn Inserts current page number in a field of `n` spaces.
- T Inserts current time and date in the format `HH:MM:SS DD MMM YYYY` using the 24-hour clock.
- '' Two successive single quotes are used to print a single quote in a heading or footing.

Figure 9.25 gives an example of the use of these commands.

Notice now that the length of the statements being used is gaining in size the further we progress through this chapter. Whilst typing in such a lengthy statement is perfectly satisfactory for *ad hoc* requests, any typing mistake will mean retyping from scratch. Hence for any ACCESS report that is a regular report or is potentially a regular report, the statement should be encompassed in a PROC. For details on how to do this, see Section 11.2.

9.3.10 Producing output in label format

The label functions of ACCESS enable information to be output in label format to cater for any type of label stationery. It is one of the winning features that keeps PICK ahead in the commercial operating system race and another of its endearing features. The ACCESS statement is built in the same way as described above except that `LIST` is replaced with `LIST-LABEL` and `SORT` with `SORT-LABEL`.

When the ACCESS statement has been accepted, additional parameters will be requested by use of a ? prompt. If the ACCESS statement has been produced in a `PROC`, these additional parameters will have to be entered either from the terminal or, preferably, via the

```
SORT STAFF BY DEPT BY NAME BREAK-ON DEPT DEPTDESC NAME
  TOTAL SALARY HEADING "PERSONNEL REPORT 'C'
  PAGE : 'PN' 'LL' " FOOTING "CONFIDENTIAL"[CR]

                          PERSONNEL REPORT                   PAGE : 1
STAFF ..... Dept Description ......... Name ............... Salary ....

006         02   ADMINISTRATION        BRIGHT, IAN          12,400.00
001         02   ADMINISTRATION        DIXON, GEORGE        12,500.00
            ***                                             24,900.00
004         11   SALES                 HARLOW, MICHAEL       9,900.00
002         11   SALES                 LEA, SHAUN           10,250.00
010         11   SALES                 RILEY, JULIE         11,550.00
***                                                         31,700.00
005         13   SW SUPPORT            MORRIS, JIM          12,500.00
003         13   SW SUPPORT            PIKE, JOHN            8,350.00
            ***                                             20,850.00
***                                                         77,450.00
:
:
:
CONFIDENTIAL
:
7 items listed. <------------------ Printed on a new page
```

Figure 9.25 The use of headings and footings.

Secondary Output Buffer. Otherwise the parameters can either be entered one at a time, in which case the ? will be displayed until all parameters are input, or all parameters can be input in one go, each separated by a comma. The parameters are in the following format:

```
?count, rows, skip, indent, size, space {,C}
```

where

`count`	represents the number of labels across each page
`rows`	represents the depth of the label in number of print lines
`skip`	represents the number of print lines between the bottom of one label and the top of the one beneath it
`indent`	represents the number of spaces to indent from the left margin, invaluable for certain printers
`size`	represents the width of the label in number of print positions

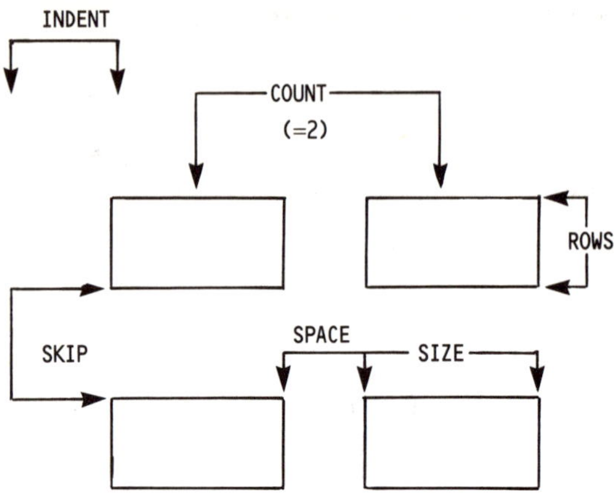


```
>SORT-LABEL STAFF BY DEPT BY NAME NAME ADDRESS
 COL-HDR-SUPP[CR]

?2,6,2,0,30,2,C[CR]

006                           001
IAN BRIGHT                    GEORGE DIXON
121 JOINERS LANE              21 GROVE LANE
WELWYN                        CRAYTHORNE
HERTS WD1 1DD                 LEICS

004                           002
MICHAEL HARLOW                SHAUN LEA
58 FOUNTAIN LANE              55 LYNDON WAY
BILLERICAY                    LONDON NW1 7SZ
ESSEX

010                           005
JULIE RILEY                   JIM MORRIS
52 HIGHMEAD                   33 MILL LANE
SUTTON COLDFIELD              REIGATE
BIRMINGHAM B12 1TT            SURREY

003
JOHN PIKE
74 WASHWOOD HEATH ROAD
BIRMINGHAM B7 7RR
```

Figure 9.26 Label production using ACCESS.

`space` represents the number of horizontal spaces between the end of one label and the beginning of the next

`C` if specified, null attributes will not be printed. This prevents blank lines appearing in some address labels where certain elements such as the county do not exist.

An example of this facility is described in Figure 9.26.

9.3.11 Miscellaneous ACCESS verbs

The COUNT verb

The ACCESS verb COUNT counts the number of items that meet specific criteria. If no selection criterion is stated it will count all the items in a file. Figure 9.27 gives examples of this.

```
>COUNT STAFF[CR]

 7 items counted

>COUNT STAFF WITH TEL = "01]" OR "021]"[CR]

 4 items counted
```

Figure 9.27 The COUNT verb.

The SUM verb

The ACCESS verb SUM generates the total of all the values of one attribute name for a selected set of items in a file. ACCESS selection options can also be applied if required. Figure 9.28 gives examples of this verb.

```
SUM STAFF[CR]

Total of STAFF = 695

SUM STAFF SALARY[CR]

Total of Salary = 77,450.00

SUM STAFF SALARY WITH DEPT = "11"[CR]

Total of Salary = 31,700.00
```

(Note to "Total of STAFF = 695":) 695 is the number of characters in the file and includes attribute and value marks as well as the four characters used in each item to define the item size. It does not include any segment marks.

Figure 9.28 The SUM verb.

The STAT verb

The STAT verb works in the same way as the SUM verb except it produces additional statistical information. Figure 9.29 gives examples of the use of this verb.

```
STAT STAFF[CR]

Statistics of STAFF :
total = 695 average = 99.28 count = 7

STAT STAFF SALARY[CR]

Statistics of STAFF :
total = 77,450.00 average = 11,064.2857 count = 7

STAT STAFF SALARY WITH DEPT = "11"[CR]

Statistics of STAFF :
total = 31,700.00 average = 10,566.6666 count = 3
```

Figure 9.29 The STAT verb.

The HASH-TEST and ISTAT verbs

Whilst these verbs have been covered in earlier sections of this book relating to item distribution, it is worth noting that they are part of ACCESS. To review their function refer to Section 5.3.

The T-DUMP and T-LOAD verbs

These verbs are covered fully in Sections 13.2.7 and 13.2.8 which discuss the various ways in which data can be secured and recovered. It is worth noting, however, that these verbs are part of ACCESS.

The REFORMAT and SREFORMAT verbs

The REFORMAT and SREFORMAT verbs are equivalent respectively to LIST and SORT except that the output is directed to another file or magnetic tape or diskette instead of to the terminal or printer. Figure 9.30 demonstrates the use of these verbs.

9.3.12 The principles and uses of 'lists'

As we have discovered, ACCESS provides an extremely powerful and flexible enquiry language which in conjunction with the strength of the dictionaries enables ready access to the database to produce a variety of

Example 1

```
>SREFORMAT STAFF BY DEPT BY NAME DEPT NAME ADDRESS
 SALARY[CR]

FILE NAME : TEMP[CR]<——— This file must exist
                         otherwise an error
                         message will occur

>
```

Example 2

```
>T-ATT 500[CR]
BLOCK SIZE: 500

>SET-FLOPPY[CR]
BLOCK SIZE: 500
[1072] Diskette set.

>REFORMAT STAFF NAME ADDRESS SALARY[CR]

FILE NAME : TAPE[CR]
    1 006
    2 001
    3 004
    4 002
    5 010
    6 005
    7 003
7 items dumped.
```

Figure 9.30 The `REFORMAT` and `SREFORMAT` verbs.

reports. In certain instances, for example restricting the input to a BASIC program, it is just sufficient to identify those items which meet specific criteria. To handle such requirements ACCESS offers two other selection verbs: `SELECT`, which selects items in random sequence, and `SSELECT`, which selects items in sorted sequence. These two verbs can be looked on as equivalents to `LIST` and `SORT` except they do not directly produce output.

The `SELECT` and `SSELECT` statement is the first step in a two-stage process. These verbs generate a list of items that meet specified selection criteria, a list which can then be used by a second and immediately following process. It is worth stressing here that unless steps are taken to save the list of item-ids from the select commands, the list produced is destroyed as soon as the next command has completed execution. Hence list processing is always a two-stage process – the first to produce the list and the second to make use of it. There are also commands to save, edit, copy and retrieve lists which are described further on.

Lists which are saved are stored in a special system file called POINTER-FILE. This file is always resident in the SYSPROG account and is 'pointed' to within other accounts by setting up a Q-pointer in their master dictionary. If such a Q-pointer does not exist you will need to establish it before saving any lists. Without it, you will only be able to use SELECT and SSELECT to create temporary lists. Whilst accessible via the editor, the POINTER-FILE pointers which contain CL in attribute 1 should *never* be altered in any way. Since these lists can take up a lot of space, and people tend to be careless in tidying up behind themselves, the POINTER-FILE should be checked from time to time and unwanted lists removed.

9.3.13 The SELECT and SSELECT verbs

The SELECT and SSELECT verbs equate to LIST and SORT except they do not directly produce output. Their purpose is to produce a temporary list containing the item-ids of the records which meet specified criteria. This list of item-ids is in random sequence if SELECT is used and in sorted sequence if SSELECT is used. All the selection criteria described above, which can be used with the LIST and SORT verbs can be used with the select verbs. Since the purpose of these select verbs is to generate a list of item-ids, facilities for control breaks, report formatting and totalling are inapplicable and if used will give spurious results.

The temporary list is referred to by the original file name that was interrogated by the select commands. To all intents and purposes it can be considered to be a subset or restricted version of the original file – for use by the next command only. Hence the list can next be processed by:

- an ACCESS command using any data dictionary name defined in the original and interrogated file;
- a BASIC program;
- the SAVE-LIST command to save the list for later use;
- the T-DUMP command to dump the items to diskette or tape.

An example of the use of these commands is given in Figure 9.31. These select verbs are most frequently used to generate sorted lists for use by a BASIC program. As is discussed in Chapter 10, PICK BASIC has no 'sort' statement and hence the selecting and sorting of data to be processed by a BASIC program is handled by the ACCESS processor and normally encompassed in a PROC hidden behind a menu and hence transparent to the user. The handling of these lists is discussed in

```
>SSELECT STAFF BY DEPT BY NAME WITH DEPT > "05"[CR]

[404] 5 items selected.
```

Since the temporary list is in sorted sequence, SORT is unnecessary

Use same name as original file interrogated

```
>LIST STAFF NAME BREAK-ON DEPTDESC TOTAL SALARY[CR]

PAGE    1                                                13:11:57  04 JAN 1986

STAFF ..... Name ................ Description ......... Salary ....

004         HARLOW, MICHAEL       SALES                    9,900.00
002         LEA, SHAUN            SALES                   10,250.00
010         RILEY, JULIE          SALES                   11,550.00
                                  ***                     31,700.00

005         MORRIS, JIM           SW SUPPORT              12,500.00
003         PIKE, JOHN            SW SUPPORT               8,350.00
                                  ***                     20,850.00

***                                                       52,550.00

5 items listed.

>LIST STAFF[CR]
```

← The temporary list was destroyed following the completion of the previous command, hence this command addresses the entire, *original* file

```
PAGE    1                                                13:25:43  04 JAN 1986

STAFF ..... Name .............Tel ............

006         BRIGHT, IAN       0244 99933
001         DIXON, GEORGE     0533 30303
002         LEA, SHAUN        01 346 2456
010         RILEY, JULIE      021 355 6060
003         PIKE, JOHN        021 359 6009
004         HARLOW, MICHAEL   0474 344255
005         MORRIS, JIM       01 345 5454

7 items listed.
```

Figure 9.31 The use of temporary lists.

Section 10.13 in the chapter on PICK BASIC and illustrated in Figure 10.72.

9.3.14 Saving and manipulating saved lists

Lists required for later use are saved using the **SAVE-LIST** command. This saves the list of item-ids and sets a pointer to them in the **POINTER-FILE** but *only* if the command is issued immediately following the **SELECT** or **SSELECT** statement. The name of the list is part of the **SAVE-LIST** command and is the name to be used when retrieving the list using the **GET-LIST** command. The **EDIT-LIST** command enables you to edit and

```
>SSELECT STAFF BY DEPT BY NAME WITH DEPT > "05"[CR]

[404] 5 items selected.

>SAVE-LIST DSTAFF[CR]

List 'DSTAFF' saved — 1 frame(s) used.

>...  }     Other TCL commands      — Use the same name as that of the
 ...  }                               original file interrogated
 ...  }

>GET-LIST DSTAFF[CR]
[404] 5 items selected.

>LIST STAFF NAME BREAK-ON DEPTDESC TOTAL SALARY[CR]

PAGE    1                                          13:11:57  04 JAN 1986

    STAFF ..... Name .............  Description ......... Salary ....

    004         HARLOW, MICHAEL     SALES                    9,900.00
    002         LEA, SHAUN          SALES                   10,250.00
    010         RILEY, JULIE        SALES                   11,550.00
                                    ***                     31,700.00
    005         MORRIS, JIM         SW SUPPORT              12,500.00
    003         PIKE, JOHN          SW SUPPORT               8,350.00
                                    ***                     20,850.00
    ***                                                     52,550.00

    5 items listed.

    >DELETE-LIST DSTAFF[CR]
    [245] List 'DSTAFF' deleted.
```

Figure 9.32 SAVE-LIST, GET-LIST and DELETE-LIST verbs.

amend the list and once the list is finished with it can be removed using the DELETE-LIST verb. Figure 9.32 shows these commands in action.

There are three other commands associated with lists:

COPY-LIST	to copy an existing list to a terminal, to another select-list or to an item in a file
QSELECT	generates a select-list from each of the attributes of an item in a file
FORM-LIST	performs the same function as QSELECT

9.4 Summary

We are now at the end of the chapter on ACCESS, and I am sure you will agree that the PICK operating system has given true consideration to the need to retrieve and report on stored data. Through the use of dictionary definition items and synonyms the PICK operating system can readily be made to understand the terminology used throughout a company. This increases its ease of use and acceptability to such an extent that people with very little training can soon produce their own enquiries and reports.

As has been demonstrated, ACCESS provides for the production of information from the database in a variety of forms, ranging from a simple list of information, to complex selections of data, sorted and formatted in a way suitable for presentation to management, all of which can be produced without the need to resort to any programming.

10 Programming in PICK BASIC

TCL verbs and general commands covered in this chapter

BASIC	CATALOG	COMPILE	DECATALOG	RUN

10.1 An introduction to PICK BASIC

The prime programming language of the PICK operating system is PICK BASIC. It is an extended and enhanced version of Dartmouth BASIC. On some systems it is called Data BASIC, and it is the language most widely used for developing application software. There is an assembler language which is only for the experienced and competent programmer, and not readily distributed. Such is the power of the assembler that any company that uses it voids their operating system warranty and indeed some manufacturers refuse to distribute it altogether.

Needless to say PICK BASIC contains all the necessary features to develop complete and comprehensive applications based around the special PICK database structure without the need to resort to assembler. It works with variable names of any length allowing sensible programmers to give them meaningful names! It also encourages structured programming by providing multiline `IF` statements, a `CASE` statement for the conditional selection of BASIC statements, a `LOOP...UNTIL...DO...REPEAT` facility and the means to call external subroutines.

PICK BASIC is a compiled BASIC protecting the original source code which can be removed from any 'live' system. The object code produced by the compiler however, is not native machine code and therefore has to be interpreted at runtime. This explains the frequently used, but often confusing, statement that PICK BASIC is a compiled interpretive BASIC. Another important feature is that the compiled program is re-entrant. This means that if more than one person is using the same program only one copy of its logic is kept in memory which everybody uses, although each user will naturally be assigned their own data area for variables.

BASIC programs are held in a file. Each program is an item in that file and normally each program statement is an attribute of the item. Since the compiler writes an object code pointer in the file dictionary of the item there are two important aspects to every BASIC program file which need to be borne in mind. Firstly it *must* contain a dictionary portion and secondly its master dictionary entry *must* contain DC in attribute 1 indicating it to be a pointer file. (Refer to Section 5.1.3 for more detail on dictionary item types.)

10.2 Creating, compiling and running BASIC programs

The first stage in programming is to create a file to hold the programs. This file is often given the name BP but obviously can be called any other name you choose. You may find such a program file already exists since it is frequently part of the SYSPROG account. If you cannot find this file, try the LISTFILES command and look for a file containing DC under the heading CODE. (Refer to Section 3.3 on the details of LISTFILES.) Any file with the DC code, other than POINTER-FILE (whose special purpose is discussed in Chapter 9 on ACCESS, Section 9.3.12), can be used as the program file. If no program file exists you must first create one using the CREATE-FILE command as discussed in Section 4.2.1. Having created the file, the next step is to edit its MD entry and change the first attribute, which defines the file type, to DC. Figure 10.1 explains how these two important steps are handled.

```
>CREATE-FILE BP 3 27[CR]

[417] FILE 'BP' CREATED BASE= 29576, MODULO=3,  SEPAR=1.
[417] FILE 'BP' CREATED BASE= 31985, MODULO=27, SEPAR=1.

>ED MD BP[CR]
TOP
.[CR]
001 D
.R[CR]
001 DC[CR]
.FI[CR]
'BP' FILED.
```

Figure 10.1 Creating a file to hold BASIC programs.

Having created the program file the next stage is to create a program. A program contains source code which consists of lines of PICK BASIC instructions, the last of which is an **END** statement. Each program requires a name that uniquely identifies it. The program is created using the editor and once created has to be compiled to generate the object code which is interpreted at run time. Compilation is handled by a TCL command, **BASIC** or **COMPILE**, both of which carry out the same task. In order to know what program to compile, whichever of these commands is used the program file name and program name have to be given. When the program has been compiled successfully, it can be run by typing the TCL verb **RUN** followed by the program file name and program name. Example 10.2 shows the development of a small program called **PROG1** through these various stages. Do not worry too much at this stage about the syntax of the program.

The program in Figure 10.2 displays on the screen five random numbers between 0 and 100. The **RND** function generates random numbers

```
>ED BP PROG1[CR]
NEW ITEM
TOP
.I
001+*THIS PROGRAM PRINTS 5 RANDOM NUMBERS[CR]
002+PRINT "5 RANDOM NUMBERS BETWEEN 0 & 100 ARE"[CR]
003+FOR I=1 TO 5[CR]
004+NUM=RND(101)[CR]
005+PRINT NUM[CR]
006+NEXT I[CR]
007+END[CR]
008+[CR]
EOI 007
.FI[CR]
'PROG1' FILED.

>BASIC BP PROG1[CR]
********
 SUCCESSFUL COMPILE!   1 FRAMES USED.

>RUN BP PROG1[CR]
FIVE RANDOM NUMBERS BETWEEN 0-100 ARE
22
26
47
90
38
```

Figure 10.2 The development stages of a program.

between 0 and one less than the number contained in brackets following RND. You may have noticed that following the instruction to compile the program (and the command COMPILE could have been used in place of BASIC), there followed a series of asterisks. If you count these you will find that one asterisk is displayed for each line in the program plus one for the program-id, hence as our program was seven lines long, eight asterisks in total are displayed.

A number of compiler options are available and these are shown in Figure 10.3.

```
>BASIC 'Program file name' 'Program name' (OPTIONS
>COMPILE 'Program file name' 'Program name' (OPTIONS
```

- A The assembled code option which generates a listing of the source code line numbers, the labels and the BASIC opcodes used by the program. This is a 'pseudo' assembly code listing which allows the user to see what BASIC opcodes his program has generated.
- C The catalogue option for fully debugged programs. It suppresses the end-of-line opcodes from the object item. Since the compiler uses the EOL opcodes to count lines for error messages it means the compiler can only show error messages as being on line 1. The advantage of this option is that it saves 1 byte for each source code line.
- E Lists error lines only.
- L Lists each line of the program as it is compiled.
- M Produces a variable map and a statement map both of which are printed after compilation. These maps show where the program data has been stored in the user's workspace.
- S Suppress the symbol table which is normally generated during compilation and which is used exclusively by the debugger.
- X Generates a cross-reference of all variables and labels which it stores in a file called BSYM which normally has to be created by the user.
- P All compilation output goes to the printer.

Figure 10.3 Compiler options.

In Figure 10.2 a lot of typing was required to run the program. We had to include the program file name and the program name so that PICK could identify the program to execute. There is a much easier way to execute a compiled program. Any compiled program can be catalogued using the TCL verb CATALOG. This places an entry of the program name in the master dictionary and from this point on the program can be run by just typing in the program name. There is just one potential problem with this process, which is not so obvious, but which can be time-consuming to resolve, and that is the cataloguing of programs of the same name in different program files.

PICK will allow you to catalogue programs even if they have been catalogued before and will not complain if the program was previously catalogued and from a different program file. All that will happen when you go to run the program is that it will run the last program to be catalogued under that name. So if one of your programs or subroutines is doing outrageous and inexplicable things, you may find this to be the reason. There is an obvious moral to this story which is that no program name should be duplicated and certainly not in the same account. It may sound obvious and without doubt it is common sense. However since all subroutines *must* be catalogued before they can be called from a program problems of this nature have been known to occur.

Please note too, that some implementations of PICK require that programs be catalogued each time a change is made (although this is not a feature of standard PICK). Having shown the way in which a program can be catalogued, it is worth mentioning that programs can also be decatalogued. This is achieved with the DECATALOG command, which not only removes the entry in the master dictionary but removes the object code as well. To reuse the program in any way after it has been decatalogued it will need to be recompiled! Like the CATALOG verb, DECATALOG requires the program file name and the program name. To catalogue or decatalogue all programs in a program file you can use the wildcard (asterisk) facility as shown in Figure 10.4.

```
CATALOG BP *
DECATALOG BP *
```

Figure 10.4 Cataloguing and decataloging all programs in a program file.

Whatever the implementation of PICK, any change to the source code will obviously require the recompilation of the program in order to generate a new object code. Figure 10.5 illustrates how program changes are handled. In this example the program shown in Figure 10.2 is changed to reflect the following requirements:

- clear the screen before displaying any data;
- request the upper limit number of the random number to be chosen by the user;
- check the user entered number does not exceed 32 767.

Do not worry if the changes in Figure 10.5 have been difficult to understand since the entire new source code is shown in Figure 10.6.

```
>ED BP PROG1[CR]
TOP
.[CR]
001 *THIS PROGRAM PRINTS 5 RANDOM NUMBERS
.I[CR]
001+LOOP[CR]
001+PRINT (-1) ; *THIS CLEARS SCREEN[CR]
001+PRINT "RANDOM NUMBER PROGRAM"[CR]
001+PRINT "CHOOSE A NUMBER BELOW 32,767"[CR]
001+INPUT MAXNO[CR]
001+UNTIL MAXNO > 32767 DO[CR]
001+PRINT "CHOOSE A NUMBER BELOW 32,767"[CR]
001+PRINT "PRESS RETURN TO CONTINUE"[CR]
001+INPUT DUMMY  [CR]
001+REPEAT[CR]
001+[CR]
.[CR]
002 PRINT "5 RANDOM NUMBERS BETWEEN 0 & 100 ARE"
.R[CR]
002 PRINT "THESE ARE 5 RANDOM NUMBERS 0 TO ":MAXNO[CR]
.I[CR]
002+MAXNO=MAXNO+1[CR]
002+[CR]
.[CR]
003 FOR I=1 TO 5
.[CR]
004 NUM=RND(101)
.R/101/MAXNO/[CR]
005 NUM=RND(MAXNO)
.FI[CR]
'PROG1' FILED.
```

Figure 10.5 Changing an existing program with the Editor.

Figure 10.6 shows how the new program is compiled, catalogued and run. In the first section of Figure 10.6 a format program is used. The purpose of this program is to format the program into logical blocks making it easier to understand and hence easier to maintain. This is achieved by indenting the source code to make it more readable. To consider the worth of this program, compare the original program in Figure 10.2 with that of Figure 10.6. Since not every implementation has this facility, a copy of the source to the format program is given in Appendix E.

```
>FORMAT[CR]

DATA/BASIC FILE NAME    - ?BP[CR]
DATA/BASIC PROGRAM NAME - ?PROG1[CR]

*THIS PROGRAM PRINTS 5 RANDOM NUMBERS
   LOOP
      PRINT (-1) ;*THIS CLEARS SCREEN
      PRINT "RANDOM NUMBER PROGRAM"
      PRINT "CHOOSE A NUMBER BELOW 32,767"
      INPUT MAXNO
   UNTIL MAXNO > 32767 DO
      PRINT "PLEASE CHOOSE A NUMBER BELOW 32,767"
      PRINT "PRESS RETURN TO CONTINUE"
      INPUT DUMMY
   REPEAT
      PRINT "THESE ARE 5 RANDOM NUMBERS BETWEEN 0 & ":MAXNO
      MAXNO=MAXNO+1
   FOR I=1 TO 5
      NUM=RND(MAXNO)
      PRINT NUM
   NEXT I
   END

--DONE--

>BASIC BP PROG1[CR]
******************
 SUCCESSFUL COMPILE   1 FRAMES USED.

>CATALOG BP PROG1[CR]
 'PROG1' CATALOGUED!

>PROG1[CR]
RANDOM NUMBER PROGRAM
CHOOSE A NUMBER BELOW 32,767
?7535[CR]
THESE ARE 5 RANDOM NUMBERS BETWEEN 0 & 7535
1695
921
6776
5936
6079
```

Figure 10.6 Formatting, compiling, cataloguing and running a BASIC program.

10.3 PICK BASIC conventions

We have already started to work with PICK BASIC in the above examples to get a feel for the language. Those of you already familiar with other BASICs will undoubtedly have understood much of the source so far. Before we start to move more seriously into BASIC, let's look at some of its conventions.

A BASIC statement can consist of two parts: the statement number and the statement itself. The statement number though, is optional and is normally only included when the statement is itself the destination of another statement. Using statement numbers in this way certainly saves the headache of renumbering programs to incorporate new codes, but remember, statement numbers, when used, must be numeric and unique within the program.

Although it is usual to have one statement on one line, it is possible and generally more efficient, to include several statements on one line, in which case each is separated by a semi-colon. It is best to do this as much as is possible without affecting the clarity of your program.

Variables can be assigned names of any length (actually restricted to 32 267 characters). They must begin with a letter and can contain any combination of letters, numbers, full stops and dollar signs. They cannot be one of the command words (see Appendix D), nor can they be one of the following reserved words:

```
AND    ELSE   GOSUB   LT        ON        THEN
AT     END    GOTO    MATCHES   OR        TO
CASE   EQ     GT      MATCH     REPEAT    UNTIL
CAT    GE     IF      NEXT      SETTING   WHILE
DO     GO     LE      NE        STEP
```

Variables should, to be sensible, be given meaningful names to assist others who may need to maintain or debug your program. Avoid the trap of being 'ultra-efficient' by using variables names as short as possible, particularly those just one letter long. Just imagine how difficult it would be to locate all the occurrences of a single-letter variable in a program!

Alphanumeric literals or constants consist of a string of characters surrounded either by single quotes, double quotes or backslashes. Numbers can exist on their own. Hence all the following literals are valid:

```
A="123"      A=123.99    A="NAME"           A='NAME'
A=\NAME\     A="B7 4BJ"  A='Say "Hello" '
```

A number can be represented in virtually any way, with or without signs or decimal points. The largest number that can be represented is 147 037 488 350 000, the smallest is the negative of the same number. PICK traditionally holds numbers to four places of decimals, although this can be altered in the program by use of the PRECISION statement. Arithmetic expressions are formed using arithmetic operators, each of which is given an order of precedence. These are:

Operator	*Operation*	*Precedence*
+	Unary plus	1 (high)
−	Unary minus	1
*	Multiplication	2
/	Division	2
+	Addition	3
−	Subtraction	3

This means that expressions like 6+4/2+3*2 are acceptable to PICK BASIC although quite frankly it is hardly clear to most people what the result might be! For the sake of completeness in this book it should be noted that where two or more operators appear that have the same precedence, the left-most is evaluated first. I trust, however, that most people will use parentheses in formulae, not just for the sake of clarity but in respect of the sanity of the person who has to maintain your program. The use of brackets transforms the previously stated equation to the expression (6+(4/2)+(3*2)) which makes it completely unambiguous and gives the same result, 14.

Within BASIC statements a series of logical and relational operators can be used. These are:

Operator	*Operation*
<	Less than
LT	Less than
>	Greater than
GT	Greater than
<=	Less than or equal to
LE	Less than or equal to
>=	Greater than or equal to
GE	Greater than or equal to
=	Equal to
EQ	Equal to
#	Not equal to
NE	Not equal to
MATCH	Matching a pattern
MATCHES	Matching a pattern
:	Concatenation
CAT	Concatenation

Any statement commencing with *, ! or REM will be considered to contain user-defined remarks and thus will be ignored by the compiler.

10.4 The control of terminals in BASIC

10.4.1 Terminal input

The INPUT statement provides the means of collecting information keyed in by the user at a terminal. The word INPUT is followed by the name of a data area in the program, called a variable, in which the BASIC compiler will place the typed in data so that the program can make use of it. Without any enhancement to the statement, as shown in Figure 10.7, the program will print a question mark on the screen and place the cursor immediately after it awaiting the input of data.

INPUT QTY	would cause the terminal to respond with a question mark as shown below
?	Any information typed in after the ? would be written in the variable QTY accessible to the program

Figure 10.7 The INPUT statement.

Input statements of this type are not very satisfactory since they only prompt the user with a question mark and do not explain what is being requested. A program full of these would be most confusing! It is a regular need to ask the user for information, but far better to do this by first explaining what the user is expected to input. This is achieved by combining the INPUT statement with the PRINT statement, as shown in Figure 10.8. (The PRINT statement is described in Section 10.4.2 on terminal output.)

PRINT 'WHAT IS THE QUANTITY SOLD' *INPUT QTY*	Program statements
WHAT IS THE QUANTITY SOLD ?	Display on screen

Figure 10.8 INPUT and PRINT statements.

In Figure 10.8 the words **WHAT IS THE QUANTITY SOLD** appear on one line whilst the question mark appears on the next. To improve the statement further, it is possible to ensure that input is made on the same line by placing a **:** at the end of the print statement. In order to control the number of characters permitted to be input, the maximum digits allowed can be specified in the **INPUT** statement. Figure 10.9 shows these improvements.

```
PRINT 'WHAT IS THE QUANTITY SOLD ':          Program
INPUT QTY,4

WHAT IS THE QUANTITY SOLD ?<-- Display on screen which
                               allows a maximum of four digits
                               to be input
```

Figure 10.9 INPUT and PRINT statement.

In Figure 10.9, we saw that the colon on the **PRINT** statement prevented the automatic carriage return and linefeed which caused the **?** to be displayed on the following line. The colon can also be applied to the input statement, again to prevent an automatic carriage return and linefeed. In Figure 10.9, as soon as the fourth digit is input, the program will execute the next statement of the program and any subsequent input will assume a carriage return and linefeed has taken place. If a colon is placed at the end of the **INPUT** statement, i.e. **INPUT QTY,4:**, the user will either have to press the **RETURN** key to send his input to the program or input the exact number of characters as specified in the **INPUT** statement before the next statement of the program is executed. PICK BASIC automatically uses the **?** as a prompt unless told otherwise. The statement to change the prompt is **PROMPT** followed by the appropriate character. Hence

```
PROMPT ":"
```

will change the prompt to a colon. The prompt character will remain in effect until another **PROMPT** statement is encountered.

Input or print statements of this nature will assume that information is to be input or displayed on the current line or the line following the current line. In many programs, however, it is necessary to input information at a specific column and row of the screen. To accept or display information at a specific position on the screen the @ function is added to the statement. The starting position is the top left of the screen addressed by the coordinates 0,0. The @ is followed by parameters, contained in parentheses, that specify the column and row position. For example:

```
INPUT @(41,2):QTY
```

would position the cursor at column 41, row 2 and await data input.

It is important to note that had the variable QTY already contained a value, that value would have been displayed first, after which the cursor would have been repositioned at the start of the displayed data waiting to receive input from the user. If the return key is pressed, the variable will remain unchanged, containing the value of the displayed data. Any other data keyed in by the user will change the variable, QTY, to the value of what is input.

The INPUT command is extremely powerful as it can optionally contain a format mask against which the data input is displayed and/or verified. This is a very complex function and you should refer to your manual for full details. Some examples of format masks are given in Section 10.4.4.

10.4.2 Terminal output

Information is displayed on the terminal by the PRINT or CRT statement. The PRINT statement will print information either on the printer or terminal, dependent on whether or not the printer has been assigned in the program. Printers are assigned and unassigned respectively with the PRINTER ON and PRINTER OFF statements. If the PRINTER ON statement is used all subsequent PRINT statements will print to the printer until a PRINTER OFF statement is encountered. All information produced by the CRT statement is sent to the terminal regardless. Most people adopt the PRINT statement for both terminal and printer output and it is worth noting here that unless told otherwise, the PRINT statement automatically produces its output on the terminal.

The PRINT statement also contains the information to be printed, which may be a string of characters contained in single or double quotes, or a variable which is given by its name as assigned in the program.

As with the INPUT statement, the @ function determines cursor positioning. Hence:

```
PRINT @(20,1):"WHAT IS THE QTY"
```

will print the message in row 1 column 20, and

```
PRINT @(30):"WHAT IS THE QTY"
```

will print the message at column 30 on the current row.

The PRINT @ statement uses cursor control to position the cursor at a specified position on the screen. However, you should be aware that some terminals will not accept implicit cursor addressing (as given in the last example PRINT @(30)...) and it is therefore recommended that the column and row positions are specified in each case to eliminate any possible difficulty in the future when the software may have to be transported to another PICK system.

Again, as with the INPUT statement, format masks can be used to specify how the information is to be printed. These masks can specify scaling factors, justification, the suppression of leading zeros and so on. (See Section 10.4.4 for further details on these masks.)

10.4.3 Special screen control functions

The @ function can be used to carry out special screen controls, such as clear screen, clear from cursor position to end of line, backspace one character and so on. These screen control functions are shown in Figure 10.10.

@(−1)	Clears the screen and places the cursor in what is known as the home position, i.e. column 0 row 0
@(−2)	Positions the cursor in the home position
@(−3)	Clears from the cursor position to the end of the screen
@(−4)	Clears from the cursor position to the end of the line
@(−5)	Starts blinking of data subsequently printed
@(−6)	Ends blinking
@(−7)	Starts a protected field, which is one that cannot be overwritten
@(−8)	Ends the protected field
@(−9)	Backspace by one character
@(−10)	Up one line

Figure 10.10 Screen control function codes.

There is a wide variety of terminals supporting a wide range of features. Not all terminals will support all the features listed in Figure 10.10, whilst most modern terminals support a great deal more. It is also possible that these attributes carry out different functions on your implementation. If you have any doubts about your terminal, or these aspects of video attributes, refer to your terminal manual or your supplier. If your terminal is not responding properly to these attributes and/or cursor control then it probably means that your terminal type is wrong. Terminal types are discussed fully in Chapter 14 (Section 14.6).

The PICK implementation for the IBM PC-XT and PC-AT supports other terminal features such as reverse video, underlining and colour. Because of the importance of the implementation on the IBM PC range, a separate chapter, Chapter 16, is devoted to it. The implementation on the IBM PC-XT sets out video attributes that future PICK implementations have included. Not all PICK systems support them, however, although it is expected that most will include them at some time in the future. These video attributes are listed in Figure 10.11.

@(−11)	Screen protect on
@(−12)	Screen protect off
@(−13)	Reverse video on
@(−14)	Reverse video off
@(−15)	Underlining on
@(−16)	Underlining off
@(−17) to (−32)	Reserved for future use

Figure 10.11 Latest video attributes.

10.4.4 Format masks

These masks provide a convenient and clever means of formatting and validating data and are discussed in detail in Chapter 9 which deals with ACCESS (see Section 9.2.1 on conversion codes). The intention of this section is to give an example of some of them and how they can be applied. The format string consists of two sections: the numeric mask and the format mask (and on some implementations the format mask needs to be enclosed in brackets). These masks immediately follow a variable name and comply with the format shown in Figure 10.12.

Please note that whatever the format characters used, the *entire* format string must be enclosed in single or double quotes. Format masks provide a convenient way to present information in a format familiar to the user. Masked input, for example, can be used to collect information in a specific form, such as a date or a money field where the input contains 2 decimal places. With masked output it is possible to specify, amongst others, that information should be left or right justified, filled with asterisks, or show commas between the thousands positions. Examples of format masks are shown in Figure 10.13.

The input format masks validate the input and will display a message on the last line of the terminal, if the validation fails. The format masks for numeric data are a little more complicated in that the format mask code, which may need to be enclosed in parentheses, follows information regarding justification, the number of decimal places and the scaling required. Figure 10.14 explains the way in which numeric format masks can be used.

```
Variable = variable "{j}{n}{m}{Z}{,}{c}{$}{(format mask)}"
```

where, for the numeric mask,

- j Justification which defaults to left. R is right and L is left
- n Number of digits to print following the decimal point. If n equals zero, no decimal point will be printed.
- m Optional scaling factor, which descales the converted number by the mth power of 10. Since BASIC assumes four decimal places unless changed by PRECISION statement, to descale by 10, m should equal 5, and to descale by 100, m should equal 6.
- Z Specifies the suppression of leading zeros.
- , Specifies the inserting of commas between every thousands positions of a value.
- c The credit indicator. The options are:
  - C causes letters 'CR' to follow negative values and two spaces to follow positive values
  - D causes letters 'DB' to follow positive values and two spaces to follow negative values
  - E causes negative values to be enclosed in pointed brackets <...>, whilst a blank follows positive values
  - M causes a minus sign to follow negative values whilst a space follows positive values
  - N causes the minus sign of negative values to be suppressed.
- $ Causes a dollar sign to be appended to the left-most position of the value prior to conversion.

For the format mask:

- $ Outputs a dollar sign in the leftmost position of the field.
- #n Fills data on a field of n blanks.
- %n Fills data on a field of n zeros.
- *n Fills data on a field of n * characters, where the asterisk can be any specified character.

Figure 10.12 The general format of format masks.

10.4.5 Limiting the data printed

Sometimes it is necessary to print part of a string, or perhaps just the first *n* characters. This is handled by referring to the starting position of the first character and the number of characters required, separated by a comma, all of which is enclosed in square brackets.

Hence, if the variable NAME contained BOURDON, ROGER JAMES and there was only room on the report to print the first ten characters, the statement X=NAME[1,10] would assign BOURDON, R to X.

INPUT @(10,1):VAR.DATE 'D' Input is only valid if it is in date format `DD/MM/YY`. Input is taken from the screen at column 10 row 1, and if it conforms to the date format mask `D`, which requires the date to be entered in the format `DD/MM/YY` what is keyed is put in the variable `VAR.DATE`.

INPUT @(10,1):AMT.DUE 'R2,' Input a number and decimal point where appropriate. Number will be displayed to two decimal places with commas in the thousands positions. The format mask of `R2` means that a number input as *1234.5* will be displayed as `1,234.50`.

INPUT @(10,1):QTY "R26(%15)" Input a number (ignore decimal positions input) and redisplay number to two decimal positions, right-justified on a field of 15 zeros.

Figure 10.13 Format masks for `INPUT` statement.

Value of NUM	*PRINT statement*	*Output result*
1234	*PRINT NUM "R26"*	*12.34*

Justification
Decimal places
Scaling factor

The number is right-justified to two decimal places. The number is descaled to the 6th power of 10, but since BASIC assumes four decimal places the number is descaled by 100.

1234567	*PRINT NUM "R26,"*	*12,345.67*

As previous example but with commas printed.

12.35	*PRINT NUM "1"*	*12.4*

Print rounded to one decimal place.

123456	*PRINT NUM "R26,M(*15)*	**********1,234.56*

Print right-justified, with commas and to two decimal places on a 15 character field of asterisks.

123456	*PRINT NUM "L(%10)"*	*1234560000*

Print left-justified in a field containing 10 zeros.

123456	*PRINT NUM "R(*10)"*	*123456*

Print right-justified in a field containing 10 spaces.

Figure 10.14 Examples of numeric format masks.

10.4.6 Sounding the bell

Most terminals have a bell or audible beep that can be sounded from a program to draw the operator's attention to the screen. This is handled by sending a special character to the screen using the CHAR statement as shown below.

```
PRINT CHAR(7)
```

10.5 The control of printers in BASIC

As was discussed earlier, the PRINT statement is used to direct information to the printer, provided that the PRINTER ON statement has been declared in the program. From this point on, and until a PRINTER OFF statement is used, the output from the PRINT statement will be produced on the printer.

At the start of a program, BASIC considers printers to be unassigned regardless of any TCL assignments that are in force. Hence, all output from the PRINT statements will be produced on the screen. If a printer is assigned using the PRINTER ON statement, all printed output is written to a spool file which is closed and printed out when the program completes its execution. If it is necessary to force printing earlier than at the end of the program, the spool file must be 'forced' closed, which is achieved by issuing a PRINTER CLOSE statement.

It is frequently necessary to produce more than one report within a program and PICK BASIC handles this by use of the PRINT ON statement. This allows the programmer to specify up to 255 printed reports to be printed simultaneously. Each report has to be given a unique number so that the PRINT ON statement can identify which report is being addressed. As with output to a single printer, none of the reports will be printed until the PRINTER CLOSE statement is encountered or until the program finishes. Figure 10.15 shows how three separate reports are produced from the same program. Notice that PRINT assumes report number 0, so a PRINT ON 0 is not needed.

```
PRINTER ON
PRINT "This is a line for report 1"
PRINT ON 1 "This is a line for report 2"
PRINT ON 2 "This is a line for report 3"
```

Writes separate report lines to three separate reports

Figure 10.15 Producing more than one report from a program.

In order to produce several reports from a program, which are to be printed on separate printers, all reports need to be spooled with the 'hold' option and manipulated to the various printers using SP-EDIT (refer to Sections 8.3 and 8.4). The assignment of the 'hold' status would have to be handled *before* the program was executed and would be achieved by use of the SP-ASSIGN command. In this situation the SP-ASSIGN command can either be typed in at TCL before the program is run, or can be included in a PROC prior to the command that runs the program.

Where several PRINT ON statements are used and where the reports can go to the same printer, only one SP-ASSIGN is necessary. If the reports are to be sent to different printers then several SP-ASSIGNs are required in the form SP-ASSIGN FnRm where n is the printer form number and m is the number given by the PRINT ON m statement in the program.

10.5.1 Headings, footings and page throws

To make life easy PICK BASIC will print automatic headings and footings (lines at the top and bottom of each page) with special commands which do not require control by the programmer. Once the commands have been encountered within the program, each page of output will automatically include the heading and/or footing without the programmer having to make checks regarding the number of lines already printed.

Headings and footings are handled with the special statements HEADING and FOOTING. Within these it is possible to have multiple lines, to have the text centred or to include the date, time or page number. Figure 10.16 shows the possible options that can be included within the text of the heading or footing. In all cases the options chosen must be enclosed in single quotes.

Option	*Meaning*
P	Current page number, right-justified
PN	Current page number, left-justified
L	Carriage return/line feed
T	Current time and date (HH:MM:SS DD MMM YYYY), e.g. 21:53:11 or 21 OCT 1985.
D	Current date (DD MMM YYYY), e.g. 21 OCT 1985
C	Centre the text

Figure 10.16 HEADING and FOOTING options.

Headings or footings can be more than one line long. Typically a heading may include a line of text for the title of the report followed by one or two blank lines and then text lines which give a heading to each column of information printed. Multiple line headings or footings are performed by including the L option at the end of each line of text. Let's assume a report with a title of 'Staff List' which prints out a list of staff showing their names, department number, age and telephone number. Figure 10.17 shows typical BASIC statements for headings and footings and their effect.

The BASIC program

```
HEADING "STAFF LIST AS AT 'DC'                    PAGE
'PLL'FULL                DEPT            TEL'L'NAME
        CODE    AGE      NUMBER 'L' "
PRINT NAME "L(#20)":DEPT "L(#10)":AGE "L(#8)":TEL "L(#20)"
```

The printed report

```
            STAFF LIST AS AT 21 OCT 1985       PAGE   1

FULL                DEPT             TEL
NAME                CODE      AGE    NUMBER

D H Houghton        004       22     01 455 1211
M Hynes             009       28     01 236 4680
   ...
   ...
       STAFF LIST AS AT 21 OCT 1985            PAGE   2

FULL                DEPT             TEL
NAME                CODE      AGE    NUMBER

G L Leech           001       34     01 111 1111
     ...
     ...
```

Figure 10.17 Use of HEADING and FOOTING.

Figure 10.17 has introduced extensions to some of the features already discussed. You will notice that the heading contains a number of options which have been combined together and contained in single quotes. The first two, DC, incorporates the date into the title and centres the entire title, including the date. The second group of options is PLL which prints the page number and spaces up two lines. Notice that the first word of the column heading FULL appears immediately after the options PLL and on the printed report appears in the first column of the first line.

Apart from the standard options shown in Figure 10.16, headings and footings can contain variables and/or variables using conversion codes. Suppose a program requested period start and end dates which you wanted to be included in a heading. The dates would be held in the program as two variables in internal format (the number of days since 31 December 1967). Let's call the variables FROM.D and TO.D. These could either be assigned to other variables in output format, such as DISP.DATE=OCONV(FROM.D,'D') after which DISP.DATE could be included in the heading, or alternatively the date could be converted *in situ*, enabling:

```
HEADING "PERIOD ":OCONV(FROM.D, 'D'):" TO ":OCONV(TO.D, 'D')
```

The PRINT statement of Figure 10.17 shows how items of information can be printed across a page one after the other. This is denoted by the colon. However, had we not applied a format mask to the information printed (the format mask is what appears in double quotes), the pieces of information printed would be bunched together, without any spaces between them and without appearing under the headings – see Figure 10.18. The purpose of the format mask, therefore, is to give a fixed length to each of the columns by effectively overlaying the data to be printed on a fixed number of spaces. Hence "L(#10)" or "L#10" requests that the information be printed left-justified on a data area containing 10 banks.

There are times when it is necessary to force the printer to throw a page and this is achieved using the PAGE statement which causes the current heading to be printed at the top of a new page. The PAGE

The BASIC program

```
HEADING "STAFF LIST AS AT 'DC'                    PAGE
                      DEPT         TEL'L'NAME     'PLL'FULL
       CODE    AGE    NUMBER 'L' "
PRINT NAME:DEPT:AGE:TEL
```

The printed report

```
          STAFF LIST AS AT 21 OCT 1985        PAGE   1

FULL             DEPT           TEL
NAME             CODE    AGE    NUMBER

D H Houghton0042201 455 1211
M Hynes0092801 236 4680
```

Figure 10.18 A report printed without format masks.

statement can optionally be followed by a number which then becomes the next page number to be used. This resetting of the page number can be useful where control totals are printed on separate pages.

10.6 File control in PICK BASIC

If you are new to PICK it is worth refreshing your mind on the special PICK data structure discussed in Chapters 2 and 5, before proceeding too far with this section. From this point on we will be using PICK terminology, explained in that chapter, to describe the file handling facilities of PICK BASIC.

10.6.1 The OPEN statement

Before you can use any file it must first be opened, and made known to the program. This is achieved using the `OPEN` statement, which can enable access to either the dictionary or data sections of the file. Remember that both the dictionary and data portions of a file are files in their own right. You can open as many files as you like at any one time but, unlike other systems, BASIC does not require, nor does it provide for, the closing of files. Files are automatically closed when the program finishes.

The filename given in the `OPEN` statement must be the name of an **existing** file. This file would previously have been created using the `CREATE-FILE` command since there is no BASIC command that will create a file. The format of the `OPEN` statement is shown in Figure 10.19.

OPEN {'DICT' ,}'FILENAME' {TO 'variable'} ELSE 'statements'

where

- The word `DICT` in single quotes is used if the dictionary section of the file is to be maintained. If this is omitted the data portion is assumed. A variable can be optionally used here which equates to `DICT`. If the data portion is being maintained, the entire expression, including the single quotes, can be ignored.
- `FILENAME` is the name of the file as held in the MD.
- `variable` is the name used from this point on in the program to refer to the file.
- `statements` are those BASIC statements that will be executed should the file specified by `FILENAME` not exist in the master dictionary (MD).

Figure 10.19 The `OPEN` statement format.

The statements following the **ELSE** are mandatory and tell the compiler how to handle the exception condition of the file not existing. It is quite feasible to tell the program to stop if such a condition occurs. Whilst this is a simple and easy option to take, it is unhelpful in 'live' operation when a program stops, giving no reason. In these situations it is extremely difficult to work out why a program has stopped for what may appear to be no reason, and is extremely unhelpful and unnecessarily time-wasting when more than one file or more than one program is in use. It is therefore more usual to pass control to an exception routine or to display a message on the terminal stating which file is missing. Figure 10.20 shows various forms of the **OPEN** statement.

OPEN "OPORDERS" TO ORD ELSE ← *PRINT "OPORDERS NOT FOUND"* *STOP* *END*	Opens data section of **OPORDERS** file
OPEN 'DICT', 'OPORDERS' TO ORD ELSE STOP ←	Opens the **DICT**ionary of **OPORDERS** file
OPEN "OPORDERS" TO ORD ELSE GOSUB 900 ←	Opens data section of **OPORDERS** **ELSE** perform subroutine 900

Figure 10.20 Use of the **OPEN** statement.

It should be noted that the variable assigned to the file is not treated as a normal variable. Hence, it cannot be assigned a value or have its contents displayed or printed. It is assigned to enable a program that handles several files to uniquely identify the file to be updated. In a program that uses external subroutines, all files should be open in the main program with the file variable being passed as a parameter. Alternatively, the file variable should be passed to the subroutine in a special part of the program called the COMMON area as defined by the **COMMON** statement.

10.6.2 The READ statement

The **READ** statement reads from the specified and *already opened* file and places the entire item (record), with the exception of the item-id (key), in the specified variable. The item-id is assigned as a variable by this statement. The format of the **READ** statement is shown in Figure 10.21.

The statements following the **ELSE** are mandatory and tell the compiler how to handle the exception condition caused by the record not existing. Figure 10.22 shows the various forms of the **READ** statement.

```
READ variable FROM { file var,} item-id ELSE statements
```

where

- `variable` contains the contents of the record
- `file var` is the name of the file variable assigned in the `OPEN` statement
- `item-id` is the key of the record
- `statements` are those BASIC statements that will be executed should the record specified by `item-id` not exist in the file

Figure 10.21 The **READ** statement format.

`READ ORDREC FROM ORD,ORDNO ELSE` `   PRINT "RECORD NOT FOUND ":ORDNO`	Reads record with a key of that held in variable **ORDNO** into the variable **ORDREC**
`READ ORDREC FROM ORD,"123" ELSE` `   PRINT "RECORD NOT FOUND '123' "`	Reads record with a key of 123 into the variable **ORDREC**
`READ ORDREC FROM ORD,ORDNO ELSE GOSUB 900`	If record not found perform error subroutine 900

Figure 10.22 The **READ** statement.

In each of the cases in Figure 10.22, assuming the record exists, an entire item (record) is read from a file called **ORDREC**, the filename as given in the **CREATE-FILE** command. In the first example in Figure 10.22, the item-id or key of the record was held in a variable called **ORDNO**; in the second example the item-id was known and a specific record with the key **123** was read. The final example showed how an error subroutine is invoked if the record is not found. In this case a separate section of the program must have a series of statements that begin with the label **900** and end with the statement **RETURN** (see Section 10.11.1).

This version of the read statement will read an entire item – which is fine if you need to work on several attributes (fields) of the item. However, you may just want to read a single attribute and this can be achieved with the **READV** statement. In this statement, since you require a specific attribute, you need to provide the position of the attribute within the item as well as its item-id. It is far more efficient to read an entire record if more than two attributes need to be referenced. The general format of the **READV** statement is shown in Figure 10.23, whilst Figure 10.24 gives examples of its use.

```
READV 'var' FROM {file-var,} exp1,exp2 ELSE statements
```

where

- `var` is the name of the variable containing the contents of the specified attribute
- `file-var` is the name of the file variable
- `exp1` specifies the item-id of the record
- `exp2` specifies the attribute number
- `statements` are those BASIC statements that will be executed if the item specified in `exp1` cannot be found

Figure 10.23 The `READV` statement format.

`READV VAT FROM ORD,ORDNO,12 ELSE` `PRINT "RECORD NOT FOUND":ORDNO`	Reads attribute 12 of the record with a key of that held in variable `ORDNO`, into the variable `VAT` from the file whose file variable is `ORD`
`READV VAT FROM ORD,"123",12 ELSE` `PRINT "RECORD NOT FOUND '123' "`	Reads attribute 12 of the record with a key of 123 into the variable `VAT` from the file whose file variable is `ORD`

Figure 10.24 The `READV` statement.

10.6.3 The `WRITE` statement

As with the read statement, there are two variants of the write statement: `WRITE` to write the entire record and `WRITEV` to write a specific attribute. Again, it is far better to write away an entire record if you have more than two attributes to update than to write them away individually. If the record or attribute specified in these statements already exists it will be overwritten; if not a new record will be created. A `WRITEV` therefore, can itself write a new record, but only to a file that already exists. The format of these commands is given in Figure 10.25.

You will probably have noticed that there is no `ELSE` clause in these statements. This is because it is always possible to write data. If the record being written does not exist, a new one will be created. The only possibility for error here is that the file has not been opened first. In both the case of the read and write statements, a runtime error will be displayed if the file has not been opened, normally `[B12] LINE n FILE HAS`

```
WRITE var1 ON {file-var,} exp1

WRITEV var2 ON {file-var,} expr1,expr2
```

where

- var1 contains the contents of the record
- file-var is the file variable
- expr1 contains the item-id of the record
- var2 contains the contents of the attribute
- expr2 specifies the attribute number

Figure 10.25 The WRITE and WRITEV statement formats.

`WRITE ORDREC ON ORD,ORDNO` ←	Writes a record whose contents are held in the variable ORDREC, on the file assigned to the variable ORD, the key being that held in the variable ORDNO
`WRITE "DATA RECORD" ON ORD, "123"` ←	In this case the record written has a key of 123 and contains the string DATA RECORD in attribute 1
`WRITEV VAT ON ORD,ORDNO,12` ←	Writes the contents of variable VAT in attribute 12 of the record on the file assigned to the variable ORD whose key is given by the contents of variable ORDNO
`WRITEV "15" ON ORD,"123",12` ←	Here attribute 12 of the record on the file assigned to the variable ORD, and whose key is 123, is assigned the value 15

Figure 10.26 The WRITE and WRITEV statements.

NOT BEEN OPENED where n is the statement number in the program trying to read or write to a non-opened file. You may remember that all error messages are held in the ERRMSG file and in this case the message has the item-id B12.

Figure 10.26 shows examples of these write statements.

The variable containing the entire record to be written away, and which reflects the format of the PICK database, is referred to as a dynamic array. The subject of dynamic arrays is discussed fully in Section 10.7.

Assuming the item MONTHS in the file 'DEMO' contains the following attributes:

```
001 FEB
002 MAR
003 APR
```

The effect of the statements:

WRITEV "JAN" ON DEMO,"MONTHS",0 ◄— Inserts at beginning of the item MONTHS the value JAN

WRITEV "MAY" ON DEMO,"MONTHS",-1 ◄— Appends the value MAY to the end of the item MONTHS

The result of a program with these statements would be an item containing these five attributes:

```
001 JAN
002 FEB
003 MAR
004 APR
005 MAY
```

Figure 10.27 Using WRITEV to add to the start and end of the attributes in a record.

The WRITEV statement has the facility to insert information at the beginning of the record and to append information to the end of the record by defining the attribute number as 0 or −1, respectively. Figure 10.27 shows the use of these two versions of WRITEV.

10.6.4 The DELETE statement

The DELETE statement is used to remove records, attributes and values from the database. Nothing will happen if the record or attribute does not exist so there is no need for an ELSE clause. However a runtime error will be displayed if the file has not been opened. This section deals with how records are deleted, whilst Section 10.10.2 explains how attributes and multivalues are removed. The format of the statement for deleting records from the database is shown in Figure 10.28, whilst Figure 10.29 gives examples of its use.

```
DELETE {file-var,} exp1
```

where

- `file-var` is the name assigned in the `OPEN` statement
- `exp1` specifies the item-id of the record

Figure 10.28 The `DELETE` statement format.

`DELETE ORD,ORDNO` ←	Deletes the record from the file assigned to the file variable `ORD`, whose key is held in the variable `ORDNO`
`DELETE ORD,"123"` ←	Deletes the record with the key of 123, held on the file assigned to the file variable `ORD`

Figure 10.29 The `DELETE` statement.

10.7 Handling arrays in BASIC

A variable is an entity in a program we can give a name to, but whose value varies. It varies because different values can be assigned to it and the values within it adjusted. When we read a record from the database we know it will consist of a number of attributes. PICK BASIC allows the record to be read into a set of variables called an **array** which consists of a number of elements, each of which can be addressed individually. Hence, when the record is read into the array, element 1 of the array will contain attribute 1, element 2 of the array attribute 2, and so on.

Arrays can be one-dimensional, when they are known as **vectors** and are used to handle items. A two-dimensional array is known as a **matrix**. The handling of records involves single-dimensional arrays. Before an array can be used, its maximum dimensions have to be defined, which is handled by the `DIM` statement. Figure 10.30 shows how arrays are defined and addressed.

Once the array has been defined, records can be read in, and written from, using the special read and write commands, `MATREAD` and `MATWRITE`. Although they perform special array-handling functions, the format of these statements, as shown in Figure 10.31, is the same as the normal `READ` and `WRITE` statements.

Where there are fewer attributes in the record than elements in the array, the remaining elements are given a null value. The problem that may occur with **real arrays** (as these arrays are called), is that the record may contain more attributes than the `DIM` statement has defined. In these

A one-dimensional array – Vector

DIM A(5)

Each element is referred to by specifying its offset position contained in parentheses:

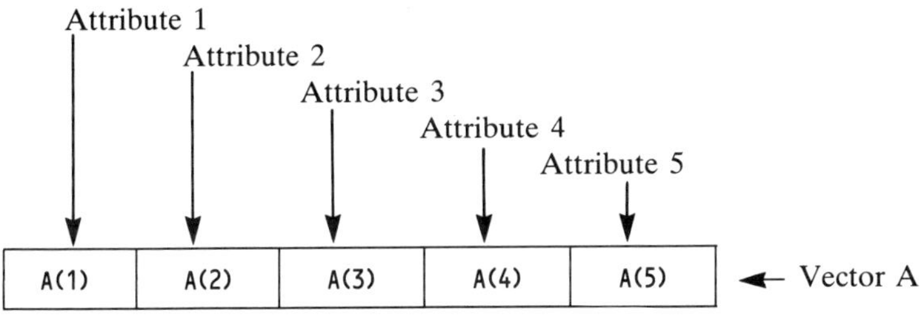

A two-dimensional array – Matrix

DIM B(4,5)

Each element is referred to by specifying its position in the array, row then column, contained in parentheses:

Matrix B

B(1,1)	B(1,2)	B(1,3)	B(1,4)	B(1,5)
B(2,1)	B(2,2)	B(2,3)	B(2,4)	B(2,5)
B(3,1)	B(3,2)	B(3,3)	B(3,4)	B(3,5)
B(4,1)	B(4,2)	B(4,3)	B(4,4)	B(4,5)

Figure 10.30 The vector and matrix.

cases most PICK implementations will place the remainder in the final element of the array. However, do beware, since in some implementations it doesn't and the final elements will be truncated and lost!

Another way of handling record processing is to use dynamic arrays, where their length is assigned dynamically by BASIC at the time the record is read, to reflect exactly the length of the record being processed.

```
MATREAD variable FROM {file variable}, item-id ELSE
statements
```

where

- `variable` contains the contents of the record
- `file variable` is the name assigned in the `OPEN` statement
- `item-id` is the key of the record
- `statements` are those BASIC statements that will be executed should the record specified by item-id not exist in the file

```
MATWRITE variable ON {file-var,} item-id
```

where

- `variable` contains the contents of the record
- `file-var` is the file variable
- `item-id` contains the item-id of the record

Figure 10.31 The `MATREAD` and `MATWRITE` statement format.

10.8 The handling of variables in BASIC

A variable is an entity in a program we can give a name to, but whose value varies. It varies because different values can be assigned to it and the values within it adjusted. Already within this chapter we have seen considerable reference to the use of variables, including the ability to assign arrays to a variable and to reference the individual elements by subscripting.

By far the most efficient way to handle variables is by use of the `EQUATE` or `EQU` statement. The general format of the command is shown in Figure 10.32.

```
EQU{ATE} var1 TO var2{,var3 TO var4...}
```

where

- `var1` is a simple variable
- `var2` can be a literal number, string, character or array element, `CHAR` function or combination thereof
- `var3` and `var4` are repeats of `var1` and `var2`

Figure 10.32 The general format of the `EQUATE` statement.

The EQUATE statement offers a number of advantages in that no storage location is generated for the variable, since its immediate value is compiled into the object code of the program at each point in which it is referenced. This means that it does not have to be reassigned and its variable location computed and accessed each time the variable is used within the program. A further advantage is that by using meaningful names, readability of the program is improved.

The use of EQUATE cannot be too highly recommended for program efficiency and clarity. Examples of the use of EQUATE are given in Figure 10.33.

Assigning a literal number

```
EQUATE PI TO 3.142
```

Assigning a CHAR function

```
EQU AM TO CHAR(254), VM TO CHAR(253)
```

Assigning the elements of an array

```
EQUATENAME TO A(1), ADDRESS TO A(2), TEL TO A(3)
```

Figure 10.33 Examples of the use of the EQUATE statement.

10.9 Multi-user aspects of file control

PICK is a multi-user operating system, which means that more than one person can use the computer at any one time. It also means that it is possible for more than one person to be using the same program at the same time. In this sort of environment, the multi-user systems environment, steps have to be taken to protect the integrity of the database. It would be foolish to enable two or more people access to the same record for updating at the same time. In such a case, as each person finished updating their record, the contents of their record would be written away overwriting what was there previously and the final state of the record would reflect only the changes made by the last person to finish.

PICK provides for control in a multi-user environment by using a locking mechanism that prevents more than one person accessing a record to be updated. In BASIC this is handled by adding a U (Update) to the end of each of the file-handling commands. Hence READ becomes READU, READV becomes READVU, and so on. The read with lock commands will remain effective until released with the RELEASE statement or until a write statement is encountered that also contains the U, such as WRITEU, or MATWRITEU.

Within many PICK implementations locking is at the group rather than item level. Remember that a group can consist of one or more frames and hence consists of a number of items (see Section 5.2.2). The important thing to bear in mind, therefore, is that by locking a group you may have also locked other items not necessarily associated with the transaction. This rarely becomes a problem, even in a very busy multi-terminal system, but when locking the group locks an item another user requires, their terminal will bleep to signify the data they need is locked. This bleeping will continue until the group is unlocked, enabling the other user to continue.

Sensible file sizing, as discussed in Sections 5.3 and 5.4, reduces the problems of group locking to a minimum. However many implementations now include true item (record) locking, which is obviously far preferable. There are a number of commands within the SYSPROG account to assist in lock situations should they become a problem. Firstly, LIST-LOCKS displays the location of the locks and, secondly, CLEAR-BASIC-LOCKS clears file locks set in BASIC.

One of the biggest worries in programming in a multi-user environment is that of conflict during updating. A process known as 'deadlock' or 'deadly embrace' can occur. This is a situation where one user has locked file A and now wants access to file B and a second user has locked file B and now needs access to file A. Neither can obviously progress forward and the only way out is then to use the CLEAR-BASIC-LOCKS command to free both terminals.

PICK does not recognize a deadlock situation so it is up to the programmer to take the utmost precautions to ensure the possibility is minimized. Sensibly, therefore, as few a number of files as possible should be opened for updating at any one time. Not only that, but the number of instructions between locking data and releasing the lock should be kept to an absolute minimum. It is also sensible to ensure that when files are updated, they are updated in the same sequence in each transaction. This means that if file A and file B are used in a number of different transactions, file A is always updated before file B in each transaction.

Some application software will provide its own locking mechanisms by using one of the attributes of the record to indicate whether or not the record is locked and in such instances may not use the U (update) facility.

There is another facility within BASIC to help overcome these problems, and that is the LOCK statement. The LOCK statement sets an execution lock of which there are 48 (0–47), which prevents another program setting the same lock number until the current process that set it has released it with the UNLOCK statement. Setting locks in this way has the advantage of being able to program exception conditions since the LOCK statement has an ELSE condition for handling lock situations not available with the read statements READU, MATREADU, etc., which enables other statements to be executed should the lock be already set.

10.10 Handling dynamic arrays in BASIC

We have seen how a complete record can be read into a variable using the READ statements. Unless defined by a DIM statement the variable will be called a **dynamic array**. Hence READ ORDREC FROM OPORDERS,ORDNO without a previous DIM statement will create the dynamic array ORDREC. Having a complete record available in this way means that we need to have the means of accessing and manipulating specific attributes, multivalues and subvalues. We can refer to a specific part of the record by surrounding its positional reference within pointed brackets rather than the standard parentheses used for real arrays as discussed in Section 10.7. Hence, to refer to attribute 1 of the dynamic array, ORDREC, we would use the form ORDREC<1> and to refer to the first multivalue of attribute 2 we would use ORDREC<2,1> and for the second subvalue of the first multivalue of attribute 3 ORDREC<3,1,2> and so on.

This same notation is used when building up a dynamic array. However, whilst they need no dimensioning, dynamic arrays have to be assigned a value, albeit a null value, before they can be referenced in any way. This value assignment enables the compiler to locate the start point of the array in its table of variables (known as the descriptor table). Figure 10.34 gives an example of building up a record in the dynamic array ORDREC which is first assigned a null value.

ORDREC=' ' ←	The dynamic array is assigned a null value
ORDREC<1>=NAME ←	Attribute 1 is assigned the value of variable NAME
ORDREC<2,1>=ADDR1 ←	Attribute 2, multivalue 1 is given the value of variable ADDR1
ORDREC<2,2>=ADDR2 ←	Attribute 2, multivalue 2 is given the value of variable ADDR2
ORDREC<2,3>=ADDR3 ←	Attribute 2 multivalue 3 is given the value of variable ADDR3
ORDREC<3>=TELNO ←	Attribute 3 is assigned the value of variable TELNO
ORDREC<4>=TLX ←	Attribute 4 is assigned the value of variable TLX

Remember that it is more efficient to use EQUATE; hence these statements should read:

```
EQU NAME TO ORDREC<1>,ADDR1 TO ORDREC<2,1>
EQU ADDR2 TO ORDREC<2,2>,ADDR3 TO ORDREC<2,3>
EQU TELNO TO ORDREC<3>,TLX TO ORDREC<4>
```

Figure 10.34 The dynamic array.

There are a number of BASIC statements used to handle dynamic arrays. These statements are able to handle attributes, multivalues and secondary values and provide powerful string handling facilities. We have looked at two already, READV and WRITEV. Among the others are:

```
COUNT     DCOUNT    DELETE
EXTRACT   INSERT
LOCATE    REPLACE
```

10.10.1 The INSERT and REPLACE statements

The format of these commands are the same, but obviously the INSERT statement will insert information into a dynamic array whilst REPLACE will replace it with some new data. The general format for these statements is shown in Figure 10.35.

```
INSERT(var,exp1,exp2,exp3;new)
REPLACE(var,exp1,exp2,exp3;new)
```

where

- var is the name of the dynamic array
- exp1 is the attribute position
- exp2 is the multivalue position
- exp3 is the subvalue position
- new is the new data to insert or the data used to replace the existing data

---

Figure 10.35 The INSERT and REPLACE statement format.

It is not necessary to specify multivalue and subvalue positions where they don't apply, but in order to make this apparent to BASIC the new data must be preceded by a semi-colon. Figure 10.36 gives examples of the use of these statements.

Using the value −1 for exp2 or exp3 in either of these commands will append to the end of the multivalue or subvalue string being updated whilst using the value 0 will insert at the beginning of the string. Notice too that it is possible and equally valid to make a direct assignment rather than use the REPLACE statement. Hence in Figure 10.36, we could have substituted REC<2,3>="YYY" for the REPLACE statement.

10.10.2 The DELETE and EXTRACT statements

The DELETE statement will delete information from a dynamic array whilst EXTRACT will extract information from it. The general format of these two

```
OPEN "OPORDERS" TO ORD ELSE
     PRINT "OPORDERS NOT FOUND"
     STOP
     END
REC=" "
* Read record whose item-id is 123
READ REC FROM ORD,"123" ELSE
     PRINT "RECORD NOT FOUND '123' "
     STOP
     END
* Insert the string XXX as multivalue 2 on attribute 2
REC=INSERT(REC,2,2;"XXX")
* Replace multivalue 3 on attribute 2 with the string YYY
REC=REPLACE(REC,2,3;"YYY")
* Insert the string AAA at the start of the multivalues
REC=INSERT(REC,2,0;"AAA")
* Add the string ZZZ at the end of the multivalues
REC=INSERT(REC,2,-1;"ZZZ")
* Write away new contents of record 123
WRITE REC ON OPORDERS,"123"
END
```

Figuire 10.36 The use of INSERT and REPLACE in dynamic arrays.

```
DELETE(var,exp1,exp2,exp3)
EXTRACT(var,exp1,exp2,exp3)
```

where

- var is the name of the dynamic array
- exp1 is the attribute position
- exp2 is the multivalue position
- exp3 is the subvalue position

Figure 10.37 The DELETE and EXTRACT statement format.

commands is shown in Figure 10.37, whilst examples of their use are shown in Figure 10.38.

Once again, reference to −1 in exp2 or exp3 will point to the last multivalue or subvalue.

```
OPEN "OPORDERS" TO ORD ELSE
     PRINT "OPORDERS NOT FOUND";STOP;END
REC=" "
* Read record whose item-id is 123
READ REC FROM ORD,"123" ELSE
     PRINT "RECORD" NOT FOUND '123' ";STOP;END
* If multivalue 3 of attribute 2 is XXX then exit program
IF EXTRACT(REC,2,3)="XXX" THEN GOTO 999
* Delete multivalue 3 of attribute 1
REC=DELETE(REC,2,3)
* Write away new contents of record 123
WRITE REC ON OPORDERS,"123"
999 END
```

Figure 10.38 The DELETE and EXTRACT statement.

It is also possible and just as accurate to replace the EXTRACT command in Figure 10.38 with a direct assignment such as IF REC<2,3>="XXX" THEN GOTO 999. Many programmers prefer the use of direct assignment as it makes the program easier to write and maintain.

10.10.3 The LOCATE statement

This is an extremely valuable statement which enables you to locate specific information. It is used not only to determine whether a particular value is present or not, but also to maintain values in ascending or descending sequence within the array, whether these values be attributes, multivalues or subvalues. The format of the statement is shown in Figure 10.39.

If neither exp1 nor exp2 is included in the statement, the LOCATE statement will search down each attribute of the record in turn looking for the appropriate value. It will look at the *entire* contents of each attribute and will not pay attention to the fact that some may contain multivalues or subvalues nor that the string to be located is a part of an attribute. Figure 10.41 gives an example of the LOCATE statement, looking for the string XYZ within in a record. Whilst the character string appears within several attributes, the LOCATE statement will not recognize it as being present because XYZ is not the complete value of any of the attributes.

The same string XYZ does exist as an exact value of one of the multivalues of attribute 3. To search a specific attribute, the attribute number is included in the LOCATE statement as EXP1. Hence, using the

```
LOCATE(value,var{,exp1,exp2};var1{;seq}) ELSE statement
```

where

- value contains the string to be located. A literal must be enclosed within single or double quotes
- var is the name of the dynamic array
- exp1 is the attribute position
- exp2 is the multivalue position
- var1 is the variable containing the position number of the string
- seq defines the sequence where appropriate (see Figure 10.42)
- statement is the BASIC statement to be executed should the string contained in value not be present

Figure 10.39 The LOCATE statement format.

Item-id = 123 as contained in dynamic array **ORD** is the record being searched and contains:

```
001 P0123
002 WATFORD HQ
003 ABC]DEF]XYZ]ZZZ
004 XYZ445
```

LOCATE("XYZ", ORD;POS) ELSE POS=0 ← Would not find the string **XYZ** so the variable **POS** would contain 0

Figure 10.40 The **LOCATE** statement.

same record shown in Figure 10.40, the variable **POS** would contain 3 after use of the statement:

```
LOCATE("XYZ",ORD,3;POS) ELSE POS=0
```

since the string **XYZ** is the *third* multivalue of one of the attributes. Similarly to search through a specific mutlivalue, looking for a string, the multivalue number must be included in the **LOCATE** statement as **exp2**.

If we were to use a format of the statement where following **ELSE** was the word **NULL**, meaning take no action, then if the string to be located was not found, the variable **POS** would contain a number one greater than the number of attributes or multivalues or subvalues searched. Hence in the case of Figure 10.41, the value of **POS** would be 5 following the use of the **LOCATE** statement.

Item-id = 123 as contained in dynamic array **ORD**

```
001 P0123
002 WATFORD HQ
003 ABC]DEF]XYZ]ZZZ  <——— Contains four multivalues
004 XYZ445

LOCATE("AAA",ORD,3;POS) ELSE NULL  <——— Would not find the string AAA in
                                        attribute 3 so the variable POS will
                                        contain 5 (4 attributes + 1)
```

Figure 10.41 The LOCATE statement for multivalues.

The LOCATE statement can be made to abandon its search part way through if you specify a sequence for the search. In this case the data it is searching is assumed to be in sequence (ascending or descending), and the position variable POS will be given a number one more than the number items it passed when it finally found the string to be out of sequence. Figure 10.42 shows how this facility can be used to maintain a series of multivalues in ascending sequence. It shows how the string GHI is added in the correct position in attribute 3 to maintain its ascending sequence of multivalues.

Item-id = 123 as contained in dynamic array **ORD**

```
001 P0123
002 WATFORD HQ
003 ABC]DEF]XYZ]ZZZ  <——— Begins with four multivalues. GHI should follow
004 XYZ445                DEF as the third multivalue

*Locate the string "GHI" held in ascending sequence in attribute 3
LOCATE("GHI",ORD,3;POS;"AL") ELSE NULL

* The variable POS now contains 3
*Insert the string "GHI" in the correct sequence in attribute 3
ORD=INSERT(ORD,3,POS;"GHI")
```

Figure 10.42 Maintaining a string sequence with LOCATE.

The sequences permitted are A or AL for ascending order, left-justified, and D or DL for descending order, left-justified. For right-justified sorting, required when sorting numbers, use AR or DR.

10.10.4 The COUNT and DCOUNT statements

The COUNT statement will count the number of occurrences of a specified string of characters within another string, returning a value of zero if the string is not found. This function will return a number equivalent to the number of characters in the string if asked to look for a null character. Figure 10.43 shows the general format of these statements whilst Figures 10.44 and 10.45 give some examples of their use.

COUNT(string1,string2)

where

- string1 is the string being examined
- string2 is the string to look for

VAR=DCOUNT(string1,string2)

VAR contains the number of occurrences of the system delimiter plus 1 specified in string2 within string1.

String2 must be a reserved system delimiter such as a value mark

---

Figure 10.43 The COUNT statement format.

```
ANS=COUNT('INITIALLY IT IS LIMITING','IT') <------ ANS will show result of
                                                    COUNT which is 3

ANS=COUNT('THE MISSISSIPPI IS A RIVER','I') <----- ANS = 6

A='THE MISSISSIPPI IS A RIVER'
B='IS'
ANS=COUNT(A,B) <---------------------------------- ANS = 3

ANS=COUNT('THE THAMES',' ') <--------------------- ANS = 10 (the number of
                                                    characters in the original
                                                    string)
```

Figure 10.44 The COUNT statement.

The DCOUNT statement is used to count the number of values separated by a specified delimiter. It is a very useful command and is used to count the number of attributes in an item, or the number of multivalues or subvalues in an attribute. A value of zero is returned if the entire string is null. Counting of attributes, multivalues and subvalues is handled by use of the CHAR conversion function which converts a number to its respective ASCII value. The values used to count attributes, multivalues and subvalues are:

Attribute mark	ASCII value 254
Value mark	ASCII value 253
Subvalue mark	ASCII value 252

Figure 10.45 gives examples of the **DCOUNT** statement.

The contents of item-id = 123 as contained in dynamic array

```
ORD
001 P0123
002 WATFORD HIGH STREET
003 ABC]DEF]XYZ]ZZZ
004 XYZ445

AND=DCOUNT(ORD,CHAR(254)) <-------- ANS = 4, the number of attributes

ANS=DCOUNT(ORD<3>,CHAR(253)) <----- ANS = 4, the number of multivalues in
                                    attribute 3

A=ORD<2>
B=' '
ANS=DCOUNT(A,B) <------------------ ANS = 3, the number of words in
                                    attribute 2
```

Figure 10.45 The use of **DCOUNT**.

10.11 Structured programming

PICK BASIC provides the means to produce well structured programs, a structured program being one that reflects the structure of the problem it solves. In this environment use is made of subroutines and loops and the word **GOTO** is frowned on as a four-letter word! Subroutines, which are routines written to handle specific tasks, can be part of the main program or completely external to it. When external, the subroutine is compiled and catalogued totally independent of the main program and just called in by the main program as required, with control then returning to the main program once the subroutine has finished.

In a structured programming environment, each task to be performed represents a separate program or subroutine, with the overall control of these functions being handled by the main program.

10.11.1 Internal subroutines

An internal subroutine is an area within a program which performs a task that is required to be repeated frequently within the program. In this situation, or one where an exception or error routine is required, an internal subroutine is used since it is not considered appropriate for the exception or error routine to be coded at exactly the place in which it occurs in the program.

A subroutine is defined by the GOSUB statement which specifies a label at which the start of the subroutine is to be found. Control is returned to the program at the instruction following the GOSUB statement, just as soon as a RETURN statement is encountered in the subroutine.

Since the return addresses of subroutine calls are held in a stack, one on top of the other, it is possible to call a subroutine within a subroutine, as required, with confidence of returning to the right part of the program afterwards, providing each has only one entry and exit point. The maintenance and understanding of such a process is another matter entirely and the 'nesting' of subroutines is not a recommended practice! Figure 10.46 shows the workings of subroutine calls.

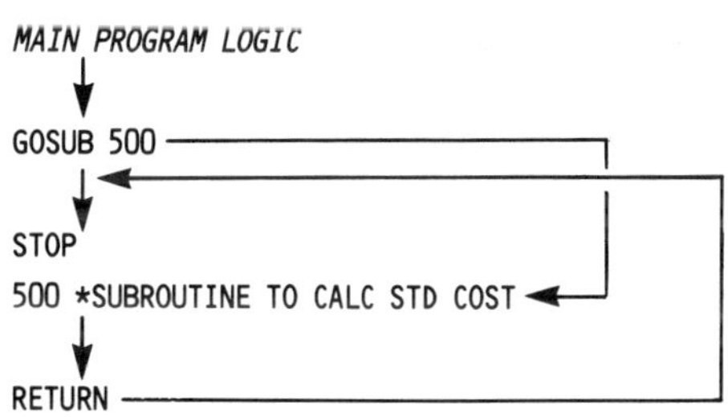

Figure 10.46 Subroutine logic.

An extension of the GOSUB statement allows for the evaluation of an expression first. This permits one of a number of subroutines to be called, depending on the value of a variable. Hence:

```
ON ANS GOSUB 500,600,700,800
```

would cause the program to branch to one of the subroutines at label 500, 600, 700 or 800, depending on the value of ANS. If ANS contains 1 then the subroutine at label 500 will be executed, if it is 2 then the subroutine at label 600 will be used and so on. If the value of ANS is less than 1 or greater than the number of statement labels, no action will be taken, so care must be taken when using this command to cater for this possibility.

10.11.2 The `IF` statement

The `IF` statement allows for the appropriate action to be taken on the results of a test. In its simplistic form the statement format is:

```
IF exp THEN statements
```

where `exp` is the test expression and `statements` are the statements executed as a result. Figure 10.47 gives examples of the simplistic form of the `IF` statement.

`IF A THEN GOSUB 500`	If `A` is non-zero then subroutine 500 is performed
`IF A = B THEN GOSUB 500`	
`IF A > 12 THEN X = 2`	
`IF A = "BLUE" THEN PRINT X`	

Figure 10.47 The simplistic `IF` statement.

An extension to the `IF...THEN` statement adds the `ELSE` condition and enables complex conditions to be handled. The general format of this statement is:

```
IF exp THEN
statements
...
...
END ELSE
statements
...
...
END
```

Figure 10.48 gives examples of the complex form of the `IF...THEN...ELSE` statement.

The various relational operators that can be used within an `IF` statement are given in Figure 10.49.

10.11.3 The `CASE` statement

Since the `IF` statement can become complicated and difficult to understand, even by the person who first wrote it, BASIC provides a simpler way of coding multiple `IF` conditions by use of the `CASE` statement. As many `CASE` statements as needed can follow each other, but

```
IF A > 0 THEN
   X=X-1
END ELSE
   X=X+1
END
```

← If A greater than zero X = X–1, otherwise X = X+1

```
IF FLD<12> = X THEN
   PRINT (10,3):"ERROR CODE ":FLD<12>
   STOP
END ELSE
   IF X = "BLUE" THEN
       A="RIGHT"
   END ELSE
      A="WRONG"
   END
END
```

← This IF statement will *only* be executed if FLD<12> ≠ X

← Set when X ≠ "BLUE"

Figure 10.48 The IF...THEN...ELSE statement.

< or LT	means 'less than'
> or GT	means 'greater than'
= or EQ	means 'equals'
# or <> or NE	means 'not equal'
<= or LE or =<	means 'less than or equal to'
>= or GE or =>	means 'greater than or equal to'
MATCH or MATCHES	means 'match pattern'

Figure 10.49 The relational operators for the IF statement.

they must all be bound within two statements, a **BEGIN CASE** at the beginning and an **END CASE** at the end. The general format is:

```
BEGIN CASE
      CASE exp
      statements
      CASE exp
      statements
END CASE
```

It is important to realize that each **CASE** statement is tested only *until* a true one is found. Once a true one is found, all statements relating to the true **CASE** statement are processed until the next **CASE** statement and then the remainder of the statements are ignored, with control being passed to the statement immediately following the **END CASE** statement. For this reason, to optimize the efficiency of your program you should ensure that the most frequently true condition is the first in the list. Figure 10.50 gives examples of the use of these statements:

```
LOOP
   PRINT (10,10):;INPUT ANS,1;
BEGIN CASE
   CASE ANS = 'Y' OR ANS = 'y'
        ANS = 'Y'
   CASE ANS = 'N' OR ANS = 'n'
        ANS = 'N'
   CASE 1;*RETRY    <- A test expression of 1 means 'always true', hence if
        ANS = 'X'               the previous CASE statements are
        PRINT (10,10):" ":      inappropriate, CASE 1 will force the
END CASE                        subsequent statements to be processed
UNTIL ANS = "Y" OR ANS = "N" DO <- setting ANS to an invalid response of X and
   NULL                         causing the loop to be restarted
REPEAT
   ...
   ...
999 STOP
    END
```

Figure 10.50 The CASE statement.

CASE statements can be nested to handle highly complex conditions. It is obviously important in this situation to think carefully about where the **BEGIN CASE** and **END CASE** statements should go. Figure 10.51 gives an example of nested CASE statements.

10.11.4 Various methods of programming loops

The FOR...NEXT loop

A loop is a set of instructions that is executed several times before the program continues further. Within the loop and for each successive iteration of the loop a variable is changed. Once the variable reaches a specified value, the loop is exited and the program continues. The **FOR...NEXT** loop is one of the most common loops of the BASIC language and can be enhanced by the addition of the **WHILE** or **UNTIL** clauses. Figure 10.52 gives examples of these.

```
BEGIN CASE
    CASE X = 1
        BEGIN CASE
          ...
          ...
        END CASE
    CASE X = 2
        BEGIN CASE
          ...
          ...
        END CASE
END CASE
```

Figure 10.51 Nested CASE statements.

In each of the examples in Figure 10.52 the counter variable was automatically incremented by 1 simply by asking for the next. In some cases it is necessary to increment by more than one at a time, which is handled by adding the STEP clause to the statement. Hence

```
FOR I=1 TO 40 UNTIL X > 50 STEP 2
...
                         statements
...
NEXT I
```

means that each time the NEXT I statement is encountered, the variable I will be increased by 2.

The LOOP...UNTIL/WHILE...DO...REPEAT loop

This kind of loop, often referred to as the DO loop, differs from the FOR...NEXT loop in that the loop is not executed a preset number of times. In the FOR...NEXT loop a variable is set equal to the number of occurrences the loop is to be executed, for example FOR I=1 TO 5, and the loop process started. In the LOOP...UNTIL/WHILE statement, the loop is executed *until* a specific condition occurs, or *while* a specific condition does not occur. So this kind of loop enables execution of the series of commands following the DO statement *until* a test condition proves positive or *while* a test condition remains negative. Whilst these conditions apply, program control will loop back to the top of the loop. Once the test condition is satisfied, control is passed to the first statement following the REPEAT statement. Figure 10.53 gives examples of these.

Example 1

```
FOR I=1 TO 5 ◄────────── First time round sets I = 1
    PRINT I
NEXT I ◄──────────────── Increments I by 1
```

Example 2

```
X="10"
FOR I=1 TO 12 WHILE X < 50 ◄─── This loop will continue until I = 12 or X ≥
    PRINT X*X                    50 whichever comes first. It actually loops
    X=X+5                        eight times.
NEXT I
```

Example 3

```
*Read order number 123
READ ORDREC FROM OPORDERS,"123"
*Count the number of multivalues in attribute 30 of ORDREC
X=DCOUNT(ORDREC<30>,CHAR(253))
*Process loop for as many occurrences as there are multivalues
FOR I=1 TO X
*Build attribute 60 of ORDREC to contain same number of
*  multivalues as attribute 30 , each being twice that held
*  in the original multivalues in attribute 30
    ORDREC<60,-1>=ORDREC<30,I>*2
*Increment loop
NEXT I
*Write record away
WRITE ORDREC ON OPORDERS,"123"
```

Figure 10.52 Examples of the `FOR...NEXT` loop.

The main program in the first example of Figure 10.53 could easily have been the first program we encountered in this chapter which generated random numbers. To insert the loop routines around this program would mean that rather than finishing after running through the program once, the program could optionally be rerun until the user, rather than the program, decided to stop.

10.11.5 The handling of external routines

As was discussed earlier, in structured programming each task becomes a separate program controlled from the main program. This is the right approach to programming, but presents a problem of how to link all these routines together. There are four ways in which your program can

Example 1

```
LOOP
   PRINT (1,20):"DO YOU WANT ANOTHER GO? (Y or N) ":
   INPUT ANS
   WHILE ANS NE "N" DO      ← Process the main program until N is input by
      ...                     the user
     main program
      ...
REPEAT
```

Example 2

```
I=0
LOOP
   I=I+1
   UNTIL ORD <3,I> = '' DO    ← Process the program routine for each
   ...                          multivalue of attribute 3 of the dynamic
 program routine                array ORD, i.e. stop when a null value is
   ...                          found
REPEAT
```

Figure 10.53 The `LOOP...WHILE/UNTIL...DO...REPEAT` statement.

interface to other programs and other parts of the system:

1. The preferred way is via a `CALL` to an external subroutine where data is passed between the two processes. Once the external subroutine has finished, control returns to the calling program.
2. The program can `ENTER` another program. In this case although data can be passed to the entered program, control is not returned to the calling program.
3. The `EXECUTE` statement enables the program to execute any TCL command, after which control is returned to the calling program.
4. The `CHAIN` statement enables the program to execute any TCL command, but control is not returned to the program.

One undocumented statement which might prove useful when using a series of external subroutines is the `X=ERROR()` statement, where the variable `X` is assigned the entire contents of the TCL statement that called the program. This makes it possible to develop a program that performs several functions dependent on the options keyed in. Beware, however, when the program is called from a `PROC`, since it is what was typed in to initiate the `PROC` which will be assigned to the variable, not the contents of the line within the `PROC` which called the program.

The external subroutine and CALL statement

An external subroutine is one that has been written, compiled and **catalogued** outside and separate to the main program. It is called into action using the CALL statement within the main program. Once the subroutine has finished execution, control is returned to the main program at the instruction following the CALL statement. The external subroutine cannot be used unless it has been catalogued and if you have forgotten to do so, the program will go into debug displaying the message, PROGRAM 'XXX' HAS NOT BEEN CATALOGUED. Another important point to bear in mind with subroutines is that they must use the same arithmetic precision as that used within the main program.

The external routine must start with the SUBROUTINE statement and end with the RETURN statement. When using external subroutines it is often necessary to pass them data collected by the main program, such as information keyed in by the user. Such information (known as the parameter list or argument list) can be passed in two ways. If the amount of information is small and limited to a few arguments, reference to these can be made following the CALL statement in the main program. If the amount of information is substantial, both the main program and external subroutine can declare a common area between them in which information can be passed. This common area can be of any size and is defined by the COMMON statement. Figure 10.53 shows how external subroutines are used, by demonstrating the calling of a program 'CALR' within a main program.

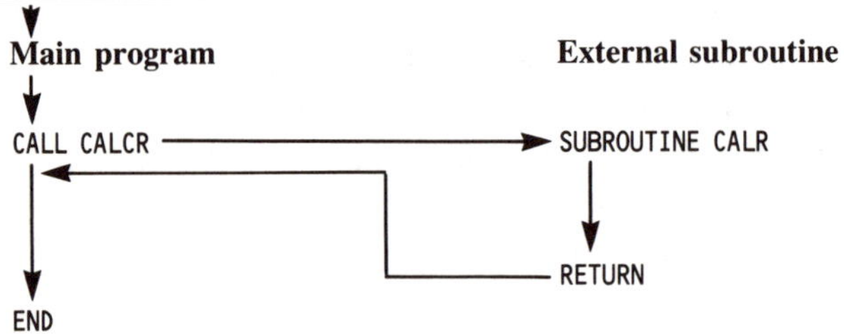

Figure 10.54 The use of external subroutines.

The CALL statement can include the list of variables to be passed to the subroutine, by containing these, each separated with a comma, within parentheses. If the argument list is used for the CALL statement the same feature *must* apply to the SUBROUTINE statement. These arguments may be called by a different name in the main program to those used within the subroutine, provided that the number of arguments in the CALL statement and SUBROUTINE statement are the same. Figure 10.55 gives an example of argument-passing where, prior to calling the subroutine, the arguments passed, A, B and C, are given values. Whilst the names of the arguments are not the same in the external subroutine, the number of arguments is identical and the values of the arguments are therefore assigned in the same order as the list in the CALL statement. Hence, in Figure 10.55, X has the same value as A, Y the same value as B, and so on.

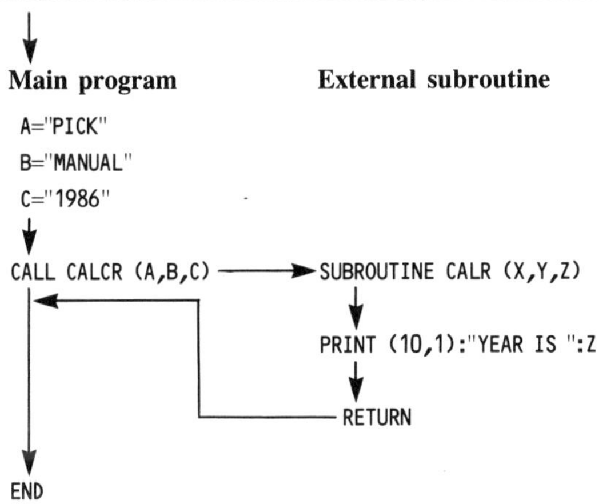

The message displayed by the subroutine is YEAR IS 1986

Figure 10.55 Passing arguments between subroutine and main program.

Arrays may be passed to a subroutine by identifying them as such. This requires using MAT prior to the variable name. The variable must first be dimensioned with the DIM command in the calling program, and the external subroutine must also dimension its variable before making use of its contents. It is quite feasible to change the array dimension, providing that the total number of elements in the array remain the same. Hence a vector (single-dimensioned array) of eight elements can be changed into a matrix (two-dimensional array) of 2×4 elements. Figure 10.56 gives an example of this.

With argument-passing the parameters are copied from the data area of the main program to the data area of the subroutine. If the amount of information to be passed is large, this not only wastes space but time. A far more efficient way of passing information in these circumstances is through the common area. This is a common data area which both the main program and subroutine access and can update. If this concept is adopted, then *both* the subroutine and main program must contain a common area, defined by the COMMON statement. Once again there is

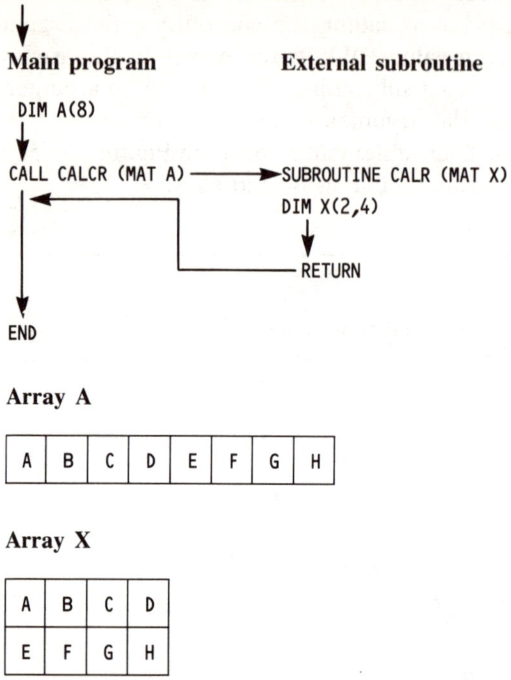

Figure 10.56 Passing arrays as arguments to external subroutines.

complete independence between the names used to describe these variables in the main program and subroutine, although it is good programming practice to use the same names in both.

The `COMMON` statement does impose some disciplines that should be borne in mind. Firstly, the `COMMON` statement must appear before the use of any of the variables contained in it. Whilst this does not dictate that it has to be placed at the start of the program or subroutine, it is generally found there. Arrays can be declared by specifying their dimensions within parentheses. Any arrays declared in this way should not be declared again in a `DIM` statement.

As with argument lists, the elements defined by the `COMMON` statement in the main program 'mask' those defined in the external subroutine. Hence, where the main program defines a common statement with the variables `A`, `B` and `C` and the subroutine declares the common statement with `X(2)` and `Y`, `X(1)` refers to `A`, `X(2)` refers to `B` and `Y` refers to `C`. Figure 10.57 shows how the `COMMON` statement is used to define a single variable, `A`, and a one-dimensional array of eight elements, `B`, in the main program which is defined as variable `X` and the two-dimensional array `Y` in the subroutine.

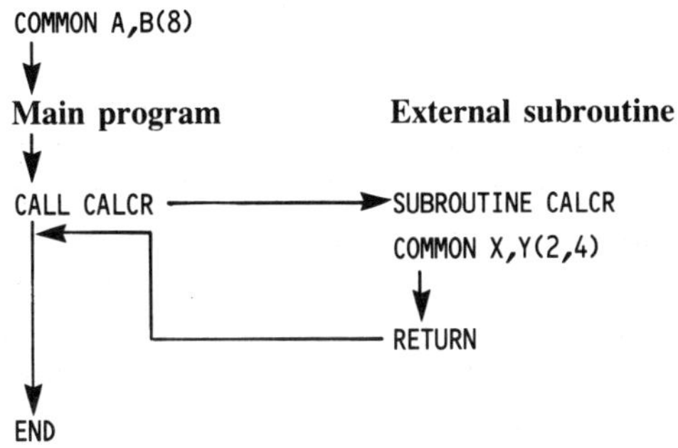

Figure 10.57 Use of the COMMON statement.

One useful aspect of the CALL statement is that it can be used to make indirect calls. This applies in the situation where one of a number of external subroutines is to be used, dependent on the result of a test condition. In this form a variable is set to contain the subroutine name and the call statement calls the variable. To indicate that the name being called is a variable, it is preceded with an @. Hence the general format of the command is:

```
CALL @subroutine {(arguments)}
```

where subroutine is the subroutine name and arguments are the arguments to be passed.

Figure 10.58 shows how the indirect call to an external subroutine is made.

```
COMMON A,B,C(8)
  ...
  ...
BEGIN CASE
    CASE ANS = 1
         SUBNAME = 'SUBR1'
    CASE ANS = 2
         SUBNAME = 'SUBR2'
    CASE ANS = 3
         SUBNAME = 'SUBR3'
END CASE
CALL @SUBNAME
  ...
  ...
END
```

Figure 10.58 The indirect subroutine call.

The external routine and ENTER statement

Use of external routines using the ENTER statements are similar to the CALL statement except for two major differences. Firstly, no argument list can be used, so data *must* be passed using the COMMON statement. Secondly, and most importantly, control is *not* returned to the calling program once the external routine has completed. It is permitted to ENTER a program that calls a subroutine, but is obviously illegal to enter a subroutine from a program because on reaching the RETURN statement in the subroutine and being unable to return to the calling program, the program would have nowhere to go! Figure 10.59 shows the use of the ENTER statement which enters another program which itself calls a subroutine. Again as with the CALL statement the indirect form of ENTER is permitted.

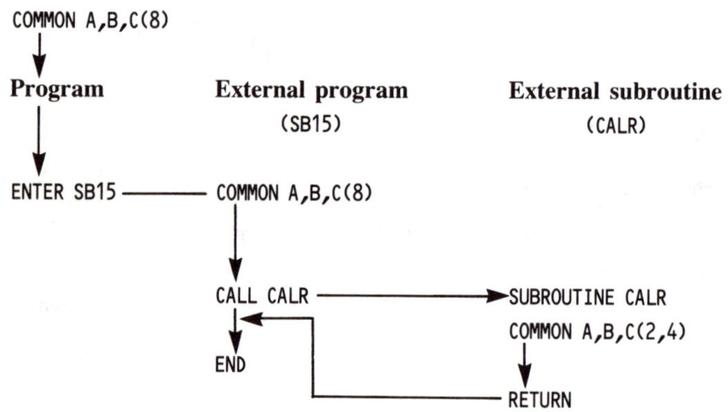

Figure 10.59 Using the ENTER statement.

External routines and the EXECUTE statement

The EXECUTE statement is a recent addition to the PICK operating system and as such is not available from every licensee. This statement provides extremely powerful facilities to the programmer, enabling the execution of any TCL command from within BASIC. After the execution of the TCL command, control is returned to the program at the statement following the EXECUTE statement. It is the introduction of this statement which is expected to see a reduction in the use of PROCs. Prior to its introduction the only way to execute a TCL command from BASIC was to use CHAIN, which does not return control to the calling program.

The only disadvantage with EXECUTE is that it requires additional workspace in which to operate. These workspaces, each 413 frames, are taken from overflow and maintained in a special workspace table for use by the EXECUTE process. When an EXECUTE is complete, the workspace it used is returned to this table and not to system overflow. If sufficient space is not available in this table, and more needs to be constructed, the process can incur a noticeable delay.

This issue of workspace becomes important in a multi-user environment, and even more important in a heavily loaded system using nested EXECUTE statements. It could become very serious indeed in a heavily loaded multi-user system using nested EXECUTE statements on a system with limited disk capacity, such as 10 or 20 Mbytes.

In general, the EXECUTE statement preserves the current working environment before executing the TCL command and restores it after the execution is complete. However, there are certain parameters that are not restored before resuming the BASIC program, these being:

1. The terminal characteristics are not restored if they are changed by a TERM command.
2. The spooler assignment is not restored if altered by a spooler command, such as SP-ASSIGN, SP-OPEN, etc.
3. Terminal output suppression (P verb) is not restored if the current execution does not have output capturing.
4. Current CPU usage statistics are not restored.
5. Tape attachment and tape record size changes with the T-ATT and T-DET verbs are not restored.

Certain TCL verbs will not return after 'execution', namely OFF and LOGTO and, from the debugger, END or OFF will not continue with the EXECUTE.

EXECUTE has a number of general formats, given in Figure 10.60, and examples of its use are given in Figure 10.61.

```
EXECUTE expr
EXECUTE expr RETURNING var1
EXECUTE expr CAPTURING var2
EXECUTE expr RETURNING var1 CAPTURING var2
EXECUTE expr CAPTURING var2 RETURNING var1
```

where

- expr is a complete TCL statement
- var1 is a variable that will contain error message numbers after the execution
- var2 is a variable to capture the output from the executed command

---

Figure 10.60 The format of the EXECUTE statement.

Input can be passed to a TCL command by means of the DATA statement, although no data can be passed to a PROC. Once the TCL command is complete, the data stack is reset.

Output from the executed command may be captured and redirected back to a variable in the calling program by use of the CAPTURING clause. If output is being redirected in this way, carriage return/linefeed pairs are converted to attribute marks and 'clear screen' sequences are removed.

```
    ...
    ...
EQU DATA TO "(BACKUP)", ITEMS TO " *", FILE TO " MASTER"
EQU OK TO 805
    ...
    ...
EXECUTE "COPY ":FILE:ITEMS RETURNING ERR CAPTURING LIST
IF ERR # OK THEN
   PRINT "COPY FAILED. ERROR WAS ":ERR
END ELSE
   PRINT "COPY SUCCESSFUL. ITEMS COPIED WERE ":LIST
END
    ...
    ...
```

Figure 10.61 Using EXECUTE and DATA statements in BASIC.

In Figure 10.61, the TCL statement COPY was used to copy the contents of the file MASTER to the file BACKUP. The variable ERR will contain 805 if the copy is successful, which is the message passed from ERRMSG. A complete list of the message numbers and their meanings can be found in Appendix A describing the ERRMSG file.

External routines and the CHAIN statement

Prior to the introduction of the EXECUTE statement, the CHAIN command was the only way in which a TCL command could be executed directly from BASIC. The CHAIN program can therefore, by definition, also execute a PROC or run another program using the TCL command RUN. Once the command is initiated full control is passed to the TCL command, so there is no ability to return to the BASIC program.

Any data to be passed to the TCL command must be done via the DATA statement in the same way as shown in Figure 10.61 using the EXECUTE statement. The general format of the statement is:

```
DATA expression CHAIN "TCL command"
```

Figure 10.62 shows an example of this command.

```
↓
Main program            TCL processor
↓
CHAIN "LISTU" ─────────►LISTU

                        CH# PCBF NAME ...... TIME .......

                        *00 0400 SYSPROG     10:39
                         01 0420 SYSPROG     10:39
                        ...
                        ...
                        >
```

Figure 10.62 The `CHAIN` statement.

10.12 Other program statements

PICK BASIC provides a number of other commands, the most useful of which have been summarized in Figure 10.63. None of them require a great deal of explanation as their use is fairly straightforward. Should you require further information you should consult your BASIC manual.

Command	Function
`ABS`	Returns the absolute value from a numeric expression regardless of sign. Hence `A=ABS(25-100)` assigns the value 75 to `A`.
`BREAK ON`	Enables the use of the `BREAK` key on the VDU to interrupt the program and enter the debugger.
`BREAK OFF`	Disables the use of the `BREAK` key.
`CLEARFILE {file var}`	Removes all data from the file specified by the file variable.
`ECHO ON`	Enables the characters typed in at the keyboard to be 'echoed' back to the VDU so what was typed in can be seen.
`ECHO OFF`	Turns off the character echo on the screen. Used where passwords are entered, that have to be interpreted by the program, but for security reasons should not be shown on the terminal.

ICONV (exp1,convexp)	Converts exp1 to internal format in accordance with the conversion code in convexp. See Chapter 9 on ACCESS for details on conversion codes.
INT	Returns the integer value from a numeric expression. Hence A=INT(7/3) assigns the value 2 to A.
LEN	Determines the length of a string. Hence A=LEN("ABC123") assigns 6 to the variable A.
OCONV (exp1,convexp)	The reverse of ICONV, where exp1 is converted into external format. See Chapter 10 on ACCESS for details of conversion codes.
REM	Returns the remainder of one number divided by another. Hence A=REM(7,2) which asks for the remainder of 7 divided by 2, assigns 1 to the variable A.
SLEEP n or RQM n	Stop program for n seconds, then continue.
SLEEP HH:MM:SS	Stop program until time reaches that given by HH:MM:SS, then continue.
SPACE	Generates a string containing *n* spaces using SPACE(n).
STR	Generates a string containing *n* characters of a specified value. Hence A=STR('*",6)) assigns ****** to A.
TRIM (exp1)	Removes preceding, trailing and redundant blanks from an expression exp1. This leaves one space between words.

Figure 10.63 Useful BASIC statements/functions.

10.12.1 The date and time

The date and time can be displayed using the commands DATE() for the date, TIME() for the time and TIMEDATE() for the combined date and time.

The DATE() statement returns the date in internal form, i.e. a number of days in relation to 31 December 1967. If the date is prior to this date the internal date is a negative number, if subsequent to it the number is positive. In this way arithmetic can be carried out on dates. In order to display dates in a meaningful way, a conversion code has to be applied to them using the OCONV statement.

Chapter 9 on ACCESS discusses conversion codes in detail. For the purpose of this section the conversion codes and their result is given in

↓

Main program

↓

```
X= DATE()
X1=OCONV(X,'D') ←—— where D is the conversion code
PRINT X1 ←———— displays date as DD MMM YYYY
```

Conversion	*Format displayed*	*Comments*
D	07 DEC 1985	
D/	07/12/1985	
D–	07–12–85	
DO	07 DEC	
DO/	07/12	Useful with US date format
D2/	07/12/85	
D2+	07+12+85	Any character can be delimiter
DD	07	The day
DM	12	The month
DY	1985	Four-digit year
D2Y	85	Two-digit year
DQ	4	The quarter

Figure 10.64 The `DATE()` statement and its conversion codes.

Figure 10.64 without further explanation, together with an example of the format of the date they display.

As was shown in Figure 10.64, it is possible to use the `OCONV` statement to convert internally held data to output format. Similarly it is possible to accept data and convert it to internal format. For example, this allows for dates to be input by the operator which, once converted into internal format, can be used in various calculations. It is important to note here, however, that although a variety of *output* conversion codes are used for dates (see Figure 10.64) there is only one valid *input* conversion code, that of `D` (see Figure 10.65).

The `TIME()` statement returns the time since midnight, converted to seconds. As with the date, an output conversion code has to be applied to display the time in a meaningful way. Figure 10.66 shows how this would be used in a program and shows the conversion codes that apply.

The `TIMEDATE()` statement returns the current time and date in external format, `HH:MM:SS DD MMM YYYY`, the general format being `X=TIMEDATE()`.

```
PRINT (10,1): "SELECT INVOICES DUE FOR PAYMENT"
PRINT (10,5): "Input FROM date ":
INPUT ANS
FROM.DATE=ICONV(ANS, 'D')
PRINT (10,6):"Input TO date ":
INPUT ANS
TO.DATE=ICONV(ANS, 'D')
IF FROM.DATE > TO.DATE THEN ERR = "INVALID DATES";GOSUB ERRORS
IF FROM.DATE = TO.DATE THEN ERR = "INVALID DATES";GOSUB ERRORS
...
...
```

Figure 10.65 The input conversion statement `ICONV`.

↓

Main program

↓

```
X=TIME()
X1=OCONV(X,'MTS') ◄——— where MTS is the conversion code
PRINT X1◄———————— displays timer as HH:MM:SS
```

Conversion	*Format displayed*	*Comments*
MT	13:15	
MTS	13:15:33	
MTH	01:15PM	
MTHS	01:15:33PM	

Figure 10.66 The `TIME()` statement and its conversion codes.

10.12.2 The SYSTEM statement

The `SYSTEM` statement will provide details of some of the system parameters. For example it will return the current page number or line number if the `HEADING` or `FOOTING` commands are in use or return a code to signify whether or not the system printer is on. The general format of the command is:

```
X=SYSTEM(n)
```

where n represents the function to be tested.

The possible functions are:

1 Returns a 1 if system printer is on and a 0 if not
2 Returns page width as defined by the TERM command
3 Returns page length as defined by the TERM command
4* Returns the number of lines remaining to print on current page, based on the current terminal characteristics previously defined with a TERM command
5* Returns current page number
6* Returns current line number
7 Returns terminal type code as defined in the TERM command
8 Returns block size at which the floppy/tape was last attached
9 Returns the current CPU millisecond count
10 Checks current stack on (STON) condition. Returns 1 if the stack is on and 0 if not.
11 Checks whether or not list function active. Returns 1 if active, 0 if not.

*Options 4, 5 and 6 are only available in conjunction with the HEADING and FOOTING commands.

10.12.3 Other string functions

The INDEX statement

The INDEX statement searches a string for the occurrence of a substring and returns the starting position of the substring. It is possible to determine the position of the *n*th occurrence of the expression by specifying *n* within the statement. The answer returned is the starting column position of the substring, with zero being returned when the string is not found. The format of the statement is:

```
INDEX(string,expression,substring,occurrence)
```

```
POS=INDEX("ABCABC","A",2)    POS is assigned value 4

X="MISSISSIPPI"
Y = "I"
POS=INDEX(X,Y,3)             POS is assigned value 8
```

Figure 10.67 The INDEX statement.

The FIELD and COL(1) and COL(2) functions

The FIELD function returns a substring from a string specifying a delimiter character and is often used in conjunction with the COL(1) and COL(2) functions which return, respectively, the column position before and after the string returned to the FIELD function.

The FIELD function is useful when a value has been subdivided by a program into a number of subvalues with a user-defined delimiter and the subvalues need to be addressed.

The general format of the function is:

```
FIELD(expr,delimiter,occurrence)
```

where

- expr is the string being searched
- delimiter is the character which separates the substrings
- occurrence equals the number of occurrences of the expression

Figure 10.68 shows how the FIELD function works together with those of COL(1) and COL(2).

```
X=15 HIGH STREET*BOW*LONDON*E3 3AB
ANS=FIELD(X,"*",3)  <----------  ANS = LONDON
START.COL=COL(1)    <----------  START.COL = 16
END.COL=COL(2)      <----------  END.COL = 23
```

Figure 10.68 The FIELD and COL(1) and COL(2) functions.

10.13 Batch processing

All the discussion so far has revolved around interactive data processing, where the keys of the records to be processed have been known or input at runtime. Whilst most of the programs will fall into this category, there is still a need for batch processing, where a batch of records are to be processed at a time. Typically this happens at the end of a month when special routines need to be applied, like ageing debts and clearing out and producing a report from the month's transactions. Another typical use of batch processing is when part of the database has to be updated to handle a special situation, such as increasing the price list by *x*% to account for inflation or changing the price list to reflect a change in VAT rate.

All these processes require a series of routines to be applied to a selection of records from the database and sometimes require the records to be input in a given sequence. The first point to note here is that, unlike some programming languages, PICK BASIC does not contain a SORT command. Whilst some implementations can now overcome this problem with the **EXECUTE** statement, the normal means of handling this requirement is to include the program in a **PROC** which handles the selection and sorting of records using an **ACCESS** statement. Not only does **ACCESS** handle sorting but it has extremely powerful selection facilities which provide the programmer with great flexibility and obviate the need to develop complex programs for record selection.

Where **ACCESS** is not used, BASIC provides the means to select and process every record in a file. This is handled by the **SELECT** statement, whose general format is shown in Figure 10.69.

```
SELECT {'file-var'} {TO 'variable'}
```

where

- `file-var` is the name of the file variable as defined in the **OPEN** statement. If omitted, the last file opened is assumed.
- `variable` is the name used from this point on in the program to refer to the file.

Figure 10.69 The **SELECT** statement.

The **SELECT** statement builds a list of item-ids which can then be processed within a program using the **READNEXT** statement, whose format is shown in Figure 10.70. This statement will retrieve each item from the selected list which can be used in the standard **READ** statement to enable the processing of each record. The loop for processing each record must be constructed by the programmer with the **READNEXT** being at the top of the loop and a **GOTO** pointing to the **READNEXT** statement being at the end.

```
READNEXT var {FROM sel-var} ELSE statements
```

where

- `var` contains the contents of the 'next' record
- `sel-var` is the name assigned in the **SELECT** statement
- `statements` are those BASIC statements that will be executed after the last record in the file has been processed

---

Figure 10.70 The **READNEXT** statement.

Figure 10.71 shows these statements in action. In this example the entire price list contained in the file, **OPPRICE** , is increased by 8% with a report on the changes being listed on the printer.

The program (PROG10)

```
      OPEN "OPPRICE" TO PRICE ELSE
         PRINT "PRICE LIST FILE NOT FOUND"
         STOP
      END
      PRINTER ON
      SELECT PRICE
      HEADING " 'C'PRICE LIST INCREASES AS AT 'D'
'LL' DESCRIPTION       ORIGINAL  INCREASE    NEW
'L' OF GOODS          PRICE     IN PRICE    PRICE 'L' "
10    READNEXT RECID ELSE
         PRINT
         PRINT "----------- END OF REPORT----------"
         STOP
      END
      READ PRICEREC FROM PRICE,RECID ELSE
         PRINT "ID NOT FOUND ":RECID
         GOTO 10
      END
      EQUATE DESC TO PRICEREC<1>
      EQUATE ORIG TO PRICEREC<2>
      EQUATE INCR TO ORIG*(8/100)
      EQUATE NEW TO ORIG+INCR
      PRINT
DESC"L(#17)":ORIG"R26(#10)":INCR"R26(#10)":NEW"R26(#10)"
      GOTO 10
   END
```

The output from the program

```
                    PRICE LIST INCREASES AS AT 25 NOV 1985

DESCRIPTION        ORIGINAL     INCREASE     NEW
OF GOODS           PRICE        IN PRICE     PRICE

WIDGETS               12.25         0.98     13.23
SCREWS                 0.24         0.02      0.26
HAMMERS                8.76         0.70      9.46
SCREWDRIVER 1"         3.33         0.27      3.60
:
----------- END OF REPORT----------
```

Figure 10.71 Using the READNEXT statement.

In order to repeat the process shown in Figure 10.71, but on a selected group of items, and to produce the report in alphabetical sequence, the program may need to be incorporated into a procedure containing an ACCESS statement that carries out the selection and sorting process. Figure 10.72 shows how this is handled. The ACCESS statement selects all records whose price is less than £10 and sorts them into alphabetical sequence of their description. Thereafter the same program shown in Figure 10.71 is run (PROG10) to increase the price of the selected items by 8%, printing a report of the increases made.

The PROC

```
PQ
HSSELECT OPPRICE BY DESC WITH PRICE < "10"
STON
HRUN BP PROG10
P
```

The output from the program

```
                    PRICE LIST INCREASES AS AT 25 NOV 1985

DESCRIPTION          ORIGINAL      INCREASE     NEW
OF GOODS             PRICE         IN PRICE     PRICE

:
HAMMERS                  8.76          0.70      9.46
:
SCREWS                   0.24          0.02      0.26
SCREWDRIVER 1"           3.33          0.27      3.60
:
---------- END OF REPORT---------
```

Figure 10.72 The use of ACCESS and PROC in BASIC.

As you may have now realized, the combination of PROC and ACCESS with PICK BASIC provide a complete and flexible systems environment. In many application systems, programs are run from behind a menu system built with PROC, which then calls other PROCs, ACCESS statements or BASIC programs. A complete hierarchy can be built up, typically starting with a procedure at the top level and ending with programs at the bottom levels.

10.13.1 The PROCREAD and PROCWRITE statements

The PROCREAD and PROCWRITE are valuable and frequently undocumented statements. They allow reading and writing to the PROC PIB (Primary

Input Buffer). The PROCREAD statement assigns the contents of the PIB to a variable whilst PROCWRITE writes the contents of a variable to the PIB. The general format of these commands is as follows:

```
PROCREAD var ELSE statements
PROCWRITE var
```

Notice the PROCREAD statement has an ELSE clause which is invoked if the program has not been run from a PROC. Figure 10.73 gives an example of the use of PROCREAD together with the PROC that called it, both of which you might find useful. The purpose of the PROC is to produce an analysis of catalogued programs from any account. If the procedure is run without the name of an account, i.e. by typing CAT, the account to which the user is logged will be used and catalogued programs within it analysed. If the analysis is required of a different account, the account name must follow the procedure name, i.e. CAT OFFICE will produce an analysis of catalogued programs in the account OFFICE.

Figure 10.73 The use of PROCREAD.

The PROC to produce a list of catalogued programs

```
PQ
C LIST CATALOGUED PROGRAMS
IF #A2 IHMD        ← If no parameter follows CAT when the PROC is called A2 is
HSSELECT             set to MD
A2
HWITH *A2 = "E6" BY *A0 BY *A6
STON
HRUN BP CAT
P
```

The program CAT

```
*CATALOGUED PROGRAM ANALYSIS
*READ PROC PIB
*
PROCREAD MDNAM ELSE MDNAM="MD"
*
*CHECK TO SEE WHETHER A PARAMETER EXISTS AFTER THE WORD
*'CAT' WHICH SPECIFIES AN ACCOUNT NAME, AND IF SO CAPTURE IT
*IN THE VARIABLE 'MDNAM'
*
IF INDEX(MDNAM," ",1) THEN MDNAM=MDNAM[INDEX(MDNAM," ",1)+1,32767]
*
```

```
*OPEN THE MD OF THE ACCOUNT
*
OPEN MDNAM TO MDID ELSE STOP 201,MDNAM
OPEN "MD" TO MMD ELSE STOP 201,"MD"
PAGENO=0
LINENO=100
DUM=''
START=1
*
*SELECT THE CATALOGUED ITEMS IN THE ACCOUNT
*
EXECUTE 'SSELECT ':MDNAM:' WITH *A2 = "E6" BY *A0 BY *A6 CAPTURING DUMMY2
FINAL=0
LOOP
*
*READ THROUGH SELECT LIST, WHEN COMPLETE DELETE ANY DUMMY
*'Q' POINTER THAT MAY HAVE BEEN USED.  'Q' POINTER GIVEN
*ID OF 'CCCBBBCCCBBB'
*
READNEXT KEY ELSE
DELETE MMD,"CCCBBBCCCBBB"
IF LINENO=24 THEN PRINT "PRESS RETURN TO CONTINUE":;INPUT DUMMY
PRINT;FINAL=1
END
UNTIL FINAL DO
READ ITM FROM MDID,KEY ELSE STOP 203
FLAG=0
*
*OPEN DICT VALUE OF ATTRIBUTE 6. CHECK TO SEE IF IT IS A
*'Q' POINTER
*
OPEN "DICT", ITM<6> TO ITMID ELSE Q=''
READ Q FROM MMD,MDNAM ELSE FLAG=1
IF Q<1> # "Q" THEN FLAG =1 ELSE
  PROC=" "
  PROC<1>="Q"
  PROC<2>=Q<2>
  PROC<3>=ITM<6>
  WRITE PROC ON MMD,"CCCBBBCCCBBB"
  OPEN "DICT","CCCBBBCCCBBB" TO ITMID ELSE FLAG=1
END
END
IF FLAG=0 THEN READ OBJ FROM ITMID,KEY ELSE FLAG=1
```

```
IF LINENO > 23 THEN
   LINENO=2
   PAGENO=PAGENO+1
   IF START THEN START=0 ELSE PRINT "PRESS RETURN TO CONTINUE":;INPUT DUMMY
   IF SEQ(DUM)=24 THEN PRINT;STOP
   PRINT (-1)
   PRINT
"PROGRAM" "L#20":"FILE" "L#20":"B/FID" "L#9":"N/F" "L#5":"COMPILE DATE"
END
PRINT
LINENO=LINENO+2
PRINT KEY"L#20":ITM<6>"L#20":
IF FLAG THEN PRINT "**** NO OBJECT CODE FOUND ****":ELSE
   PRINT OBJ<2>"L#9":OBJ<3>"L#5":OBJ<5>
END
REPEAT
END
```

Figure 10.73 The use of PROCREAD.

The typical output produced by the above procedure shown in Figure 10.73 is shown in Figure 10.74.

10.14 The interactive debugger

No chapter on BASIC is complete without discussion of its debugger, the means to debug programs and find out what is going wrong. The PICK debugger enables full control of the execution of the program allowing you, amongst other things, to step line by line through the program, to display the original source code and to list and change variables.

The BASIC debugger can be entered on demand at runtime by pressing the BREAK key (if your terminal has no BREAK key, press CTRL and C together). Or take the debug option (D with the RUN command. In some cases the program will automatically go into debug where it encounters a situation it cannot understand. In all cases the BASIC debugger is represented by an asterisk prompt.

Having arrived at the debugger prompt, a number of options are available. The most likely initial requirement will be to display a part or all of the source code of the program. Whilst all manuals explain that the L command handles this function, they do not clearly explain that unless the Z function is used first the debugger will display the words NO SOURCE. The Z function makes available to the debugging session the source of *any*

```
PROGRAM       FILE        B/FID   N/F  COMPILE DATE

BMRK.DYNAMIC  BENCH       4474    1    21:29:43  29 APR 1985
BMRK.ICONV    BENCH       4477    1    21:29:45  29 APR 1985
BMRK.MATH     BENCH       4475    1    21:29:44  29 APR 1985
BMRK.OCONV    BENCH       4476    1    21:29:45  29 APR 1985
BMRK.R/W      BENCH       4472    1    21:29:41  29 APR 1985
CHKLNK        SYSTEM-BP   4337    3    17:28:30  17 JUN 1985
FORMATTER     BP          12087   3    10:15:34  01 FEB 1986
PASSWORD      SYSPROG-PL  4528    1    19:43:33  27 OCT 1983
POVFX         SYSTEM-BP   4356    3    17:29:00  17 JUN 1985
ROBOT         BP          4362    10   19:36:19  27 OCT 1983
PRESS RETURN TO CONTINUE
------------- ( End of first screen ) -------------------------

PROGRAM       FILE        B/FID   N/F  COMPILE DATE

SET.PORT      BP          4346    6    08:21:55  22 MAR 1984
SOLIT         BP          4340    4    17:28:42  17 JUN 1985
```

Figure 10.74 The output from the program CAT.

program held within the account, that has been compiled without the S option. (The S option is used to suppress the symbol table during compilation). Figure 10.75 gives an example of using the debugger on the program shown in Figure 10.71. The example shows how to list the first ten lines of source code of the program being debugged. Following this listing the program is allowed to finish normally using the G command. Figure 10.75 gives just one use of the L command. A full summary of all debugger commands is given at the end of this section.

Having established the way to list out a program in the debugger, the next likely requirement is to look at and possibly change the contents of variables at a particular point in the program. This is handled by stopping the program at a given line number. Stopping the program at a specific line number requires setting a 'breakpoint' equal to that line number by using the command B$=nn where nn equals the line number. There are four separate breakpoints that can be set at any one time (1–4). Any one of them can be removed with the Kn command to kill a specific breakpoint, numbered n, or K which will remove them all.

The contents of a variable are displayed by preceding the variable name with a '/'. When the contents are displayed they will be followed by an equals sign. If the content of the variable is to remain unchanged,

```
>RUN BP PROG10 (D[CR]   <-- Initiate the debugger

*I1   <-- The current line number
*Z[CR] FILE/PROG NAME?BP PROG10   <-- The program whose source is to be displayed

*L1-10   <-- List line 1-10 of the program
0001      OPEN "OPPRICE" TO PRICE ELSE
0002         PRINT "PRICE LIST FILE NOT FOUND"
0003         STOP
0004      END
0005      SELECT PRICE
0006      HEADING " 'C'PRICE LIST INCREASES AS AT 'D'
          'LL'DESCRIPTION
          ORIGINAL  INCREASE    NEW 'L'OF GOODS
          PRICE     IN PRICE    PRICE 'L' "
0007 10    READNEXT RECID ELSE
0008         PRINT
0009         PRINT "---------- END OF REPORT---------"
0010         STOP
*G   <-- Resume execution of program from current line number
                        PRICE LIST INCREASES AS AT 25 NOV 1985

DESCRIPTION        ORIGINAL     INCREASE     NEW
OF GOODS           PRICE        IN PRICE     PRICE

WIDGETS               12.25         0.98     13.23
SCREWS                 0.24         0.02      0.26
HAMMERS                8.76         0.70      9.46
SCREWDRIVER 1"         3.33         0.27      3.60

---------- END OF REPORT---------
```

Figure 10.75 The Z and L commands of the debugger.

press the return key, otherwise enter the new value of the variable and press the return key.

Figure 10.76 shows the setting of a breakpoint at line 21 of the program, which enables the description on the first line of the report to be changed. The breakpoint is then removed to enable the rest of the program to complete as usual.

There is a further use of the breakpoint which is extremely useful and that is in setting conditional breakpoints. In this situation the logic to be applied is written at the debugger prompt. Hence to stop the program as

```
>RUN BP PROG10 (D[CR] ←——— Initiate the debugger

*I1 ←——————————————— Current line number
*BS$=21[CR] + ←—————— Set breakpoint on line 21, system responds
                       with + to indicate OK
*G ←————————————————— Continue program until breakpoint reached
                         PRICE LIST INCREASES AS AT 25 NOV 1985

DESCRIPTION      ORIGINAL    INCREASE    NEW
OF GOODS         PRICE       IN PRICE    PRICE

*B1 21←——— Breakpoint 1 reached, program halted at line 21
*/DESC[CR] WIDGETS=NUTS 3mm[CR] ←—— Display contents of variable DESC and
                                     change it
*K1[CR] - ←————————————————————————— Remove breakpoint 1, system res-
                                     ponds with – to indicate OK

┌——————————————————————————————Resume program to completion
↓
*G NUTS 3mm          12.25       0.98      13.23
SCREWS               0.24        0.02      0.26
HAMMERS              8.76        0.70      9.46
SCREWDRIVER 1"       3.33        0.27      3.60

---------- END OF REPORT----------
```

Figure 10.76 The use of breakpoints to change variables in the debugger.

soon as the variable `RECID` equals 1, the following would be input at the debugger prompt:

```
BRECID="1"
```

It is all well and good setting a breakpoint in a program providing you reach the condition or the line of the program specified. In some programs, however, when the program just aborts for no apparent reason or enters a part of the program it has no reason to be in, you need to trace what is going on by looking at the sequence of program statements that are executed. The command `En` is used to step through the program n statements at a time each time a `G` command is executed. The step-by-step process is turned off by entering an `E` followed by **RETURN** at the debug prompt. Figure 10.77 shows the use of the `E` command which is first used to step a single statement at a time, then two statements at a time through the program until the exercise is abandoned and the program run to completion using the `G` command.

These are the main debug commands, but there are several others which are summarized below for completeness. For details of their use refer to your BASIC manual.

Command	*Function*
Bexp	Set breakpoint based on expression exp
B$nn	Set breakpoint when line number nn reached
D	Display breakpoint and trace tables
DE	Enter system debugger (denoted by an !)
DEBUG	As with DE above
En	Execute n statements at a time. E[CR] turns it off
END	End execution of program and return to TCL
G	Proceed from breakpoint
Gn	Go directly to line n. Do not execute other statements in between
K	Kills all breakpoints
Kn	Kills breakpoint n
Ln-m	List program lines from line n to line m
LP	All output forced to printer
Nn	Ignore the next n+1 breakpoints
N	Resets the Nn command above. Breakpoints are processed
OFF	Log off
P	Toggles whether output is displayed or not
PC	Force printer closed and send report to spooler
R	Removes address from top of stack, forcing program to return from current subroutine as though a RETURN statement had been encountered.
S	Display subroutine stack
T	Toggle trace function
Tvar	Sets variable var in trace table
U	Remove all variables from trace table
Uvar	Remove variable var from trace table
Z	Use symbol table (including source code) from specified program
$	Current statement number
/var	Display value of variable var
/a(x)	Print value of point x in array a
/a(x,y)	Print value of point x,y in array a
/a	Print the entire array a
/*	Display entire symbol table
[x,y]	Set left margin x and right margin y for debugger display
[	Remove limits from [x,y] command

```
>RUN BP PROG10 (D[CR] <——— Initiates the debugger

*I1[CR] <——— Current statement number in program
*E1[CR] <——— Execute a statement at a time
*G[CR] <——— Proceed
*I4 <——— Current statement number in program
*G[CR] <——— Proceed
*I5 <——— Current statement number in program
*E2[CR] <——— Execute two statements at a time
*G[CR] <——— Proceed
*I7 <——— Current statement number in program
*G[CR] <——— Proceed

                  PRICE LIST INCREASES AS AT 25 NOV 1985

DESCRIPTION        ORIGINAL     INCREASE     NEW
OF GOODS           PRICE        IN PRICE     PRICE

*I12 <——— Current statement number in program
*E[CR] <——— Turn off the E command
  ┌——————— Proceed
  ↓
*G[CR] WIDGETS        12.25        0.98      13.23
SCREWS                0.24         0.02      0.26
HAMMERS               8.76         0.70      9.46
SCREWDRIVER 1"        3.33         0.27      3.60

---------- END OF REPORT----------
```

Figure 10.77 Following the execution of statements in the debugger.

10.15 BASIC optimization techniques

1. **How to reduce frame faults during program execution**
   a) Reduce the number of runtime lines of code.
   b) Maximize the efficient use and organization of internal storage.
   c) Reduce the amount of data handled.
2. GOSUB
   a) Subroutines called only once should be incorporated into the main body of the program.
   b) Small subroutines executed two or three times should be incorporated into the main body of the program.
   c) The runtime code generated for a GOSUB statement is small compared to the reduction in program size created by its use.

   d) Careful placement of the GOSUB statement can help to reduce frame faults. Keep the number of statements between the GOSUB and the subroutine itself, to a minimum.

3. CALL
   a) The CALL statement generates a large overhead and therefore should be used sparingly.
   b) It should be used to reduce the runtime code of large programs widely used in a multi-user environment.
   c) It should be used where the program size exceeds the maximum item size.
   d) When passing parameters, use the COMMON statement rather than argument list.
4. GOTO
   a) The use of GOTO is widely recognized as poor programming practice and hence its use should be kept to a minimum.
   b) Where possible replace them with ON...GOTO statements.
   c) Reduce the number of instructions skipped between the GOTO and its destination to a minimum.
5. REM
   Remarks should be placed at the end of a statement line rather than on a separate line.
6. **Stack-related statements**
   Stack-related statements should be kept on the same statement line. In essence as so many statements are stack related, it is best to include as many statements as possible on a single line, so long as clarity is unaffected.
7. **Assignment statements**
   a) Do not assign any constants to variables within loops.
   b) Do not re-evaluate expressions; assign them once only to a variable.
   c) Initial values should be assigned in the initialization section.
   d) Eliminate all variables that are not used.
   e) Concatenation is time-consuming and should be kept to a minimum.
8. **Literals**
   a) Literals are not stored in the descriptor table which contains the contents of variables.
   b) Descriptor tables of only one frame tend to remain in main storage.
   c) Literals appear in runtime code, exactly as they appear in the source code.
   d) String literals (value enclosed in quotes), require 2 bytes plus the length of the literal in runtime code.

e) Numeric literals (value not enclosed in quotes), are converted to 6-byte binary numbers and require 7 bytes of runtime code.
f) It takes only 3 bytes of runtime code to reference a variable.
g) A frame fault is normally required to access a variable.
h) In order to maximize the chance of variables being located in the descriptor table in main memory, re-use variable names wherever possible, providing the clarity of the program is unaffected.

9. **Dynamic arrays**
   a) Use dynamic arrays when dealing with data files.
   b) Use standard arrays for internal tables.
   c) If the same information is needed more than once assign it to a variable rather than continually `EXTRACT`ing it.
   d) Use the `REPLACE` statement for replacing two or three values in large dynamic arrays.
   e) Use `MATREAD` and `MATWRITE` statements when building, accessing or updating large dynamic arrays.
   f) Use standard arrays only when necessary since the object code it creates is greater than for simple variables.
   g) Do not enlarge source code by using arrays simply to avoid using subscripted variables.

10. **Space**
    a) For six spaces or less use `bb.b` where `b` is the number of blanks needed.
    b) For more than six spaces use `SPACE(n)` where `n` is the number of blanks needed.

11. `STR`
    a) Where the string is nine characters or less use `cc.c` where `c` is the character desired.
    b) Where the string is greater than nine characters use `STR('c' ,n)` where `c` is the desired character and `n` its number of occurrences.

12. `ICONV/OCONV`
    a) These conversions are executed quite rapidly in most cases.
    b) When a definite field width is desired, use format masks.
    c) If the format is to be used often, assign it to a variable.

13. **@ Position cursor**
    Each parameter takes up 7 bytes of runtime code and therefore these statements should be used sparingly.

14. `IF`
    a) Multiple `IF` statements containing `AND` and/or `OR` conditions are not optimized. The entire statement is evaluated.
    b) Therefore use the complex `IF` statement wherever possible.
    c) There is an overhead associated with every `IF`. Use them sparingly.

15. FOR...NEXT **and** LOOP
    a) FOR...NEXT statements execute faster than building a FOR/NEXT with the LOOP statement.
    b) If the index variable is not used within the loop use the LOOP statement with the WHILE or UNTIL clause.
    c) Avoid repetition of deriving the same value for both the UNTIL/WHILE test within the loop.
    d) FOR/NEXT have initial and terminal conditions – make use of them!
16. EQUATE
    a) The immediate value is compiled into object code.
    b) They do not access variable locations during runtime.
    c) The array address is computed during compilation.
    d) They should be used to predefine attribute marks, value marks, subvalue marks, array elements and literals.
    e) Extensive use of the EQUATE statement is highly recommended to improve program efficiency and program clarity.
17. a) ENTER is faster than CHAIN to execute a BASIC program.
    b) The programs executed must be CATALOGued.
    c) Use caution as ENTER does not initialize the variables used in the ENTERed program.
18. CASE

    Ensure that the condition most frequently expected to be found true is tested first.

11 The Procedure Language – PROC

TCL verbs and general commands covered in this chapter

LISTPROCS

11.1 An introduction to PROC

PROC is the procedure language of the PICK operating system. It is a powerful processor which provides a means of storing a number of commands together which can then be invoked from the terminal by a single command. Any sequence of commands that can be typed in at a terminal can be prestored using PROC. In addition, it is possible to take in input from the terminal and validate it, format screens (which makes it eminently suitable for building menu systems), run subroutines and set test conditions and branch in accordance with the results. In essence PROC is the equivalent of a powerful Job Control Language simplifying the day-to-day use of the system.

PROC is not a programming language and was never intended to be so, although it does offer some facilities like conditional branching found in programming. `PROC`s are held as items (records) in files and are interpreted at runtime. They are maintained via the system editor and the single command name used to call the `PROC` must exist as an item in the master dictionary. To identify a `PROC` amongst the other items of the MD, attribute 1 of *all* `PROC`s must be `PQ`.

Indeed, there is a `PROC`, `LISTPROCS`, which has been written to list out all the `PROC`s in an account! If the `PROC` is short, then its entire contents can be held in the master dictionary (MD). However, if the `PROC` is long and involved, the MD should just contain a pointer to the `PROC` and the `PROC` itself should be held on a separate file. The whole purpose of keeping large files outside the MD is to minimize the possibility of having the MD in overflow where the initial contigous space allocated to it is extended by additional linked frames. Such a situation is to be avoided at all costs because of the dramatic effect it has on response times. To store a pointer to a PROC in the MD uses just two lines, the first containing PQ and the second containing the name of the procedure file and the name of the procedure contained in parentheses (as shown in Figure 11.1).

```
>CT MD PROC1
    PROC1
001 PQ
002 (PROCFILE PROC1)
```

Figure 11.1 The format of a PROC in the master dictionary.

PROC's power and flexibility is achieved by providing four buffers, each with a special purpose, in which data can be manipulated. These are:

PRIMARY INPUT BUFFER (PIB)
SECONDARY INPUT BUFFER (SIB)
PRIMARY OUTPUT BUFFER (POB)
SECONDARY OUTPUT BUFFER (SOB)

As you can see there are two input buffers and two output buffers and all the processing handled by a PROC is handled within these buffers. However, only *one* input buffer and only *one* output buffer can be active and in use at any one time. There are commands in PROC to activate and deactivate each of these buffers and to pass information between them.

The **primary input buffer** is used to contain the exact and total contents of the phrase that was typed at TCL to invoke the procedure and will automatically be selected as the current input buffer. If it was just the name, such as PROC1 then the primary input buffer would just contain the word PROC1. If however the command was longer because it included parameters (extra data), required by the procedure then this would all be placed in the PIB. Hence invoking a procedure by typing in PROC1 A123 B456 would mean the PIB would contain PROC1 A123 B456. Each character string separated by a space is called a parameter and can be manipulated independently. Hence if the input buffer contains the string PROC1 A123 B456 it contains three parameters:

```
PROC1
A123
B456
```

The **secondary input buffer** contains data subsequently input from the keyboard by the user in response to an IS command and is also used to hold data from several system processes, notably the spooler. The data is usually checked here before being moved to the secondary output buffer, referred to as the stack. Subsequent data input to this buffer overwrites what was previously held. As has probably been realized, the contents of this buffer are extremely volatile and should be viewed as a temporary storage area.

The **primary output buffer** is used to build up the command that will ultimately be executed at the TCL level. This is the only buffer that enables a TCL command to be executed.

The **secondary output buffer** is referred to as the stack. It has the ability to stack-up lines of data which can be passed to the procedure one at a time for processing. It is the only buffer whose data can be stacked up in this way.

Figure 11.2 shows how these buffers interrelate. Do remember that many PROC commands are designed to work on the currently active buffer, and only one input and one output buffer can be active at any one time. Thus, when moving data between buffers, the source is the currently active input buffer and the destination is the currently active output buffer.

Another important aspect of the buffers worth noting is that they each have a pointer that points to the current position within the buffer. The purpose of these pointers is to point to a character position within the respective buffers which enables specific strings of characters to be moved to specific positions within the buffers, all of which will become apparent later on. A summary of PROC commands is shown in Figure 11.3.

11.2 A simple PROC using the C, H, P and STOFF commands

With so many commands in the PROC language, it is obviously not possible to cover them all here. The easiest way to explain the important ones is to see them in action; the others you should look up in your manual.

The P command will take the contents of the POB and pass it to TCL just as though it had been typed in at the terminal. After the command has been initiated, it will automatically clear both output buffers. A fairly obvious use of PROCs therefore is to hold frequently used and lengthy ACCESS commands. Not only does this speed up their execution, because you don't have to type in the commands each time, but it obviously removes the possibility of typing error! Figure 11.4 shows an example of a PROC containing an ACCESS statement. It also introduces the C command which is used to provide comments within the PROC.

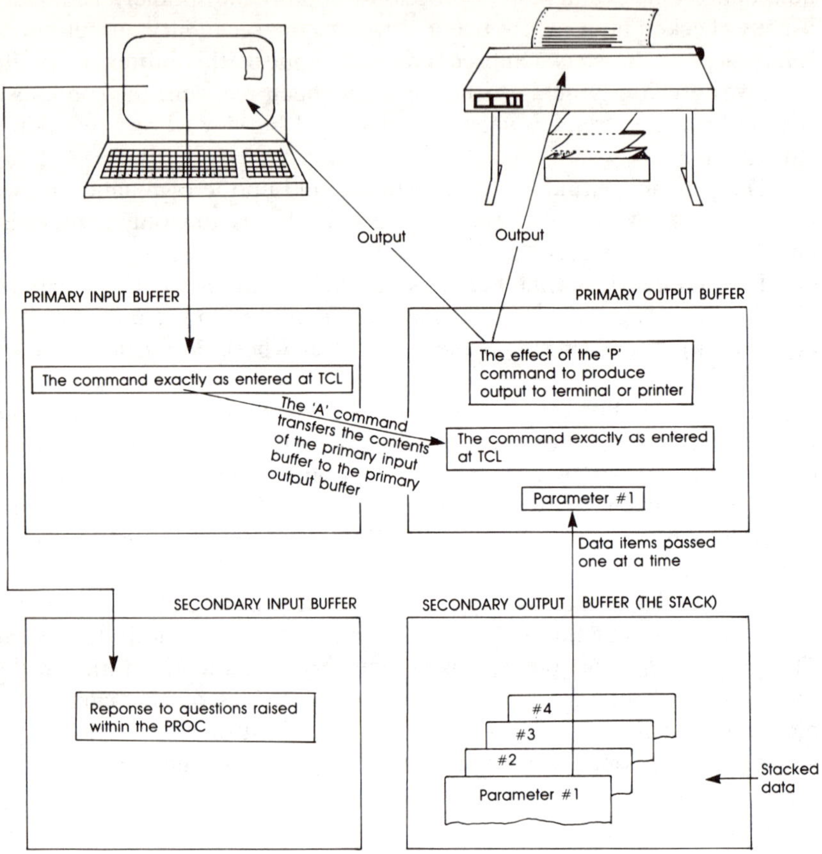

Figure 11.2 The PROC processor buffers and their interaction.

Figure 11.4 shows how a simple ACCESS statement can be stored in a PROC. As we saw in the chapter on ACCESS, it is important to realize that these statements can get very lengthy indeed. The H command for the POB places the buffer pointer at the very end of the string it contains. This allows any subsequent H command to append data after it. The buffer pointer will then move to the end of the entire string. It is not until it encounters the P command that the POB contents will be sent to the TCL processor. Using this knowledge therefore we can build a PROC to handle lengthy ACCESS statements, an example of which is shown in Figure 11.5. Notice in this case that the second and subsequent H statements are followed by a space. This is because they are concatenated immediately onto the end of the previous line's data, where trailing spaces are ignored.

Command	*Description*
A	Moves data from current input to current output buffer
B	Moves current input buffer pointer back one parameter
BO	Moves current output buffer pointer back one parameter
C	Comment
D	Display contents of current input buffer on terminal
F	Moves current input buffer pointer forward one parameter
G	Go to a specified statement label
GO	Go to a specified statement label
H	Moves text string to the current output buffer
IF	A test condition to execute specified commands
IH	Moves text string to the current input buffer
IP	Input from terminal into current input buffer
IS	Input from terminal to secondary buffer
IT	Input from tape label into current input buffer
O	Outputs text string on terminal
P	Execute command in primary output buffer
PH	As with P, but suppress the output produced by the command
PP	As with P, but also display contents of both output buffers
PW	As with PP, but wait for user response first
PX	As with P, but return to the TCL prompt not the PROC
RI	Clear (reset) both input buffers
RO	Clear (reset) both output buffer
S	Position the pointer in the current input buffer
SP	Select primary input buffer
SS	Select secondary input buffer
STOFF	Select primary output buffer (stack off)
STON	Select secondary output buffer (stack on)
T	Format output on the terminal
U	Exit to user-defined subroutine
X	Exit to TCL, or calling PROC
+b	Add a number to the parameter in the current input buffer
+n	Subtract a number to the parameter in the current input buffer
()	Call another PROC
[]	Call subroutine, either local at a statement label or to an external PROC

Figure 11.3 The PROC processor commands.

Contents of a procedure called PROC1

```
    PROC1
001 PQ      ← Defines this as a PROC
002 C – ACCESS enquiry on STAFF     ← Comment for clarity
003 HSORT STAFF BY NAME NAME AGE DEPT    ACCESS statement moved to POB
004 P    Execute command in POB by passing it to TCL
```

The results of using PROC1

```
>PROC     ← Execute the PROC; results shown below
PAGE   1                              11:42:44  24 OCT 1985

STAFF.. NAME                   AGE       DEPT

002     Appleby, J             21        Accounts
011     Atkin, PL              24        Sales
171     Barnett, R             32        Accounts
           ...
           ...
35 ITEMS LISTED.
```

Figure 11.4 A simple PROC carrying out an ACCESS command.

11.3 The use of the STACK

Within procedures there is often the need to pass parameters. Consider the TCL command COPY, which following its use, for example COPY STAFF 020[CR], will prompt with the question 'TO:' and await input. We can handle this in a PROC by ensuring the necessary response is contained in the secondary output buffer, since the procedure processor will first look in the SOB for these answers. If it cannot find any data in the stack then it will prompt for the data on the terminal. Figure 11.6 gives an example of the use of the stack. Notice that any input placed on the stack is followed by a < to simulate a carriage return.

Whilst Figure 11.6 just showed one line being added to the stack it is possible to add as many lines to the SOB as required. Assuming we were running a program that required four separate parameters, we could easily include these in a PROC and Figure 11.7 shows how this would be handled. Beware: when building your PROC only build the stack relating to the next command to be executed using the P statement – the P command clears *both* output buffers.

Contents of a procedure called PROC2

```
     PROC2
001 PQ      ← Defines this as a PROC
002 C – ACCESS enquiry on STAFF ← Comment for clarity
003 HSORT STAFF BY DEPT BY NAME ← ACCESS statement moved to POB
004 H BREAK-ON DEPT  } Continuation of ACCESS statement (notice these start
005 H NAME AGE DEPT  } with a space)
006 P    ← Execute command in POB by passing it to TCL
```

The results of using PROC2

```
>PROC2    ← Execute the PROC; results shown below

PAGE   1                                          11:42:44  24 OCT 1985

STAFF.. NAME                  AGE    DEPT

002     Appleby, J            21     Accounts
171     Barnett, R            32     Accounts
                                     ***
045     Johnson, JK           28     Administration
          ...
          ...
35 ITEMS LISTED.
```

Figure 11.5 A PROC to carry out a lengthy ACCESS command.

```
     PROC3
001 PQ– –←Defines this as a PROC
002 C – – TCL COPY command  ← Comment for clarity
003 HCOPY STAFF 010 ← TCL COPY statement moved to POB
004 STON     ← Turn stack on and make SOB active
005 H098<    ← Store data on stack – notice the <
006 STOFF    ← Turn stack off and make POB active
007 P        ← Execute command in POB by passing it to TCL

>PROC3[CR]  ← Execute the PROC; results shown below
     1 010 to 98

1 ITEMS COPIED
```

Figure 11.6 A simple PROC using the STACK.

```
PROC4
PQ ← Defines this as a PROC
C -- RUN PROGRAM PROG1 ← Comment for clarity
STON ← Turn stack on and make SOB active
HA123< ← Store data on stack – notice the <
HB456 ← The second line on the stack
HC789< ← The third line on the stack
HD012< ← The fourth line on the stack
STOFF ← Turn stack off and make POB active
HRUN BP PROG1 ← Write this into the POB
P ← Execute command in POB by passing it to TCL
```

Figure 11.7 A PROCtaking data from the STACK.

11.4 Screen formatting and cursor control

Formatting a screen and controlling the cursor are handled by the T command. The command has the following format:

```
T {function}, {function}, ...
```

the T must be followed by one of the following options:

"string"	Displays the string of characters at the current cursor position
B	Sounds the terminal bell
C	Clear screen
Inn	Displays the integer character nn
Xnn	Displays the hex character nn
(x,y)	Positions the cursor at column x, row y
(–1)	Clears the screen
(–2)	Positions the cursor in the home position (0,0)
(–3)	Clears from cursor position to end of the screen
(–4)	Clears from cursor to the end of the line
(–5)	Starts blinking
(–6)	Stops blinking
(–7)	Starts protected field
(–8)	Ends protected field
(–9)	Backspace by one character
(–10)	Up one line

Figure 11.8 illustrates the T command.

The result of Figure 11.8 is to produce a screen layout that offers

```
TEXT-MENU
PQ
10 C - - - - - DISPLAY MENU
T (-1)      ← Clear screen
T (25,0)."T e x t  P r o c e s s i n g" ← Display
T (0,3),"└------------------------------------┘"
T (0,5),"FILE MANAGEMENT"
T (20,5)" 1 : List Text Files"
T (20,6)," 2 : Create Text File"
T (20,7)," 3 : Delete Text File"
T (0,9),"DOCUMENT MANAGEMENT"
T (20,9)," 4 : List Documents"
T (20,10)," 5 : Word Process Document"
T (20,11)," 6 : Edit Document"
T (20,12)," 7 : Copy Document"
T (20,13)," 8 : Delete Document"
T (20,14)," 9 : Print Document"
T (0,19),"PRINTER CONTROL"
T (20,19),"13 : List Printer Output"
T (20,20),"14 : Kill Printer Output"
100 C ----- INPUT OPTION
T (0,2),"SELECT MENU OPTION              ",(19,2)
RI     ← Clear INPUT buffers
RO     ← Clear OUTPUT buffers
IP     ← Accept input from the terminal
```

Figure 11.8 Screen formatting within a PROC.

text-processing options and which would be presented to the user as shown in Figure 11.9.

In Figure 11.8 we have been introduced to three commands which are relatively self-explanatory: RI, RO and IP. These stand for reset (clear) input buffers, reset output buffers and input to current input buffer, respectively. The IP command can optionally be followed by a character which represents the prompt character to be used. Hence IP? would cause a question mark to be displayed at the current cursor position and the cursor would await for data to be entered.

Data input by IP is placed in the PIB and replaces the parameter being pointed to, or if the pointer is at the end of the data, appends the inputted data to it.

```
                        Text Processing

SELECT MENU OPTION _
------------------------------------------

FILE MANAGEMENT         1 :  List Text Files
                        2 :  Create Text File
                        3 :  Delete Text File

DOCUMENT MANAGEMENT     4 :  List Documents
                        5 :  Word Process Document
                        6 :  Edit Document
                        7 :  Copy Document
                        8 :  Delete Document
                        9 :  Print Document
                       10 :  Merge & Print Document
                       11 :  Runoff Document
                       12 :  Merge & Runoff Document

PRINTER CONTROL        13 :  List Printer Output
                       14 :  Kill Printer Output
```

Figure 11.9 The screen presented to the user from the PROC listed in Figure 11.9.

11.5 Moving parameters with the A command

The A command moves one parameter from the currently active input buffer to the currently active output buffer. The command has the following format:

```
A {c} {p} {,n}
```

where

c is the character that surrounds the parameter
p is the position of the parameter being moved
n is the count of the number of characters to be moved

If the surround character is omitted, the parameter will be moved exactly as it is with surrounding blanks. If the surround character is a backslash (\), the surrounding blanks are omitted. If the position parameter is left out the parameter that will be moved is the one currently being pointed to. The surround character is extremely valuable in building an ACCESS statement where the input from the terminal has to be enclosed in double quotes.

After the execution of the A command the input buffer pointer points to the very next character after the string that was moved.

Figure 11.10 shows an example of the A statement where input from the terminal is used to build an ACCESS statement.

The contents of a procedure called PROC5

```
PROC5
PQ                    ← Defines the file as a PROC
10 C ----- DISPLAY MENU ← Comment for clarity
T (-1)                ← Clear screen
C Display headings and display request for dept
T (25,0),"E n q u i r y  b y  D e p t"
T (4,3),"-----------------------------------------"
T (10,5),"Input Dept Number (001-012)"
STOFF                 ← Stack off, primary output buffer active
HSORT STAFF BY NAME WITH ← Start of ACCESS command
H DEPTNO =
C POB now contains 'SORT STAFF BY NAME WITH DEPTNO ='
T (38,5)              ← Position cursor ready for input of data
SP                    ← Select PIB as active
IP                    ← Data input moved into PIB
A"1                   ← Move 1st parameter of PIB to POB
                        enclosed in double quotes
C POB - SORT STAFF BY NAME WITH DEPTNO = "nnn"
H NAME AGE DEPTNO ← Remainder of ACCESS statement
P                     ← Execute command from POB
```

The results of using PROC5

```
>PROC5 ← Execute the PROC; results shown below

                    E n q u i r y  b y  D e p t
------------------------------------------------

                Input Dept Number (001-012):001

PAGE   1                                   17:20:47  27 OCT 1985

STAFF..  NAME              AGE   DEPT

002      Appleby, J        21    001
171      Barnett, R        32    001
           :
           :
12 ITEMS LISTED.
```

Figure 11.10 The use of the A command within PROC.

11.6 Conditional operations with IF and GO

The IF statement allows you to test for a condition and take action dependent on the result. The format of the IF statement is:

```
IF {#}A–cmd PROC–cmd
```

where

equates to NOT
A–cmd is any valid form of the A command
PROC–cmd is any valid PROC command

The GO or G statement transfers control unconditionally to the PROC statement which starts with the label. The label must be a number and the statement containing the label must start with the label and can contain any PROC command, but the command must follow on from the single space following the label number. If the label referenced does not exist, the PROC will continue to the next sequential statement following the branch command.

These two statements are used together and Figure 11.11 shows how they are used to check the validity of the department number input. This check is incorporated in the example of a PROC shown in Figure 11.10.

The IF statement can also be used to check for a specific pattern of characters in a string. The pattern specification is enclosed in parentheses and consists of any combination of the following:

- an integer number followed by the letter N which tests for that number of numeric characters;
- an integer number followed by the letter A which tests for that number of alphabetic characters;
- an integer number followed by the letter X which tests for that number of alphanumeric characters;
- a literal string, enclosed in single or double quotes.

Hence IF # (2A'–'3N) G 50 would go to the statement label 50 if the string was not in the format, two alpha characters followed by a hyphen followed by three numeric characters.

11.6.1 Further forms of the IF statement

The IF command can be used to test for system generated errors as specified in the ERRMSG file. The format of the command is:

```
IF {#} E {ERRMSG number} proc–cmnd
```

You can check whether *any* system error has occurred without having to

```
PROC5
PQ
10 C ---- DISPLAY MENU
RI
RO
T (-1)
T (25,0),"E n q u i r y  b y  D e p t"
T "(0,3)," -------------------------------------
T (38,10),"
  "
T (38,11),"
  "
T (10,5),"Input Dept Number (001-012)"
STOFF
HSORT STAFF BY NAME WITH
H DEPT =
T (38,5)
SP
IP
IF #A1 G 900 ← If parameter 1 missing go to 900
IF A1 < 001 G 900 ← Test value input. If it is out of
IF A1 > 012 G 900    range go to label 900
A"1
H NAME AGE DEPT
P
G 999
900 T (38,10),"THAT NUMBER IS OUT OF RANGE, SILLY"
T (38,11),"PRESS RETURN TO CONTINUE"
IP
G 10
999 X
```

Figure 11.11 The use of conditional statements in PROC.

check for a specific error message number by using IF E. It is possible however to check for specific error message numbers by including the error message number in the statement. Thus IF E 1169 G 50 would go to statement label 50 if the error message 1169 (an illegal printer number) was encountered.

This facility is often used to check the existence of a file (ERRMSG number 201) or to check whether any items have been selected by ACCESS (ERRMSG number 401) before a report is run. A complete list of error message numbers and their meanings can be found in Appendix A.

Another useful version of the IF command, is the IF S which is used to test the presence of a LIST as generated by a SELECT, SSELECT, QSELECT or GET-LIST verb. Figure 11.12 gives an example of its use.

```
PQ
HGET-LIST
OENTER LIST NAME+
IP?
A
STON
H
P
IF #S XNON EXISTENT LIST!
HSORT STAFF BY DEPT DEPT NAME TEL
P
```

Figure 11.12 Use of IF to check the existence of a list.

11.7 Linking to other PROCs

11.7.1 Transferring control to another PROC

A command in one PROC can transfer control directly to another, which may be resident in a dictionary or data file. This is achieved by enclosing the location of the PROC in parentheses and has the general format:

```
({DICT} filename {item-id}) {n}
```

where

filename	is name of file containing PROC
item-id	is the name of the PROC
n	is optional. If used, control is passed to the line whose label is n

Figure 11.13 shows an example of linking PROCs in this way. In this example, control is passed to the item in the file MASTERPROCS whose item-id matches the input from the IS command, providing it is in the range 001–080.

11.7.2 Using another PROC as a subroutine

If instead of passing implicit control to another procedure, you require to use a PROC as a subroutine within another, the called PROC has to be enclosed in square brackets. Once the called PROC has completed, control

```
PQ
10 T (-1)
T (0,2)."INPUT TASK TO BE RUN"
IS?
IF #A G 900
IF A < 001 G 900
IF A > 080 G 900
(MASTERPROCS#A)
900 XILLEGAL RESPONSE
G 10
```

Figure 11.13 Transferring control to another PROC.

is returned to the PROC that initiated the call. The general format of the command is:

```
[{DICT} filename {item-id}] {n}
```

where

filename	is name of file containing PROC
item-id	is the name of the PROC
n	is optional. If used, control is passed to the line whose label is n

This principle is used extensively in menu systems where a main menu controls a series of submenus. When a program is run from a submenu and is complete, the submenu is redisplayed. Pressing [CR] at the submenu recalls the main menu enabling an alternative submenu to be called. Figure 11.14 gives an example of this principle.

Figure 11.14 The calling of PROCs as subroutines.

```
The PROC TEXT-MENU
PQ
10 C ----- DISPLAY MENU
T (-1)                ← Clear screen
T (25,0),"T e x t  P r o c e s s i n g"
T (0,3),"-------------------------------------"
T (0,5),"PRINTER CONTROL"
T (20,6),"1 : List Printer Output"
T (20,7)," 2 : Kill Printer Output"
100 C ----- INPUT OPTION
T (0,2),"SELECT MENU OPTION        ",(19,2)
RI                    ← Reset both input buffers
```

```
RO                      ← Reset both output buffers
IP                      ← Input response from terminal
IF #A1 G 900            ← If null response, i.e. [CR] exit
IF A1 = 1 G 500
IF A1 = 2 G 500
G 100                   ← If invalid response rerun PROC
500 C ----- PROCESS OPTION
IF A1 = 1 [PICK.UTILITY TEXT-OUTPUT] ← Call PROC TEXT-OUTPUT
IF A1 = 2 [PICK.UTILITY TEXT-KILL]   ← Call PROC TEXT-KILL
T (0,23),"Press Return To Continue "+ Point at which
IP:                                  PROCs return
G 10                    ← Rerun PROC
900 C ----- END TEXT PROCESSING
T (-1)                  ← Clear screen
OTEXT SYSTEM FINISHED ← Display message, return to TCL
```

The PROC TEXT-OUTPUT

```
PQ
HSP-LIST
P   ← End of PROC, return to calling PROC
```

The PROC TEXT-KILL

```
PQ
10 C ----- DISPLAY SCREEN
T (-1)
T (13,0),"T e x t  P r o c e s s i n g - Kill Printer
Output"
T (0,3),"--------------------------------------"
100 C ----- INPUT OPTIONS
T (20,5),"Printer Number  0"
T (35,5)
S1
IHO
IP
IF #A1 G 900
500 C ----- PROCESS
T (0,18)
RO
HSP-KILL
A1
P
X
900 C ----- EXIT ← End of PROC return to calling PROC
```

Figure 11.14 The calling of PROCs as subroutines.

Appendix F contains a series of procedures that can front-end JET, the word processor most frequently found on PICK systems, and RUNOFF PICK's own text processor. These PROCs use the concept of a main PROC calling others as subroutines.

11.8 Printer control under PROC

Printers can be controlled within PROCs using information from the error message handler and the verb LISTPTR, both of which feed information into the secondary input buffer. Do remember that the information in the secondary input buffer is volatile. Hence, if the information needs to be held, it should first be saved.

Figure 11.15 shows the output from a typical LISTPTR verb and the data it passes to the secondary input buffer.

Normal output from LISTPTR

```
Printer assignments                              10:56:30
Printer        Form queues      Page  Dev or   Status
Type    Number                  Skip  Line #
SERIAL     0   0   2               1       2   INACTIVE
SERIAL     1   1                   1       3   ACTIVE
```

Information passed to Secondary Input Buffer

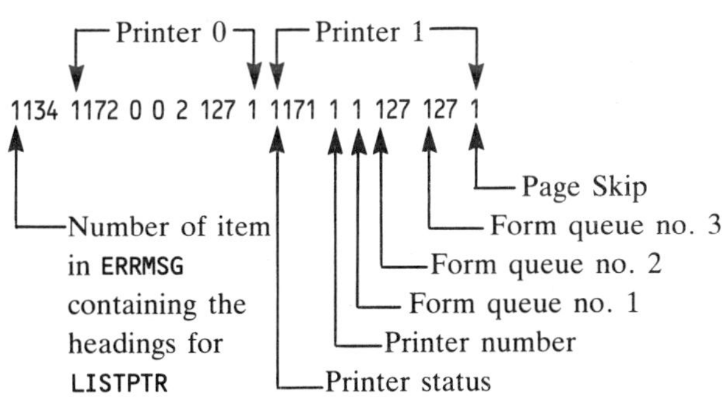

Note: a form queue number of 127 means that the form queue number has not been assigned

Figure 11.15 The data passed by LISTPTR to the SIB.

```
PQ
HSTOPPTR 0        ← Stop the printer
P                 ← Execute the command
SS                ← Select secondary input buffer (SIB)
B                 ← Move pointer for SIB back one parameter
10 IF #A G 30          ← If no more data go to label 30
IF A = 1171 G 100      ← If printer inactive go to label 100
IF A = 1174 G 100      ← If printer unallocated go to 100
IF A = 1172 G 20       ← If printer busy go to label 20
G                      ← Get next parameter
G 10                   ← Loop around the test
20 HSLEEP 5            ← Sleep for five seconds
30 HLISTPTR 3          ← List printer status
P                      ← Execute LISTPTR command
SS                     ← Select SIB
B                      ← Move pointer for SIB back one parameter
40 IF A = 1134 G 10    ← Test for correct ERRMSG number
IF # A G 999           ← Incorrect ERRMSG number
F                      ← Get next parameter
G 40                   ← Loop around test
50 F                   ← Get next parameter
IF # A G 999           ← Nothing present
IF A = 1171 G 100      ← If printer inactive go to label 100
IF A = 1174 G 100      ← If printer unallocated go to 100
IF A = 1172 G 60       ← If printer busy go to label 60
XTHE BUFFER CONTAINS BAD DATA  ← An unknown printer status
60 OTHE PRINTER IS ACTIVE DO YOU WANT TO WAIT(Y/N)+
SP                     ← Set pointer to primary input buffer
IP?                    ← Input response to question
IF A = Y G 20          ← Continue, pausing for 5 seconds
X                      ← Execute PROC
100 HSTARTPTR 3,2,2,S2      ← Start printer as form queue 2
P                           ← Execute the command
        :
(remainder of PROC)
        :
999 OFINISHED               ← End of PROC
```

Figure 11.16 The control of printers using PROC.

If you run into difficulties building procedures using these principles, the contents of the secondary input buffer can be displayed by including the statements SS and DO following the P. Hence the information shown in Figure 11.15 can be displayed using:

```
PQ
HLISTPTR
P
SS
DO
```

Checking the status of printers within PROCs can become necessary where a printer in general use has to be allocated to a specific task. Figure 11.16 explains the way in which this is handled.

Whilst providing an extremely useful, flexible and powerful facility, the buffer principle of PROC is difficult to grasp and its language a little forbidding to the uninitiated! The EXECUTE statement in BASIC obviates the need to learn PROC and for new incumbents to the PICK operating system this may be helpful. It should be borne in mind, however, that PROC is still a major element of the PICK operating system and one still widely used.

12 RUNOFF – the Text Processor

TCL verbs and general commands covered in this chapter

```
RUNOFF
```

12.1 An introduction to RUNOFF

RUNOFF is a PICK utility that facilitates the preparation of documents and manuals. RUNOFF text is prepared using the Editor or a word processor and contains control codes within the text to indicate such features as headings, footings, page numbering, bold text, underlined text and so on. In addition RUNOFF can compile a table of contents and an index, which makes it ideal for the preparation of manuals. Indeed most of the PICK manuals have been printed using RUNOFF. As the use of RUNOFF is straightforward it requires little discussion since it can easily be picked up from the user manual. However, in addition to the summary of commands, this section does highlight some useful and not so obvious features.

12.2 RUNOFF command summary

RUNOFF commands are preceded with a full stop and most have an abbreviated form. The commands must be on a line on their own, and must start at the beginning of the line. It is possible to have a number of commands together on the same line, in which case no delimiter is required between them and one follows on immediately after the other.

The summary of RUNOFF commands is as follows:

`.*`	Comment line – rest of text in the line is a comment only.
`.BEGIN PAGE` or `.BP`	Begin a new page.
`.BOX n,m`	Causes text following to be enclosed in a box starting at positon `n`, ending at position `m`.
`.BOX` or `.BOX OFF`	Disables the `BOX` function and prints the bottom line of the box. Text to be put in a box is preceded with `.BOX n,m` and succeeded with `.BOX` or `.BOX OFF`.
`.BREAK` or `.B`	Causes any partially filled line to be output before processing next line.
`.CAPITALISE SENTENCES`	Automatically capitalizes the first letter after a full point, question mark or exclamation mark that is followed by a space. Also it follows these characters and the characters (`:`) and (`;`) by two spaces.
`.CENTER` or `.C`	Centres text found on the line following this command.
`.CHAIN {f} i`	Transfers control to a specified item name.
`.CHAPTER`	Causes the subsequent text to be used as the chapter heading.
`.CONTENTS`	Outputs a table of contents based on previous `.CHAPTER` and `.SECTION` commands encountered.
`.CRT`	Directs output to the terminal.
`.ENDCASE` or `.EC`	Disables any previous `.LC` or `.UC` command.
`.FILL` or `.F`	Words are output one at a time until a line has been filled.
`.FOOTING`	Causes text found on line following this command to be printed at the foot of every page.
`.HEADING`	Causes text found on line following this command to be printed at the top of every page.
`.HILITE x`	Causes character `x` to be displayed at the extreme right-hand margin for every line until turned off.

.HIGHLITE OFF	Disables HIGHLITE.
.INDENT n or .I n	Indents following line by n spaces.
.INDENT MARGIN n or IM n	Indents margin by n spaces. Causes break to occur.
.INDEX 'text'	Causes text, enclosed in single quotes, to be compiled into index together with current page number.
.INPUT	Prompts for text from the terminal which is then incorporated into the document.
.JUSTIFY or .J	Justifies to the right-hand margin.
.LEFT MARGIN n	Sets left margin to n.
.LINE LENGTH n	Specifies width of line, ignoring margin.
.LOWER CASE or .LC	Causes all subsequent text to be printed in lower case.
.LPTR	Directs output to the spooler.
.NOCAPITALISE SENTENCES or .NCS	Disables .CAPITALISE SENTENCES.
.NOFILL or .NF	Disables fill and justification and outputs text exactly as shown.
.NOJUSTIFY or .NJ	Disables justification although line fill still operates.
.NOPARAGRAPH	Disables .PARAGRAPH function.
.PAGE NUMBER n	Sets page number to n, defaults to 1.
.PAPER LENGTH n	Sets page length to n lines. Unless specified, length used is as defined by the TCL TERM command.
.PARAGRAPH n or .P n	Causes any blank line or line starting with a space to be treated as the start of a new paragraph. A break occurs and text is indented n characters.
.PFILE n	Directs subsequent output to print file n.
.PRINT	Prints next line of text on users terminal.
.PRINT INDEX	Causes index to be printed in two-column output.

`.READ {DICT} {f} i`	Causes RUNOFF to read the filename `f` and the itemname `i`.
`.READNEXT`	Reads next item from a preselected list using `SELECT` or `SSELECT` ACCESS statements. Used for mailmerge techniques.
`.SAVE INDEX f`	Causes index information to be saved in the filename '`f`'. This filename *must* be different to the text filename containing the RUNOFF text.
`.SECTION n text`	Denotes next section at level `n`, which together with text is included in table of contents.
`.SET TABS`	Specifies tab settings.
`.SKIP {n}` or `.SK {n}`	Causes a `.BREAK` after which `n` lines are skipped before printing continues.
`.SPACE n` or `SP n`	Ignores `.SPACING` after which `n` lines are skipped before printing continues.
`.SPACING n`	Sets standard line spacing. Hence double spacing means `n` = 2.
`.STANDARD`	Sets a series of default parameters: `.CS.F.J.UC.LEFT MARGIN 0.CRT.HEADING .FOOTING.PARAGRAPH 5.LINELENGTH 70.`
`.TEST PAGE n` or `.TP n`	Causes a `.BREAK` and advances to a new page when there are less lines than `n` left on a page.
`.UPPER CASE` or `.UC`	Causes all subsequent text to be printed upper case.

12.3 Special control characters in RUNOFF

RUNOFF handles underlining and bold print by use of special control characters. These characters are & for underlining and @ for bold. On their own they affect only the single character immediately following the control character. To underline or to embolden strings of characters these control codes should be placed at either end of the string, preceded by the up arrow (^) and followed by the backslash (\) as demonstrated in Figure 12.1.

Emboldened, underlined text can be achieved by combining the two control codes together and again encompassing a string of text with the up arrow and backslash characters.

To be able to use the @ and & as characters in their own right in the text, these special control characters have themselves to be preceded with

RUNOFF text	*Resulting output*
@A single bold character	**A** single bold character
@^A bold string@\	**A bold string**
&A single underline	A single underline
&^An underlined string&\	An underlined string

Figure 12.1 RUNOFF control codes.

a special control character, the underscore (_). The underscore denotes that the character following it is to be treated as text.

Two other useful control codes are the less than and greater than signs. Less than, <, denotes that the next word is to start at the next tab position whilst greater than, >, means that the word is to finish at the next tab position.

12.4 Using RUNOFF

When using RUNOFF to produce manuals or lengthy documents it is usual to create a file to contain the documents and to create within it a separate item for each subject or chapter.

One of these items is the master item containing a series of `.READ` commands, each relating to the separate items containing each subject or chapter in RUNOFF text. In the case of manuals, this master item would also contain the `.CONTENTS` and `.PRINT INDEX` commands to generate the table of contents and the index. An example of this is shown in Figure 12.2 where the file `WP` contains four items, the first containing the master RUNOFF control instructions and the other three, separate chapters of a book.

The entire manual would be output by the command `RUNOFF WP MASTER`, and would be suffixed with an `LPTR` or `(P` to produce the report on the printer rather than terminal. The following RUNOFF options that can be used with the TCL verb are:

`C` Suppress the `.CHAIN` and `.READ` commands.

`I` Outputs the next item name. Useful for tracing when `.CHAIN` in use.

`N` Causes output to be continuous to a terminal, otherwise RUNOFF pauses at the bottom of each page awaiting a carriage return.

Contents of the file WP

Item-id Contents

```
MASTER      .READ CHAPTER1
            .READ CHAPTER2
            .READ CHAPTER3
            .PRINT INDEX
            .CONTENTS
```

Contents of CHAPTER1, CHAPTER2 and CHAPTER3

```
CHAPTER1     .STANDARD
             .HEADING
             Introduction                    'L'
             .FOOTING
             'L' THE ART OF WRITING          'P'
             .BOX 1,75.CENTER
             @^I N T R O D U C T I O N@\
             .BOX.J
             .SK 4
             .CHAPTER @^INTRODUCTION@\
             .SK 2
             .SECTION 2 An introduction to writing concepts
             .SK 2
             ...   }      Text of Chapter 1
             ...   }

CHAPTER2           }
  ...              }
  ...              }      Contents are similar to CHAPTER1
CHAPTER3           }      in that they contain text
  ...              }      interspersed with RUNOFF command
  ...              }      lines
```

Figure 12.2 A typical RUNOFF file.

Nnn Indicates the number of times to overstrike on emboldening, where nn represents an integer number.

P Directs output to the spooler.

S Suppresses underlining and emboldening when being output to the terminal.

U Produces all output in upper case.

12.5 Some useful tips

12.5.1 The BOX command

Text can be highlighted by enclosing it in a box. This is achieved by inserting a .BOX command before and after the text to be highlighted. The first .BOX command specifies the left and right margins for the box. The box will be as long as is necessary to contain the entire text. The top and bottom lines of the box will be printed on the next line before or following the text. If you require a blank line between the box lines and text you will have to force it using the .SK n command.

The RUNOFF processor will take no note of the maximum number of print characters as defined by the TCL verb TERM, so it is up to you to ensure that your .BOX parameters are sensible. Figure 12.3 shows an example of its use.

```
 ┌── Right margin for the box, character position 1
 │  ┌── Left margin for the box, character position 50
 │  │    ┌── Centre the text that follows within the box
 ▼  ▼    ▼
.BOX 1,50.CENTER
THE TEXT PROCESSOR
.BOX   ← No resetting of justification required
```

The result:

```
 ______________________________________
|    THE TEXT PROCESSOR                |
 ______________________________________
```

Figure 12.3 The use of the BOX command.

12.5.2 The PARAGRAPH command

The .PARAGRAPH command causes any blank line, or any line that starts with a space, to be considered as the start of a new paragraph. This enables the subsequent text to be justified in accordance with the parameter of the .PARAGRAPH command.

It is extremely valuable where paragraphs of text need to be numbered in a format where the number is to be 'hung' outside of the normal justified text (see Figure 12.4). To achieve this the normal left margin is changed, say to start in column 5, whilst the paragraphs are set to start in column 1, by following the .PARAGRAPH command by a negative number, say −4, which says that paragraphs are to be inset 4 character positions *before* the start of the left margin. If the number following .PARAGRAPH command were positive, the first line of each paragraph would be inset n characters after the start of the left margin. It is much easier than it sounds and Figure 12.4 shows how this works.

The RUNOFF text

```
.STANDARD
If problems appear to occur with the spooler there are a
number of checks that should be made:

 1. Make sure the printer is switched on and in a state
ready to receive data.,
 2. Make sure you have defined the correct printer type, i.e.
serial or parallel.,
 3. Check that the baud rate of the printer matches that of
the speed of the line. Refer to your printer manual for the
baud rate for the printer.,
 4. Make sure the printer is known to the system by using the
'LISTPTR' command. If not, use 'STARTPTR'.

The ':STARTSPOOLER' command will re-initialize the spooler at
the TCL prompt without going through the normal coldstart
procedures.
```

The results

```
If problems appear to occur with the spooler there are a
number of checks that should be made:

 1. Make sure the printer is switched on and in a state
    ready to receive data.

 2. Make sure you have defined the correct printer type,
    i.e. serial or parallel.

 3. Check that the baud rate of the printer matches that of
    the speed of the line. Refer to your printer manual
    for the baud rate for the printer.

 4. Make sure the printer is known to the system by using
    the 'LISTPTR' command. If not, use 'STARTPTR'.

The ':STARTSPOOLER' command will re-initialize the spooler at
the TCL prompt without going through the normal coldstart
procedures.
```

Figure 12.4 Use of the PARAGRAPH command.

12.5.3 The TEST PAGE command

The test page command enables a test to be carried out of the number of lines left on a page. If this is less than the number you specify, a page break will occur. This is invaluable where it is necessary for a certain part of your text to appear together, rather than be split across pages. It is frequently used where text is boxed, since the .BOX command will not recognize the bottom of a page and continues printing the sides of the box until a new .BOX command is encountered. Figure 12.5 shows this in use.

```
.TP 13                         ← Test to ensure there are at least 13 lines left
.SK 2                                          ← Lines 1 & 2
.BOX 1,75                                      ← Line 3
.NOFILL
.SK1                                           ← Line 4
INSERT(var,exp1,exp2,exp3,new)                 ← Line 5
REPLACE(var,exp1,exp2,exp3,new)                ← Line 6
where — var is the name of the dynamic array   ← Line 7
      — exp1 is the attribute position         ← Line 8
      — exp2 is the multivalue position        ← Line 10
      — new is the new data to insert          ← Line 11
.SK 1                                          ← Line 12
.BOX                                           ← Line 13
.FILL.J
.SK 1
```

This ensures all thirteen lines are printed together

Figure 12.5 Use of the TEST PAGE command.

12.5.4 The FILL, NOFILL and JUSTIFY commands

The .FILL command fills up the line with words from the text until there is no more room, without starting a new line. If the .JUSTIFY command is also in effect, spaces are added at random between the words to create a straight right-hand margin. If justify is not in effect, the right-hand margin will be ragged.

The .NOFILL command not only cancels the effect of the .FILL command but also the .J command. When .NOFILL is in effect, text is printed exactly as edited. In order to resume justification after this command, remember to issue a .J or .JUSTIFY command.

12.5.5 Mailmerge techniques using READNEXT and CHAIN

Whilst most people now use a word processor for their day-to-day requirements, including its mailmerge facilities, for those without a word processor it's encouraging to know that the editor, ACCESS and RUNOFF between them can provide such a facility.

The technique requires the following steps:

1. Create the letter, using the editor, in the dictionary portion of the file containing the data to be merged into the letter. Place a **.READNEXT** command where text is to be merged into the letter. At the bottom of the letter include a **.BP** to start the next letter on a new page and **.CHAIN name**, where name is the name of the document being edited. This ensures that RUNOFF knows which document it should next print after throwing the page.
2. Use ACCESS to select the relevant data from the file and save it in a list. This must be run *immediately* prior to the RUNOFF command.
3. RUNOFF the letters using a special form of the command which specifies the dictionary and filename of the file on which the ACCESS was performed, this also being the dictionary which contains the master letter.

Figure 12.6 shows the preparation necessary before a mailmerge exercise can take place and uses the **STAFF** data files referred to in Section 9.3 on ACCESS. In order to display the salary details correctly, attribute 8 of the dictionary item **SALARY** is altered. Figure 12.7 shows how the letters are produced from the tasks performed in Figure 12.6.

The preparation

The letter – item-id LETTER

```
>ED DICT STAFF LETTER[CR] ← Notice it is edited into the dictionary

NEW ITEM
TOP
.I[CR]
001+.SK 8[CR]
002+ Dear[CR]
003+.READNEXT[CR]
004+Our records show you are in the [CR]
005+.READNEXT[CR]
006+department which is being transferred to our Bristol
office next Spring. Your current salary of £[CR]
007+.READNEXT[CR]
```

continued over

continued

```
008+will be incremented by a further £500 in consideration
of any inconvenience this may cause.[CR]
009+.SK 1[CR]
010+                 Yours sincerely,[CR]
011+.SK 3[CR]
012+                  M K L CROCHET[CR]
013+                  Personnel Officer[CR]
014+.BP
015+.CHAIN LETTER[CR]

016+[CR]
TOP
.FI[CR]
'LETTER' filed
```

Amend the dictionary definition of salary
(This is necessary to force the decimal point to be printed within RUNOFF)

```
>ED DICT STAFF SALARY[CR]
TOP
.8[CR]
008
.R[CR]
008 A;6(MR2,):"."[CR]
.FI[CR]
'SALARY' filed
```

The ACCESS statement to select the required data

```
>SSELECT STAFF WITH DEPT = "02" FNAME DEPT SALARY[CR]

[404] 6 items selected
```

Figure 12.6 Preparation for mailmerge using RUNOFF.

12.5.6 The HEADING and FOOTING commands

The text output from RUNOFF can contain optional headings and footings – text printed respectively at the top and bottom of each page output. This is achieved using the `.HEADING` and `.FOOTING` commands. Following each of these commands can be one line containing a combination of text and special characters. Both the `.HEADING` and `.FOOTING` commands can contain the following special characters:

`C` Centres the text on the current line.

The contents of the select list

```
GEORGE
ADMINISTRATION
12,500.00
IAN
ADMINISTRATION
12,400.00
```

The RUNOFF command and its results

```
>RUNOFF DICT STAFF LETTER (P)

Dear GEORGE

Our records show you are in the ADMINISTRATION department
which is being transferred to our Bristol office next
Spring. Your current salary of £12,500.00 will be
incremented by a further £500 in consideration of any
inconvenience this may cause.

    Yours sincerely,

    M K L CROCHET
    Personnel Officer

Dear IAN

Our records show you are in the ADMINISTRATION department
which is being transferred to our Bristol office next
Spring. Your current salary of £12,400.00, will be
incremented by a further £500 in consideration of any
inconvenience this may cause.

    Yours sincerely,

    M K L CROCHET
    Personnel Officer
```

Figure 12.7 The production of letters using RUNOFF.

D Inserts the date in the form DD MMM YYYY.

F Inserts the name of the file being processed.

Fn Causes the file name to be included, left-justified in a field of n blanks, where n is a decimal number.

- `i` Inserts the item name being processed.
- `in` Causes the item name to be included, left-justified in a field of `n` blanks, where `n` is a decimal number.
- `L` Specifies the start of a new line, allowing for multiple line headings and footings.
- `P` Inserts current page number right-justified in a field of four blanks.
- `Pn` Inserts page number in a field of `n` spaces.
- `T` Inserts current time and date in the format `HH:MM:SS DD MMM YYYY` using the 24-hour clock.

12.5.7 Producing an index

Any word or phrase can be stored in an index list by the command `.INDEX`. The text must be enclosed in single quotes. The word or phrase is put in a sorted index list which is printed out using the `.PRINT INDEX` command.

It is worth noting that each index column is just 25 characters wide, so the subject text for the index must be kept short, particularly where there are several page references to it!

13 Security and Integrity

TCL verbs and general commands covered in this chapter

ACCOUNT-SAVE	ACCOUNT-RESTORE	CHARGES	CHARGE-TO
CLEAR-FILE	FILE-SAVE	FLUSH	LIST-FILE-STATS
PASSWORD	SEL-RESTORE	SET-HALF	SET-FLOPPY
SET-SCT	T-ATT	T-BCK	T-CHK
T-DET	T-EOD	T-EOF	T-FWD
T-RDLBL	T-READ	T-REW	

13.1 An introduction to security

On any multi-user system where a number of people can be accessing the system at any time, the subject of security becomes a major issue. It is important to ensure that those using the system are authorized users, and as such are only able to access the information they are entitled to. This becomes an even bigger problem where access to the system can be gained remotely over telephone lines. With the capabilities of the so-called 'hackers' it could be said that the only secure system is one that does not have electricity connected to it!

In managing the privacy and protection of your data, it is necessary to appoint a System Administrator to be responsible for setting up the necessary control procedures. Apart from the aspects of security of access, he should also ensure that regular backups are taken to ensure that the data of the system can be restored if necessary.

PICK provides for security of access to the system in a number of ways. Firstly each account can be given a password. This password, held on the System Dictionary, prevents unauthorized access to accounts. If the password is typed in wrongly, the user is returned to the logon prompt. Once a user has access to an account, the files he can access can be restricted using retrieval lock codes, and the files he is permitted to update, by use of update lock codes. The user privileges assigned to a user when he logs on, also restrict the facilities made available to him. The final restrictions that can be applied are by removing specific TCL verbs from his account and preventing him access to TCL altogether which means he can only work within the confines of the application software. A further aid to the System Administrator is the provision of a comprehensive system history via a usage recording and reporting system.

13.1.1 Password protection

The top level of security is that associated with accounts. An account can be protected with a password by using the command `PASSWORD`. This TCL command is available from the `SYSPROG` account and prompts for the account name and password. An encrypted version of the password is then stored in attribute 7 of the system dictionary item for the account. Once applied the password will be requested before access to the account is given. Without giving the correct password the user is returned to the logon prompt. Individual users can be given their own user-ids to accounts which can contain passwords in a similar fashion.

It is obviously crucial to password-protect the `SYSPROG` account, otherwise anyone could freely gain access to all system utilities and password protection on any other account would be useless! It is obviously equally sensible to change passwords from time to time and to avoid the use of obvious passwords such as user initials, christian names or forenames, or two-character passwords, all of which can be readily broken. Any combination of characters is acceptable making password protection a realistic proposition.

Once applied, the password will be requested immediately following a `LOGTO` command or immediately before access is given to the account. With the use of the editor and access to the system dictionary the encrypted password can be removed so access to both of these facilities should be removed from each user account. This is achieved by removing the Q-pointer entry `SYSTEM` and the verbs `ED` and `EDIT` from the master dictionary if present. Doing so restricts access to the password utility to the `SYSPROG` account which itself should be restricted to the System Administrator by means of password protection.

13.1.2 System privilege levels

System privilege levels are assigned to each account at the time the account is created. They can only subsequently be amended by using the editor on the item in the system dictionary relating to the account. Each account created generates an item in the system dictionary with an item-id of the account name. In this item amongst others is the encrypted password in attribute 7 and the privilege level which is held in attribute 8.

There are three privilege levels that can be used. At the lowest level is `SYS0`, then follows `SYS1` with `SYS2` being at the top level. Those with

SYS1 privileges cannot use the debugger, the DUMP verb, the assembler and the FILE-SAVE and FILE-RESTORE processes. In addition to these, those with SYS0 privileges cannot create files, delete files or clear data from files and are not allowed to update the master dictionary.

13.1.3 Update (L/UPD) and retrieval (L/RET) lock codes

These lock codes are provided to protect the most sensitive files of your system and provide the most detailed level of security. The retrieval locks prevent a file being read, whilst the update locks prevent a file being updated. By using these codes, even an authorized user with sufficient technical knowledge to create Q-pointers to other accounts, or even to the system dictionary itself, will be excluded from accessing confidential data.

These lock codes are placed in the file definition item in the master dictionary. The retrieval lock is placed in attribute 5 whilst the update lock is placed in attribute 6. These locks are compared with those of the user and provided they tally, the files can be read and/or updated. The user's retrieval and update lock codes are held in attributes 5 and 6 respectively of the account entry in the system dictionary.

If you refer back to Section 4.1.1 on creating an account, you will notice that the retrieval and update lock codes were requested at the time the account was created. It is these codes that are assigned to the user. In order to provide varying levels of access to the same account it is possible to create Q-pointer entries to an account. These are held in the system dictionary and effectively create user-ids. Section 6.2 explains how this is handled.

The entire update or retrieval code given to a file, read left to right, must match completely all or part of the user's code. Hence if a file has a lock code of ABC anyone with that exact code will have access to the file. Likewise, anyone with a lock code which starts with ABC, i.e. ABC1, ABCD, etc. However anyone whose code is AB or BC or any other subset of the full code will not gain access.

To provide complete protection to the system dictionary these lock codes can be applied to both the SYSPROG and SYSTEM entries in the system dictionary. The codes applied to both of these should be identical to ensure that the only person able to gain access to the system dictionary is the person who can log to the SYSPROG account. You must take extreme care if you decide on this course of action, since to make a mistake will lock you out from the system dictionary and may require you to reload from a previous backup. As the system dictionary is at the top of the hierarchy in the PICK system, any security system must first protect the system dictionary and work down from there.

There are two places you should never put an update or retrieval lock

1. On the SYSTEM entry of SYSTEM.
2. On the MD of an account.

13.1.4 Restricting TCL access

With anything other than the highest privilege level (SYS2), access to the system debugger and assembler is restricted. Further within an application program as we have seen, it is possible using the BREAK OFF statement to prohibit use of the BREAK key to get into the system debugger. Providing the application software is robust and proven and the system administrator is capable, there is no reason why a user should ever need to be given access to TCL.

If the user has SYS2 privileges, however, and the BREAK key is enabled, then by pressing the BREAK key or using a designated alterative the user gains access to the system debugger, denoted by an !. By typing END at this point the system may return to the TCL prompt > and thereafter the user can make use of whatever is available to him. It is possible, however, to stop people gaining access to TCL in this way, thereby confining them to the application software. This is achieved by another security code in attribute 9 of the item in the system dictionary. This is normally set to L, but if it is changed to an R the system will execute the LOGON PROC for that account when END is entered at the debug prompt !, thereby ensuring the user cannot accidentally or deliberately gain access to TCL. The R or L code in attribute 9 can be followed by an optional U which denotes that usage of the account is to be monitored on the System Accounting History file ACC.

13.1.5 Restricting use of TCL verbs

If the user has access to TCL, it may be sensible to remove certain verbs from his account. The obvious verbs relate to the use of the editor, which, as was discussed fully in Chapter 7, enables anyone to access any piece of data and change it. Whilst the retrieval and update locks prevent access to confidential files, it is unlikely that all files in your system will use them. In that case any file without them is open to abuse by the editor. Be aware that the editor leaves no audit trail, so its use should be restricted to just those who need to use it.

Removing TCL verbs from an account is purely a matter of identifying those in question and deleting them using the DELETE verb (see Section 4.3.2).

13.1.6 The System Accounting History file ACC

The System Accounting History file, known as ACC, records users' activities and is one of the mandatory files of the PICK system. It is activated by placing a U alongside the L or R in attribute 9 of the system dictionary entry for the account. Once set, each time a user logs onto the system his connect time and CPU usage, together with the number of pages sent to the spooler, are recorded up to and including the time he logs off. This is an extremely useful mechanism for controlling security since it holds details of:

- the time and date of logon;
- the time and date of logoff;
- the length of time the user was connected to the computer;
- the number of CPU units used;
- the number of pages of print sent to the spooler.

The details displayed to the user as he logs off, prior to being given the logon prompt, are in the form shown in Figure 13.1.

```
<CONNECT TIME = 3 MINS.; CPU = 20 UNITS;LPTR PAGES = 0    >
<LOGGED OFF AT 12:23:14          ON 7 DEC 1985            >

*******************************************************************************
*                                                                             *
*                                                                             *
*******************************************************************************
LOGON TO XXXXXX AT HH:MM:SS  :
```

Figure 13.1 Details displayed to the user as he logs off.

This charging information can also be displayed by the TCL command `CHARGES`. The PICK system maintains the `ACC` file and creates items within it which are a concatenation of the user-id (the logon name) and the port number for completed sessions, for example, `SYSPROG#1` and a hex number, usually starting at `0400`, for active sessions. This hex number bears a direct relationship to the FID of the user's PCB and is explained fully in your user manual. The number is also given under the heading `PCBF` in the output from the command `LISTU` – list users. It is mentioned here to draw your attention to the fact that logged on and logged off users are handled differently in the `ACC` file and it is only the completed sessions, the non-active user sessions, which can be reported on in detail.

If a user wishes to charge his computer usage to another cost centre or project he can use the command `CHARGE-TO` followed by the cost centre or project name. PICK will create a new item on the `ACC` file which records activities from the time the `CHARGE-TO` command is entered to the time the user either logs off or enters a new `CHARGE-TO` command. The item-id of this new record is the concatenation of the user-id (logon name), an asterisk, the cost centre or project name and the port number, for example `SYSPROG*PROJECT1#1`. It will be included in the reports in the same way as any other item.

Producing reports from the ACC file is by use of the ACCESS processor which is described fully in Chapter 9. The ACC dictionary names that can be used in the ACCESS statement, together with the attribute positions they define, are shown in Table 13.1.

Table 13.1 The ACC file dictionary definition items.

ACC dict. Name	*Attribute number*	*Active user*	*Accounting history item (non-active user)*
NAME	1	Hex number of PCB FID	Concatenation of user-id and line no.
DATE	2	Date logged on	Not used
TIME	3	Time logged on	Not used
DATES	4	Not used	Dates logged on, multivalued
TIMES	5	Not used	Times logged on, multivalued
CONN	6	Not used	Connect time, i.e. the time between logon and logoff, multivalued
UNITS	7	Not used	Charge units, multivalued
PAGES	8	Not used	

Notes

CONN	The length of time connected, i.e. the time between logon and logoff
DATES	The date logged on
PAGES	The number of pages spooled to the printer
TIMES	The time logged on
UNITS	The number of charge units

Since most implementations define these attributes as default headings (there are DICT entries for 1–5 for the file ACC) the simple ACCESS statements LIST ACC or SORT ACC are all that are needed to produce a complete report, an example of which is given in Figure 13.2.

Since the charge units, connect times and spooled pages are held as multivalued attributes, it is a simple task to define other dictionary items in ACC that will enable a summary report to be produced. Figure 13.3 shows how this can be done by defining new dictionary items TOT-UNITS, TOT-CONN and TOT-PAGES.

One great danger with the use of system accounting is to forget it is being used, since there is no automatic facility to clear it down. Provided this history monitoring is activated, entries will continue to be added to the ACC file until it uses all the spare disk space! Whilst the file has usually been sized to allow for a sensible number of entries, if it is overlooked it

```
LIST ACC[CR]

PAGE   1                                                11:41:09 20 DEC 1985

ACC....... DATE  TIME... CONN...        UNITS PAGES
                   *       *       *          *
0440
SYSPROG#0  02/11 00:08     19:09       347397
           10/12 08:22    295:53      1185107    25
           19/12 16:16     40:36       624017   114
           20/12 08:53     00:00           21
04200
0400
SM#0       18/12 16:13     01:04          301
OFFICE#1   03/12 11:41     00:04           60
           10/12 09:41     15:15        23778    10
           16/12 14:15     00:00           19

6 items listed.
```

Active users

Figure 13.2 Sample accounting history report.

will link in additional frames to contain the history detail to an extent that will noticably increase logon and logoff times and noticably reduce the amount of free disk space.

The ACC file can be cleared down either completely or selectively. To clear it down completely use the CLEAR-FILE DATA verb which is described in Section 4.2.4. To clear it down selectively use an ACCESS SELECT statement to identify the records to be removed, then remove them using the DELETE verb. Figure 13.4 shows how these two options work.

Note however, that the deletion of records shown in Figure 13.4 removes the entire item containing *all* the information for a user/port. Hence, to base the selection on one of the multivalued attributes such as logon dates would be unlikely to be of value since selective removal of multivalued attributes is not possible without writing a PICK program. Since it is the entire item that is removed using the selection techniques described in Figure 13.4, and hence all reference to the user/port, in practice the accounting history file tends to be completely cleared out each time.

Dictionary items in ACC

Item-id →	TOT-UNITS	TOT-CONN	TOT-PAGES
Attr.			
001	A	A	A
002	7	6	8
003	Total Units	Total Connect	Total Pages
004			
005			
006			
007		MT	
008	AS(7)	AS(6)	AS(8)
009	R	R	R
010	10	10	8

```
LIST ACC TOT-UNITS TOT-CONN TOT-PAGES[CR]
PAGE   1                                         11:41:09  20 DEC 1985

ACC....... Total Units Total Connect Total Pages

0440               0        00:00          0
SYSPROG#0    2156542       355:40        139
0420               0        00:00          0
0400               0        00:00          0
SM#0             301        01:04          0
OFFICE#1       23857        15:19         10

6 items listed.
```

Figure 13.3 Using totals-only dictionary items in ACC.

```
CLEAR-FILE DATA ACC[CR] <———————— Clears down entire file

SELECT ACC WITH *A0 = "SM]"[CR] <—— Select records to
                                    be deleted and
[40] 1 items selected               delete them
>DELETE ACC[CR] <———————————————————┘
'SM#0' deleted
```

Figure 13.4 Removing items from the ACC file.

13.2 An introduction to integrity

The integrity of the database is equally as important as its security and in some respects is more important. Integrity involves ensuring that what is contained within the database is a correct reflection of the masterfile data and its transactions. It also means establishing, and where necessary carrying out, procedures at the time of a system failure to recover the database from previous backups and to bring the database up to date. In some cases this will involve the rekeying of transactions, which means that some form of manual recording procedure has to be put in place.

To be able to recover from failure it is necessary to ensure that adequate backup copies of the database are taken. Whilst anyone would agree that the thought of losing their entire data is abhorrent, there are regretfully many companies who are either so convinced of the reliability of their hardware or generally relaxed and uncaring about their data or even too lazy to spend the time backing up, that a failure means the loss of months of work. It is at times like these that the user realizes the value of support and will place considerable and unnecessary pressure on the supplier to help them recover data! There can be no doubt that it is the responsibility of System Administrators to ensure that backups are carried out frequently enough to provide an adequate level of security for their company and each company's responsibility to recognize these responsibilities and to support the System Administrator when backup time conflicts with an 'urgent' task. No task can be more urgent than securing your data!

There are four ways in which the database is secured, these being:

1. *System generation* – a complete save of all data including the operating system;
2. *File save* – a complete save of all accounts;
3. *Account save* – a backup of specified accounts;
4. *File backup* – a backup of specified files.

The frequency and type of backup taken is very much a function of individual needs. Most people will take an account save once a day, with a complete file save being taken on a weekly and/or monthly basis. In each case several versions of the backup should exist, to protect against the unlikely but disastrous event that a backup tape is found to be corrupt.

The minimum backup should be carried out on what is known as a 'grandfather/father/son' basis where a cycle of three tapes is rotated. In this system, three tapes are used, labelled, for example, A, B and C. Today's backup is written to tape A, tomorrow to tape B and the day after to tape C. When all the tapes have been used once, the eldest (the grandfather), tape A, is reused, overwriting the oldest backup copy. In this way three independent backup copies are retained. This is not to say that three is all that is needed. For a nominal cost, particularly in relation to the value of the data, additional tapes can be added to the cycle, perhaps providing a complete set of backup tapes for each day of the working week, or even the working month with additional tapes being held for the weekly and/or monthly backups.

Whatever the number of tapes used, it will be essential to clearly identify and mark each tape and to keep a log of which tape was used, on which day and for which type of backup. In addition, all backup tapes and the log should be kept in a fireproof safe, with additional copies of the weekly, monthly or annual backups being kept off-site in a secure place, such as in a bank or with a security company. If all of this sounds dramatic, so is the loss of your data!

13.2.1 Tape and floppy disk handling

The original backup medium handling commands written for PICK were written for ½-inch magnetic Tape and hence commence with the letter T. As hardware evolved, other backup devices have been introduced, namely floppy disk and ¼-inch cartridge tape. The original backup medium commands have not changed and are equally applicable to ¼-inch tape and floppy disks. In order to tell PICK which backup device you are addressing, these commands need to be preceded by a `SET` command, even when using ½-inch tape. This command is followed by the device to be addressed. While these commands vary between implementations they are typically:

`SET-FLOPPY`	Floppy disk
`SET-HALF`	Magnetic tape (½-inch)
`SET-SCT`	Cartridge tape (¼-inch)

Following one of the above commands the verbs shown in Figure 13.5, whilst specifically referring to the tape unit, will carry out the same function for all media. There is one additional command which is required specifically for floppy disks and is the command to format the physical floppy disk. No floppy disk can be used until it has been formatted. Again the verb to perform this function varies between implementations, but is typically:

```
FORMAT-FLOPPY
FORMAT-DISKETTE
FFORMAT
```

`T-ATT {BLOCKSIZE}`
Attaches the tape unit to the port number on the system of the terminal carrying out the command. Only one port at a time can have access to the backup medium. If another port is using it, the message `DEVICE ATTACHED TO LINE n` will be displayed showing which terminal has control of the backup devices. If they are no longer using it, either carry out a `T-DET` from the controlling terminal or a `T-DET (U` from your own terminal. The blocksize normally has a default when the device is attached. This can be overridden by specifying one here within the limits for that device.

`T-BCK {number of records}`
Move the tape back a specified number of records. If a number is not given, one is assumed.

`T-CHK {A}`
Check current tape file for parity errors. If `A` option is used the check is made to the end of the tape.

`T-DET {(U)}`
Detaches the device from the current process making it available to others. The `U` unconditionally frees it.

`T-EOD`
Moves the tape forward to the end of the data on the tape.

`T-EOF`
Moves the tape forward to the end of the current file.

`T-FWD {number of blocks}`
Moves the tape forward a specified number of blocks. If no number is specified, one is assumed.

`T-RDLBL {(reel number)}`
Reads a tape label from the specified reel number. If no number is specified, the current one is assumed.

`T-READ {(Options)}`
Reads a records from tape and displays it on the terminal. The options are:

- `A` dumps alphanumeric segment after conversion to ASCII
- `X` dumps in hexadecimal format
- `P` dumps to the printer
- `n-{m}` dumps from block `n` to block `m` inclusive

It should be noted that not all these commands will work for every device on every implementation.

Figure 13.5 Device-handling commands.

13.2.2 System generation backup and restore processes

A system generation tape is a copy of the entire data on your disk including the PICK operating system. It is obviously advisable to take such a backup upon receiving your system and at regular intervals thereafter. Not all manufacturers enable you to create your own system generation copy, but, if you can, the instructions for doing so will be in your manual. If you are unable to do this then you will only have *one* copy of the operating system, which should naturally be treated with every precaution. If this copy gets lost or damaged and you need to recover the operating system the only way would be by a replacement from the manufacturer, which could involve costly delays.

The method of restoring the system from a system generation tape is to reboot the system with the system generation tape/diskette loaded in the system. Once the operating system has been loaded from the backup, the message `OPTIONS (X,F) =` will be displayed. If the file system is satisfactory an `X`, to execute, is the correct entry, which will initialize the recovered PICK operating system. If, however, the file system is also to be restored, the tape/floppy containing the latest file save copy (this could be on the same tape or floppy diskette as that containing the system generation data used to reload the operating system), must be placed in the machine and the `F` option chosen. The file system will be restored and a cold-start procedure initiated. This is discussed further in Section 3.1.

13.2.3 The `FILE-SAVE` backup and restore processes

The `FILE-SAVE` procedure will back up all data, with the exception of the operating system, to a backup medium. This process is normally handled by a `PROC` in the `SYSPROG` account supplied by your manufacturer and called `FILE-SAVE`. This `PROC` will handle all aspects of the backup process through a question and answer session after which a security copy of your data will be available.

During the procedure, file statistics are recorded in a file called `STAT-FILE`. Whilst an option is available to print these statistics as they are being collected, they can be reproduced thereafter by the command `LIST-FILE-STATS` or by use of a simple ACCESS enquiry. In order to establish the dictionary items available for ACCESS enquiries, carry out the command `SORT ONLY DICT STAT-FILE` which will list them for you.

The `STAT-FILE` provides useful information about file sizes which enables the System Administrator to keep a watchful eye on files which may need resizing. Additionally, of course, it will show up files that are bigger than they should be, for example word-processing files, because unwanted items have not been removed.

Figure 13.6 shows some of the information from the file statistics report, which is an invaluable aid in determining incorrectly sized files. It will also show file utilization and padding (the amount of unused space). From this information it is possible, using the formula given in Section 5.2.5, to determine whether a file needs resizing. If so, refer to Section 5.4 on the method for so doing.

```
PAGE   1                                                   10:28:50  08 JAN 1986

NAME.............. BASE M S    ... ...SIZE... ITEMS. FRAMES

ACC                9681 1 1              79      3      1
ACC                9682 1 1           3,113     96      7
ACC*ACC            9683 11 1            990     12     11
                                 ----------        ------

*** TOTALS FOR USER- ACC              4,182             19

BENCH-TEST         3957 101 1        14,933    547    102
PROCS              4058 1 1              32      1      1
PROCS*PROCS        4059 37 1            850      4     37
TESTFILE           4096 7 1             377     11      7
TESTFILE*TESTFILE  4103 3 1           1,171     10      3
PROGS              4106 17 1            358      8     17
PROGS*PROGS        4123 17 1          3,898      6     22
BACK-UP            4155 7 1              33      1      7
BACK-UP*BACK-UP    4162 1 1               0      0      1
                                 ----------        ------

*** TOTALS FOR USER- BENCH TEST      21,652            197
:
:
:

*** TOTALS FOR USER- XXX             19,948            377
                                  2,609,470          9,451

314 items listed.
```

Figure 13.6 Output from the STAT-FILE.

Since a file save operation is highly time-consuming, there may be certain accounts or certain files you may not wish to back up each time. These accounts can be marked with a DX in attribute 1 of the system dictionary, whilst the files not to be backed up need to have a DX in attribute 1 of the master dictionary item. Whilst this is an extremely useful facility to reduce backup times, it is dangerous in that should the system need to be recovered from the file save tape, the contents of the file save tape are used to *completely* overwrite the file system. Hence any files or accounts not included on the file save tape will not be restored and will, therefore, no longer exist. In certain cases this could mean that valuable data is lost forever!

There are valid reasons for DXing accounts, for example where the account rarely changes and adequate backups already exist. It is also possible to use DY in place of DX in file definition items which means that the files will be restored empty of data following a file restore process. This process has its uses for certain types of transaction file. File definition item types are discussed further in Section 5.1.3.

To reload the file system from backup, reboot the system to initiate a cold-start process. When the OPTIONS (X,F) = message is displayed, place the latest file save backup in the machine (this could have been a system generation backup tape from which the system was booted), and take the F option.

13.2.4 Checking the data secured

Once the data has been backed up it should be checked to see that the copy contains readable data. This is achieved by using a selective restore command SEL-RESTORE, which is given a fictitious item name to restore. It forces the entire backup tape/diskette to be read from start to finish. Whilst this doubles the backup time, it can save a lot of heartache and wasted time when things go wrong and when the backup tape has to be relied on to recover data. This philosophy is demonstrated in Figure 13.7.

13.2.5 The ACCOUNT-SAVE backup processes

An ACCOUNT-SAVE command saves all the data of an individual account to tape or diskette. This procedure has no tape-handling commands embedded into it, so the normal procedure to follow would be as given in Figure 13.7 which shows how the account ACCOUNTS would be backed up to floppy disk.

```
>SET-FLOPPY[CR]        <—— indicates backup device
BLOCK SIZE 500         <—— default block size for this
[1072] Diskette set.       device

>T-REW[CR]

 DEVICE ATTACHED BLOCK SIZE 500

>ACCOUNT-SAVE[CR]

 BLOCK SIZE 500
 TAPE LABEL IF DESIRED = [CR]
```

```
 ACCOUNT NAME = ACCOUNTS[CR]

1      1 ACCOUNTS
1      2  SLTRANS
1      3   SLTRANS
1      4  SLMASTER
1      5  SLMASTER
1      6  DEPT
1      7  SLBALS
1      8   SLBALS
```

- file name
- file sequence number
- floppy diskette number (used to cater for multiple floppies/tapes)

```
...
...
ANOTHER ACCOUNT (Y) ?N[CR]
 BLOCK SIZE:  500
[94] End of file.

>T-REW[CR]
 BLOCK SIZE 500
```

must be an existing file on the hard disk

```
>SEL-RESTORE SLMASTER XXXXXX[CR]
```

fictitious item name

```
ACCOUNT NAME ON TAPE?XXXX[CR]
FILE NAME?XXXX[CR]
```

fictitious names

```
 ACCOUNTS 1
  SLTRANS 2
   SLTRANS 2
  SLMASTER 4
   SLMASTER 5
  DEPT 6
  SLBALS 7
   SLBALS 8
```

reading through backup tape to prove the data can be read

```
...
...
[992] 0 ITEM(S) HAVE BEEN RESTORED.
```

Figure 13.7 The ACCOUNT-SAVE dialogue.

13.2.6 The ACCOUNT-RESTORE process

The ACCOUNT-RESTORE command will restore an account from a security copy. The account must not already exist on disk otherwise the message EXISTS ON FILE will be displayed. This is a protection mechanism to prevent you from overwriting a working account. Where the account you are restoring still exists, you will first need to remove it using the DELETE-ACCOUNT verb discussed in Section 4.1.2.

The ACCOUNT-RESTORE process is the reverse of ACCOUNT-SAVE in that it restores the data from an individual account from a security copy. A typical dialogue is shown in Figure 13.8 where the account ACCOUNTS is restored.

It is also possible to restore an account under a different name, by using the command ACCOUNT-RESTORE newname where the ACCOUNT NAME ON TAPE is given under its original name. In this way several copies of an account may be kept on file. This can be useful, for example, when new programs are being tested.

```
>SET-FLOPPY[CR] <---------- indicates backup device
 BLOCK SIZE 500 <---------- default block size for this
 [1072] Diskette set.       device

>T-REW[CR]

 DEVICE ATTACHED BLOCK SIZE 500

>ACCOUNT-RESTORE ACCOUNTS[CR]

ACCOUNT NAME ON TAPE? ACCOUNTS[CR]
 BLOCK SIZE 500
ACCOUNTS
  ACCOUNTS 11205,29,1       location of MD for ACCOUNTS
   SLTRANS 11352,7,1        location of DICT of SLTRANS
    SLTRANS 13155,17,1      location of data of SLTRANS
   SLMASTER 11279,11,1
    SLMASTER 10228,71,1
   DEPT 11326,1,1
    DEPT 11327,1,1
   SLBALS 11328,7,1
    SLBALS 11335,3,1
      ^     ^    ^ ^
      |     |    | |________ separation
      |     |    |__________ modulo
      |     |_______________ base FID number
      |_____________________ file name
```

Figure 13.8 The ACCOUNT-RESTORE process.

13.2.7 The file backup process using T-DUMP

An individual file may be backed up by means of the `T-DUMP` command, which was briefly discussed in Section 9.3.11 on ACCESS. This command is also used to selectively back up records from a data or dictionary file to tape and/or diskette since the command can optionally include selection criteria as described in Section 9.3.7. Without any qualification, the entire file will be secured. It is important to note that the data and dictionary portions of a file are held in separate files. Hence, to back up an entire file, the dictionary file must be dumped in the same way and as well as, the data, and similarly it must be restored independently. A typical `T-DUMP` process is illustrated in Figure 13.9 where the file `SLMASTER` is backed up to floppy disk.

```
>SET-FLOPPY[CR]<----------- indicates backup device
 BLOCK SIZE 500 <---------- default block size for this
 [1072] Diskette set.       device

>T-REW[CR]

 DEVICE ATTACHED BLOCK SIZE 500

>T-DUMP DICT SLMASTER[CR]

 BLOCK SIZE 500

    1  ADDRESS
    2  NAME
    3  CRLIMIT
    ...
    ...
10 items dumped.

>T-DUMP SLMASTER[CR]

 BLOCK SIZE 500

    1  A0007
    2  C0018
    3  A0003
    4  D0003
    5  D0004
    ^  ^
    |  |_________ item name
    |____________ sequence number

    ...
    ...
53 items dumped.
```

Figure 13.9 Using `T-DUMP` to back up a file.

```
>SET-FLOPPY[CR] <———— indicates backup device
 BLOCK SIZE 500 <———— default block size for this
 [1072] Diskette set.   device

>T-REW[CR]

 DEVICE ATTACHED BLOCK SIZE 500

>T-LOAD DICT SLMASTER[CR]

 BLOCK SIZE 1000

   1  ADDRESS
   2  NAME
   3  CRLIMIT
   ...
   ...
   10 item(s) loaded.

     >T-LOAD SLMASTER[CR]

   BLOCK SIZE 500

   1  A0007
   2  C0018
   3  A0003
   4  D0003
   5  D0004
   ↑    ↑———— item name
   └————————— sequence number

   ...
   ...
 53 item(s) loaded.
```

Figure 13.10 Using the `T-LOAD` command.

13.2.8 The file restore process using `T-LOAD`

The `T-LOAD` process is the reverse of `T-DUMP` and can only be used from a `T-DUMP` backup. In exactly the same way as with `T-DUMP`, the `T-LOAD` statement can contain selection criteria to qualify the records of a file that is restored.

Without this qualification, all records are restored. The file must already exist, otherwise the error message `[10] File name missing` will be displayed. If the item being restored already exists on the file, a message will be displayed to that effect; the original item will not be overwritten.

If the file being restored does not exist it will have to be created using the CREATE-FILE command, which is described in Section 4.2.1. These T-DUMP and T-LOAD commands can be used to create test data in test accounts, which contain a subset of the live data. Figure 13.10 shows a typical dialogue from the use of the T-LOAD command.

13.2.9 Selective restores

Selective accounts can be restored from a file save tape using the standard ACCOUNT-RESTORE command. In the case of an extreme emergency you might like to know that it is possible to restore an account from a system generation tape, again using the ACCOUNT-RESTORE verb, but after having T-FWDed past the ABS frames at the beginning of the tape. PICK will look consecutively through the tape from start to finish, so in order to save wasted time rewinding and researching through the tape, accounts selected for restore should be selected in the order in which they were originally saved. The file statistics report produced will give you this sequence.

Individual files may be selectively restored from a file save or account save tape. The means of doing this is with the SEL-RESTORE command. The selective restore can be initiated from any tape of a multitape backup, which saves wasting time searching from the first tape produced. Again the statistics file report will enable you to determine which volume the data is held on.

Finally, selected records may be restored to a file based on the selection criteria of the ACCESS command T-LOAD. Hence all records whose name starts with the letter R could be restored from a T-DUMP backup, using the command T-LOAD SLMASTER WITH NAME = "R]".

13.2.10 Controlled shutdown

The way in which the system is shut down is extremely important. The PICK system is a virtual memory system and frequently frames of data are held in memory for long periods before they are written away to disk. This means that simply powering off the system could mean a substantial loss of data.

Unless the manufacturer has a recommended procedure to follow, ensure that all other users are logged off the system and allow half a minute to pass before powering off. If your implementation has the FLUSH verb or its own controlled shutdown procedure, this should be used in place of the wait. This procedure will force the system to write to disk any data held in memory that should be written to disk. Once this command has finished, which is a matter of moments, the TCL prompt is displayed and the system can be switched off in the secure knowledge that the integrity of the database has been secured.

14 Managing Your System

General commands and TCL verbs covered in this chapter

COMPARE	DUMP	ECHO ON	ECHO OFF	FLUSH
GROUP	HASH-TEST	ISTAT	ITEM	LISTU
LISTPROCS	POVF	MSG	TERM	TIME
SET-BAUD	SET-DATE	SET-TERM	SET-TIME	STAT
VERIFY-SYSTEM		WHAT	WHERE	WHO

14.1 The role of the System Administrator

This section completes the description of the PICK operating system and summarizes the role of the System Administrator. In earlier chapters we have reviewed the structure of the PICK database and covered, in detail, the functional workings of the various facets of the operating system. Undoubtedly you will have realized that this is a substantial operating system whose strengths can best be realized by a detailed understanding of its operation. In this respect, as with all other computer systems, at least one person, whom I have called the System Administrator, needs to gain an intimate understanding of PICK in order to manage any day-to-day difficulties and the security of the system.

This chapter summarizes the role of the System Administrator. It encompasses several functions not discussed earlier and also those referenced in earlier chapters. It is intended that the System Administrator should be able to use this chapter to answer his problems, either directly or by reference to other chapters.

14.2 System start up and close down

The first aspect of managing your system is being able to start up and close down your system in a controlled manner. These functions are mostly implementation-dependent and you should refer to your manual for those specific to your system. Few problems should be experienced in this area if you follow the instructions properly. For information on typical procedures refer to Section 3.1.

Do remember that the start-up and close-down messages are displayed on the terminal plugged into port 0 and that unless you have a special close-down procedure provided by your supplier, you must wait a few minutes after all others have logged off or, if available on your implementation, carry out a `FLUSH` command, to flush the memory to disk, before powering off (see Section 13.2.10).

The cold-boot mechanism provides the means to restore the complete file system. This is touched on in Section 3.1.1 and discussed more fully in Section 13.2.3.

14.3 Logging on and logging off

Logging on and off the system is a simple process provided the necessary accounts exist and any passwords to them are correctly entered. These processes are discussed in Sections 3.2 and 3.3. If a particular terminal has 'hung' then the command `LOGGOFF` should send the 'hung' terminal to the logon message. Similarly the use of the `BREAK` key or `CTRL/C` function followed by `OFF` at the debug prompt ! should cure the problem. In certain circumstances, where neither of these options works, the only way out is to close down the system and carry out a cold-start initialization procedure.

The other aspect of logging on is that of security and of creating account synonyms or user-ids. System security, from password protection to system usage reporting is covered in Sections 13.1.1–13.1.5, whilst the creation of user-ids is to be found in Section 6.2.

14.4 Setting the date and time

Before using the system, it may be necessary to set the date and time. On some systems, however, a battery-backed clock is provided, and this process is obviated. Even so, at some stage you will need to make changes, even if it is just to cater for Summer Time! The command `TIME` displays the current date and time whilst `SET-DATE` and `SET-TIME` change the date and time, respectively, as Figure 14.1 illustrates.

```
>TIME[CR]
12:20:54   18 JAN 1986

>SET-TIME 13:20[CR]
13:20:00   18 JAN 1986

>SET-DATE 19JAN86[CR]
13:20:39   19 JAN 1986
```

Figure 14.1 Changing the date and time.

14.5 Control of printers

One of the most common areas for a System Administrator to spend his time is looking after printers and, for this reason, the whole of Chapter 8 was devoted to this topic, with Section 8.5 covering problem-solving.

Most problems arise through being unclear of the difference between printer number and form queue number when using the spooler commands, or through having the printer available to a large number of users in a multi-user environment. In these circumstances the user's report may have been produced on the wrong stationery, or in the wrong quality of print, which causes him to require assistance.

The page width and page length is set automatically to 132 columns and 64 lines, but can be changed, if necessary, using the TERM and SET-TERM commands. Since these commands are also, and most frequently, used for setting terminal characteristics, they are covered in the next section on controlling terminals.

One other area that is worth mentioning here is that of baud rates. Each port on the computer operates at a particular speed, called the baud rate. This is normally 9600 baud, and must be identical to that of the devices attached to it, be they terminals or printers. Whilst the majority of printers can operate at this speed some can only operate at lower speeds, such as 2400 baud. In order to use the lower speed printer on the system, the port the printer is attached to must also be set to this lower speed. This is achieved through the SET-BAUD command. The general format of this command is shown in Figure 14.2 as are the possible baud rate settings.

14.6 Control of terminals

Provided terminals are plugged in, switched on and operating with the correct terminal type, at the correct baud rate, they will give no problems until they develop a hardware fault. The setting of baud rate is unlikely to

```
>SET-BAUD n,rate
```

where n is the port number and rate is the baud rate

Meaningful baud rate

50	Forced to 110
75	Forced to 110
110	
134.5	Forced to 150
150	
300	
600	
1200	
1800	Forced to 2400
2000	Forced to 2400
2400	
3600	Forced to 4800
4800	
7200	Forced to 9600
9600	
19200	

Figure 14.2 The SET-BAUD verb and baud rate settings.

arise, though if it does, Figure 14.2 above describes how to change it. The main difficulty likely to occur relates to the terminal type. This is normally taken care of by your supplier, but should you buy an alternative VDU for your system you need to know how to change the terminal type.

The command TERM is used to display the current terminal and printer characteristics and TERM followed by parameters, to change these characteristics. The command TERM sets the characteristics for the terminal even whilst it is logged on. Once the terminal is logged off, future use will revert back to the system default characteristics which can be altered using SET-TERM. Both TERM and SET-TERM use the same options and have the same general format, which is described in Figure 14.3.

To change a particular characteristic, you do not have to specify them all in order to incorporate the change. You can omit those unaltered, by entering a comma in their place. Hence TERM ,25 will change the number of lines for display on a terminal to 25, leaving the number of characters across a page at 79. Similarly TERM ,,,,,,,50 will change the page length for each report page to fifty lines. The terminal type must be the last parameter option, and since PICK is smart enough to differentiate between letters and numbers, TERM W will set the terminal type as W and

```
>TERM sw,sd,ls,lf,ff,bs,pw,pd,tt

>SET-TERM sw,sd,ls,lf,ff,bs,pw,pd,tt
```

where

- sw is the terminal screen width in columns; defaults to 79
- sd is the terminal screen depth in lines; defaults to 23
- ls is the terminal line skip in lines, defaults to 0. The sum of sd and ls must equal the number of lines of the VDU
- lf is the number of delay characters output after a linefeed. This is for terminals that require a pause after such an operation because they cannot cope with the speed the processor sends data
- ff is the number of delay characters output after a top-of-page is encountered. This affects both terminals and printers
- bs is the backspace character
- pw is the page width of the printer in columns; defaults to 131
- pd is the page depth of the printer in lines; defaults to 64
- tt is the terminal type which defines the way in which the cursor addressing is to be handled. If this is incorrect, the information will be displayed in a jumbled form on the screen. Whilst these vary from implementation to implementation they are defined by a single letter and are typically:
  - A Adds 580
  - B Ampex 210
  - C Citoh VT52
  - D Datamedia
  - L Lear Seigler ADM-3A
  - M Ampex 80
  - P Pertec 701
  - R Adds Regent
  - T TEC 2402
  - V Adds Viewpoint
  - W Wyse 50

Figure 14.3 Terminal and printer characteristics.

TERM 131 the terminal screen width to 132 columns.

There is one other problem that may arise and this will undoubtedly confuse you the first time it happens. A user may tell you that although he is typing his commands into the terminal, the cursor is not moving and no characters are appearing on the screen! Whilst this can be a hardware failure, it is more likely to occur because the terminal echo, which echos (redisplays) the characters typed in onto the screen, has been turned off. Although the echo is turned off the system will react to the instructions in exactly the same way, the only difference being that you cannot see what you've typed in! The echo can be turned on and off with the commands `ECHO ON` and `ECHO OFF`.

14.7 Sending messages

The command `MSG` enables messages to be sent to all users, users on a specific port or users operating within a specific account. Whilst this has its uses, it immediately interrupts the user with the message, rings the VDU bell and in the process disturbs his cursor which is moved to the end of the displayed message. Since this disturbs the data on the user's screen, he is often thrown by it, not being sure whether the message will be considered as part of the data he is inputting, which of course, it is not.

To send a message to all users, known as an all-ports broadcast, use `MSG * message text`. For messages to a specific port the asterisk is replaced with an exclamation mark, followed by the port number, i.e. `MSG !n message`. And for messages to users of a specified account the asterisk is replaced by the account name, i.e. `MSG account-name message`.

14.8 Handling disk usage

The handling of disk usage can be a severe management task in a volatile system with limited disk space. Fortunately, disk capacity these days is relatively cheap, and should not represent much of a problem. The first step, of course, is to keep a regular eye on the amount of free disk space and how it is organized.

Free disk space can be determined from the TCL command `WHAT` which also gives additional information about the active processes and printers. The available space, in frames, is given under the heading 'Avail overflow' in Figure 14.4.

In addition to giving information about the spare disk space, Figure 14.4 shows how other information is displayed. For example it also shows the amount of memory on the system (256K) and the number of physical lines, 3. (Yes it is 3 and not 4. Remember 1 of the 4 shown is the phantom process for the spooler.) The location of the start of the system files (`SYSBASE`) is also shown. By virtue of giving the `MAXFID`, the maximum number of frames on the disk, you can determine the disk size (number of ABS frames × 2048 bytes plus the remainder of frames × 512 bytes, which works out for Figure 14.4 at $((1023 \times 2048) + ((39212 - 1023) \times 512)) = 21\,647\,872$ bytes or approximately 21 Mbytes.

A disk should not operate at more than 80% of its capacity, to allow for sorts, spooler and other temporary files. If you find your system working regularly above this figure you should seriously consider a disk upgrade.

```
14:00:12 19 JAN 1986                                      Avail.
Core Line PCBO WSstart WSsize Sysbase/Mod/Sep Maxfid Overflow
256K    4 1024  1152   127    2676  11  1   39212     26512
```

Spare space 26512 frames of 512 bytes each

```
00 00 00 00 00 00 00 00 00 00 00 00 00 00 00 00
00 00 00 00 00 00 00 00 00 00 00 00 00 00 00 00
00 00 00 00 00 00 00 00 00 00 00 00 00 00 00 00

00 00 00 00 00 00 00 00 00 00 00 00 00 00 00 00
00 00 00 00 00 00 00 00 00 00

*00 0400 FF00     121.000 121.1AC 166.58E
 01 0420 ED00     351.0D0
 02 0440 BF00     170.1CA 170.096
 03 0460 BF00     170.1CA 170.12E

 The spooler is inactive.

Printer # 0 is serial, inactive, and on line.
The printer is running on line 2.
Assigned output queues: 0.
The number of inter-job pages to eject is 0.
```

Figure 14.4 Output from the WHAT command.

Having established the amount of spare space available, it is important to find out how it is distributed on the disk. Spare frames scattered all over the disk in small groups cause the condition known as fragmentation. Fragmentation will lead to long response times and may restrict the use of the system, particularly where new files are concerned, since new files have to have the required initial allocation of frames provided as a contiguous block. The command POVF shows where the free space is available, an example of which is shown in Figure 14.5.

The POVF table can normally only hold 32 entries. When the table is full, the last entry is used to chain together references to all other spare frames and the system is then said to have 'linked overflow'. This demonstrates a severely fragmented system which should be immediately reorganized by performing a FILE-SAVE and restore. You should also be aware that GFEs are far more likely to occur when the system has linked overflow. Linked overflow is signified from the POVF command by virtue of the first entry showing a number in parentheses, that number being the number of linked frames. Figure 14.6 gives an example of this.

Another area to keep a watchful eye on is the system accounting

```
>POVF[CR]
                              ┌── From FID location
                              │     ┌── To FID location
                              │     │        ┌── Spare frames
                              ▼     ▼        ▼
 3957-  4163 :   207   9829- 10215 :   387
13262- 13268 :     7  13276- 13276 :     1
13303- 39212 : 25910

Total number of contiguous frames   : 26512 — Total number
                                              of spare frames
```

Figure 14.5 Output from POVF.

```
34179 (     17)
14936- 14967 :    32   14983- 14984 :    2
15003- 15004 :     2   15040- 15044 :    5
15057- 15057 :     1   15059- 15059 :    1
15061- 15061 :     1   15068- 15068 :    1
15073- 15073 :     1   15084- 15084 :    1
15098- 15200 :   103   15902- 15902 :    1
16298- 24021 :  7724   24157- 24157 :    1
35899- 35899 :     1   36328- 36328 :    1
36852- 36852 :     1   37888- 37889 :    2
37892- 37892 :     1   38177- 38177 :    1
38346- 38346 :     1   38529- 38529 :    1
38785- 38787 :     3   40000- 40000 :    1
40004- 40005 :     2   40328- 40340 :   13
40351- 40479 :   129   52444- 52444 :    1
52447- 52447 :     1   52884- 52884 :    1
53165- 80109 : 26945

Total number of contiguous frames   : 34981
```

Figure 14.6 Linked overflow.

history file (ACC), which should be cleared out regularly, and word-processing files, which users rarely tidy up behind them. Both these could be using considerable disk space unbeknown to you. The STAT verb, see Section 9.3.11, will tell you the size of a specific file, whilst the file statistics produced from a file save operation will give you a complete analysis of your files (see Section 13.2.3).

If a file grows considerably it will link on additional frames, gradually causing a degradation in response wherever that file is used. In those circumstances it will be necessary to reorganize the data in a larger file. Where file resizing is necessary, the existing distribution of data can be checked using ISTAT (Section 5.3) and new file sizes tested, before they are created using HASH-TEST (Section 5.3.1). This testing of alternatives enables file sizes to be optimized, from which the physical reorganizing, described in Section 5.4, can be carried out.

The other aspects of disk usage management are the control of accounts, their creation and deletion (covered in Sections 4.1.1 and 4.1.2) and the management of data files (explained in Section 4.2).

14.9 Optimizing response time

Response times can be affected by hardware or software factors. On the hardware side, apart from hardware failures such as hard disk errors causing the system to force the Winchester disk controller to continually retry to read the data until it is read successfully, the two main factors affecting response are the available RAM and the hard disk speed.

Since PICK is a virtual memory system, it will use the spare space on the hard disk as an extension of its real memory. It will page information out of real memory when it needs the space to work on something else. Hence, the more memory it has available, the more information it can ratain before paging data to disk. Working from real memory is a great deal faster than having to access data from disk – from RAM access is virtually instant.

Paging information to and from disk is a fundamental function of the PICK operating system. Apart from this, the operating system and all of the data it works on is stored on disk. It is fairly obvious, therefore, that the speed at which the disk works is an instrumental factor of the system's performance.

Whilst the hardware elements are important, invariably poor response is caused by software. This can be a function of the application software in handling excessively large items or making more disk accesses than are necessary, but more often than not is caused by poorly sized files or a fragmented disk. The previous section, which covered the POVF command, talks about how to check for fragmentation and how to put it right.

Poorly sized files can have a dramatic effect on response. If response times seem to be slowing down you should look very carefully at all the files on the system, *including* the master dictionary. Since the master dictionary is the central reference point for all activities within an account, the file that will have the greatest impact on response time, if wrongly sized, is the master dictionary. File sizing and optimizing is covered in Sections 5.3 and 5.4.

14.10 Handling system hangs and system errors

When an individual terminal hangs it is possible to break from the process using the BREAK key or the CTRL/C keys and type OFF to logoff and start again. This process should be handled with extreme care when the activity involves the updating of files. When all the terminals stop and none seem to respond to the break process, life becomes a little more difficult! The first step is to move a terminal to an unused port and see if you can logon. If so, carry out a controlled shutdown and reboot the system. If this does not work, the only alternative is to reboot the system. In these circumstances some work may be lost, and if you are unsure of what has been lost, you must assess whether you should restore from backup tapes and rekey subsequent transactions.

Whenever you have retrieved the situation from a system hang, you should carry out the command VERIFY-SYSTEM, which checks each frame on the system. This process generates a checksum for each frame which it compares to the original values held in the item CHECK-SUM in ERRMSG. Those frames which do not verify are displayed with their old and new checksums. If there are errors you should reload the operating system. If there are errors after you have reloaded the operating system you should contact your supplier.

There are certain rare problems which do occur on PICK systems, known as Group Format Errors (GFEs). A GFE can occur because of a hardware failure, a glitch in the power supply, an uncontrolled shutdown such as a total power failure or a reboot occurring whilst file updating is in progress, incorrect use of assembler programs or even static electricity. A GFE is reported, and reported without any prior warning, when one of the following conditions occurs:

1. The actual size of an item in a group differs from that recorded by the first four bytes which define the item size and which precede the item data.
2. A terminator is of the wrong type or is missing.
3. Backward frame linkages are incorrect.
4. Forward frame linkages are incorrect.

The message displayed is GROUP FORMAT ERROR nnnnnn, where nnnnnn is the number of the first frame in the group containing the GFE. The message is displayed on the terminal that was using the file in which the group format error was found. The first and immediate step is to stop all other users working whilst the error is located and corrected.

Whilst correcting GFEs and use of the system debugger is outside the scope of this book it must be pointed out that to correct these errors requires the assistance of a highly skilled PICK technician who knows the PICK operating system intimately and is competent in the use of the

System Debugger. The file in which the GFE occurred must be traced and an analysis carried out to see whether all data can be recovered or, in the case of linkage errors, whether these can be put right without any loss of data. In most cases, for the sake of integrity, it will mean recovering a file or an account from a backup, and if these files or accounts affect others, it may be sensible to reload the entire system from a backup.

It is this type of problem, which comes without giving any sort of warning, which emphasizes the importance of adequate backup procedures. It is worth repeating, without wishing to sound overdramatic, that only you can determine the frequency and type of backups that should be taken to secure your own system.

Other GFEs relate to forward or backward link errors. These occur for similar reasons and make themselves known by the message `Forward link error` or `Backward link error`. In a similar way, strong technical expertise is required to put these problems right. If you want to check the linkages the `DUMP nnnnnn L` will show you the forward and backward linkages of a group whose first frame is nnnnnn, as is illustrated in Figure 14.7.

```
>DUMP 10318 L[CR]
```

Backward link FID
Forward link FID
FID
The same table in hexadecimal format

```
  FID: 10318 : 0  10340      0   0 ( 284E : 0  2864     0 0 )
+ FID: 10340 : 0  10341  10318   0 ( 2864 : 0  2865  284E 0 )
+ FID: 10341 : 0  10342  10340   0 ( 2865 : 0  2866  2864 0 )
+ FID: 10342 : 0  10343  10341   0 ( 2866 : 0  2867  2865 0 )
+ FID: 10343 : 0  10344  10342   0 ( 2867 : 0  2868  2866 0 )
+ FID: 10344 : 0  10345  10343   0 ( 2868 : 0  2869  2867 0 )
+ FID: 10345 : 0      0  10344   0 ( 2869 : 0     0  2868 0 )
```

Figure 14.7 Checking the linkages of a group.

One other message that may be encountered, again requiring technical help, is `Referencing illegal frame`. This message occurs when a frame links to one which is below 0 or above `MAXFID`, i.e. a frame that does not exist on the system. Fortunately all these errors are rare and not impossible to resolve. If they do occur it is generally because of a hardware fault, so if they start to occur regularly you should call in a hardware engineer.

There are two useful commands that will help in the location of

```
GROUP STAFF[CR]

3980 <——— Base FID of group
0023 006 <— Item-id '006' is 35 bytes long
0021 003
2 ITEMS 68 BYTES 0/68 FRAMES
3981
0025 001
0026 004
0024 010
0019 1
4 ITEMS 136 BYTES 0/136 FRAMES
3982
0022 002          ┌──── Number of full frames
0023 005          │ ┌──────── Number of bytes in the last frame
0019 2            ▼ ▼
3 ITEMS 94 BYTES 0/94 FRAMES
```

Figure 14.8 The GROUP command.

GFEs, namely GROUP and ITEM, which as their names suggest provide information about group and item structure. The GROUP command, illustrated in Figure 14.8, displays the base FID of each group of the specified file. In addition every item-id in the group is listed along with its character count in hex (see Appendix G for a full list of hex codes). At the end of the display for each group is a summary of its contents.

The ITEM command provides exactly the same information as the group command, but only for the group in which the specified item is located. Figure 14.9 shows an example of this.

```
>ITEM STAFF 006[CR]

3980
0023 006
0021 003
2 ITEMS 68 BYTES 0/68 FRAMES
```

Figure 14.9 The ITEM command.

14.11 Backup procedures

The System Administrator should ensure that regular backups are taken to secure the company's database. These procedures should ensure that several copies of the backup are rotated. This is to protect against the extremely unlikely circumstances of needing to recover from the backup tape and finding the tape unreadable. In addition, at regular, perhaps monthly, intervals, a copy of the database should be placed outside the company, perhaps in a bank or at another branch, to protect against fire damaging the computer and all its backup copies.

Section 13.2 covered all the various ways in which data can be backed up together with all the commands necessary to handle tapes and floppy disks.

14.12 Other useful commands

There are a few other commands that the System Administrator might find useful. The verb `WHO` tells you which account and which port you are logged to. `WHERE` shows which ports and which system frames are in use, and hence which function (see Appendix H) the users are located in. `COMPARE` compares two items and points out the differences.

Two other commands which may prove helpful are `LISTU` which lists the users logged into the system and the time and date they logged in and `LISTPROCS` which lists all `PROC`s associated with the account in use.

15 PICK and Application Generators

15.1 An introduction to application generators

The PICK operating system encourages the development of application generators more than any other operating system. The reason for this is probably obvious – the superb and efficient, integrated variable length database system. All application generators, often referred to as fourth-generation application generators, fourth-generation languages or 4GL products, require a powerful database or ISAM (Indexed Sequential Access Method) file system to be able to operate.

Since other operating systems require a database or ISAM file system to be purchased or developed, the creation of 4GL products becomes far less convenient. Either complex and expensive data handling facilities need to be developed before a 4GL product can be produced or a database has to be purchased. In both cases, but particularly in the latter, there is then a question over the portability of the software to other hardware and hence the potential revenue. Additionally, where a third-party database is concerned the price of the total development package can become expensive. At least with the PICK operating system the database is consistent on all implementations and included with each PICK system.

Having explained why PICK attracts 4GL products more than any other operating system, we should define what is meant by fourth-generation languages. A fourth-generation language is merely a development aid, but a development aid that permits people, generally without any data processing experience, to develop computer application systems. Dependent on the features of individual 4GL products, these could develop merely skeletal systems requiring considerable work to complete or entire systems without the need for any further development or programming.

The computing industry has come a long way since the early fifties when highly skilled specialists programmed huge electronic-valve-based computers in machine code, a language of noughts and ones. In the late fifties electronic valves were replaced by transistors and then in the late sixties by ultra-miniaturized circuits which today have been replaced with VSLI (Very Large Scale Integration), usually containing over 10 000 circuits on a chip.

Developments in software have been just as impressive as those in hardware. Machine code languages were replaced with second-generation assembler languages, to be followed by the third generation of high-level languages like Pascal, COBOL and FORTRAN. In recent years, 4GL products have grown in number, acceptance and use.

Historically, computer users have suffered from being at the mercy of data processing specialists; data processing specialists who speak a technical language of their own, who are unable to understand a problem sufficiently to develop a system exactly as the user required, whose developments are rigid and always behind schedule and who are either unkeen or unable to change an existing development without the user incurring significant delay and/or significant cost.

It is hardly surprising, therefore, that users have pressed for development aids. These originally came in the form of report generators and developed in sophistication to include simple data entry facilities. At the same time programmer aids were also developed to speed up the production of working lines of program code. Finally, with the introduction of databases and, in particular, with the increasing use of the PICK operating system, has come the age of fourth-generation application generators.

Whilst 4GL products enable non-experienced users to develop application software, invariably there will be a small amount of 'programming' required where sophisticated, multi-file, transaction processing systems are developed. Whilst these tools have gone a long way to placing the power of the computer in the hands of the user, there is a misconception that they can produce miracles. Regardless of how clever the application generator, users still have to understand their applications sufficiently to define them in terms of 'files' and 'data relationships'. In other words, these 4GL products are no different from the earliest software development languages in that they still require systems to be 'designed' – something that not everyone is capable of doing. If you know what you want from a system, these tools enable you to develop it, simply, easily and in a fraction of the time taken using conventional third-generation programming languages. If you don't know what you want or you have not analysed the problem properly, then your application will still be a failure, but by using a 4GL product you will know about it sooner!

15.2 How the PICK 4GL products work

Whilst each generator has its own idiosyncrasies, all start off by providing a simple means of creating files and building dictionaries. These facilities, as with its others, are generally hidden behind a series of menus and question and answer proformas which ultimately produce a working application. The additional facilities these products offer include producing data entry screens, creating reports, building menus, defining multifile updating procedures, and producing system documentation and operating manuals.

There are, primarily, two types of generator: those that generate parameters from the user's responses and those that generate program code.

Those that generate parameters enable systems to be developed extremely quickly, since the users' responses are converted into a series of parameters which are interpreted immediately at runtime. The advantage of this type of generator is the speed at which systems can be developed and subsequently modified, enabling and encouraging the prototyping of systems. Once a change has been made to the parameters, the change can be tested immediately, without the need to generate and compile source code. The main disadvantage of this method is that the developed application is generally slower in operation than a compiled program, a degradation in response which is noticeable most when in use by a large number of users. Examples of such products are: *ALL*, *APPGEN*, *LIBRA*, *SYSTEM BUILDER*, *UPDATE* and *X-Y-Z (3D)*.

In contrast, a system that generates source code will be faster in operation but, since source code must be generated and compiled for *every* change, however minor, development is much longer. In addition this type of approach tends to discourage prototyping and specifically discourages minor modifications. Further to cope with the enormous variety of possible application requirements, source code generators tend to produce voluminous code, making them less efficient and requiring more disk storage than specifically written programs. Examples of such products are: *CREATOR*, *GHOSTWRITER*, *G/CODE*, *SYSTEM BUILDER*, *TPS*, *WIZARD II*.

The product the author is most familiar with is *System Builder*, which is marketed by a Swiss company, Atech System Builder, and was originally released on the Pertec system on which the Aston Technology Crystal product range was originally based. System Builder is unusual in that it offers both interpretive and source code generation options, and is now available on most PICK systems, including the IBM PC-XT and IBM PC-AT. Whilst I am not trying to promote System Builder above other 4GL products, it is an outstanding product and I am familiar with it, and for that reason I am using it here as a basis for demonstrating the typical facilities offered by this type of product.

The first part of any application generator is the main menu, which lists the available tools for developing a system. From this menu lead other menus and finally proforma screens for developing the application, a hierarchical structure which is depicted in Figure 15.1.

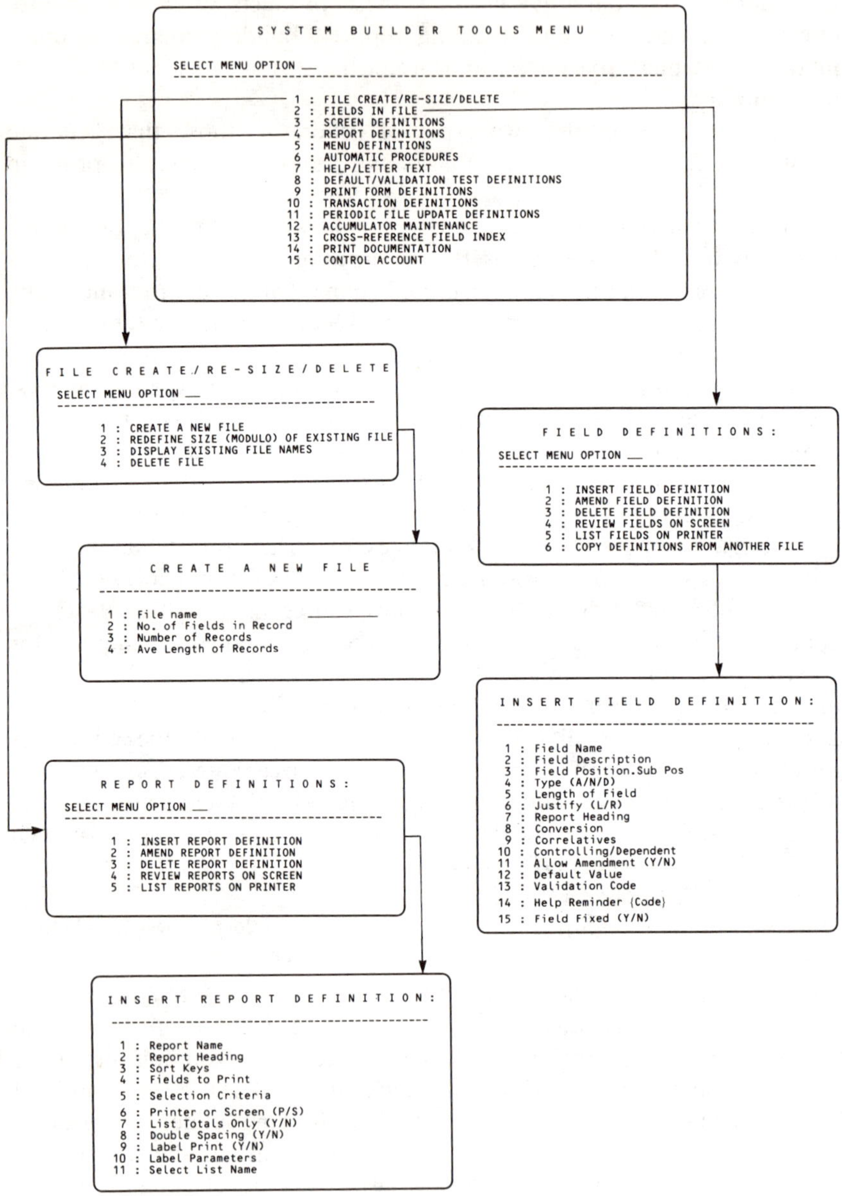

Figure 15.1 Some of the menus within System Builder.

Figure 15.1 shows what is behind three of the menu options, but all of them have further menus and ultimately proforma screens. If we examine the final proforma screens we can see that System Builder provides a user interface to the PICK operating system. Figure 15.2 examines the first menu option in more detail, showing the results of creating a file. As may be apparent, System Builder calculates the modulo size of both the dictionary and data portions of the file from the answers given by the developer, which it then passes to the `CREATE-FILE` command. This results in the file being created and the standard PICK messages being displayed, after which control is returned to System Builder and the application developer.

If we consider the way in which fields (attributes) are defined, using System Builder, again it will be apparent that it is a user front end to building dictionaries, which otherwise would have to be created using the

```
                         FILE CREATE/RESIZE/DELETE

SELECT MENU OPTION .....
-----------------------------------------------------------------------

          1 :  CREATE A NEW FILE
          2 :  REDEFINE SIZE (MODULO) OF EXISTING FILE
          3 :  DISPLAY EXISTING FILE NAMES
          4 :  DELETE FILE
```

Performs a `CREATE-FILE` command based on responses given in the next screen in the hierarchy

```
                    C R E A T E   A   N E W   F I L E

ENTER FIELD NO TO AMEND (0=OK) 0.
------------------------------------------------

1:  File Name                STAFF .......
2:  No of fields in Record   24.
3:  Number of Records        130 ...
4:  Ave length of Records    160 ..

                              SYSTEM NOW

                          CREATING FILE STAFF

[417] File 'STAFF' created; based = 3980,modulo = 5,separ = 1

[417] File 'STAFF' created; base = 3985,modulo = 47,separ = 1
```

Figure 15.2 Creating a file using a 4GL product.

editor. Whilst in normal use each dictionary item contains ten attributes, System Builder extends each item using up to 20 attributes, to offer additional features to the user. This enhancement to the dictionaries is specifically for System Builder, and in no way affects the PICK operating system. Hence ACCESS, the editor or any other PICK function will work equally well on a System Builder file as on a file created using standard PICK utilities.

Figure 15.3 examines the final proforma screen for creating a dictionary item, showing its relationship to the standard dictionary definition and how this has been enhanced.

Figure 15.3 shows how a dictionary item is created using System Builder. All attributes except attribute 1, the attribute definition attribute which System Builder automatically fills in, are able to be defined from the answers to the proforma screen presented. In addition System Builder enables the application developer to have different text to describe an item on the screen to that used in the heading on a report. This is achieved by requesting a field description (line 2) and a report heading (line 7). It allows the developer to define a default value to be displayed (line 12); it permits extensive validation to be carried out by use of a series of validation codes (line 13 – the `M:` used in Figure 15.3 means the field is mandatory, so that a record cannot be created without some positive entry being made in this field); and it also enables the developer to define help messages to be displayed, on request, to an inexperienced user (line 14). All of these additional features are aimed at enabling a person who knows what he wants from a computer system to be able to develop it without having to resort to programming.

In a similar way to creating files and building dictionaries, System Builder allows data capture and enquiry screens to be produced. System Builder produces a proforma screen, in this case a blank screen, onto which the defined fields and any headings and text are 'painted'. This simple process enables the screen to be used for the full file maintenance functionality of creating, amending and deleting of records. This development, which takes a matter of a few minutes, is an exercise that could readily take upwards of half a day using conventional methods!

The production of reports results from the responses to the report definition screen, and provides a front end to the ACCESS processor. This is illustrated in Figure 15.4, which shows how System Builder would be used to produce the report shown in Figure 10.43, which required quite a detailed understanding of ACCESS. Again you will notice that System Builder asks the developer questions in terms that a non-DP professional or non-PICK expert would understand.

Once familiarity has been gained with these 'foundation' tools, which enable simple systems to be built to handle file maintenance, enquiry and reports, System Builder enables the developer to advance into sophisticated multi-file transactional processing systems, all built in the same question and

```
                 F I E L D   D E F I N I T I O N S :   S T A F F

SELECT MENU OPTION .....
--------------------------------------------------------------------------------

          1 :  INSERT FIELD DEFINITION
          2 :  AMEND FIELD DEFINITION
          3 :  DELETE FIELD DEFINITION
          4 :  REVIEW FIELDS ON SCREEN
          5 :  LIST FIELDS ON PRINTER
          6 :  COPY DEFINITIONS FROM ANOTHER FILE
```

Creates an item in the DICT (dictionary) portion of the file STAFF based on responses provided in the next screen in the menu hierarchy

```
I N S E R T   F I E L D   D E F I N I T I O N   :   S T A F F
                                           Standard dictionary
ENTER FIELD NO TO AMEND (0=OK) 0           attribute positions
-------------------------------------------

 1:  Field Name              FNAME          ← item-id
 2:  Field Description       First name and initials
 3:  Field Position.Sub Pos  1              ← attr  2
 4:  Type (A/N/D)            A
 5:  Length of field         20             ← attr 10
 6:  Justify (L/R)           L              ← attr  9
 7:  Report Heading          First Name     ← attr  3
 8:  Conversion                             ← attr  7
 9:  Correlatives            G1,1           ← attr  8
10:  Controlling/Dependent                  ← attr  4
11:  Allow Amendment (Y/N)   Y
12:  Default Value
13:  Validation Code         M:
14:  Help Reminder {Code}    At least one christian name
is required
15:  Field Fixed (Y/N)       Y
```

Figure 15.3 Building a dictionary with a 4GL product.

answer fashion. Transactional systems are those which take in one set of data and use it to update several files. For example, the information on an invoice would be used to maintain information on the customer file, the salesman file (for commission calculations), the sales analysis file and so on.

As you can see, therefore, 4GL products are extremely valuable

```
               R E P O R T   D E F I N I T I O N S   :   S T A F F

SELECT MENU OPTION .....
----------------------------------------------------------

           1 :  INSERT REPORT DEFINITION
           2 :  AMEND REPORT DEFINITION
           3 :  DELETE REPORT DEFINITION
           4 :  REVIEW REPORTS ON SCREEN
           5 :  LIST REPORTS ON PRINTER
```

Builds a file of standard reports which are produced using the ACCESS processor

```
I N S E R T   R E P O R T   D E F I N I T I O N   :   S T A F F

ENTER FIELD NO TO AMEND (0=OK) 0.
------------------------------------

 1:  Report Name              STAFFREPT1
 2:  Report Heading           PERSONNEL REPORT
 3:  Sort Keys                DEPT NAME
 4:  Fields to Print          KEY DEPT(B) DEPTDESC NAME
                              SALARY(T)
 5:  Selection criteria       DEPT > "?"
 6:  Printer or Screen (P/S)  S
 7:  List Totals Only (Y/N)   N
 8:  Double Spacing (Y/N)     N
 9:  Label Print (Y/N)        N
10:  Label Parameters
11:  Select List Name
12:  Preferred Heading
13:  Footing                  'LL' CONFIDENTIAL
```

Figure 15.4 Defining a report using a 4GL product.

development aids, which when used in conjunction with the PICK operating system generate flexible systems, capable of being developed and modified even when 'live'. In addition they give a useful introduction to the PICK operating system for those who come to use it, since many of its features have been 'incorporated' in a user-oriented shell.

15.3 The case for fourth-generation languages

15.3.1 Advantages of fourth-generation languages

- Applications can be developed very quickly, in fractions of the time taken with traditional programming methods. Using an application generator, typically what takes 1–2 days to develop using conventional programming will take less than an hour.
- Customizing or changing the application is very easy. This is for two reasons. Firstly, the PICK database system, being dictionary-driven, enables systems to be modified even when 'live'. This is because a simple change to the dictionary definition item, even to the key of the file, is instantly reflected throughout the system. Secondly, because 4GL products themselves have been designed to handle such changes, this occurs speedily and easily. These facilities, coupled with the speed of initial development, encourage prototyping. This gives greater credibility to the application, enables earlier discussion on user requirements and shows up problems and potential problems far quicker.
- Maintenance of the application is substantially easier. This is because either the source code generated is written to a common format, or there is no source code to maintain at all!
- The completed application works reliably, immediately it has been developed. There is no time wasted in 'debugging' programs.
- Applications can be developed by inexperienced non-data processing professionals, with a minimum of programming effort.
- Application generators are easy to learn and easy to use which means that development staff need less training and are more productive than those using conventional programming languages.
- Application generators provide a useful introduction to the PICK operating system, by incorporating many of its features in a user-oriented shell.

15.3.2 Disadvantages of fourth-generation languages

- Application generators are rarely able to develop an entire application, leaving a small, and often minute, part of the system to be programmed in BASIC.
- Application generators will not improve the design and workings of an application. A poorly designed system will remain a poor system in operation.
- The completed application may run less efficiently and/or utilize

greater disk space than customized programs.

- Some application generators are not portable between hardware suppliers.
- Multi-user use of the software may degrade response.
- There is a learning curve required with any 4GL product, regardless of however easy it is supposed to be.

15.4 Summary

None of the above drawbacks outweigh the advantages of using 4GL products. Conventional programming methods are now seen to be outdated, and users are pressing for 4GL tools, to develop their own applications and reduce their reliance on data processing professionals.

Whilst application generators do not solve every problem, they are well suited to most commercial applications. In addition they provide users with a simple and easy method of developing speedily and with the minimum of programming by non-DP specialists.

16 PICK on the IBM PC and Compatibles

TCL verbs and general commands covered in this chapter

COLOR	COPYDOS	COPYPICK	FDISK	FORMAT
FFORMAT	MONO	PRINT	POWER-OFF	REBOOT
SET-BAUD	SET-DATE-EUR	SET-DATE-STD	SET-FLOPPY	SET-FUNC
SET-KBRD	SET-SCT	T-STATUS		

16.1 An Introduction to PC PICK

The implementation of PICK for the IBM PC is significant for a number of reasons:

1. It is the first implementation to be sold directly by PICK Systems.
2. It enables the product to be made more widely available and hence increases market awareness.
3. It is one of the few operating systems that makes the PC multi-user.

The implementation for the PC is the full PICK operating system and includes all the facilities described in this book, such as ACCESS, TCL, BASIC, Editor and so on. The entire system, originally only available for large systems, can now operate on a personal computer, in a multi-user environment with as little as a 10 Mbytes Winchester disk and 256 Kbytes of RAM. On the original IBM PC-XT a total of three users are supported whilst on the later IBM PC-XT286 there are three versions of PICK, for 1–3 users, for 1–6 users and for 1–10 users, with prices for the entire operating system starting at around £495, little more than the price of a single-user database manager! The PC-AT also supports these three versions.

The PICK operating system co-resides on the fixed disk with up to three other operating systems. The disk is effectively partitioned into sections with each operating system resident on the disk, each with its own area of contiguous disk space. The operating system to be used is marked 'active' by the FDISK command, under either DOS or PICK and then the 'active' operating system invoked by rebooting the machine. Take note that PICK will not operate with less than 300 tracks or 15 cylinders of contiguous space. The amount of free space available can be checked with FDISK under DOS.

As soon as the IBM PC product was released in 1984, PICK Systems was faced with the difficult problem of support for PC compatibles and quite rightly explained that their product was developed and hence supported on the IBM PC. For that reason and in view of the myriad of compatibles, so-called compatibles and add-on cards and disks, PICK Systems gave the warning *caveat emptor* – let the buyer beware! It adopted the view, and quite rightly so, that providing the product was truly compatible, the operating system *should* work. They did, however, test the operating system on a number of alternative systems and have collated information from around the world on successes and failures. This never-ending task is continually documented and the results published regularly for PICK dealers.

With hard disks the compatibility issue is simpler. In essence PICK expects to communicate via an IBM or compatible hard disk controller. With that proviso, therefore, it is also possible to attach a variety of disks of either the same or different sizes.

16.2 PC-specific software features

There are a number of new software options developed for the PC. Firstly, since the standard IBM monitor differs from standard asynchronous terminals attached to RS232 ports, in that it is a memory-mapped monitor, a special terminal device driver has been written and added to the list of term types. The term type for the memory mapped monitors is 'I'.

16.2.1 COLOR and MONO verbs

Two new verbs, COLOR (spelt the American way) and MONO are available to support the two types of IBM monitor. The general format of these commands is as shown in Figure 16.1, whilst examples of their use are given in Figure 16.2.

16.2.2 The PRINT @ functions

New functions have been added to the "PRINT @" statement in BASIC and the "T" command in PROC to support memory-mapped monitors. These statements can set foreground and background colours in the same way as

```
COLOR {foreground colour}{,background colour}{switches}
```

where supported colours are:

BLACK
BLUE
GREEN
CYAN
RED
MAGENTA
BROWN
WHITE

and supported switches are:

/B or /BLINK	Set character blinking
/NB or /NOBLINK	Cancel character blinking
/F or /FULL	Set foreground in full intensity
/H or /HALF	Set foreground in half intensity
/R or /REVERSE	Set reverse video
/NR or /NOREVERSE	Cancel reverse video

```
MONO {switches}
```

where supported switches are as above with the following additions:

/U or /UNDERLINE	Set underlining
/NU or /NOUNDERLINE	Cancel underlining

Figure 16.1 The COLOR and MONO verbs.

COLOR RED	Set foreground colour to red
COLOR,GREEN	Set background colour to green
COLOR BLUE,WHITE	Set foreground colour to blue, and the background white
COLOUR BLUE,WHITE/R/H	Set foreground colour to blue, the background colour to white, activate reverse video and set the foreground colour in half intensity
MONO /U/B	Set screen to monochrome, and activate underlining and blinking

Figure 16.2 Examples of the COLOR and MONO verbs.

defined by a `COLOR` statement using the negative integer concept. Section 10.4.3 explains the concept and this has been extended for the PC implementation as follows:

−1 to −10	As shown in Section 10.4.3
−11 to −16	As shown in Section 10.4.3
−17 to −32	Reserved for future use

For the IBM PC implementation:

−33 to −40	Define background colours
	−33 White
	−34 Brown
	−35 Magenta
	−36 Red
	−37 Cyan
	−38 Green
	−39 Blue
	−40 Black
−41 to −48	Define full-intensity foreground colours
	−41 White
	−42 Brown
	−43 Magenta
	−44 Red
	−45 Cyan
	−46 Green
	−47 Blue
	−48 Black
−49 to −56	Reserved for future use
−57 to −64	Define half intensity foreground colours
	−57 White
	−58 Brown
	−59 Magenta
	−60 Red
	−61 Cyan
	−62 Green
	−63 Blue
	−64 Black
−65 to −88	Reserved for future use
−89 to −96	Define IBM memory-mapped monitor modes
	−89 Monochrome
	−93 Colour 80 × 25
	−94 Black and White 80 × 25
−97 to −127	Reserved for future use

Hence the following PROC activates the colour/graphics mode and sets the foreground in blue and the background in white:

```
PQ
T(-93),(-47),(-33)
```

In BASIC the statement would be:

```
PRINT @(-93):@(-47):@(-33)
```

There is a program in the SYSPROG-PL file within the SYSPROG account called DEMO which demonstrates the extended support provided for the memory-mapped monitors. It is worth bearing in mind that these functions only work for the memory-mapped monitors and will not function on standard asynchronous terminals linked to the PC in multi-user mode.

16.2.3 Defining the keyboard functions

There are a couple of commands which enable keyboard functions to be redefined. These are SET-KBRD which defines the keyboard in use on line 0 and SET-FUNC which enables the function keys to be redefined. The system boots up using a USA keyboard and without the function keys defined.

Defining your keyboard character set

There are a number of standard keyboard layouts already defined, these being:

```
BRITISH
FRENCH
GERMAN
ITALIAN
SPANISH
USA
```

One of the above keyboard definitions can be invoked by the command SET-KBRD KEYBOARDS name where name is one from the above list held as an item in the file KEYBOARDS to be found in the SYSPROG account. Hence SET-KBRD KEYBOARDS BRITISH would invoke the English keyboard definition.

Other keyboard definition items can be set up and added to the file KEYBOARDS. The specific keys which can be redefined are:

Row 1 ESC across to backspace
Row 2 Tab across to carriage return
Row 3 A across to hyphen
Row 4 Backslash across to slash

Simple keyboard definitions redefine the keyboard on a one-to-one basis in that each keystroke results in a specific user-defined character being displayed on the screen. The following is the content of the item BRITISH in the file KEYBOARDS:

```
*
* Define BRITISH keyboard
*
* Reminder: FF or 00 means ignore this keystroke
*
1B21229C24255E262A28295F2B08        UPPER CASE, ROW 1
0051574552545955494F507B7D0D        UPPER CASE, ROW 2
FF415344464748A4B4C3A407E           UPPER CASE, ROW 3
FF7C5A584356424E4D3C3E3FFF00FF20FF  UPPER CASE, ROW 4
*
1B3132333435363738393O2D3D08        LOWER CASE, ROW 1
097177657274797569 6F705B5D0D       LOWER CASE, ROW 2
FF6173646667686A6B6C3B2723          LOWER CASE, ROW 3
FF5C7A786376626E6D2C2E2FFF2AFF20FF  LOWER CASE, ROW 4
*
1BFF00FFFFFF1EFFFFFFFF1FFF7F        CONTROL KEYS, ROW 1
FF11170512141915090F101B1D0A        CONTROL KEYS, ROW 2
FF011304060708 0A0B0CFFFFFF         CONTROL KEYS, ROW 3
FF1C1A180316020E0DFFFFFFFFFFFF20FF  CONTROL KEYS, ROW 4
```

Whilst this may look a little overpowering it can be simply understood using the following rules:

1. Any line (attribute) starting with * is a comment line.
2. Any line not starting with an * is a data line and all data up to the first space encountered will be used. The rest of the line is ignored and therefore can be used to contain comments.
3. The data must consist of *exactly* 174 key definitions grouped into three groups of 58 characters each.
4. Each group is divided into four lines and represents a keyboard row.
5. Each character definition is composed of two ASCII hexadecimal characters (see Appendix G).
6. A definition of FF or 00 means that nothing is displayed when the key is pressed.
7. Key definitions 01 to 1F will display unusual looking characters, such as happy faces, hearts and diamonds.

When setting up your own keyboard definition item remember the following:

1. Definitions are in *hexadecimal* not *decimal*. Appendix G contains a full list of hex characters.
2. Set them up carefully and ensure there are exactly 174 character definitions.
3. It is probably easiest to copy an existing definition and modify it,

rather than start from scratch.

4. Use comments freely – they may be very useful later on!

Redefining function keys

Whilst you are unlikely to need to redefine the keyboard character set, you may want to define the function keys. This is only permissible for the keyboard attached to line 0, i.e. the PC keyboard, and each function key can only be assigned a single character.

The function keys are set by use of the command SET-FUNC FUNCKEYS name where name is an item in the file FUNCKEYS which is held in the SYSPROG account. The rules are very similar to those in setting up a keyboard:

1. Any line (attribute) starting with '*' is a comment line.
2. Any line not starting with an '*' is a data line and all data up to the first space encountered will be used. The rest of the line is ignored and therefore can be used to contain comments.
3. The data must consist of *exactly* 40 key definitions grouped into four lines of 10 characters each.
4. Each character definition is composed of two ASCII hexadecimal characters (see Appendix G).
5. A definition of FF or 00 means that nothing is displayed when the key is pressed.
6. Key definitions 01 to 1F will display unusual looking characters, such as happy faces, hearts and diamonds.

The following is the content of the item TEST in the file FUNCKEYS which assigns the letters of the alphabet in upper case to the function keys, and after the first 26 characters have been defined, the remaining 14 are assigned the value of the first 14 characters of the alphabet in lower case:

```
001 *
002 * Setting up function key values
003 *
004 *1 2 3 4 5 6 7 8 9 0
005 4142434445464748494A        Function key
006 4B4C4D4E4F5051525354        Function key + SHIFT
007 55565758595A61626364        Function key + CTRL
008 65666768696A6B6C6D6E        Function key + ALT
```

16.2.4 Setting baud rates

Baud rates can only be set for any additional terminals attached to the system on lines 1 and/or 2. The baud rate for line 0 (the memory-mapped monitor) is always 9600. To set the baud rate follow the instructions given in Section 14.5.

16.2.5 Use of storage media

The `FFORMAT` verb is used to format floppy diskettes on the PC-XT whilst `FORMAT` is used on the PC-AT. Newly purchased floppy disks must be formatted before they can be used on the PC. Once they have been formatted under PICK they can be reused time and time again without reformatting.

The disk format under PICK is not the same as that under DOS, hence the diskettes are not interchangeable. On the PC-XT disks are formatted in standard density in drive A. On the PC-AT, however, disks can optionally be in high density and can be formatted in drive B and options can be applied to the `SET-FLOPPY` command to denote this:

`H` – high density (1.2M)
`S` – standard density (320K)
`A` – drive A
`B` – drive B

Hence `SET-FLOPPY (SB` followed by the format command will format a diskette in drive B to standard format. The default setting for drive A is high density and if standard density diskettes are used, the commands which address the diskette will appear to work initially and will then give parity errors. If you are getting parity errors whilst using floppy disks on the PC-AT, check the current settings for the drive are correct. These are given by the command `T-STATUS`.

The commands to switch between using floppy disk and $\frac{1}{4}$-inch tape are:

```
SET-SCT
SET-FLOPPY
```

Only certain tape drives are supported by PICK, so take care when purchasing your system. The present versions support the Colorado Memory Systems and the Techmar QIC-60 tape drives. Although the hardware is manufactured by Wangtek, the controller firmware was written by Colorado Memory Systems.

16.2.6 Setting the date format

There are two date formats that are supported, European and non-European. To set the date to European format (DD/MM/YY) use the command `SET-DATE-EUR`; for the non-European format (MM/DD/YY) use the command `SET-DATE-STD`.

16.2.7 Moving data between PICK and DOS

There are two verbs for transferring data between the two operating environments, PICK and DOS – COPYDOS which transfers data from a DOS partition to PICK and COPYPICK which performs the operation in reverse, i.e. from PICK to DOS.

Transferring data from PICK to DOS

The COPYPICK utility allows data in the PICK database to be transferred into the DOS partition. Since the transfer is performed from the DOS partition, a separate DOS diskette is required (available from the distributors of PICK for the PC). It comprises two utilities, BRIDGE-EXE and BASRUN.EXE, which are copied to the hard disk with the command COPY A:*.* C:.

The use of the command, run from DOS, is shown in Figure 16.3.

```
C>COPYPICK[CR]

Enter PICK account name: OFFICE[CR]
Enter PICK filename (or dict,dataname): CUSTOMER[CR]
Enter PICK item name or <cr> for all: [CR]
Enter DOS receive filename: CUST[CR]

45 item(s) 488 records/attributes

Enter PICK account name: [CR]

c>
```

Figure 16.3 An example of the COPYPICK command.

Since each of PICK's attribute marks (hexadecimal FE) are replaced with line feeds (hexadecimal 0A), it effectively means that each PICK attribute becomes a DOS record.

Transferring data from DOS to PICK

The COPYDOS verb transfers data from a DOS file into the PICK environment. The general format of the command is given in Figure 16.4 and an example of the use of COPYDOS in Figure 16.5.

The general rules applied are as follows:

1. If neither S nor R is specified, then S (sequential) is assumed.
2. If neither the F nor T option is specified, the DOS hex string 0A (line feed) is converted to hex FE (attribute mark), meaning that each DOS line becomes a PICK attribute.

```
COPYDOS DOSpathname {(options)}
TO:(filename {itemname}    ← the ( after TO: is displayed by PICK and not
                             input by the user
```

where options are:

- F To enable specific strings to be flagged
- M To split data transferred into a number of items
- O Overwrite existing PICK item if already present
- R DOS data is in random file mode
- S DOS data is in sequential file mode
- T To translate certain characters transferred into others

The syntax for the DOS pathname is:

```
drive:\subdirectory\subdirectory\DOSfilename
drive:\DOSfilename
```

Figure 16.4 General format of the COPYDOS command.

3. If the DOS file is too large to fit into a PICK item and the M option has not been specified, the data will be split across several items each numbered sequentially: itemname1, itemname2, itemname3 and so on.
4. No item is created with the name given in the command line. A number is always appended to the item name.

The M option enables the item size to be regulated. If the option is specified a secondary prompt will be given:

```
ENTER LENGTH OF RECORD (OR Dn):
```

The response can either be a number, to indicate the number of bytes in length to make each PICK item, or a D followed by a number, indicating the number of PICK attributes there should be in each PICK item. Using the Dn option will cause PICK to translate linefeeds as attribute marks.

All items created are given an item-id, equal to the item name given in response to the TO:(prompt, concatenated with the next in the sequence of numbers starting at 0, i.e. itemname0, itemname1, itemname2 and so on. No item is created using just the item name alone.

If the T option is chosen up to 16 different hex bytes can be translated. The system will respond alternately with REPLACE: and WITH: until a carriage return is given to a REPLACE: prompt after which an OKAY(Y/N): is offered so that the translate specifications can be re-entered if an error has been made.

The F option enables up to 16 different hex bytes to be flagged by placing the hex string '00' in front of them. If the F option is taken, following the response to the TO:(prompt, the system will display **REPLACE:** and await a response. After entering the hex character to translate or pass, the system displays **WITH FLAGGED:**. Upon entry of the same character or a replacing one, the system will prompt for up to a further 15 times to flag.

```
>COPYDOS C:\DIR1\DIR2\CUSTOMER (SMT[CR]
TO: (CUSTOMER ADDRESS[CR]

ENTER LENGTH OF RECORD (OR Dn): D6[CR]

     REPLACE: 0D[CR]          WITH: FE[CR]
     REPLACE: 0A[CR]          WITH: FD[CR]
     REPLACE: 2C[CR]          WITH: 2A[CR]
     REPLACE: [CR]

OKAY (Y/N): Y[CR]
                 READING DIRECTORY
                        DIR1
                        DIR2
                        CUSTOMER
                 WRITING ITEM
                        ADDRESS0
                        ADDRESS1
                        ADDRESS2
                          ...
                          ...
                        ADDRESS76
                 END OF FILE
```

Figure 16.5 Using the COPYDOS command.

16.2.8 Powering off and rebooting

The PC implementation has a special verb, POWER-OFF which should be used before the system is closed down. This disables all users, causes the memory buffers to be flushed to disk and halts the system. From this state the system can be switched off or rebooted using the CTRL/ALT/DEL keys – all being depressed at the same time.

The system can be rebooted from the TCL prompt by the command REBOOT but only from line 0. This is useful where the active partition has been altered using FDISK and you now wish to return to a non-PICK operating system.

16.3 Making PICK run on a compatible

In view of the demand for PICK to run on a wide variety of compatibles, Pick Systems released a version of the operating system for the PC-XT which enabled the software to be 'customized' in the knowledge that it would suit most requirements. Note this may not work with all controllers and/or all compatibles.

The installation menu provides for customization through the option 99, allowing new drives and systems to be tested out. The following information for handling such an operation is as supplied by PICK Systems and is published courtesy of PICK Systems:

1. Boot DOS.
2. Run the DOS program, DEBUG.
3. DEBUG will respond with a – prompt.
4. At the prompt enter:

   ```
   -D 0:0104
   ```

   DEBUG will dump some hexadecimal output to the screen similar to:

   ```
   0000:0104    08 04 00 C8 00 00 00 00 00 00 00 00
   0000:0110    00 00 00 00 00   and so on.
   ```

6. We are interested in the first line of output that follows the 0000:0104. Write down the next eight digits displayed. In the example above, this would be 080400C8.
7. For the next step we need to rearrange the data. If the eight digits written down are represented by 12345678 then they must be re-arranged in the form 78563412. In the above example this would be C8000408. This data, C800 and 0408 is a vector, or pointer, to the information describing the system's hard disk to DOS.
8. Using the rearranged data (all of the following steps will refer to the above example) enter at the DEBUG prompt:

   ```
   -D C800:0408   [CR]
   ```

9. DEBUG will once again display some hexadecimal output which will look similar, but not identical to the following:

   ```
   C800:0408   32 01 04 00 00 32 01 0B
   C800:0410   17 0C B4 28 00 00 00 00-E1 01 08 00 00 00 01 00
   C800:0420   17 20 FF 40 00 00 00 00-32 01 04 32 01 00 00 0B
   C800:0430   07 0C B4 28 00 00 00 00-64 02 02 00 00 64 02 0B
   C800:0440   07 10 D4 38 00 00 00 00-   and so on.
   ```

   The data we've just dumped is the data describing the hard disk to DOS. It is still in machine-readable hexadecimal form so we'll have to do some manipulating to get it into a form that is easily understandable and usable.

10. Ignore the data on the left hand side, which is in the form XXXX:YYY. It is the address data and doesn't concern us. What we want to do is to write down the first 128 hexadecimal digits. In our example, we would begin writing with the data on the first line where it says 320104.., but, *before* you begin writing, read on because we want to write them down in a special way.
11. Get a piece of paper and down the left side number:

    1.
    2.
    3.
    4.

    On line one neatly write down the first 32 digits from the hexadecimal display. Then go to line 2 of your paper and write down the next 32 digits and continue until all 128 are recorded. Your paper should look like:

    1. 32 01 04 00 00 32 01 0B 17 0C B4 28 00 00 00 00
    2. E101 08 00 00 00 01 0B 17 0C B4 28 00 00 00 00
    3. 32 01 04 32 01 00 00 0B 07 0C B4 28 00 00 00 00
    4. 64 02 02 00 00 64 02 0B 07 10 D4 38 00 00 00 00

12. At the debug prompt enter the following:

    ```
    -I 322 [CR]
    ```

13. Two hexadecimal digits will be displayed. The right digit is the one we're interested in. Based on what the right digit is, we are going to select one of the four lines on your paper as our line and we will cross out the others:

Right digit was	*Line to select*
0 or 4 or 8 or C	1
1 or 5 or 9 or D	2
2 or 6 or A or E	3
3 or 7 or B or F	4

14. Now that we have isolated our data down to one of the four lines on our paper, get a second sheet of paper and set it out as follows:

	Hex	*Rev*	*Dec*
Cylinders			
Heads			
Write current			
Starting precomp			

15. Using the chosen line (the one not crossed out), copy the following information under the heading 'Hex':

    – the first four digits into 'Cylinders'

- the next two digits into 'Heads'
- the next four digits into 'Write current'
- the next four digits into 'Starting precomp'

Ignore the rest of the data on the line.

16. When you are done your sheet should look like this:

	Hex	*Rev*	*Dec*
Cylinders	3201		
Heads	04		
Write current	0000		
Starting precomp	3201		

17. We are going to fill in the 'Rev' column, if necessary. At this point you will need to be able to translate hexadecimal numbers into decimal numbers. (For a full list see Appendix G.)

    Translate the 'Cylinders' number to decimal. In the above example, 3201 (hex) becomes 12801 (decimal).

    Now reverse the hexadecimal form of the number. In the above example 3201 would become 0132.

    Translate the reversed number to decimal. Hence 0132 (hex) becomes 306 (decimal).

    Compare the two decimal numbers generated. If the reversed number is smaller, then you must fill in the 'Rev' column, otherwise you can skip it. In the above example, 306 (reversed) is smaller than 12801 (unreversed), so we will have to use the 'Rev' column.

    If you *are* using the 'Rev' column, proceed to step 18. If you *are not* using the 'Rev' column, proceed to step 20.

18. For 'Cylinders', 'Write current' and 'Starting precomp' copy the digits in the 'Hex' column into the 'Rev' column, reversing the pairs. For example if the 'Hex' column holds 3201, then write 0132 into the 'Rev' column.

    For 'Heads' just copy the two digits into the 'Rev' column without reversing them.

19. Translate the numbers in the 'Rev' column from hexadecimal to decimal and write the results in the 'Dec' column. Proceed to step 21.

20. Translate the numbers in the 'Hex' column from hexadecimal to decimal and write the results in the 'Dec' column.

21. At this point we have what we want. We have the hard disk parameters that DOS is using to communicate with the hard disk. Once we pass those to PICK, it should be able to use the hard disk too. In the above example, the worksheet should look like:

	Hex	*Rev*	*Dec*
Cylinders	3201	0132	0306
Heads	04	04	4
Write current	0000	0000	0000
Starting precomp	3201	0132	0306

This table tells us, for example, that our drive has 306 cylinders, 4 heads, uses 0 write current and 306 cylinders of starting precomp. It is exactly this information which will be asked for when we install PICK using option 99.

22. Let's try to install PICK using this information. Using the PICK installation instructions, follow them implicitly until the installation menu appears.
23. At this point enter **99** to select option 99.
24. The first four prompts will be for cylinders, heads, write current and starting precomp. Enter the numbers in decimal from the worksheet.

    The remaining prompts are parameters which we do not care about. Enter carriage returns for them. This will cause the system to use IBM standard defaults. These standard defaults are acceptable.
25. The system will give you the opportunity to correct any errors. Unless you've made some errors, depress the carriage return.
26. At this point PICK will attempt to install itself. If the parameters are correct *and* the system's hardware is compatible with the IBM PC-XT then the installation should succeed.

16.4 The IBM PC-AT

Whilst the above steps may seem complicated, in practice the process is relatively straightforward. For the PC-AT the way in which PICK supports non-IBM products is different. In this release PICK supports any drive conforming to one of 14 drive types. The particular drive type is made known during the **SET-UP** program run under DOS when the hard disk is installed. When PICK is installed it uses the entry set up by the diagnostic to configure itself on the hard disk. Remember the hardware disk configuration is done under DOS not PICK. The table of supported disks is as shown in Figure 16.6.

Since the IBM PC-AT is capable of supporting up to 10 users concurrently, Pick Systems has had to become involved in a number of hardware issues, the main one being that of non-IBM add-on serial cards. PICK is much more complex and powerful than DOS and exercises the hardware in fundamentally different ways, and this means that hardware which works well with DOS does not always work with PICK.

	1	2	3	4	5	6
Cylinders	306	615	615	940	940	615
Heads	4	4	6	8	6	4
Capacity (MB)	10.6	21.4	32.1	65.4	49.0	21.4

	7	8	9	10	11	12
Cylinders	462	733	900	820	855	855
Heads	8	5	15	3	5	7
Capacity (MB)	32.1	31.9	117.5	21.4	37.2	52.0

	13	14
Cylinders	306	733
Heads	8	7
Capacity (MB)	21.3	44.6

Figure 16.6 Supported disks.

In order to assist with the use of these products PICK Systems released a PICK PC-AT Installation Guide, to which the remainder of this chapter is dedicated. I am indebted to its author, Jeffrey Hunt, Director of Product Support, and to PICK Systems, for allowing me to publish it.

16.4.1 PC-AT serial I/O ports

The PICK system for the IBM PC-AT is produced in three port configurations, one supporting three users, one supporting 6 users and one supporting 10 users. The first port is always the memory-mapped monitor. Two, five, or nine serial ports are supported by each system. Each serial port can be used for either a terminal or a printer.

There are two interrupt channels allocated to serial I/O devices,

IRQ4 and IRQ3. Each of these channels accommodates one serial I/O card; a maximum of two cards may be installed. The cards may be of different types. Each card must be set for a unique interrupt channel.

The system does not need to be configured with the hardware to support the maximum number of serial ports. However, workspace will be set aside for the maximum number of users (3, 6 or 10). This allows the maximum number of ports to be added later. If the system is configured with hardware to support more than the maximum number of ports, any serial devices on the extra ports should be disconnected before PICK is booted.

The following table illustrates different configurations possible with 3-, 6- or 10-user PICK PC-AT systems.

	Users	*First card*	*Second card*
	1	Empty	Empty
3-user	2	IBM on IRQ4	Empty
	3	IBM on IRQ4	IBM on IRQ3
	5	4 Port card on IRQ4	Empty
6-user	6	IBM on IRQ4	4 Port card on IRQ3
	9	4 Port card on IRQ4	4 Port card on IRQ3
10-user		8 Port card on IRQ4	Empty
	10	IBM on IRQ4	8 Port card on IRQ3

Each serial port is set up at boot time as follows:

Baud rate = 9600 Baud
Parity = None
Stop bits = 1
Data bits = 8

The **SET-BAUD** verb is used to set serial lines to other baud rates. It can also be used to reinitialize the serial lines in case of problems. The form of the command is as follows:

```
>SET-BAUD line. no, baud.rate
```

On the PC-AT and PC-XT Ver. 2.0 systems the SETUP.SIO program (see ADDENDA file) can be used to reset parity, stop, and data bits as required. This facility is not available on previous releases.

Serial terminals

On the PC-AT, a number of different serial cards are supported. The connectors on these cards vary, as do the styles of cable supplied. For this reason, we suggest use of the following generic cables, together with a card-specific connector.

```
Female DB25                                              Male DB25
  AT side                                                CRT side
  TD 2      -------------------------------------------- > 2 RD
  RD 3  <   -------------------------------------------- > 3 TD
 GND 7  <   -------------------------------------------- > 7 GND
 CTS 5  < ---- ]                                   [ ---- > 1 GND
 DSR 6  <  ---- ]
 DTR 20    ---- ]   Jumpered on connector

          Card-specific              Generic             CRT
          connector                  cable
PC-AT     cable
  I                                                       I
  I    ]  ---------- [ ] ------------------------- [ ]    I
  I                                                       I
```

The card-specific cable should be 1–2 ft in length. The generic cables will be interchangeable throughout your system.

Configuring specific cards

The following tables define specific configurations for serial I/O cards and card-specific connector cables used with the PICK PC-AT system. Alternate configurations may work, but are unsupported by PICK.

The hexadecimal address range shown with each card represents the 8-byte contiguous range used by a UART or latch. All cards use either the INS8250 or the NS16450 UART.

All I/O addresses must not conflict with the addresses of any other hardware installed.

Throughout this *Installation Guide* hexadecimal references are in the form X nnnn.

IBM serial/parallel adaptor

The IBM serial/parallel cards are configured by orienting the jumper block at J1.

```
                         IRQ4                    IRQ3
                     ------------            ------------
UART address            X'3F8'        or        X'2FB'

                         - -                     ----
Jumper orientation       - -                     ----
                         ----                    - -
                         ----                    - -
```

The serial port on the IBM Serial/Parallel card requires a male DB09 connector. In order to maintain configuration flexibility, the following adaptor cable is suggested.

Female DB09 *IBM card*		*Male DB25* *CRT side*
RD 2 ‹	--------------------------	2 TD
TD 3	-------------------------- ›	3 RD
CTS 8 ‹	--------------------------	5 CTS
GND 5 ‹	-------------------------- ›	7 GND
DSR 6 ‹	--------------------------	6 DSR
DTR 4	-------------------------- ›	20 DTR

Both the ALR challenger and Basic Time AT4×4 are multi-function cards which can be configured to emulate the IBM serial/parallel adaptor. The AST four-port /AT asynch card can also be configured to address a pair of IBM-compatible serial ports. Although these configurations are known to work, they will not be discussed here and are unsupported.

AST four-port /AT card

AST Research is located in Irvine, Ca. The AST four-port /AT asynch card is supported in the 'non-compatible' mode. The card is configured by DIP switch S1. S1-1 sets the mode, S1-8 sets the address range. The others set the interrupt level. DIP switches should be set as follows: 0 indicates ON, 1 indicates OFF.

	IRQ4	IRQ3
Address range	X'2A0'-'X 2B8	X'1A065-X'1B8'
	12345678	12345678
DIP switch S1	11101110	11011111

The following adaptor cable is suggested for use with the AST four-port AT card. This adaptor cable allows interchanging of any serial terminal cable and/or custom serial printer cable.

Male DB37 *AST card*		*4 male DB25* *CRT side*
	Channel 1	
RD 37 ‹	--------------------------	2 TD
TD 19	-------------------------- ›	3 RD
CTS 36 ‹	--------------------------	5 CTS
DSR 17 ‹	--------------------------	6 DSR
GND 35 ‹	-------------------------- ›	7 GND
DTR 16	-------------------------- ›	20 DTR
	Channel 2	
RD 14 ‹	--------------------------	2 TD
TD 33	-------------------------- ›	2 TD
CTS 13 ‹	--------------------------	5 CTS

```
 DSR 31 ‹ --------------------------    6 DSR
 GND 12 ‹ -------------------------- ›  7 GND
 DTR 30   -------------------------- › 20 DTR
                  Channel 3
  RD 28 ‹ --------------------------    2 TD
  TD 10   -------------------------- ›  3 RD
 CTS 27 ‹ --------------------------    5 CTS
 DSR  8 ‹ --------------------------    6 DSR
 GND 26 ‹ -------------------------- ›  7 GND
 DTR  7   -------------------------- › 20 DTR
                  Channel 4
  RD  5 ‹ --------------------------    2 TD
  TD 24   -------------------------- ›  3 RD
 CTS  4 ‹ --------------------------    5 CTS
 DSR 22 ‹ --------------------------    6 DSR
 GND  3 ‹ -------------------------- ›  7 GND
 DTR 21   -------------------------- › 20 DTR
```

The above adaptor cable (called an 'octopus' cable) is also available from AST Research. The above wiring configuration corresponds to the '002' type octopus cable, (please note that the four-port /XN card from AST is the same as the /AT card; however, the cable supplied is not supported for use with the PICK system).

Arnet COM4 module and PLUS4 extender

The Arnet Controls Multiport card is from Arnet Controls, Nashville, Tenn. The COM4 provides 4 serial ports and, with the addition of the PLUS4 'piggy back' extender, provides 8 serial ports. The base address of the serial ports is configured by DIP switch S1, and the address of the global interrupt latch by S2. The following specifications apply to the 1.2 version of this card. Switches should be set as follows: 0 indicates ON, 1 indicates OFF. For more information, see Appendix D in the *Multiport Users Manual*.

		IRQ4		IRQ3	
COM4 only Address range		X 280–X 298		X 180–X 198	
COM4 with PLUS4 Address range		X 280–X 2B8		X 180–X 1B8	
COM4 with or without PLUS4 DIP Switches		1234567		1234567	
	S1:	00101	(280)	00110	(180)
	S2:	0001101	(2C0)	0001110	(1C0)
	S3:	110111	(IRQ4)	101111	(IRQ3)

The following adaptor cable is suggested for use with the Arnet Com4 and Plus4 cards.

```
 Male DB25                                 Male DB25
 Arnet card                                CRT side

   RD  2 ‹  --------------------------        2 TD
   TD  3    --------------------------  ›     3 RD
  CTS  5 ‹  --------------------------        5 CTS
  DSR  6 ‹  --------------------------        6 DSR
  GND  7 ‹  --------------------------  ›     7 GND
  DTR 20    --------------------------  ›    20 DTR
```

Digigraphics Extend COM-8 card

The Digigraphic System Corporation (Minnetonka, Minn.) Extend COM-8 card allows individual configuration of each serial port, in addition to the configuration of the global interrupt latch. Each DIP switch should be set as follows. 0 indicates ON, 1 indicates OFF.

		IRQ4		IRQ3	
Address range		X 288,X 298–X 2D0		X 188,X 198–X 1D0	
DIP switches		12345678		12345678	
Interrupt latch	DS9:	10100010	(X 288)	01100010	(X 188)
Serial ports	DS8:	10100110	(X 298)	01100111	(X 198)
	DS7:	10101000	(X 2A0)	01101001	(X 1A0)
	DS6:	10101010	(X 2A8)	01101011	(X 1A8)
	DS5:	10101100	(X 2B0)	01101101	(X 1B0)
	DS4:	10101110	(X 2B8)	01101111	(X 1B8)
	DS3:	10110000	(X 2C0)	01110001	(X 1C0)
	DS2:	10110010	(X 2C8)	01110011	(X 1C8)
	DS1:	10110100	(X 2D0)	01110101	(X 1D0)

The following adaptor cable is suggested for use with the Digigraphics card to reverse pins 2 and 3.

```
 Female DB25                               Male DB25
 Digigraphics card                         CRT side

   TD  3    --------------------------  ›     2 RD
   RD  2 ‹  --------------------------        3 TD
  CTS  5 ‹  --------------------------        5 CTS
  DSR  6 ‹  --------------------------  ›     6 DSR
  GND  7 ‹  --------------------------  ›     7 GND
  DTR 20    --------------------------  ›    20 DTR
```

Digiboard Digicom COM8/COM4 (Supported on PC-AT Ver. 2.0)

The Digiboard Digicom cards are from Digigraphics Systems Corporation of Minnetonka, Minnesota.

COM8 is an 8-port serial card, COM4 is the same card with 4 ports

0 indicates ON, 1 indicates OFF

DS1 to DS5 apply to the Digiboard COM4 Board
DS1 to DS9 apply to the Digiboard COM8 Board

	IRQ4	IRQ3
Address range	X 289,X 2B0–X 2E8	X 188,X 1B0–X 1E8
	1 2 3 4 5 6 7 8 9 10	1 2 3 4 5 6 7 8 9 10
DS1 (latch)	1 0 1 0 0 0 1 0 0 0	0 1 1 0 0 0 1 0 0 0
DS2 (2B0)	1 0 1 0 1 1 0 0	0 1 1 0 1 1 0 0
DS3 (SB8)	1 0 1 0 1 1 1 0	0 1 1 0 1 1 1 0
DS4 (2C0)	1 0 1 1 0 0 0 0	0 1 1 1 0 0 0 0
DS5 (2C8)	1 0 1 1 0 0 1 0	0 1 1 1 0 0 1 0
DS6 (2D0)	1 0 1 1 0 1 0 0	0 1 1 1 0 1 0 0
DS7 (2D8)	1 0 1 1 0 1 1 0	0 1 1 1 0 1 1 0
DS8 (2E0)	1 0 1 1 1 0 0 0	0 1 1 1 1 0 0 0
DS9 (2E8)	1 0 1 1 1 0 1 0	0 1 1 1 1 0 1 0
	Jumpers J1 to J8 are jumpered 2 to 3	Jumpers J1 to J8 are jumpered 1 to 2
	Jumpers J9 and J10 are jumpered 2 to 3	Jumpers J9 and J10 are jumpered 2 to 3
Connector P2	Remove jumper	Jumpered 2 to 3
Connector P3	Jumpered 2 to 3	Remove jumper

Use the same cable adaptor as the Digigraphics card (previous page).

ALR Challenger and Basic Time AT4×4

ALR Corporation is located in El Toro, California. The Advanced Logic Research Challenger and Basic Time AT4×4 (also sold under the name Qubie) are multi-function cards which incorporate memory, serial I/O, parallel I/O, and game I/O. The cards come with one serial port and have an option for another on the main board. Two more serial ports can be added with a 'piggy back' board. This provides a great deal of flexibility in configuring these cards. With only one or two ports, these cards are configured to emulate IBM Serial/Parallel Adaptors. With the addition of the piggy back, they become a unique configuration which is valid only on interrupt level IRQ4. DIP switches should be set as follows: 0 indicates ON, 1 indicates OFF, and X indicates a switch used to configure other features on these cards.

		IRQ4		IRQ3
		----------		----------
Single port				
Address range		X 3F8		X 2F8
		12345678		12345678
DIP switch	SW2:	XX01XX00		XX01XX10
RS232 INT straps	:	Jumper 4		Jumper 3
Dual port				
Address range		X 3F8	and	X 2F8
			12345678	
DIP switch	SW2:		XX00XX00	
RS232 INT straps	:		Jumpers 4 & 1	
Quad port				
Address range			X 3F8,X 290,X 298,X 2A0	
			12345678	
DIP switch	SW2:		XX00XX01	
RS232 INT straps	:		Jumpers 2 & 5	

The first serial port uses an adaptor cable as per the IBM serial/parallel adaptor. The remaining three serial ports use adaptor cables as per the Digigraphics Extend Com-8 card.

Hostess Four Way card

The Hostess Four Way card is supplied by Control Systems of Minneapolis, Minnesota. One 25-pin D-shell female connector is provided for each port.

For the following dip switch settings 0 indicates on, 1 indicates off.

	IRQ4	IRQ3
	------------	------------
Address range	X 240–X 258	X 140–X 158
	1 2 3 4 5 6 7 8	1 2 3 4 5 6 7 8
Dip switch SW1	0 1 0 0 1 0 0 0	0 1 0 1 0 0 0 0
Dip switch SW2	1 1 1 0 1 1 1 0	1 1 0 1 1 1 1 0

The Hostess card uses the same adaptor cable as the Digigraphics card (2–3 crossover), except the board side connection should be male.

16.4.2 Installing parallel printers

XT releases	*Number of parallel printers supported*
1.3	1
2.0	3

AT releases	*Number of parallel printers supported*
1.0	1
2.0	3

Physical vs. logical printers

When IBM XT or AT systems boot, the ROM BIOS firmware checks for the presence of Parallel Printer Adaptors (PPA). Three physical addresses have been defined by IBM for PPAs. These are:

1. X 03BC
2. X 0378
3. X 0278

They are checked for by the ROM BIOS in the order shown. If none are found, then there are no logical printers assigned. Otherwise the first one found becomes Logical printer 1 and the second one found becomes Logical printer 2, and so on. The table below shows the logical printer names DOS and PICK assign:

	PICK	*DOS*
Logical Printer 1	P0	LPT1:
Logical Printer 2	P1	LPT2:
Logical Printer 3	P2	LPT3:

For example, if a system only had PPAs at physical ports X 0378 and X 0278 then the following assignments would be made:

Logical Printer 1 @ X 0378 as P0 or LPT1:
Logical Printer 2 @ X 0278 as P1 or LPT2:
Logical Printer 3 not assigned

Note: You CANNOT have two or more PPAs using the same physical address. The results will be unpredictable.*It is your responsibility to ensure that each PPA in your system, whether on stock IBM adaptor cards or on cards from other manufacturers, is at a unique physical address*.

To see what PPAs your system has, you can use the PICK Software DeBugger (SDB). Enter the SDB by typing CTRL-ALT-BREAK. At the SDB prompt, enter the following: M40:8<cr>.

The SDB will display a line of hexadecimal memory dump. The three words at 40:8, 40:A and 0:C will hold the physical port addresses of the assigned logical printers. For a situation like the one above where the PPAs are at X 0378 and X 0278 the SDB display would show:

```
Segm:Ofst 00 01 02 03 04 05 06 07 08 09 0A 0B 0C 0D 0E 0F ...
0040:0000 .. .. .. .. .. .. .. .. 00 02 78 03 78 02 00 00 .. .. ...
```

The word at `40:8` (under the `08` and `09`) shows `78 03` (the bytes are reversed, this is normal). The word at `40:A` shows `78 02` and the word at `4C` shows `00 00`. The `00 00` indicates no parallel printer is assigned as logical printer 3.

PC-AT System PPAs

The IBM PC-AT system has two types of PPAs available; the Monochrome and Parallel Printer Adaptor card (M-PPA) and the Serial/Parallel Adaptor card (S-PPA). These cards can be set up for the following PPA physical addresses:

M-PPA `X 03BC`
S-PPA `X 0378` or `X 0278`

The M-PPA address cannot be changed. IBM has hard-wired it. The S-PPA card can be configured as either `X 0378` or `X 0278` by reversing the jumper block at J2 on the board.

PC-XT System PPAs

The IBM PC-XT system has two types of PPAs available; the Monochrome and Parallel Printer Adaptor card (M-PPA) and the Parallel Adaptor card (P-PPA). These cards can be set up for the following PPA physical address:

M-PPA `X 03BC`
P-PPA `X 0378` or `X 0278`

The M-PPA address cannot be changed. IBM has hard-wired it. The P-PPA card is hard-wired at physical address `X 0378`.

The `COLDSTART PROC` (executed at each power-on) activates the P0 parallel printer and assigns it to form queue 0. Therefore, P0 is the default printer. Each of the other parallel printers will need to be started with the `STARTPTR` command. (See p. 330 of the *Reference Manual* to determine the correct parameters and options.)

16.4.3 Installing serial printers

Any serial port on the PICK PC-XT or PC-AT systems may be used with a serial printer. To install a serial printer, we will need a serial printer, cable, and a serial line not in use by a terminal.

The following generic printer cable should be used together with a card-specific connector.

Serial printer cable

Because the connectors on cards vary, as do the cables supplied, we suggest that the following generic cables be used, together with a card-specific adaptor.

```
Female DB25                          Male DB25
AT side                              Printer

   RD  2 < ___________________________  2 TD
   TD  3   ___________________________ > 3 RD
  DSR  6 < ___________________________  ? BSY†
  GND  7 < ___________________________ > 7 GND
  CTS  5 < ____ ]
  DTR 20   ____ ]  Jumpered on connector
```

† Varies from printer to printer; usually this is pin 20 or 11; see printer manual for more information. Do not cable a BSY line if your printer uses X-ON/X-OFF (see below).

Most serial printers can be driven at baud rates higher than their effective printer speed by capturing incoming data in an on-board buffer before printing. When a buffer becomes full, the printer must be able to tell the sending computer that it cannot accept any more data. This is called busy/not-busy handshaking. This handshaking is typically accomplished in one of two ways, by an RS-232 control line (see cable diagram) or by X-ON/X-OFF.

X-ON and X-OFF is simply a process of sending ASCII characters, usually DC1 (`X 11`) and DC3 (`X 13`), through the data lines to signal the computer to stop, or start sending data again. When you type in **CTRL/S** and **CTRL/Q** at the keyboard to stop/start the display on a terminal, you are doing exactly the same thing.

Both Pick PC-XT and PC-AT systems support X-ON and X-OFF on all serial lines. The following two commands are used to start and stop X-ON/X-OFF:

```
MODEM-ON
MODEM-OFF
```

Before hooking up a serial printer, make sure that the serial line is running correctly by hooking up a terminal. Then make sure that X-ON/X-OFF is turned on by executing **MODEM-ON** at TCL.

Finally, for some printers, jumpering pins 5,6,8,20 together on the printer side's DB25 connector may be additionally required.

Once the serial printer is installed, the following example command should be executed to start the printer:

```
> STARTPTR 1, 1, 0, S1
```

This instruction starts the printer as printer 1, and assigns it to form queue 1. To vary the port number, or queue number assigned to the printer, please see p. 330 of the *User Reference Manual*.

To assign your port's printer output to this printer (instead of the default parallel printer 0) use the following example command line:

```
> SP-ASSIGN F1
```

16.4.4 Slave printers

Slave printers can be connected to any terminal that contains an auxiliary output. A control sequence (refer to each terminal's reference manual), is used to activate the auxiliary port. This control sequence can be entered through the keyboard, or through a program run on that port. Once the auxiliary port is activated, all output to the terminal will also be sent through the auxiliary port to the printer. A spooler hold file may be printed on a slave printer by the following sequence:

1. Execute a `TERM` command so that your `TERMINAL PAGE WIDTH` and `TERMINAL PAGE DEPTH` match your slave printer's page width and depth.
2. Activate your auxiliary output port on your terminal.
3. `SP-EDIT` your hold file.
4. `SPOOL` using `TN` option (see p. 327 of Peripherals chapter of *Reference Manual*).

16.4.5 Installing modems

Any serial port on the PICK PC-XT or PC-AT system can be connected to a modem for use by a remote terminal. However, special cabling may be required depending upon the modem used. The following cable diagram is suggested for use with modems; note that in this diagram more lines are brought through than with the adaptor/generic terminal cables.

```
 Serial card                          Modem
 connection                           connection

   RD   2 ‹ --------------------------      2 TD
   TD   3   -------------------------- ›    3 RD
  RTS   4 ‹ ---- ]              [ ---- ›    4 RTS
  CTS   5 ‹ ---- ]              [ ---- ›    5 CTS
  DSR   6 ‹ ---- ]              [ ---- ›    6 DSR
  GND   7 ‹ -------------------------- ›    7 GND
  DCD   8 ‹ -------------------------- ›    8 DCD
  DTR  20 ‹ -------------------------- ›   20 DTR
```

The DCD line connection is supported in PC-AT Ver. 2.0; for all releases previous to PC-AT 2.0 lines 8 and 20 should be jumpered together on both the serial connection and modem connection.

A low signal on the DCD line (caused by a line disconnect) will LOGOFF the process.

Internal modems are not supported on the PICK PC-XT or PC-AT systems.

16.4.6 Hard disk installation

Almost any hard disk which can be installed in a PC-AT is compatible with PICK. The hard disk must be 17 sectors per track, and must be installable using standard IBM utilities. Do not use special format utilities supplied by some hard disk manufacturers.

After physically installing a new hard disk, you will need to use the SETUP utility found on the diagnostic diskette for IBM Personal Computer AT. The hard disk manufacturer usually specifies which drive type you should use. When you have this information, boot the system with the diagnostics diskette, and take the SETUP option. This is a self-explanatory system of menus, which will allow you to configure several hardware options of your system. When asked, give the number of hard disk drives installed, and the drive types for each hard disk drive (usually, the manufacturer of the hard disk specifies the drive type to be used). Then, allow the system to reset.

The following table shows the standard drive type table entries of the IBM ROM BIOS:

DRIVE TYPE	1	2	3	4	5	6	7	8	9	10	11	12	13	14
Cylinders	306	615	615	940	940	615	462	733	900	820	855	855	306	733
Heads	4	4	6	8	6	4	8	5	15	3	5	7	8	7
Size (MB)	10	21	32	65	49	21	32	32	117	21	37	52	21	45

After the SETUP utility is run, the PICK PC-AT System can usually be installed normally. In some cases (see section on hardware-related error messages), a low-level reformat of the hard disk needs to be done before PICK can be installed. For this, you will need the advanced diagnostics for IBM Personal Computer AT. To use the hard disk format utility, boot the advanced diagnostic diskette, and choose the following options:

- 0 system checkout – the current system configuration displayed. If this information is correct, answer y.
- 0 run tests – the list of available hardware tests is displayed.
- 17 fixed disk test – the fixed disk diagnostics menu is displayed.
- 7 format menu – the fixed disk format menu is displayed.

At this point, you may choose either the conditional or the unconditional format utility. If you choose the unconditional format, you will need to enter all defects (use the hard disk defect map supplied by the hard disk manufacturer). Otherwise, use the conditional format. To proceed, enter the option number and the drive name as directed. When the prompt says 'Prepare system for desired operation,' you are ready to install the operating system(s).

If any DOS partitions are desired, they should be installed now, within the first 33 megabytes of the fixed disk. Now, boot the system from your PICK PC-AT system diskettes.

The first operating system loaded on your PC-AT system establishes the Master Fixed Disk Boot Record (MFDBR, Sector 1). If PICK is loaded first, it will set up this sector; if DOS is loaded first, DOS will set up this sector. If problems occur later when booting from the hard disk, generally it means that a non-standard DOS, or an old version of DOS, was used to initially establish the MFDBR. The only way to re-establish the MFDBR is to do a low-level reformat, which deletes the MFDBR, then boot up PICK or DOS. Make sure, however, to use an IBM PCDOS.

Both the PICK PC-AT and PC-XT systems are able to run more than one hard disk. On a two-drive system, there must be enough room on the first drive for the PICK monitor and ABS (the contents of the system diskettes). Leave at least 2 megabytes of partitioned cylinders on the first drive and the second completely open. The PICK system will consider the two disks as contiguous, and does not distinguish (from the end user's point of view) between drives 1 and 2; it is all one pool of file and workspace.

PC-XT hard disk installation – the 99 option

On PICK PC-XT systems a special INSTALLATION MENU will appear as part of the virgin installation process (this is not present on PICK PC-AT systems). This menu will prompt for the type of hardware that is being used. The menu includes the standard stock IBM configurations along with some popular compatibles. If you have installed your own hard disk, you must use the CUSTOM DRIVE DEFINITION (or 99 Option). The CUSTOM DRIVE DEFINITION must also be used if your hard disk configuration does not exactly match any of the other INSTALLATION OPTIONs.

A common scenario that calls for use of the 99 option is when more disk space is required (most stock PC-XTs come with a 10-megabyte hard disk). A higher-capacity hard disk is added to the PC-XT, followed by a virgin install of the PICK PC-XT system. In this case, the CUSTOM DRIVE DEFINITION (99 option) must be taken.

Note. To add a higher-capacity hard disk to the PC-XT requires the addition of a compatible hard disk controller. It is the responsibility of the installer to match and configure an appropriate controller for the hard disk. Once the unit is installed, FDISK in DOS can be executed before loading PICK to determine if all cylinders are being recognized.

Once the PICK PC-XT system is booted, and the 99 option taken, the following physical characteristics of the installed hard disk will be prompted for:

1. ENTER MAX # OF CYLINDERS
2. ENTER MAX # OF HEADS
3. ENTER STARTING REDUCED WRITE CURRENT
4. ENTER STARTING PRECOMPENSATION

5. `ENTER MAX ECC DATA BURST LENGTH`
6. `ENTER CONTROL BYTE`
7. `ENTER STANDARD TIMEOUT VALUE`
8. `ENTER TIMEOUT VALUE FOR FORMAT DRIVE`
9. `ENTER TIMEOUT VALUE FOR CHECK DRIVE`

The PICK PC-XT system uses this information to set up a table in RAM. This table enables the PICK PC-XT system to read and write to the hard disk directly. (*Note*: In PC-AT systems there is a set of 14 hard disk table entries that are resident in the PC-AT ROM BIOS, see above. The SETUP program activates one of these entries, and the PICK system uses this active table. On PC-XT systems the ROM BIOS does not contain these entries, therefore it is necessary to create the table using the 99 option.)

In most cases, only prompts 1–4 need to be entered; a carriage return can be entered for the 5–9 prompts. The information for prompts 1–4 can be obtained from the hard disk manufacturer, or your PICK dealer. The appendix at the end of this manual is a table of the 99 option entries for some of the most popular hard disks.

16.4.7 Installing tape backup

The PICK System supports the Colorado Memory Systems and Tecmar QIC-60 cassette tape units. Colorado Memory Systems is located in Loveland, Colorado; Tecmar is located in Solon, Ohio. Both these units are made up of a combination of physical hardware manufactured by Wangtek, controller cards manufactured by Wangtek or Everex Corp., and firmware Proms from Colorado Memory Systems. The PICK System is designed to interface directly to the Rev A17 and A18 firmware from Colorado Memory Systems, and is therefore incompatible with any other types of tape units and controllers.

The following is a breakdown of PICK systems software releases and supported CMS and Tecmar tape units:

XT releases	CMS and Tecmar units
1.3	Non-supported
2.0	Both internal and external (also supports the WANGTEK internal drive)

AT releases	CMS and Tecmar units
1.0	External only
2.0	Both internal and external (also supports the WANGTEK internal drive)

There are two types of controller cards that come with these tape units. The PC-36 (or long card) comes with the internal tape unit, and with the combination tape and hard disk system. The QIC-02 (or short card) comes with the external tape units. These cards are functionally identical. The following are the physical settings that must be made on the controller cards to support the PICK system:

PC-XT systems

IRQ = 2
DMA = 1 (DRQ = 1, DACK = 1)
PORT ADDRESS = hex 338

PC-AT systems

IRQ = 5
DMA = 3 (DRQ = 3, DACK = 3)
PORT ADDRESS = hex 338

When installing these tape units, we recommend that the following procedure be used to insure that your tape unit is functioning properly:

1. Set the physical controller board as described above.
2. Boot up DOS.
3. Start the CMS or Tecmar menu software.
4. Choose the utilities option, then the change configuration file option.
5. Change the first four parameters of the configuration file to match the physical controller settings.
6. Follow the CMS or Tecmar manual, and exercise the tape unit by doing some file-by-file and mirror image backups.
7. Boot up PICK.
8. Log to `SYSPROG`, execute a `SET-SCT` . . . your tape unit is now the active PICK tape device.

Tape troubleshooting tips

- *Parity errors after installation* – The PICK system is probably not sensing your tape drive. Check all controller settings, and make sure your controller ROMS are A17 or A18, reboot PICK. If problems still occur contact your PICK dealer.
- *Parity errors during a write operation* – Choose `Q` – Quit option to stop processing. Rewind the tape and execute a `T-ERASE`. If problems continue try a new tape.
- *Parity errors during a read operation* – Choose `Q` – Quit option to stop processing. Rewind the tape and execute a `T-RETEN`, then retry.
- *Intermittent parity errors* – Unplug your ribbon cable from the back of your tape and controller. Make sure all pin male connections are straight. Clean your tape heads as per the CMS or Tecmar manual.
- *A final tip* – On important system `SAVE` tapes, execute a `T-CHK (A)` to

ensure that the tape is free of parity errors. The `T-CHK` will read all the data on your tape and display any errors.

16.4.8 Hardware-related error messages

The following is a summary of some of the more common hardware-related error messages with suggested corrective actions:

- `F/D ERROR xx` This is a floppy disk error. It usually indicates that the diskette in use is defective, but may also be caused by a dirty, or defective, floppy drive. It is suggested that the diskette be loaded into another PC to determine if the diskette is defective. If so, your dealer will replace your set of PICK diskettes.
- `H/D ERROR xx` This is a hard disk error. It can occur when the PICK system is booting up on incompatible or defective hardware (usually hard disk, disk controller, or ROM BIOS). If the hardware is a supported IBM system, or compatible, contact your dealer for service.
- `R/W MFDBR ERROR` This is a virgin installation error that is caused when the PICK system is attempting to read the Master Fixed Disk Boot Record (sector 1) of the hard disk and cannot read this sector. This operation is the first hard disk read attempted by the PICK system, and indicates a total failure of hard disk I/O. Usually, this type of error occurs when installing PICK for the first time on incompatible or defective hardware. If the hardware is a supported IBM PC-AT system or compatible, a complete re-installation is suggested (see section on Hard Disk Installation); contact your dealer for further information.
- `CAN NOT LOAD SEED ABS FRAMES` This error message is issued when the PICK system is attempting to start up virtual processing by reading from the hard disk the first ABS frames. It usually indicates that the CPU is out of phase with the hard disk I/O, and is timing out before the read is completed. This type of error may occur when special speed enhancement cards have been added to the system. If this is not the case, have the hard disk controller checked out.
- `NOT ENOUGH ROOM FOR PICK` This error message is issued when the PICK system is initializing the hard disk and determines that there are insufficient unallocated cylinders to install the system. Check the partitions under DOS using FDISK to verify that there are at least 70 cylinders that are available (unallocated) for PICK; make sure that the total number of cylinders displayed by FDISK matches the capacity of your hard disk. If problems continue, kill your DOS partition, then establish it. On PC-XT systems (only) this error message can occur when incorrect hard disk parameters are entered during a virgin install (the 99 option).

- `MAXIMUM PARTITIONS EXIST` This error message is issued during the boot process when the PICK system determines by reading the MFDBR that all available partitions (there is a maximum of four possible) are occupied. Boot up DOS and execute `FDISK` to display the partitions. Delete the extra partitions and reinstall PICK. If the problem still occurs, do a low-level reformat (see the section on Hard Disk Installation) and then reinstall PICK.
- `TOO MANY BAD TRACKS` This error message is issued when the PICK system is initializing the hard disk and determines that there are too many defective tracks for the defect table. The PICK system assigns 2% of the PICK partition for defective tracks. It is rare that a hard disk will have more defective tracks than the 2%; therefore this message usually indicates hard disk I/O problems. It is suggested that a full reinstallation process be done, including a low-level reformat (see section on Hard Disk Installation). If the problem still occurs, have the disk controller checked out. On PC-XT systems (only) this error message can occur when incorrect hard disk parameters are entered during a virgin install (the 99 option).
- `I/O ERROR` See H/D or F/D error. This error message can occur during either a floppy or hard disk boot operation. If a floppy disk I/O is taking place refer to F/D ERROR. If hard disk I/O is taking place refer to H/D error.
- `PROTECTION VIOLATION` This message is issued when the PICK system attempts to verify the copy protection of the System #1 diskette and determines that the verification fails. This may be a defective diskette, so return your PICK diskettes to your dealer.
- `PARITY ERRORS` This message usually indicates defective media, either floppy diskette or tape. For tape I/O see the section on troubleshooting in Installing Tape Backup. For floppy I/O, on the PC-AT, make sure that you have the correct density set for your diskette (`SET-FLOPPY` with (`S`) for standard, or (`H`) for high density); make sure a `T-REW` is done; and if all else fails reformat your floppy (`FORMAT` command) and try again.
- `PARITY CHECK xx` This is a ROM BIOS error message indicating hardware memory read or write errors. Immediately contact your dealer for service.
- `&&&& ...` These ampersands are issued by the PICK system during virtual (multi-user) processing when the hard disk controller is sending read or write errors. This usually indicates hardware deterioration of the hard disk controller. The following procedure is suggested:

  1. Back up the PICK System and do a virgin install, this will reinitialize the hard disk (flag defective tracks).

2. If 1 does not resolve the problem, do a full low-level reformat of the hard disk (see section on Hard Disk Initialization); then a full virgin install of PICK.
3. If both 1 and 2 do not resolve the problem, contact your dealer for service on your hard disk controller and/or hard disk. At this point, usually swapping out the hard disk controller resolves the problem.

- `GROUP FORMAT ERROR xxxx` This is the PICK system error message that occurs when a PICK file is damaged (the item-to-item links are destroyed). This is not a software error, but individual GFEs can be corrected through the software. Contact your dealer. Most often these errors are caused by hard disk I/O problems; see above on ampersands for corrective action.

17 PICK: Its Place as an Operating System

17.1 Other major operating systems

Having devoted an entire book to the PICK operating system, it will be impossible to do justice to others here in the same way. In order to highlight PICK's strengths and weaknesses, however, it is important to identify the other principal operating systems and to discuss how PICK compares with them.

Every computer needs an operating system and in the early days the computer manufacturers developed their own, which effectively 'locked' a user into a specific manufacturer's systems. To the user not only was the portability of their application software in question, but to change to a new range of hardware meant their investment in gaining competence in the original operating system would invariably be wasted. Further the lack of standards was causing software houses and manufacturers high costs and timely delays in porting popular application packages. The market needs for portability and standardization came with the advent of the supermicro and the personal computer. This arrival, which has seen a flood of systems introduced from a vast number of manufacturers, has come the move towards standardization which has meant that most manufacturers have, in the last few years, adopted one of the following operating systems:

1. BOS
2. CP/M
3. CTOS
4. MS-DOS
5. MUMPS
6. OASIS
7. PICK
8. TURBODOS
9. UCSD p-System
10. UNIX

Whilst extremely popular, both CP/M and MS-DOS are single-user operating systems; the remainder, with the exception of BOS and UNIX, address limited machine marketplaces. Whilst BOS is available on a wide range of systems, it is still little known outside the UK. It is popular, particulary in the micro market, since it offers true portability across all machines it runs on and has a wide range of proven application software written for it. Perhaps its most limiting factor is that it only supports one language – Microcobol.

Without doubt, the prime operating system seen to 'compete' with PICK is UNIX. Developed by scientists at Bell Laboratories over 20 years ago, UNIX is seen as the leading contender to become the *de facto* standard operating system for multi-user machines. With the increased awareness of PICK and its availability on the IBM PC-XT and IBM PC-AT, the two operating systems are now seen to be battling for this prime role. In essence, however, they *both* have their place in the market and as you would expect both have their strengths and weaknesses.

17.2 A brief overview of UNIX

The UNIX operating system was developed at Bell Laboratories originally to run on DEC (Digital Equipment Corporation) equipment, at first on the PDP-7 and then on the PDP-11/70 where it gained widespread acceptance. During the early seventies, universities and colleges, many of whom used PDP-11/70 systems, were either given a UNIX licence or paid a nominal sum for it. It is this clever marketing exercise which has seen the acceptance of, and has dramatically increased the awareness and demand for, UNIX.

UNIX was originally written in an assembly language and then rewritten by Ken Thompson in a higher-level language called B, all of which was extensively modified by Dennis Ritchie in 1973 and the language was then rechristened C. It is the use of C which provides for the portability of UNIX.

The main features of UNIX are:

- **Hierarchical file system** Information is held in a series of hierarchical directories, starting at the top, known as '/' (the root). From there information is broken into logical groups or directories, which in turn can be broken into other logical groupings or subdirectories and so on as illustrated in Figure 17.1. Each directory and file offers three levels of access security, each of which can offer combinations of read, write and execute privileges.

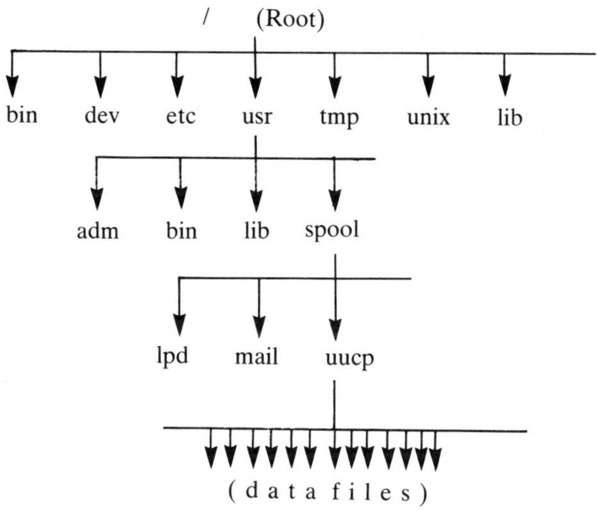

Figure 17.1 Hierarchical structure of UNIX file system.

- **Command language** A major strength of the UNIX system is its command language, which is made up of hundreds of commands. Each command has been built to carry out one task and to perform it perfectly. Most commands have a series of options that can be applied, each denoted by a single letter. Further, any of these commands can accept its input from any other command and can 'pipe' its output to any other command. This feature of 'pipes' enables many commands to be linked together to perform a series of tasks like a simple program.
- **Procedural language** The procedural language is known as the C-shell or Command Language Interpreter. It enables a sequence of operations to be executed by a single command, and is effectively a job control language in which parameters can be passed, programs run and input and output redirected. It also permits the inclusion of 'IF. . .THEN. . .ELSE' logic.
- **Multi-language support** UNIX includes a C compiler and assembler,

but can support a variety of languages which can be purchased separately, e.g. Ada, APL, a full macro assembler, BASIC, COBOL, FORTRAN, LISP and Pascal.

- **Program development environment** UNIX provides a complete program development environment. It offers a number of standard software routines, which the programmer can utilize, in its standard libraries. It also offers a system known as SCCS (Source Code Control System) which keeps control of program versions and dependencies. Further it offers archiving facilities and, naturally, a debugger, called ADB.
- **Editors** There are two editors, a line editor, known as 'ed' and a full screen editor known as 'vi'. Both of these use mnemonics and control keys to provide functionality.
- **Text processing** One of the strengths of UNIX is its text processing capabilities. It offers a whole series of facilities including:

  nroff – a text formatter for line-printers
  troff – a text formatter for typesetters
  ms – macros for type changes, cover sheets and multi-column formatting
  ptx – a utility to generate an index

- **System accounting** A utility for recording and reporting on system usage. This can provide detail at almost any level, ranging from the system usage and number of pages printed, to the individual commands used.
- **Spooler** A print spooler for controlling printing – essential in a multi-user environment.
- **Communications** UNIX offers a mail and news system for users and provides two utilities for machine-to-machine communication – 'cu' to connect a foreign system and 'uucp' a UNIX-to-UNIX copy program.
- **Concurrent processing** It is possible to spawn other processes from the terminal so that more than one task can be activated concurrently. This can be very useful, where a large time-consuming task, such as a print program or compile, can be activated and whilst it is being processed, at a lower priority in the background, the terminal can still be used for other work.

17.3 How PICK and UNIX compare

Undoubtedly PICK makes highly efficient use of the hardware on which it runs. It offers virtual memory management, and a realistic multi-user capability on small systems. It would not be unrealistic to consider up to four users on a 68000-based system with 256 Kbytes memory (the 68000 is an industry-standard processor chip), whilst, by virtue of not offering virtual memory, the UNIX operating system typically requires 384 Kbytes to run, limiting a system with 512 Kbytes memory to a single-user environment. Further instead of taking around 3 Mbytes of disk space for the operating system as PICK does, UNIX typically takes 13 Mbytes and some implementations take more, in some cases nearly twice as much. Taken as a whole, therefore, with a UNIX system, the overall hardware cost is higher, performance is reduced and the number of users that can be connected to a system, compared with PICK, is lower.

In its favour, however, is that UNIX is available on a much wider variety of systems, that it has been available longer and that it supports multiple languages. Whilst it can be argued that PICK applications, written in a single language, are easier to maintain, the industry has grown up with a wide range of languages and the likelihood is that your favourite application is written in something other than PICK BASIC. Whilst the UNIX operating system supports C, a whole variety of programming languages can be purchased for it. These are typically, Ada, APL, Assembler, BASIC, COBOL, FORTRAN, LISP and Pascal.

There is undoubtedly a much larger volume of software available for UNIX than for PICK, which is a factor of its age and the number of programing languages available. This does not mean, however, that there is a shortage of good PICK software, far from it. Both PICK and the IDBMA publish catalogues of PICK software running into many hundreds of application packages, covering the everyday word processor, graphics package and spreadsheet to the systems for specialized (vertical) markets, such as the legal profession, hospital administration, oil companies and manufacturing.

This variety of programming languages has, though, led to a variety of file structures, typically sequential, single and multiple key ISAM and relative record files. This multiplicity of file structures often causes a problem of integration when two or more applications need to share or transfer information. Such a problem is unknown to PICK since *all* its data is held in one common format. Under UNIX, therefore, it may be necessary to build 'bridges' to pass data between one application and another.

The obvious strength of PICK compared to UNIX is its integrated variable length database manager. We have just talked about how this provides integration of applications, but obviously, in its ability to handle variable length data, it also minimizes disk usage. A number of databases are available under UNIX, the more popular being Informix, Unify, Ingres and Mistress. Again these are additional to raw UNIX and apart from their cost can provide further headaches in integrating application software.

Probably PICK's greatest weakness is in the area of communications. In its native form PICK offers no communication tools, whereas UNIX offers two, 'cu' to connect to the UNIX system and 'uucp', a UNIX to UNIX copy program. As you would expect there are many third-party software and hardware products written to handle communication protocols on both operating systems. However, UNIX is readily accepted as being easier to communicate with and easier to network in that, having a hierarchical directory structure, it can more readily accept another higher level, that of the system node (a node being the point at which a system is linked to a network).

No-one would argue that there are substantially more UNIX users than PICK users and there are three main reasons for this. Firstly, UNIX has been available longer; in the region of five years. Secondly, Pick historically has been selective to whom he made the operating system available and thirdly, until very recently, the PICK operating system has had little marketing strength behind it. UNIX gained widely in popularity following its free issue to a large number of universities. The operating system, developed as tool for the scientific and academic market, was widely used by university graduates who gained an affinity for it and who promoted its use in industry thereafter. This exercise, seen as one of the best promotions of any operating system in the history of the computing industry, undoubtedly accelerated its growth and acceptance quite dramatically.

The PICK environment promotes the use of 4GL products far more than any other operating system. As discussed in Section 15.1, the prime reason for this is the superb database common to all PICK systems. Requiring a database or ISAM (Indexed Sequential Access Method) file system to operate, 4GL products are more widely available on PICK than UNIX, since there is no question of portability of the completed generator, nor that of procuring or writing a database manager or ISAM file system. The major 4GL tools for UNIX are Appgen, Oracle and Sculptor whilst most database products now offer some form of 4GL product. Those for PICK are discussed in Chapter 15.

The dictionary-driven PICK database enables changes to be made to the data structure, simply and speedily, by a simple change to the data dictionary. To change the maximum length of an attribute throughout the entire application software, takes just seconds, whereas with UNIX, depending on the application, such a change could take many hours, if not days. The flexibility offered by the PICK database enables systems to be introduced gradually, at the pace of the user, and enables them to be modified, even when live.

UNIX offers concurrent processing, a feature available on only some implementations of PICK and known as phantom processing.

It is debatable which is the most portable. In my view PICK comes out the winner since there are far more versions of UNIX than there are

PICK. Both operating systems are addressing the issue of portability, UNIX by establishing version V as its standard and PICK by setting up a standards committee, which met for the first time in October 1985.

If you look closely at these products it is apparent that they both have a place in the market. PICK is the better choice for general and commercial data processing, whilst UNIX is best for specialist systems and scientific work. In any case, when buying a system for the first time, the most important aspect is the application software. Having found the best package, only then is it worth worrying about the operating system it runs under or reviewing the hardware it will work with.

17.4 PICK's weaknesses

In its raw form PICK has a number of shortcomings, most of which are currently being addressed by Pick Systems. For most people its biggest weakness is communications. In this area, native PICK offers no standard tools. There are plenty of proprietary products however that handle:

- machine-to-machine communications;
- PICK to MSDOS and vice versa;
- X25;
- 3270;
- 2780/3780.

Another shortcoming is its handling of arithmetic, which traditionally holds numbers to four decimal places. Again there are floating point software products, offered by third parties that can increase this up to 14 digits. Since its arithmetic cannot gain the benefit of a mathematics coprocessor, such as the 8087 on the IBM PC, PICK is not seen as a scientific product.

Whilst most implementations now incorporate item locking, there are still some that only lock groups. Although this is rarely a problem in operation, some people will see it as a deficiency.

Another limitation of the PICK system is the item size limit of 32 Kbytes (32 000 characters). Whilst rarely a problem today, it will disappear tomorrow under the new release of PICK known as Open Architecture, where an item can be of any size.

To a number of people, particularly those familiar with other programming languages, PICK's single program language support is seen as a difficulty. The word 'BASIC' to most people conjures up an image of a home computer language. Many don't realize just how powerful PICK BASIC really is; it is just BASIC to them and it suffers, therefore, by association.

Apart from these few points, there are few other real complaints. A number of poeple would like to see automatic recovery, improved security and a full screen editor. In order to find out market demands a survey was undertaken by Pick Systems in 1985, which was published in their quarterly journal, *PICKWORLD*. The survey listed some 30 new features and each respondent was asked to prioritize his top five requirements. The results, in order of importance, were:

1. Communications
2. Expanded arithmetic
3. Item locks
4. Full screen editor
5. Transaction logging
6. Faster file save
7. Security enhancements
8. TCL stacker
9. Expanded documentation
10. Graphics protocols
11. ENGLISH enhancements
12. Auto file reallocation
13. PICK standards committee
14. New word processor
15. BASIC extensions

It is good to note that Pick Systems is addressing many of these issues. In addition, other licensees are starting to release a number of these features on their existing R83 systems, ahead of Open Architecture in which the vast majority of these features will be available.

18 PICK in the Commercial World

18.1 The problems besetting the businessman

Historically the data processing (DP) function has been a centralized operation with DP specialists charged with the corporate responsibility of developing and installing management information and control systems. As well as this, DP departments have been responsible for the operation of the computer, including all aspects of its security and integrity.

Once in place, these systems have tended to need additional work, either by changing their functionality to cater for misunderstandings in the design, or to incorporate additional facilities or to satisfy the need for *ad hoc* management information. In this respect it is not uncommon for centralized DP departments to be months, if not years, behind in fulfilling user requirements.

The advent of a vast range of low-cost, powerful, multi-user computers is bringing computing to the fingertips of the mass market and distributing computing power throughout most companies. Whilst these systems are also purchased by central DP departments, they are mainly finding their way onto the desks of the users. Users are now much more 'computer-literate' than ever before and are able to build their own financial models and use enquiry languages to produce their *ad hoc* reports. They buy computers for the very reasons they were bought in the past:

- better control of their business;
- simplified administration;
- elimination of errors;
- reduction in paperwork;
- receipt of better and more timely information;
- better decision-making resulting from all the above.

Experience in practice demonstrates reasonable levels of attainment in all these areas, so you could be forgiven for thinking that these installations have been a success. However, in a large number of cases this success is coupled with a feeling of being let down and by frustration with the limitations and restrictions that have been found. Contrary to general belief this is not primarily associated with the quality of the application software, but in much more commonsense areas frequently overlooked.

The businessman expects that it should be easy to put information into his system. He expects the system to recognize and cope with his information, which varies in size, in shape and in form. He becomes a little unhappy when he realizes that to make real progress with his system he has to understand new terms such as files, fields, records and so on.

The user expects that the system will take care of everything within itself and expects to be able to develop his system at his own pace. He still views it as the cure to all his problems – a miraculous tool. He becomes disappointed when he realizes he must understand the aspects and importance of file structure, file maintenance and file security. He gets very upset when he discovers that he should have got everything worked out at the *beginning* and not as he goes along, which is the way he expected to implement his systems. In some cases he may find it bordering on the impossible to develop his system the way he wanted because of something not considered at the beginning.

He also finds it strange that the computer that he purchased as his business system doesn't understand the peculiarities of his business, a business that has its own terminology, its own peculiarities and its own idiosyncrasies. The computer requires that his business conforms to its design and to its need to call each piece of information by just one name.

He further believes that if he has put the information in once, then it really should be there for all other purposes. In many systems, however, he soon discovers that he is putting in the same information more than once. It gradually begins to dawn on him that files have a discrete nature; that the operating system is not the same, and has nothing to do with, a database management system, and that neither of these have anything to do with report generation.

It's with output when for him everything starts to go wrong. The whole essence of the computer system was to get vital control information from it, from which he was *hopefully* going to run his business more efficiently. Having made extreme efforts to get his information in, he now realizes that if he didn't define a report in the first place, which he's suddenly realized he should already have thought of, he may be involved in new programs, additional cost and undoubtedly delay. Further if the information he requires is contained in two separate files, the costs and delays he incurs could escalate dramatically.

All this indicates that the businessman requires and should be given control of the computer systems necessary to manage his business and for them to be implemented at his pace and in his way.

18.2 The problems besetting the computing industry

The computing industry has seen tremendous change over the last thirty years such that today's pocket calculator is more powerful than the world's largest computer of 1954. The development of hardware, which has become smaller, more powerful and cheaper, has culminated in changes in software, from machine-specific operating systems and machine-specific programming languages to standards being established for both. The industry has seen a move from specialized, tailored software towards packages, database management systems and program and application generators. The intention has been that software and its development should be brought to those people who use it and who know what they want from it. For those reasons software development tools have to be more powerful and easy to use.

It is hardly surprising to find that four major problems have beset the computing industry and are still there today:

- meeting project deadlines;
- recruiting suitably qualified staff;
- predicting future technology;
- maintaining existing programs.

The computing industry has to cater for the needs of the businessman. As we have discussed, the businessman is becoming far more 'computer aware' and as such expects far more from his system. The software, if developed centrally, has to be developed or tailored to suit his needs, modified simply and quickly to meet the changing needs of his business and be sufficiently flexible to grow as his business grows. It also needs to be able to work in a way that requires the minimum of development effort, support and maintenance resources.

All this indicates the wider use and acceptance of software development tools, the so-called application generators, fourth-generation languages (4GL products), generally associated with powerful database management systems.

18.3 What PICK and 4GL products provide

It is apparent that the PICK operating system and fourth-generation application generators like System Builder satisfy the needs of both the businessman and the computing industry. PICK uniquely puts control in the hands of the businessman. It eliminates all the limitations, all the restrictions, all the difficulties mentioned earlier. It makes it easy for the businessman to relate to it, because it relates to *his* business. It takes account of the peculiarities of his business and he can progress on a step-by-step basis.

It accepts and stores information in its natural form. It understands the end of one thing and the beginning of the next, by something similar to punctuation marks, and we are all accustomed to those. There is no inherent restriction on the size, shape or form of information; it is always there in its natural, readable form. There is no conversion to, or from, a whole series of codes like binary, binary-coded decimal, hexadecimal, packed decimal and so on. The individual pieces of information are referred to by names, within the computer itself, that have actually been defined by *him* and the people who work for and around him. The sales department can refer to 'models' whilst the production department can refer to 'products' and the service department can refer to 'parts'. In each case the element of information is stored *once* and referred to by each of these names.

In its natural form data varies in length. Addresses, for example, each line of which is normally a different length, can be long or short. The PICK system readily copes with these, and allows them to be added, deleted or changed at will. PICK allows data to expand and contract in line with business demands.

The PICK system breaks away from convention in a way that is important to both the businessman and the computing industry. The businessman is not only interested in standard software systems – the accounting, stock, order processing systems. He frequently only needs to control information which has to be kept up-to-date and from which management information can be retrieved and reported. This needs to be done, *simply and easily*. The new generation of software products, fourth-generation application generators like System Builder, enable the businessman, without previous DP experience, to create and maintain these files and to produce the required reports, simply and easily and without the need for costly experienced DP resources.

18.4 PICK the right approach?

Hopefully by now, you too will be convinced that PICK is the right approach for the commercial world, whether it be for the DP department or the businessman himself. Its friendly, flexible approach makes it a winner to all who come in contact with it. To summarize its benefits, therefore, I would say that PICK:

- **Offers hardware independence** There are now over 30 manufacturers offering PICK on their systems, from the single-terminal PC, to several thousand terminals linked to mainframes. This provides the user with security and protects his software and technical investment in the event that he decides to change his hardware.

- **Offers efficient system usage** The operating system has generally been optimized to the hardware on which it runs. In addition it offers virtual memory management and stores data in variable length, using a powerful database manager. This efficient use of variable length data alone offers savings in the size of disk that may be required. The overall environment is one that enables bigger applications with many more terminals to be run on smaller, less powerful and hence less expensive equipment.
- **Offers upward compatibility** PICK applications are portable to the extent that should you need to upgrade your system, or even have to buy a system from a different supplier, you will always be able to find a system to run your software without having a major conversion exercise to undertake.
- **Uses the terms of the business** PICK's powerful dictionary-driven system enables the terms of the business to be adopted. New terminology can be added at will. No longer need the businessman conform to the terms of the system. It can talk to him in terms he understands.
- **Accommodates variation in data** PICK not only facilitates data entry, by taking in and storing data in its raw form, but it is designed to accommodate variations in form, shape and length of information. It recognizes that some addresses have more lines than others and that some of these lines are longer than others. It does not force information to be entered in a fixed space, with the inherent wasted space and inefficient data handling that fixed length data handling implies.
- **Enables speedier development and easier maintenance** PICK provides a complete environment to allow systems to be developed and maintained, simply and easily. The increased use of 4GL tools encourages this environment even further. This helps remove the substantial maintenance headaches that have beleaguered the computing industry.
- **Enables systems to be developed at the businessman's pace** Since all data is held in a common format, integration of applications is far simpler. Additionally the data dictionary concept enables new data elements to be readily defined and existing ones amended. All of this, coupled with an easy-to-use enquiry language for regular or *ad hoc* reports, provides an environment in which the businessman can build his systems in way he wants and at the pace he is able to cope with.
- **Provides a comprehensive reporting system** The most important part of any system is its output. Having put the information in, it is essential to get management information out. PICK's ACCESS

report utility is one of its most powerful and beneficial features. It provides an easy-to-use enquiry system allowing regular and *ad hoc* reports to be produced using an English-like enquiry language. By use of such vocabulary, users with little training can soon produce their own enquiries and reports.

- **IN SHORT PICK PRODUCES CONTROL BY PROVIDING CONTROL**

All these issues prove adequately and without doubt, the value and significance of the PICK system to the businessman, the computing industry and the commercial world. There is no doubt in my mind that PICK is the right approach.

18.5 The future of the PICK operating system

PICK is already addressing the majority of its few shortcomings and some of these, such as item locking, are starting to appear in the market, including PICK's own version for the IBM PC, the XT and AT. Information on what is being developed and when it will be available has not been released. What is known however, is that PICK will be basing its future developments around Open Architecture.

Open Architecture is probably the most significant development in the history of PICK and was first released in October 1985. It offers a totally new design of the underlying virtual sytem with the objective of opening up the architecture of the operating system to facilitate, amongst others, the use of communications and other compilers.

In its first version, Open Architecture (OA), standardizes the frame size, with all of them being 1K. It removes the 32K item size limit, so that items can be of any size. It permits multiple ABS areas and instead of setting up fixed workspaces for each process, these are set up and linked as required. Further enhancements include performance monitoring and phantom processing, the ability to run concurrent tasks from a terminal.

Whilst there are some important and fundamental differences in Open Architecture, PICK is absolutely committed to application portability, hence any PICK BASIC programs written under R80/R83 will run under Open Architecture. Perhaps the most visible change of all is that of the TCL prompt, which has changed from '>' (greater than) to ':' (colon)!

The future of the PICK operating system is assured. In my view it will continue to go from strength to strength, gaining wider acceptance and use as it becomes available on a wider range of computers. It has set a standard that others can only hope to follow. At long last we have a system that recognizes what the data processing industry is all about, that of processing data and processing it in a way that we, mere mortals, can readily understand and control.

Appendices

A Error Messages

The ERRMSG file

No.	Description
1	Uneven number of delimiters (' ").
3	Verb?
5	The word "A" is illegal.
7	A value must follow the HEADING, FOOTING, TAG or GRAND-TOTAL connective.
8	A window specification string must follow the "WINDOW" connective.
9	System dl/id missing.
10	File name missing.
11	Frame locked at location X'A'.
13	Data level descriptor (filename in dictionary) is missing.
15	The file-name is preceded by an illegal connective.
17	"WITHIN" is valid only in Count/List/Sum or Stat statements.
18	The last word may not be a connective.
19	A value without an attribute name is illegal.
20	Error in the 'USING' syntax.
21	Meaningless item-id in statement.
22	"TO" before item-id valid only in a change statement.
24	The word "A" cannot be identified.
25	The connective "WITH" may not immediately precede a value.
26	Attribute values may not both precede and follow an attribute name.
29	At least one item-id must be specified for a "WITHIN"-type statement.
30	Error in the verb definition.
53	Set in MD7/8/18: id list required for WITHIN.
71	An illegal connective modifies the word 'A'.
72	The value "A" is meaningless.
79	The number of SEPARATE and CLAUSE sets cannot exceed 9.
80	A system error has occurred in mode: A. This may be due to sort-key(s) preceding selection criteria.

No.	*Description*
82	Your system privilege level is not sufficient for this statement.
89	No data detected.
91	End tape/diskette check — A file(s).
92	End of recorded data — A file(s).
93	Attach the tape/diskette unit.
94	End of file.
95	Tape/diskette attached to line 'A'.
96	Load point.
97	End of tape/diskette.
98	Parity error.
99	Block transfer not completed.
101	Tape/diskette error — procedure exited.
102	End of account restore.
103	Tape attached.
118	The form 'with attribute and attribute' is undefined.
120	'A' negative balance not permitted.
158	An illegal connective of the form "A" modifies " A.
163	An A-, F-, or T- correlative has failed compilation.
164	Total or control break connective not followed by an attribute definition.
166	The A-correlative attribute name 'A' is illegal.
167	Missing terminal quote ("/') in A-correlative: 'A'.
168	Illegal A-correlative.: 'A'.
169	Missing left parenthesis in A-correlative: 'A'.
170	Missing right parenthesis in A-correlative: 'A'.
173	Missing semi-colon in A-correlative.
191	End tape/diskette check — A File(s) A Record(s).
192	This is an erroneous object string.
193	Basic object code cannot be copied to an item.
194	Do not copy to the same item in the same file.
195	'A' is not a list.
196	'A' is too large to be an item.
197	This GET-LIST or SAVE-LIST specification is incorrect.
198	The list pointed to by pointer item 'A' is defective.
199	Insufficient work space for item 'A'.
200	File name ?
201	'A' is not a file name.
202	'A' not on file.
203	Item name?
204	File definition 'A' is missing.
205	No statements to be assembled.
206	'A' assembled.

No.	*Description*
207	Undefined symbols.
208	Error in item-id list.
209	Columns must be in range 1–80.
210	File 'A' is access protected.
211	Mode 'A' no assembled code can be found.
212	Mode 'A' has no frame statement.
213	Mode 'A' location counter error at line no. A
214	Mode 'A' overflows frame A at line no. A
215	Mode 'A' Hex error at line no. A
216	Mode 'A' loaded; Frame = A Size = A Cksum = A
217	Mode 'A' verified; Frame = A Size = A Cksum = A
218	Mode 'A' frame = A has A mismatches.
219	Illegal command: A
220	'A' exited.
221	'A' filed.
222	'A' deleted.
223	'A' exists on file.
224	'A' is a pointer item. It may not be loaded into a non-pointer file.
225	TSYM must be DICT & DATA MOD/SEP 1,1 37,1
226	Tape/diskette format error.
227	Frame # A — verified.
228	Frame # A — A mismatches.
229	'A' is not a valid account name.
234	Item size exceeds 32000 bytes.
235	Attempt to write into update protected file.
237	'A' successfully compiled. A frame(s) used.
239	List 'A' saved — A frame(s) used.
240	A "SELECT" or "SSELECT" must be used preceding a 'SAVE-LIST' statement.
241	Successful compile. A frame(s) used.
242	'A' decataloged.
243	List 'A' saved — A frame(s) used.
244	'A' cataloged.
245	List 'A' deleted.
246	'A' is no longer a list, or is no longer on file.
247	'A' is basic object code.
249	Syntax error.
250	Command error.
251	Done.
252	Frame: A Size: A; Shortened: A; Hardness: A; Lines: A
260	Invalid batch lock command: A
265	PROC stack overflow.

No.	*Description*
267	PROC transfer to 'A' cannot be completed.
268	The destination of the PROC "GO" statement: A, cannot be found.
269	Input to PROC buffer cannot exceed 298 characters.
270	Format error in the PROC statement: A
272	A value exists for the attribute referenced by the element: A
273	Error in column-number/field-width or format specification at : A
274	Unrecognizable batch-string element : A
275	Y or F sub-element error at batch-string element : A
276	D-2 update without D-1 being specified, at batch-string element : A
277	J element missing at batch-string element : A
278	Error in processing secondary batch-string element: A
279	Incorrect scaling factor in F* batch-string element: A
280	File-definition batch element error at : A
281	D1 must have Y11 storage correlative ... Error at : A
282	Invalid parameter for select list.
289	Terminal Printer
	Page width:
	Page depth:
	Line skip :
	LF delay :
	FF delay :
	Backspace :
	Term type :
290	The range of the parameter "A" is not acceptable.
291	'A' file-definition is missing.
292	The input parameters are not in the proper format.
293	Total number of contiguous frames : A
298	Format error in specifications.
316	Numeric parameter missing.
331	The account file is missing.
335	**
	* PICK SYSTEMS RELEASE R83 *
	**
	LOG ON :
336	Logged off at A on A
337	User is not logged on.
338	Account file statistics were not updated due to either:
	1. Insufficient work-space to contain the account file item, or
	2. System dictionary changed while you were logged on.
340	< Connect time = A mins.; CPU = A units; 1ptr pages = A
341	R83 system verified.

No.	*Description*
342	R83 system does not verify. There are A frames with mismatches.
390	'A' loaded.
391	'A' verified.
398	The maximum of 20 levels for a "WITHIN"-type statement has been exceeded.
399	The file or dl/id requires a V(ertical) correlative for this statement.
401	No items present.
403	End of list.
404	A items selected.
405	A items listed.
406	Item count= A, byte count= A, avg. Bytes/item= A, avg. Items/groups= A, std. Deviation= A, avg. Bytes/group= A
407	A items counted.
408	One item counted.
409	Item 'A' is not in the secondary file.
410	A synonym (Q-type) file cannot be specified in this statement.
411	'DICT' or 'DATA' must be specified in a CLEAR-FILE statement.
412	Insufficient disk space available for the file.
413	The file name already exists in the master dictionary.
414	Illegal or missing modifier used in defining the file area(s).
415	Item 'A' exists on file.
416	Range error in modulo or separation parameter.
417	File 'A' created; base = A, modulo = A, separ = A.
418	File definition item 'A' not copied.
419	The specified file cannot be cleared or deleted.
420	Dictionary file deletion cannot be done without deletion of data-section(s) first.
421	Statistics of A :total = A average = A count = A
422	Byte statistics for : A Total = A average = A items = A cksum = A bits = A
423	Total of A = A
424	Frame id : A device address A unit number .. A cylinder ..... A head .... A sector .... A
425	Invalid frame-id request.
426	Data file already exists.
427	There is no data section for this file.
428	'A' object pointer not found.
429	'A' program object verifies.
430	'A' program object does not verify.
431	Unable to copy out of a pointer file.
432	'A' item-name used in program-file dictionary, compile aborted.
520	What?........

No.	*Description*
521	Too many characters in word to block.
522	Block-convert file missing or improperly defined.
523	Block output would exceed page width.
524	The letter 'A' is not in the BLOCK-CONVERT file.
525	Input character 'A' is improperly formatted in BLOCK-CONVERT file.
530	Already logged on.
531	Process roadblocked.
532	Illegal user id.
533	Logon successful.
534	Logoff successful.
535	Illegal line number.
536	Already logged off.
550	A required numeric parameter is missing or invalid.
551	Specify number of lines to skip.
552	Item 'A' has invalid format.
630	'STOP' in effect. Use 'RESUME'.
631	Spooler is waiting for printer cable to be attached.
632	Spooler is waiting because the printer is off-line.
633	Spooler is waiting for the tape/diskette to be detached.
634	Spooler is waiting for the printer to be detached.
635	Spooler is waiting because the tape/diskette is off-line.
636	There was a parity error on writing a spooled file.
637	The spooler needs the next reel of tape/diskette to continue.
638	The spooler is writing a file on tape/diskette.
640	The spooler is printing a file on the printer.
641	Hold file #A added;
644	An open file for line #A is being processed.
645	A closed file for line #A is being processed.
646	The current job has been aborted.
651	Spooler is not active.
652	Too many pages.
653	No file being output or file originated on another line.
654	Illegal output string length.
655	Not attached.
656	End of spool queue.
657	Not a hold file.
658	Illegal number, use SP-STATUS.
659	Line printer ready.
660	Insufficient privileges; or device is attached to a spooler.
700	Run-time F-correlative abort.
701	Invalid function correlative definition : A

No.	Description
705	Illegal conversion code : 'A'
706	The translate conversion-code : A is illegal.
708	'A' cannot be converted.
781	'A' added
782	'A' updated
783	'A' deleted
800	Formatting complete.
801	Diskette/tape device not selected.
802	A items dumped.
803	A item(s) loaded.
805	A items copied.
806	A items updated.
810	Options: I — International date format (DD-MM-YY) U — U.S.A date format (MM-DD-YY) Enter I or U +
811	Date is now in International format (DD-MM-YY).
812	Date is now in U.S.A Format (MM-DD-YY).
813	Date format unchanged.
816	End of Account.
819	File not found.
830	Process left unfinished. Need some disk space before trying any other process. To make some disk space, you can delete some obsolete records, files, or accounts.
831	Please: — Logoff this terminal — Log back on and delete the above unfinished account — Then delete some additional files or accounts to make more room before trying the process again.
870	Running the PICK O/S version — A
950	Linkfield error — group at A — frame A links: A A A
951	Illegal forward link group at A frame A links A A A
952	Illegal backward link group at A frame A links A A A
953	Should link back to: group at A frame A links A A A
954	A New error items created in DICT 'TSYM'
990	Error in ABS-dump frame limits specifications.
992	A item(s) have been restored.
993	Account name must be specified.
999	Core Lines PCBO WSstart WSsize Sysbase/Mod/Sep Maxfid Avail. Overflow A A A A A A A A A A

No.	Description
1000	Which attributes ?
1001	Coupled set specification error.
1002	Window and tag connectives not allowed.
1003	Dictionary attribute 13 improperly formatted.
1011	Error in the selection processor. Call your system software support group.
1050	That is an obsolete BASIC verb (RUN or CATALOG).
1051	That is a program catalogued under pre-R80 protocols. Please catalogue the program again.
1059	The device is not configured.
1060	This option is not currently supported.
1061	Diskette device not set.
1070	Half-inch tape set.
1071	Cartridge tape set.
1072	Diskette set.
1074	There are no diskette devices configured on the system.
1075	No device present.
1080	Bit 8 is turned off (being stripped off).
1081	Bit 8 is turned on (not being stripped off).
1099	Hold entry #
1100	Start code locked.
1101	Null printer number.
1102	Printer number too big.
1103	No form number.
1104	Illegal character.
1105	Printer must be stopped.
1106	Form number too big, it must be less than 126.
1107	Too many pages in the page skip. Must be less than 10.
1108	Negative number.
1109	Too many print files.
1110	Illegal printer type, it must be S.
1111	Illegal line number.
1112	Illegal parallel printer number.
1113	Illegal serial printer number.
1114	The device or line which you specified is being used as another printer on system.
1115	Allocation attempted on an uninitialized printer.
1116	There is no job enqueued for output on the forms that you specified. Alignment is not possible.
1117	Your align was aborted by someone. Start the align process over.
1118	The printer control block has been initialized, and the printer has been started.

No.	*Description*
1119	You are attempting to start printer A on line A, which is not stopped.
1120	You must not start a printer on the spooler line.
1121	You are improperly logged on.
1122	Your output specification is no output. Reassign your line if you wish to output a hold file.
1123	Line #A is already logged on.
1126	Printer #A control block initialized.
1127	Illegal printer number, must be 0–7.
1129	A form queue elements unlinked.
1130	PRINTER LIST ELEMENTS Stat lk ln Curpos Begfid Cp Fo Frms Date Time Acct
1131	SPOOLER ENTRIES Entry Forms No. Stat Lk Ln Statuses Copies Que Frames Date Time Account
1132	A queue elements.
1133	A frames in use.
1134	Printer assignments. Printer Output queues Page Dev or Status Type Number Page Line #
1135	A form queue #
1140	Your open files were closed.
1141	Line Status Cop Form # ies #
1143	Align terminated; printer stopped.
1144	The tape/diskette is in use.
1145	Illegal specification number A.
1147	Not attached.
1148	Tapeout terminated because of assign T or null assignment.
1149	Report this error condition to your system support group.
1150	There is something wrong with the syntax of your verb's options.
1151	Entry # A
1160	Your output specification is no output. Reassign your line if you wish to output a hold file.
1161	End of requested print files.
1162	End of print file control block.
1169	Illegal printer number. Must be between 0 and 7 inclusive.
1170	Printer #A set to stop
1171	and is inactive.

No.	Description
1172	But is still active.
1173	Printer #A control block cleared and initialized.
1174	Is unallocated.
1176	Serial printer #A has been deleted, and its process sent to logon.
1177	Printer #A is inactive.
1178	The job being output on printer #A is not your print file.
1179	Job aborted on printer #A
1180	Print file #A was not unlinked because it is being output.
1181	Print file #A was not unlinked because it is unused.
1182	Print file #A was not unlinked because it is not spooled.
1183	Print file #A was not created on the account onto which you are now logged.
1184	Print file #A was unlinked and is available as a hold file.
1200	The spooler is inactive.
1201	The spooler is active.
1202	Needs to start printers.
1203	Needs to log disk errors.
1209	The control block for printer #A is in an ambiguous state. Delete the printer from the spooler system.
1210	Printer #A is A
1211	unallocated.
1212	Serial
1213	parallel
1214	, inactive+
1215	, active+
1216	, stopped+
1217	, and on line.
1218	, and off line.
1221	The printer is defined as a parallel printer.
1222	The printer is running on line A.
1229	Print file being output is element A, A
1230	Open file for line # A
1231	Closed file for line # A
1232	Generated on account A
1233	, which is A frames long.
1234	And the output is choked.
1235	.
1239	Erroneously, the printer has no output queues assigned to it.
1240	Assigned output queues: A
1241	, A
1242	, A
1243	The number of inter-job pages to eject is A.

PICK BASIC error messages

No.	Description
B1	Run-time abort at line A
B10	Line A variable has not been assigned a value; zero used.
B11	Line A tape/diskette record truncated to tape/diskette record length.
B12	Line A file has not been opened.
B13	Line A null conversion code is illegal; no conversion done.
B14	Line A bad stack descriptor
B15	Line A illegal opcode: A
B16	Line A non-numeric data when numeric required; zero used.
B17	Line A array subscript out-of-range
B18	Line A attribute number less than 1 is illegal.
B19	Line A illegal pattern.
B20	Line A col1 or col2 used prior to executing a field statement; zero used.
B21	Line A MATREAD: number of attributes exceeds vector size.
B22	Called program is not a subroutine.
B24	Line A divide by zero illegal; zero used.
B25	Program 'A' has not been catalogued.
B26	Line A 'UNLOCK A' attempted before LOCK.
B27	Line A RETURN executed with no GOSUB.
B29	Calling program must be CATALOGed.
B32	Line A page heading exceeds maximum of 1400 characters.
B33	Line A precision declared in subprogram 'A' is different from that declared in the mainline program.
B34	Line A file variable used where string expression expected.
B100	Line A compilation aborted; no object code produced.
B101	Line A Missing "END", "NEXT", "WHILE", "UNTIL", "REPEAT" or "ELSE"; compilation aborted, no object code produced.
B102	Line A bad statement.
B103	Line A label 'A' is missing.
B104	Line A label 'A' is doubly defined.
B105	Line A 'A' has not been dimensioned.
B106	Line A 'A' has been dimensioned and used without subscripts.
B107	Line A "ELSE" clause missing.
B108	Line A "NEXT" statement missing.
B109	Line A variable missing in "NEXT" statement.
B110	Line A "END" statement missing.
B111	Line A "UNTIL" or "WHILE" missing in "LOOP" statement.
B112	Line A "REPEAT" missing in "LOOP" statement.
B113	Line A terminator missing.

No.	*Description*
B114	Line A maximum number of variables exceeded.
B115	Line A label 'A' is used before the equate statement.
B116	Line A label 'A' is used before the common statement.
B117	Line A label 'A' is missing a subscript list.
B118	Line A label 'A' is the object of an equate statement and is missing.
B119	Line A Warning — precision value out of range — ignored.
B120	Line A Warning — multiple precision statements — ignored.
B121	Line A label 'A' is a constant and can not be written into.
B122	Line A label 'A' is improper type.
B123	The program contains an unrationalizable equate.
B124	Line A label 'A' has literal subscripts out of range.
B125	Line A label 'A' has a jump greater than 32K bytes.
B126	Object code exceeds 64K.
B127	Object code and symbol table exceed 64K.
B128	Line A label 'A' equated array subscript out of range.
B154	'FOR' statement with no 'NEXT' statement.
B199	Format error in source file definition.
B209	Line A file is update protected.
B210	Line A file is access protected.

B Table of Prime Numbers

1	2	3	5	7	11	13
17	19	23	29	31	37	41
43	47	53	59	61	67	71
73	79	83	89	97	101	103
107	109	113	127	131	137	139
149	151	157	163	167	173	179
181	191	193	197	199	211	223
227	229	233	239	241	251	257
263	269	271	277	281	283	293
307	311	313	317	331	337	347
349	353	359	367	373	379	383
389	397	401	409	419	421	431
433	439	443	449	457	461	463
467	479	487	491	499	503	509
521	523	541	547	557	563	569
571	577	587	593	599	601	607
613	617	619	631	641	643	647
653	659	661	673	677	683	691
701	709	719	727	733	739	743
751	757	761	769	773	787	797
809	811	821	823	827	829	839
853	857	859	863	877	881	883
887	907	911	919	929	937	941
947	953	967	971	977	983	991
997	1009	1013	1019	1021	1031	1033
1039	1049	1051	1061	1063	1069	1087
1091	1093	1097	1103	1109	1117	1123
1129	1151	1153	1163	1171	1181	1187
1193	1201	1213	1217	1223	1229	1231
1237	1249	1259	1277	1279	1283	1289
1291	1297	1301	1303	1307	1319	1321
1327	1361	1367	1373	1381	1399	1409
1423	1427	1429	1433	1439	1447	1451

1453	1459	1471	1481	1483	1487	1489
1493	1499	1511	1523	1531	1543	1549
1553	1559	1567	1571	1579	1583	1597
1601	1607	1609	1613	1619	1621	1627
1637	1657	1663	1667	1669	1693	1697
1699	1709	1721	1723	1733	1741	1747
1753	1759	1777	1783	1787	1789	1801
1811	1823	1831	1847	1861	1867	1871
1873	1877	1879	1889	1901	1907	1913
1931	1933	1949	1951	1973	1979	1987
1993	1997	1999	2003	2011	2017	2027
2029	2039	2053	2063	2069	2081	2083
2087	2089	2099	2111	2113	2129	2131
2137	2141	2143	2153	2161	2179	2203
2207	2213	2221	2237	2239	2243	2251
2267	2269	2273	2281	2287	2293	2297
2309	2311	2333	2339	2341	2347	2351
2357	2371	2377	2381	2383	2389	2393
2399	2411	2417	2423	2437	2441	2447
2459	2467	2473	2477	2503	2521	2531
2539	2543	2549	2551	2557	2579	2591
2593	2609	2617	2621	2633	2647	2657
2659	2663	2671	2677	2683	2687	2689
2693	2699	2707	2711	2713	2719	2729
2731	2741	2749	2753	2767	2777	2789
2791	2797	2801	2803	2819	2833	2837
2843	2851	2857	2861	2879	2887	2897
2903	2909	2917	2927	2939	2953	2957
2963	2969	2971	2999	3001	3011	3019
3023	3037	3041	3049	3061	3067	3079
3083	3089	3109	3119	3121	3137	3163
3167	3169	3181	3187	3191	3203	3209
3217	3221	3229	3251	3253	3257	3259
3271	3299	3301	3307	3313	3319	3323
3329	3331	3343	3347	3359	3361	3371
3373	3389	3391	3407	3413	3433	3449
3457	3461	3463	3467	3469	3491	3499
3511	3517	3527	3529	3533	3539	3541
3547	3557	3559	3571	3581	3583	3593
3607	3613	3617	3623	3631	3637	3643
3659	3671	3673	3677	3691	3697	3701
3709	3719	3727	3733	3739	3761	3767
3769	3779	3793	3797	3803	3821	3823
3833	3847	3851	3853	3863	3877	3881
3889	3907	3911	3917	3919	3923	3929

3931	3943	3947	3967	3989	4001	4003
4007	4013	4019	4021	4027	4049	4051
4057	4073	4079	4091	4093	4099	4111
4127	4129	4133	4139	4153	4157	4159
4177	4201	4211	4217	4219	4229	4231
4241	4243	4253	4259	4261	4271	4273
4283	4289	4297	4327	4337	4339	4349
4357	4363	4373	4391	4397	4409	4421
4423	4441	4447	4451	4457	4463	4481
4483	4493	4507	4513	4517	4519	4523
4547	4549	4561	4567	4583	4591	4597
4603	4621	4637	4639	4643	4649	4651
4657	4663	4673	4679	4691	4703	4721
4723	4729	4733	4751	4759	4783	4787
4789	4793	4799	4801	4813	4817	4831
4861	4871	4877	4889	4903	4909	4919
4931	4993	4937	4943	4951	4957	4967
4969	4973	4987	4993	4999	5003	5009
5011	5021	5023	5039	5051	5059	5077
5081	5087	5099	5101	5107	5113	5119
5147	5153	5167	5171	5179	5189	5197
5209	5227	5231	5233	5237	5261	5273
5279	5281	5297	5303	5309	5323	5333
5347	5351	5381	5387	5393	5399	5407
5413	5417	5419	5431	5437	5441	5443
5449	5471	5477	5479	5483	5501	5503
5507	5519	5521	5527	5531	5557	5563
5569	5573	5581	5591	5623	5639	5641
5647	5651	5653	5657	5659	5669	5683
5689	5693	5701	5711	5717	5737	5741
5743	5749	5779	5783	5791	5801	5807
5813	5821	5827	5839	5843	5849	5851
5857	5861	5867	5869	5879	5881	5897
5903	5923	5927	5939	5953	5981	5987
6007	6011	6029	6037	6043	6047	6053
6067	6073	6079	6089	6091	6101	6113
6121	6131	6133	6143	6151	6163	6173
6197	6199	6203	6211	6217	6221	6229
6247	6257	6263	6269	6271	6277	6287
6299	6301	6311	6317	6323	6329	6337
6343	6353	6359	6361	6367	6373	6379
6389	6397	6421	6427	6449	6451	6469
6473	6481	6491	6521	6529	6547	6551
6553	6563	6569	6571	6577	6581	6599
6607	6619	6637	6653	6659	6661	6673

6679	6689	6691	6701	6703	6709	6719
6733	6737	6761	6763	6779	6781	6791
6793	6803	6823	6827	6829	6833	6841
6857	6863	6869	6871	6883	6889	6907
6911	6917	6947	6949	6959	6961	6967
6971	6977	6983	6991	6997	7001	7013
7019	7027	7039	7043	7057	7069	7103
7109	7121	7127	7129	7151	7159	7177
7187	7193	7207	7211	7213	7219	7229
7237	7243	7247	7253	7283	7297	7307
7309	7321	7331	7333	7349	7351	7369
7393	7411	7417	7433	7451	7457	7459
7477	7481	7487	7489	7499	7507	7517
7523	7529	7537	7541	7547	7549	7559
7561	7573	7577	7583	7589	7591	7603
7607	7621	7639	7643	7649	7669	7673
7681	7687	7691	7699	7703	7717	7723
7727	7741	7753	7757	7759	7789	7793
7817	7823	7829	7841	7853	7867	7873
7877	7879	7883	7901	7907	7919	7927
7933	7937	7949	7951	7963	7993	8009
8011	8017	8039	8053	8059	8069	8081
8087	8089	8093	8101	8111	8117	8123
8147	8161	8167	8171	8179	8191	8209
8219	8221	8231	8233	8237	8243	8263
8269	8273	8287	8291	8293	8297	8311
8317	8329	8353	8363	8369	8377	8387
8389	8419	8423	8429	8431	8443	8447
8461	8467	8501	8513	8521	8527	8537
8539	8543	8563	8573	8581	8597	8599
8609	8623	8627	8629	8641	8647	8663
8669	8677	8681	8689	8693	8699	8707
8713	8719	8731	8737	8741	8747	8753
8761	8779	8783	8803	8807	8819	8821
8831	8837	8839	8849	8861	8863	8867
8887	8893	8923	8929	8933	8941	8951
8963	8969	8971	8999	9001	9007	9011
9013	9029	9041	9043	9049	9059	9067
9091	9103	9109	9127	9133	9137	9151
9157	9161	9173	9181	9187	9199	9203
9209	9221	9227	9239	9241	9257	9277
9281	9283	9293	9311	9319	9323	9337
9341	9343	9349	9371	9377	9391	9397
9403	9413	9419	9421	9431	9433	9437
9439	9461	9463	9467	9473	9479	9491

9497	9511	9521	9533	9539	9547	9551
9587	9601	9613	9619	9623	9629	9631
9643	9649	9661	9677	9679	9689	9697
9719	9721	9733	9739	9743	9749	9767
9769	9781	9787	9791	9803	9811	9817
9829	9833	9839	9851	9857	9859	9871
9883	9887	9901	9907	9923	9929	9931
9941	9949	9967	9973	10007		

C TCL Verbs and General Commands

Alphabetical list

`:ABSLOAD`	Reloads the ABS frames from a `FILE-SAVE` tape
`:FILELOAD`	Reloads the file system from a `FILE-SAVE` tape
`:STARTSPOOLER`	Totally re-initializes spooler after serious system or spooler problems. Should only be used as a last resort
`:SWD`	Switches E-pointers to D-pointers
`:SWE`	Switches D-pointers to E-pointers
`:SWX`	Switches second character of attribute 1 to an X
`:SWZ`	Switches second character of attribute 1 to a Z
`ACCOUNT-RESTORE`	Restores an account from a device
`ACCOUNT-SAVE`	Saves the full contents of a user account to a device
`ADDD`	Adds two decimal numbers together
`ADDX`	Adds two hexadecimal numbers together
`BASIC`	Initiates the compilation of a BASIC program
`BLOCK-PRINT`	Outputs strings of characters in a large block print form
`CATALOG`	Creates a reference to the compiled program in the user's MD which enables the program to be executed merely by using the program name
`CHARACTERS`	Prints a continuous loop of the ASCII character set. Can only be stopped by the `BREAK` key or `CTRL/C`
`CHARGE-TO`	Specifies a project name to which future charges for system usage are to be made
`CHARGES`	Displays the system usage statistics for a logon session

`CHECK-SUM`	Generates checksums for specified file items
`CLEAR-FILE`	Clears out the items from the dictionary or data portion of a specified file
`COMPARE`	Compares two items and highlights the differences
`COMPILE`	Initiates the compilation of a BASIC program
`COPY`	Copies specified items of a file to a device or a different file
`COPY-LIST`	Copies a previously saved list to a different file or item list
`COUNT`	Displays a count of the number of items that meet a specified criterion
`CREATE-ACCOUNT`	Creates a new user account
`CREATE-FILE`	Creates a new file (dictionary, data or both) within the user account
`CT`	Copies specified items to the screen or printer
`DECATALOG`	Reversal of the `CATALOG` command which also removes the object code. To reuse a program which has been decatalogued it will have to be recompiled
`DELETE`	Deletes a specified list of items from a specified file
`DELETE-ACCOUNT`	Deletes a user account and all its files
`DELETE-FILE`	Deletes a specified file (dictionary, data or both) from a user account
`DELETE-LIST`	Removes an item list from the file `POINTER-FILE`
`DIVD`	Divides two decimal numbers
`DIVX`	Divides two hexadecimal numbers
`DTR`	Converts a decimal number to a specified radix (base)
`DUMP`	Dumps the data contents of a specified frame
`ECHO`	Toggles the echo of the characters typed in from the keyboard to the screen. Each `ECHO` causes the characters to be displayed or not displayed, dependent on the previous state
`ED`	Initiates the line editor
`EDIT`	Invokes the line editor (as with `ED`)
`EDIT-LIST`	Activates the editor on a saved list

EXCHANGE	Switches the item-id of two items leaving their contents unchanged
FILE-SAVE	Saves the entire contents of the system to tape
FLUSH	Flushes internal computer memory to disk, updating the affected files
GET-LIST	Retrieves an existing list
GROUP	Displays the base frame-id of each group in a specified file, giving its item-ids and its size
HASH-TEST	Displays the item distribution of a specified file using a test modulo entered by the user
ISTAT	Displays the item distribution of a specified file based on its actual distribution
ITEM	Displays group statistics for the group a specified item-id hashes to
LIST	Outputs the contents of the items in a file in the sequence in which they are stored
LIST-FILE-STATS	Produces a report of statistics of the files saved by the latest FILE-SAVE or ACCOUNT-SAVE commands
LIST-ITEM	Lists the contents of a selected list of items
LIST-LABEL	Outputs the specified contents of selected items in label format
LIST-LOCKS	Displays the location of locked groups
LISTABS	Lists the current spooler assignments for each port
LISTACC	Produces a report from the system accounting file
LISTCONN	Displays the connectives in a specified file
LISTDICT	Displays the contents of the dictionary items of a specified file
LISTFILES	Displays a list of all the files and Q-pointers in the user's account
LISTPEQS	Lists all the current spooler entries
LISTPROCS	Lists the PROCs in a specified file
LISTPTR	Lists the current status information of all devices controlled by the spooler
LISTU	Lists the users logged on

LISTUSERS	Lists the users logged on
LISTVERBS	Lists all the verbs in the specified file – defaults to MD
LOCK-FRAME	Locks a specified frame into memory until unlocked by UNLOCK-FRAME
LOGOFF	Logs off a specified channel
LOGON	Logs a specified channel onto a specified account
LOGTO	Logs to a specified account
MESSAGE	Sends a message
MLIST	Produces a formatted assembly source code listing
MLOAD	Loads assembled object code
MSG	Sends a message
MULD	Multiplies two decimal numbers
MULX	Multiplies two hexadecimal numbers
MVERIFY	Verifies assembled object code
OFF	Logs off the system
PASSWORD	Sets a password for a specified account
POVF	Displays the available frames
QSELECT	Creates a select list from each of the attributes of an item in a file
RECOVER-FD	Recovers an item deleted via an FD command. It must *immediately* follow the FD else the item will be lost
REFORMAT	Enables selected items in a specified file to be output in a different format, i.e. with a different sequence of attributes, to that held on the original file
RTD	Converts radix (base) to decimal
RUN	Activates a compiled BASIC program
RUNOFF	Invokes the RUNOFF processor on a specified file and item
S-DUMP	Copies selected items to a device in a sorted sequence
SAVE-LIST	Saves a list of items in a file, usually POINTER-FILE, from the results of the previous SELECT or SSELECT commands

SEL-RESTORE	Restores selected items or files
SELECT	Creates a list of items meeting specified selection criteria in random sequence
SET-BAUD	Sets the baud rate for a specified port
SET-DATE	Sets the system date to that specified
SET-FILE	Sets a Q-pointer in the item QFILE of the user's MD
SET-FLOPPY	Directs spooled output from normal spooler 'tape' commands to the floppy disk
SET-HALF	Directs subsequent spooled output using 'tape' commands to the ½-inch reel-to-reel tape
SET-SCT	Directs spooled output using normal 'tape' commands to ¼-inch cartridge tape
SET-TERM	Sets the default terminal and printer characteristics
SET-TIME	Sets the current system time
SLEEP	Suspends the terminal for a specified period (particularly useful in PROCs for rolling demonstrations)
SORT	Outputs the specified contents of a specified file in a specified sorted sequence
SORT-ITEM	Displays the contents of selected items in the sorted sequence specified
SORT-LABEL	Outputs selected attributes of selected items in label format in a specified sequence
SP-ASSIGN	Sets a spooler output assignment which remains in effect until changed by a further SP-ASSIGN
SP-CLOSE	Closes a print file previously opened by an SP-OPEN command
SP-EDIT	Enables access to the entries in the spool queue to facilitate changes to their status and processing to be made
SP-KILL	Aborts the current spool process. It can also be used to remove a device from the control of the spooler
SP-OPEN	Keeps access to the spooler open to enable a number of reports to be printed together. Must be closed by SP-CLOSE
SP-STATUS	Displays the status of all devices controlled by the spooler

SP-TAPEOUT	Converts reports spooled to 'tape' back onto the spool queue
SREFORMAT	Enables selected items in a specified file to be output in a different format, i.e. with a different sequence of attributes, to that held on the original file and enables these new items to be held in a sorted sequence
SSELECT	Creates a list in sorted sequence from the selected items from a specified file
STARTPTR	Initializes the use of a printer
STAT	Outputs statistics of the selected items of a specified file
STOPPTR	Stops the printer when it has completed the report in the process of being printed
SUBD	Subtracts two decimal numbers
SUBX	Subtracts two hexadecimal numbers
SUM	Adds together the contents of a specified attribute in selected items in a file
T-ATT	Attaches the tape device and assigns the specified block length
T-BCK	Moves the tape back a specified number of records
T-CHK	Checks the specified backup medium for parity errors
T-DET	Detaches the tape device
T-DUMP	Copies to a device all selected items
T-EOD	Moves the tape forward to the end of data
T-EOF	Moves the tape to the end of the current file
T-FWD	Moves the tape forward a specified number of files
T-LOAD	Copies from a device all selected items to a file
T-RDLBL	Displays the contents of the tape label
T-READ	Displays the contents of the next 'tape' record
T-REW	Rewinds tape device to beginning
T-SPACE	Moves the tape forward a specified number of records
T-WEOF	Writes an end-of-file mark

T-WTLBL	Writes a tape label
TERM	Displays and sets user terminal and printer characteristics
TIME	Displays current system date and time
UNLOCK-FRAME	Removes previous memory lock on a frame made with the LOCK-FRAME command
VERIFY-SYSTEM	Verifies the state of the system and displays those frames which do not check against a table held in ERRMSG
WHAT	Produces a system status display with information on memory, disk space, users and spooler
WHERE	Displays which ports are in use
WHO	Displays the port number and account being used by the user

Listed by function

System accounting

CHARGE-TO	Specifies a project name to which future charges for system usage are to be made
CHARGES	Displays the system usage statistics for a logon session
LISTACC	Produces a report from the system accounting file

ACCESS

COPY-LIST	Copies a previously saved list to a different file or item list
COUNT	Displays a count of the number of items that meet a specified criteria
DELETE-LIST	Removes an item list from the file POINTER-FILE
EDIT-LIST	Activates the editor on a saved list
GET-LIST	Retrieves an existing list
LIST	Outputs the contents of the items in a file in the sequence in which they are stored

`LIST-LABEL`	Outputs the specified contents of selected items in label format
`QSELECT`	Creates a select list from each of the attributes of an item in a file
`REFORMAT`	Enables selected items in a specified file to be output in a different format (i.e. with a different sequence of attributes) to that held on the original file
`SAVE-LIST`	Saves a list of items in a file, usually `POINTER-FILE`, from the results of the previous `SELECT` or `SSELECT` commands
`SELECT`	Creates a list of items meeting specified selection criteria in random sequence
`SORT`	Outputs the specified contents of a specified file in a specified sorted sequence
`SORT-ITEM`	Displays the contents of selected items in the sorted sequence specified
`SORT-LABEL`	Outputs selected attributes of selected items in label format in a specified sequence
`SREFORMAT`	Enables selected items in a specified file to be output in a different format, i.e. with a different sequence of attributes, to that held on the original file and enables these new items to be held in a sorted sequence
`SSELECT`	Creates a list in sorted sequence from the selected items from a specified file

Accounts

`CREATE-ACCOUNT`	Creates a new user account
`DELETE-ACCOUNT`	Deletes a user account and all its files

Assembler

`MLIST`	Produces a formatted assembly source code listing
`MLOAD`	Loads assembled object code
`MVERIFY`	Verifies assembled object code

Backup/restore and tape handling

`:ABSLOAD`	Reloads the ABS frames from a `FILE-SAVE` tape

`:FILELOAD`	Reloads the file system from a `FILE-SAVE` tape
`ACCOUNT-RESTORE`	Restores an account from a device
`ACCOUNT-SAVE`	Saves the full contents of a user account to a device
`FILE-SAVE`	Saves the entire contents of the system to tape
`S-DUMP`	Copies selected items to a device in a sorted sequence
`SEL-RESTORE`	Restores selected items or files
`SET-FLOPPY`	Directs spooled output from normal spooler tape commands to the floppy disk
`SET-HALF`	Directs subsequent spooled output using tape commands to the $\frac{1}{2}$-inch reel-to-reel tape
`SET-SCT`	Directs spooled output using normal 'tape' commands to $\frac{1}{4}$-inch cartridge tape
`T-ATT`	Attaches the tape device and assigns the specified block length
`T-BCK`	Moves the tape back a specified number of records
`T-CHK`	Checks the specified backup medium for parity errors
`T-DET`	Detaches the tape device
`T-DUMP`	Copies to a device all selected items
`T-EOD`	Moves the tape forward to the end of data
`T-EOF`	Moves the tape to the end of the current file
`T-FWD`	Moves the tape forward a specified number of files
`T-LOAD`	Copies from a device all selected items to a file
`T-RDLBL`	Displays the contents of the tape label
`T-READ`	Displays the contents of the next tape record
`T-REW`	Rewinds tape device to beginning
`T-SPACE`	Moves the tape forward a specified number of records
`T-WEOF`	Writes an end-of-file mark
`T-WTLBL`	Writes a tape label

BASIC

`BASIC`	Initiates the compilation of a BASIC program

CATALOG	Creates a reference to the compiled program in the user's MD which enables the program to be executed merely by using the program name
COMPILE	Initiates the compilation of a BASIC program
DECATALOG	Reversal of the CATALOG command which also removes the object code. To reuse a program which has been decatalogued it will have to be recompiled
RUN	Activates a compiled BASIC program

File and data handling

CLEAR-FILE	Clears out the items from the dictionary or data portion of a specified file
COMPARE	Compares two items and highlights the differences
COPY	Copies specified items of a file to a device or a different file
CREATE-FILE	Creates a new file (dictionary, data or both) within the user account
CT	Copies specified items to the screen or printer
DELETE	Deletes a specified list of items from a specified file
DELETE-FILE	Deletes a specified file (dictionary, data or both) from a user account
DUMP	Dumps the data contents of a specified frame.
EXCHANGE	Switches the item-id of two items leaving their contents unchanged
HASH-TEST	Displays the item distribution of a specified file using a test modulo entered by the user
ISTAT	Displays the item distribution of a specified file based on its actual distribution
LIST-ITEM	Lists the contents of a selected list of items
LISTFILES	Displays a list of all the files and Q-pointers in the user's account
STAT	Outputs statistics of the selected items of a specified file

General-purpose utilities

BLOCK-PRINT	Outputs strings of characters in a large block print form
CHARACTERS	Prints a continuous loop of the ASCII character set. Can only be stopped by the BREAK key or CTRL/C
ECHO	Toggles the echo of the characters typed in from the keyboard to the screen. Each ECHO causes the characters to be displayed or not displayed, dependent on the previous state
ED	Initiates the line editor
EDIT	Invokes the line editor (as with ED)
FLUSH	Flushes internal computer memory to disk, updating the affected files
LISTVERBS	Lists all the verbs in the specified file – defaults to MD
MESSAGE	Sends a message
MSG	Sends a message
RUNOFF	Invokes the RUNOFF processor on a specified file and item
TIME	Displays current system date and time
WHO	Displays the port number and account being used by the user

Logging on and logging off

LOGOFF	Logs off a specified channel
LOGON	Logs a specified channel onto a specified account
LOGTO	Logs to a specified account
OFF	Logs off the system

Management functions

:SWD	Switches E-pointers to D-pointers
:SWE	Switches D-pointers to E-pointers
:SWX	Switches second character of attribute 1 to an X
:SWZ	Switches second character of attribute 1 to a Z

CHECK-SUM	Generates checksums for specified file items
GROUP	Displays the base frame-id of each group in a specified file, giving its item-ids and its size
ITEM	Displays group statistics for the group a specified item-id hashes to
LIST-FILE-STATS	Produces a report of statistics of the files saved by the latest FILE-SAVE or ACCOUNT-SAVE commands
LIST-LOCKS	Displays the location of locked groups
LISTCONN	Displays the connectives in a specified file
LISTDICT	Displays the contents of the dictionary items of a specified file
LISTPROCS	Lists the PROCs in a specified file
LISTU	Lists the users logged in
LISTUSERS	Lists the users logged in
LOCK-FRAME	Locks a specified frame into memory until unlocked by UNLOCK-FRAME
POVF	Displays the available frames
RECOVER-FD	Recovers an item deleted via an FD command. It must *immediately* follow the FD else the item will be lost
SET-BAUD	Sets the baud rate for a specified port
SET-DATE	Sets the system date to that specified
SET-TERM	Sets the default terminal and printer characteristics
SET-TIME	Sets the current system time
SLEEP	Suspends the terminal for a specified period (particularly useful in PROCs for rolling demonstrations)
SUM	Adds together the contents of a specified attribute in selected items in a file
TERM	Displays and sets user terminal and printer characteristics
UNLOCK-FRAME	Removes previous memory lock on a frame made with the LOCK-FRAME command
VERIFY-SYSTEM	Verifies the state of the system and displays those frames which do not check against a table held in ERRMSG

`WHAT`	Produces a system status display with information on memory, disk space, users and spooler
`WHERE`	Displays which ports are in use

Mathematical Functions

`ADDD`	Adds two decimal numbers together
`ADDX`	Adds two hexadecimal numbers together
`DIVD`	Divides two decimal numbers
`DIVX`	Divides two hexadecimal numbers
`DTR`	Converts a decimal number to a specified radix (base)
`MULD`	Multiplies two decimal numbers
`MULX`	Multiplies two hexadecimal numbers
`RTD`	Converts radix (base) to decimal
`SUBD`	Subtracts two decimal numbers
`SUBX`	Subtracts two hexadecimal numbers

Q-pointers

`SET-FILE`	Sets a Q-pointer in the item `QFILE` of the user's MD

Security

`PASSWORD`	Sets a password for a specified account

Spooler

`:STARTSPOOLER`	Totally re-initializes spooler after serious system or spooler problems. Should only be used as a last resort
`LISTABS`	Lists the current spooler assignments for each port
`LISTPEQS`	Lists all the current spooler entries
`LISTPTR`	Lists the current status information of all devices controlled by the spooler
`SP-ASSIGN`	Sets a spooler output assignment which remains in effect until changed by a further `SP-ASSIGN`
`SP-CLOSE`	Closes a print file previously opened by an `SP-OPEN` command

SP-EDIT	Enables access to the entries in the spool queue to facilitate changes to their status and processing to be made
SP-KILL	Aborts the current spool process. It can also be used to remove a device from the control of the spooler
SP-OPEN	Keeps access to the spooler open to enable a number of reports to be printed together. Must be closed by SP-CLOSE
SP-STATUS	Displays the status of all devices controlled by the spooler
SP-TAPEOUT	Converts reports spooled to 'tape' back onto the spool queue
STARTPTR	Initializes the use of a printer
STOPPTR	Stops the printer when it has completed the report in the process of being printed

D BASIC Functions

Term	*Description*	*Section reference*
@(-n)	Screen control functions	10.4.3
@(x,y)	Cursor positioning	10.4.2
ABORT	Terminates program and returns to TCL	
ABORT {"err",p}	Terminates program and any PROC. Optionally can display message from the ERRMSG file using parameter(s) p	
ABS(n)	Returns the absolute value of the numeric expression n	10.12
ALPHA(e)	Returns value of 1 if the string e contains only alphabetic characters, otherwise it returns 0	
ASCII(e)	Returns the ASCII value of the EBCDIC string e	
BEGIN CASE	Initiates the CASE statement	10.11.3
BREAK OFF	Disables BREAK key	10.12
BREAK ON	Enables BREAK key	10.12
BREAK e	Disables BREAK key when expression e evaluates to zero; enables it when not zero	
CALL "n"	Passes control to external subroutine n which must have been catalogued	10.11.5
CASE	A means of defining multiple conditional expressions – a multiple IF statement	10.11.3

Term	*Description*	*Section reference*
CAT or :	Denotes concatenation	
CHAIN	Executes a TCL command and returns control to TCL	10.11.5
CHAR(n)	Returns the ASCII value of a numeric expression	
CLEAR	Initializes all variables to zeroes	
CLEARFILE	Performs the same function as the TCL verb. It removes all items in a specified file	10.12
COL1()	Returns beginning column position of the last FIELD statement executed	10.12.3
COL2()	Returns ending column position of the last FIELD statement executed	10.12.3
COMMON	Defines the variable list to be shared by programs and subroutines	10.11.5
COS(n)	Computes the cosine of the angle given by the expression n	
COUNT(a,b)	Counts the number of occurrences of the string b in the string a	10.10.4
CRT	Outputs information to the terminal	10.4.2
DATA	Stores data for use in subsequent CHAIN, ENTER, EXECUTE or INPUT statements	
DATE()	Returns the system date in internal format	10.12.1
DCOUNT(a,b)	Returns the number of occurrences of string b in string a and adds one to the result	10.10.4
DEBUG	Transfers control to the symbolic debugger	
DELETE	Deletes a value or item	10.6.4 and 10.10.2

Term	*Description*	*Section reference*
DIM	Defines a dimensioned array	10.7
EBCDIC(e)	Converts an ASCII expression e to EBCDIC	
ECHO	Toggles echo	10.12
ECHO OFF	Turns off terminal character echo	10.12
ECHO ON	Initiates terminal character echo	10.12
END	Terminates a program or multiline IF statement	10.11.2
END CASE	Terminates CASE statement	10.11.3
ENTER	Transfers control to another catalogued program	10.11.5
EQU{ATE}	Assigns variables or constants	10.8
EXECUTE	Executes a TCL command and returns to the program	10.11.5
EXP(n)	Returns value of e to power n	
EXTRACT	Extracts a part of a dynamic array	10.10.2
FIELD(a,b,c)	Returns a substring from the string expression a by specifying a delimiter b and its number of occurrences c	10.12.3
FOOTING	Defines the text to appear at the foot of each page of a report	10.5.1
FOR...NEXT	FOR. . .NEXT loop function	10.11.4
FOR...UNTIL	Executes a loop UNTIL a condition is true	10.11.4
FOR...WHILE	Executes a loop WHILE a condition is true	10.11.4
GOSUB	Branches to an internal subroutine	10.11.1
GOTO	Unconditional branch	10.11
HEADING	Specifies the text to appear as the heading on each page of the report	10.5.1

Term	*Description*	*Section reference*
ICONV(e,f)	Converts the expression e to internal format according to the conversion code f	10.12
IF...THEN...ELSE	A conditional structure	10.11.2
INDEX(a,b,c)	Returns the starting column position of c occurrences of string b in string a	10.12.3
INPUT	Prompts for entry from the keyboard	10.4.1
INPUT (x,y)	Prompts for input from the keyboard on the terminal at position column x row y	10.4.1
INPUTERR a	Displays message a on status line of the terminal	
INPUTNULL a	Defines character a as null character on subsequent INPUT statements	
INPUTTRAP a	Checks for character a in an INPUT statement and allows a function to be performed if found	
INSERT (a,b,c,d,e)	Inserts element e in a dynamic array specified by a,b,c,d	10.10.1
INT(n)	Returns the integer value of expression n	10.12
LEN(a)	Returns the length of the string a	
LN(e)	Returns the log of the expression e	
LOCATE	Locates a string within a dynamic array	10.10.3
LOCK n	Sets an execution lock, number n	10.9
LOOP...UNTIL	Loops until a specified condition is reached	10.11.4
LOOP...WHILE	Loops while a specified condition is true	10.11.4
MAT	Assigns array variables	10.11.5

Term	*Description*	*Section reference*
MATCH{ES} a	Validates a string against the pattern string of a	
MATREAD	Reads an item and assigns the value of each attribute to each element of the array	10.7
MATREADU	Reads an item and assigns the value of each attribute to each element of the array and sets the group (or item) lock	10.9
MATWRITE	Writes a file item from an array	10.7
MATWRITEU	Writes a file item from an array and releases the group (or item) lock	10.9
MOD(x,y)	Generates the remainder of x divided by y. The REM and MOD functions are identical	
NEXT	The statement which terminates a FOR. . .NEXT loop	10.11.4
NOT	A logic checking function where 1 is returned if true and 0 is returned if false	
NULL	Specifies no operation	
NUM(e)	Returns 1 if expression e is numeric and 0 if not	
OCONV(e,f)	Converts expression e to output format based on conversion code f	10.12
ON...GOSUB	Transfers control to a subroutine based on the value of an expression. Provides a multiple branch facility	10.11.1
ON...GOTO	Transfers control to a statement label based on value of an expression. Provides a multiple branch capability	
OPEN	Opens a file	10.6.1
PAGE	Causes a page throw	10.5.1
PRECISION n	Defines the number of decimal places	10.3

Term	*Description*	*Section reference*
PRINT	Outputs to the device selected by the PRINTER statement (defaults to the terminal)	10.4.2
PRINT ON	Enables output to a specified print file number	10.5
PRINTER CLOSE	Closes print file and sends to spooler reports produced by program	10.5
PRINTER OFF	Sends output from subsequent PRINT statements to the terminal	10.5
PRINTER ON	Directs output from PRINT statements to the printer, via the spooler	10.5
PROCREAD	Reads the Primary Input Buffer of the calling PROC	10.13.1
PROCWRITE	Writes a variable to the Primary Input Buffer of the calling PROC	10.13.1
PROMPT a	Changes the prompt character from the default of ? to a	10.4.1
PWR(e,f)	Raises e to the power of f	
READ	Reads an item from a file	10.6.2
READNEXT	Reads the next item from a select list	10.13
READT	Reads a tape record	
READU	Reads an item from a file and locks the group or item	10.9
READV	Reads a single attribute from a file item	10.6.2
READVU	Reads a single attribute from a file item and locks the group or item	10.9
RELEASE	Releases all group or item locks	10.9
REM or ! or *	Defines a comments line	10.3 and 10.12
REM(x,y)	Generates the remainder of x divided by y. The REM and MOD functions are identical	

Term	*Description*	*Section reference*
REPEAT	Terminates the DO portion of a LOOP. . .WHILE statement	10.11.4
REPLACE(a,b,c,d,e)	Replaces an element of a dynamic array	10.10.1
RETURN	Terminates the processing of a subroutine	10.11.1
RETURN TO	Terminates an internal subroutine and passes control to a specified statement label	
REWIND	Rewinds a magnetic tape	
RND(n)	Generates a random number between zero and n–1, inclusive	10.2
RQM	Terminates program's current quantum (time-slice) effecting a 'sleep' action. **RQM** and **SLEEP** statements perform the same task	10.12
SELECT	Creates a list of item-ids which, when used in conjunction with the **READNEXT** statement, provide for sequential access through a file	10.13
SEQ(a)	Converts ASCII character **a** to its numeric equivalent	
SIN(n)	Calculates the sine of angle n	
SLEEP	Terminates program's current quantum (time-slice) effecting a 'sleep' action. **RQM** and **SLEEP** statements perform the same task	10.12
SPACE(n)	Generates a string containing n spaces	10.12
SQRT(n)	Calculates the square root of n	
STOP	Stops the program	
STR(a,n)	Generates a string containing n occurrences of the character **a**	10.12

Term	*Description*	*Section reference*
SUBROUTINE	Defines a program as an external subroutine	10.11.5
SYSTEM	Enables access to certain system functions such as the TERM parameters, CPU count, etc.	10.12.2
TAN(n)	Returns the tangent of the angle n	
TIME()	Returns the current time in internal format	10.12.1
TIMEDATE()	Returns the current date and time in internal format	10.12.1
TRIM(a)	Removes excess blanks from the string a	10.12
UNLOCK n	Releases execution lock n	10.9
UNTIL	Part of the LOOP. . .WHILE and FOR. . .NEXT loops	10.11.4
WEOF	Writes an End-of-File mark on a tape	
WRITE	Writes an item from a dynamic array	10.6.3
WRITET	Writes a record to magnetic tape	
WRITEU	Writes an item on a file and unlocks the group or item lock	10.9
WRITEV	Writes an attribute to an item	10.6.3
WRITEVU	Writes an attribute to an item releasing any group or item lock	10.9

E Formatting Program

```
FORMAT
*********************************************************
*  THIS PROGRAM FORMATS A DATA/BASIC PROGRAM TO         *
*  DISPLAY BLOCK STRUCTURING BY INDENTING LINES         *
*********************************************************
*---- DEFINITIONS
10    SP = 6              ;* LEFT MARGIN COLUMN NUMBER
      ID = 3              ;* NUMBER OF SPACES TO INDENT
*---- INITIALIZATION
      SPX = SP
      LINE.NO = 0
*---- INPUT FILE NAME AND PROGRAM NAME
      PRINT; PRINT
      PRINT 'DATA/BASIC FILE NAME    - ':;INPUT FILE
      IF FILE = '' THEN STOP
      OPEN '',FILE ELSE
         PRINT 'CANNOT OPEN FILE - ': FILE
         GOTO 10
      END
      PRINT 'DATA/BASIC PROGRAM NAME - ':;INPUT NAME
      IF NAME = '' THEN GOTO 10
      NEWITEM = ''
      READ ITEM FROM NAME ELSE
         PRINT 'CANNOT FIND THAT PROGRAM'
         GOTO 10
      END
*---- GET NEW LINE, IF NONE THEN DONE
100   LINE.NO = LINE.NO + 1
      LINE = EXTRACT(ITEM,LINE.NO,0,0)
      IF LINE = '' THEN
         WRITE NEWITEM ON NAME
         PRINT; PRINT; PRINT '--DONE--'; GOTO 10
```

```
        END
        LABEL = ''
*—————  STRIP OFF LEADING/TRAILING SPACES
200     IF LINE[1,1] = ' ' THEN LINE = LINE[2,32767]; GOTO 200
210     IF LINE[LEN(LINE),1] = ' ' THEN LINE = LINE[1,LEN(LINE)-1]; GOTO 210
*—————  LOOK FOR A COMMENT ('*','!', OR 'REM')
        IF LINE[1,1] = '*' THEN GOTO 1500
        IF LINE[1,1] = '!' THEN GOTO 1500
        IF LINE[1,3) = 'REM' THEN GOTO 1500
*—————  LOOK FOR 'FOR'
        IF LINE[1,4]='FOR ' AND INDEX(LINE,'NEXT ',1)>0 THEN GOTO 2000
        IF LINE[1,4] = 'FOR ' AND INDEX(LINE,'NEXT ',1) = 0 THEN GOTO 1000
*—————  LOOK FOR 'END'
        IF LINE = 'END' THEN GOTO 1100
        IF LINE[1,4] = 'END ' THEN
           IF LINE[LEN(LINE)-4,5] = ' ELSE' THEN GOTO 1200
        END
*—————  LOOK FOR 'NEXT'
        IF LINE[1,5] = 'NEXT ' THEN GOTO 1100
*—————  EXTRACT LEADING NUMERIC LABEL
        IF LINE[1,1] MATCHES '1N' THEN
           L = 2
300        IF LINE[L,1] MATCHES '1N' THEN L=L+1; GOTO 300
           LABEL = LINE[1,L-1]
           LINE = LINE[L,32767]
           GOTO 200
        END
*—————  LOOK FOR LINE ENDING IN 'ELSE' OR 'THEN' ('IF' OR 'READ')
        X = LINE[LEN(LINE)-4,5]
        IF X = ' THEN' THEN GOTO 1000
        IF X = ' ELSE' THEN GOTO 1000
*—————  THIS IS JUST ANOTHER LINE, THEREFORE NO CHANGE
        GOTO 2000
*—————  INDENT ON SUBSEQUENT LINES
1000    SP = SP + ID
        GOTO 2000
*—————  OUTDENT ON THIS AND SUBSEQUENT LINES
1100    SP = SP - ID
*—————  OUTDENT THIS LINE ONLY
1200    SPX = SPX - ID
        GOTO 2000
*—————  PRINT WITH NO INDENTATION
1500    SPX = 0
*—————  WRITE NEW LINE
2000    NEW.LINE = LABEL : STR(' ',SPX-LEN(LABEL)) : LINE
```

```
        PRINT NEW.LINE
        NEWITEM = REPLACE(NEWITEM, LINE.NO,0,0,NEW.LINE)
        SPX = SP
        GOTO 100
    END
```

Published courtesy of Pick Systems

F PROCs for JET and RUNOFF

To use these procedures without modification, create a file called PICK.UTILITY and edit in each of the PROCs with the item-id as given in bold face at the start of each PROC.

TEXT-MENU

```
PQ
10 C ——— DISPLAY MENU
T (-1)
T (25,0),"T e x t   P r o c e s s i n g"
T
(0,3),"————————————————————————————————————————————————————————"
T (0,5),"FILE MANAGEMENT"
T (20,5)," 1 : List Text Files"
T (20,6)," 2 : Create Text File"
T (20,7)," 3 : Delete Text File"
T (0,9),"DOCUMENT MANAGEMENT"
T (20,9)," 4 : List Documents"
T (20,10), " 5 : Word Process Document"
T (20,11), " 6 : Edit Document"
T (20,12), " 7 : Copy Document"
T (20,13), " 8 : Delete Document"
T (20,14)," 9 : Print Document"
T (20,15),"10 : Merge & Print Document"
T (20,16),"11 : Runoff Document"
T (20,17),"12 : Merge & Runoff Document"
T (0,19),"PRINTER CONTROL"
T (20,19),"13 : List Printer Output"
T (20,20),"14 : Kill Printer Output"
100 C ——— INPUT OPTION
1 (0,2),"SELECT MENU OPTION        ",(19,2)
RI
```

```
RO
IP
IF #A1 G 900
IF A1 = 0 G 900
IF A1 = 1 G 500
IF A1 = 2 G 500
IF A1 = 3 G 500
IF A1 = 4 G 500
IF A1 = 5 G 500
IF A1 = 6 G 500
IF A1 = 7 G 500
IF A1 = 8 G 500
IF A1 = 9 G 500
IF A1 = 10 G 500
IF A1 = 11 G 500
IF A1 = 12 G 500
IF A1 = 13 G 500
IF A1 = 14 G 500
G 100
500 C ——— PROCESS OPTION
IF A1 = 2 [PICK.UTILITY TEXT-FILES]
IF A1 = 2 [PICK.UTILITY TEXT-CREATE]
IF A1 = 3 [PICK.UTILITY TEXT-DELETE]
IF A1 = 4 [PICK.UTILITY TEXT-LIST]
IF A1 = 5 [PICK.UTILITY TEXT-IN]
IF A1 = 6 [PICK.UTILITY TEXT-EDIT]
IF A1 = 7 [PICK.UTILITY TEXT-COPY]
IF A1 = 8 [PICK.UTILITY TEXT-DEL]
IF A1 = 9 [PICK.UTILITY TEXT-OUT]
IF A1 = 10 [PICK.UTILITY TEXT-OUT-SEL]
IF A1 = 11 [PICK.UTILITY TEXT-RUNOFF]
IF A1 = 12 [PICK.UTILITY TEXT-RUNOFF-SEL]
IF A1 = 13 [PICK.UTILITY TEXT-OUTPUT]
IF A1 = 14 [PICK.UTILITY TEXT-KILL]
T (0,23),"Press Return To Continue "+
IP:
G 10
900 C ——— END TEXT PROCESSING
HMM
PX
```

TEXT-FILES

```
PQ
10 C ——— DISPLAY SCREEN
```

```
T (-1)
T (15,0)."T e x t   P r o c e s s i n g  —  List Text Files"
T
(0,3),"————————————————————————————————————————————————————————————————"
100 C ——— INPUT OPTIONS
T (20,5),"Printer or Screen P/S S    "
T (20,6),"Printer Number       0    "
T (43,5)
RI
S1
IHS
IP
IF #A1 G 900
IF A1 = S G 500
IF A1 # P G 100
T (43,6)
S2
IHO
IP
IF #A2 G 10
RO
HSP-ASSIGN F
A2
P
500 C ——— PROCESS
T (0,18)
RO
HSORT MD USING PICK.UTILITY WITH *A0 = "TEXT*]" TEXT.FILE
TEXT.FILEDESC
H ID-SUPP HDR-SUPP
H HEADING "TEXT PROCESSING FILES — AS AT 'T'          PAGE
'PN' "
IOF A1 = P H (P
P
X
900 C ——— EXIT
(PICK.UTILITY TEXT-MENU)
```

This PROC uses the following dictionary items in the file PICK.UTILITY, the file which contains these PROCs.

Item-id	**TEXT.FILE**	**TEXT.FILEDESC**
Attr 1	A	A
Attr 2	0	11
Attr 3	File Name	Description

```
Attr  4
Attr  5
Attr  6
Attr  7
Attr  8   G1*1
Attr  9   T                T
Attr 10   15               40
```

TEXT-CREATE

```
PQ
10 C —— DISPLAY SCREEN
T (-1)
T (15,0),"T e x t  P r o c e s s i n g  –  Create Text File"
T
(0,3),"————————————————————————————————————————————————————————————————————"
100 C —— INPUT OPTIONS
T (20,5), "Text File Name"
T (20,6),"File Description"
T (37,5)
RI
S1
IP
IF #A1 G 900
T (37,6)
S2
IP
500 C —— PROCESS
T(0,18)
RO
HCREATE-FILE TEXT*
A1
H 1 51
P
IF E # 417 G 510
HED MD TEXT*
A1
STON
H10<
HI<
A2,40
H<
H<
HFI<
```

```
PH
510 C ———
X
900 C ——— EXIT
(PICK.UTILITY TEXT-MENU)
```

TEXT-DELETE

```
PQ
10 C ——— DISPLAY SCREEN
T (-1)
T (15,0),"T e x t   P r o c e s s i n g  —  Delete Text File"
T
(0,3),"————————————————————————————————————————————————————————————"
100 C ——— INPUT OPTIONS
T (20,5),"Text File Name          "
T (20,6),"Are You Sure ?  N       "
T (36,5)
RI
S1
IP
IF #A1 G 900
T (36,6)
S2
IHN
IP
IF A2 = N G 10
IF A2 # Y G 10
500 C ——— PROCESS
T (0,18)
RO
HDELETE-FILE TEXT*
A1
P
X
900 C ——— EXIT
(PICK.UTILITY TEXT-MENU)
```

TEXT-LIST

```
PQ
10 C ——— DISPLAY SCREEN
T (-1)
t (15,0),"T e x t   P r o c e s s i n g  —  List Documents"
```

```
T
(0,3),"————————————————————————————————————————————————————————————"
100 C —— INPUT OPTIONS
T (20,5),"Text File Name                   "
T (20,6),"Printer or Screen P/S S          "
T (20,7),"Printer Number        0          "
T (43,5)
RI
S1
IP
IF #A1 G 900
T (43,6)
S2
IHS
IP
IF #A2 G 10
IF A2 = S G 500
IF A2 # P G 100
T (43,7)
S3
IHO
IP
IF #A3 G 10
RO
HSP-ASSIGN F
A3
P
500 C —— PROCESS
T (0,18)
RO
HSORT TEXT*
A1
H USING PICK.UTILITY TEXT.REF TEXT.DESC TEXT.OWNER TEXT.DATE
H ID-SUPP HDR-SUPP
H HEADING " 'F15' FILE LISTING AS AT 'T'              PAGE 'PN' "
IF A2 = P H (P
P
X
900 C —— EXIT
(PICK.UTILITY TEXT-MENU)
```

This PROC assumes that the first line of the document contains a ruler and the second, third and fourth lines contain, respectively, a description of the document, the owner and date created, each of these preceded with * – the backslash asterisk tells the JET word processor to ignore the line on output. The PROC uses the following dictionary items in the file PICK.UTILITY to produce the output report.

Item-id	TEXT.REF	TEXT.DESC
Attr 1	A	A
Attr 2	0	2
Attr 3	Reference	Description
Attr 4		
Attr 5		
Attr 6		
Attr 7		
Attr 8		G1*1
Attr 9	T	T
Attr 10	15	40

Item-id	TEXT.OWNER	TEXT.DATE
Attr 1	A	A
Attr 2	3	4
Attr 3	Owner	Date
Attr 4		
Attr 5		
Attr 6		
Attr 7		
Attr 8	G1*1	G1*1
Attr 9	T	T
Attr 10	10	11

TEXT-IN

```
PQ
10 C ——— DISPLAY SCREEN
T (-1)
T (12,0),"T e x t  P r o c e s s i n g  — Word Process
Document"
T
(0,3),"————————————————————————————————————————————————————"
100 C ——— INPUT OPTIONS
T (20,5),"Text File Name"
T (20,6),"Document Name"
T (37,5)
RI
S1
IP
```

```
IF #A1 G 900
T (37,6)
S2
IP
IF #A2 G 10
500 C ——— PROCESS
T (0,18)
RO
HJET-IN TEXT*
A1
A2
P
X
900 C ——— EXIT
(PICK.UTILITY TEXT-MENU)
```

TEXT EDIT

```
PQ
10 C ——— DISPLAY SCREEN
T (-1)
T (16,0),"T e x t   P r o c e s s i n g  —  Edit Document"
T
(0,3),"————————————————————————————————————————————————————————"
100 C ——— INPUT OPTIONS
T (20,5),"Text File Name"
T (20,6),"Document Name"
T (37,5)
RI
S1
IP
IF #A1 G 900
T (37,6)
S2
IP
IF #A2 G 10
500 C ——— PROCESS
T (0,18)
RO
HJET-EDIT TEXT*
A1
A2
P
X
```

```
900 C ——— EXIT
(PICK.UTILITY TEXT-MENU)
```

TEXT-COPY

```
PQ
10 C ——— DISPLAY SCREEN
T (-1)
T (16,0),"T e x t  P r o c e s s i n g  —  Copy Document"
T
(0,3),"————————————————————————————————————————————————————————"
100 C ——— INPUT OPTIONS
T (0,5),"SOURCE"
T (20,5),"Text File Name"
T (20,6), "Document Name"
T (20,7),"Delete After Copy   N"
T (0,9),"DESTINATION"
T (20,9),"Text File Name"
T (20,10),"Document Name"
T (20,11),"Overwrite          N"
T (38,5)
RI
S1
IP
IF #A1 G 900
T (38,6)
S2
IP
IF #A2 G 10
T (38,7)
S3
IHN
IP
IF #A3 G 10
T (38,9)
S4
IP
IF #A4 G 10
S5
IH*
IF A2 = * G 110
T (38,10)
S5
IP
```

```
IF #A5 G 10
110 C ———
T (38,11)
S6
IHN
IP
IF #A6 G 10
500 C ——— PROCESS
T (0,18)
RO
HCOPY TEXT*
A1
A2
H (
IF A3 = Y HD
IF A6 = Y HO
STON
H(TEXT*
A4
H
IF A5 # * A5
H<
P
X
900 C ——— EXIT
(PICK.UTILITY TEXT-MENU)
```

TEXT-DEL

```
PQ
10 C ——— DISPLAY SCREEN
T (-1)
T (15,0),"T e x t   P r o c e s s i n g  –  Delete Document"
T
(0,3),"————————————————————————————————————————————————————————————"
100 C ——— INPUT OPTIONS
T (20,5),"Text File Name"
T (20,6),"Document Name"
T (20,7),"Are You Sure ?   N"
T (36,5)
RI
S1
IP
IF A#1 G 900
```

```
T (36,3)
S2
IP
IF #A2 G 10
110 C ———
T (37,7),"N",(36,7)
S3
IHN
IP
IF A3 = N G 10
IF A3 # Y G 110
500 C ——— PROCESS
T (0,18)
RO
HB/ADD DICT PROCLIB :DEL
STON
H'
HTEXT*
A1
H'
A2
H<
H<
P
X
900 C ——— EXIT
(PICK.UTILITY TEXT-MENU)
```

TEXT-OUT

```
PQ
10 C ——— DISPLAY SCREEN
T (-1)
T (15,0),"T e x t   P r o c e s s i n g  —  Print Document"
T
(0,3),"————————————————————————————————————————————————"
10;0 C ——— INPUT OPTIONS
T (20,5),"Text File Name"
T (20,6),"Document Name"
T (20,7),"Suppress Random Justify    N"
T (20,8), "View Mode                  N"
T (20,9),"Show Line Numbers           N"
T (20,10),"Printer/Aux/Screen  P/A/S  P"
T (20,11),"Printer Number              0"
```

```
T (46,5)
RI
S1
IP
IF #A1 G 900
T (46,6)
S2
IP
IF #A2 G 10
T (46,7)
S3
IHN
IP
IF #A3 G 10
T (46,8)
S4
IHN
IP
IF #A4 G 10
T (46,9)
S5
IHN
IP
IF #A5 G 10
110 C ———
T L(47,10),"P",(46,10)
S6
IHP
IP
IF #A6 G 10
IF A6 = G 500
IF A6 = S G 500
IF A6 # P G 110
T (46,11)
S7
IHO
IP
IF #A7 G 10
RO
HSP-ASSIGN F
A7
P
500 C ——— PROCESS
T (0,18)
RO
```

```
HJET-OUT TEXT*
A1
A2
IF A6 = P H (P
IF A6 = A H (CN
IF A6 = S H (
IF A3 = Y HR
IF A4 = Y HV
IF A5 = Y HL
P
X
900 C ——— EXIT
(PICK.UTILITY TEXT-MENU)
```

TEXT-OUT-SEL

```
PQ
10 C ——— DISPLAY SCREEN
T (-1)
T (11,0),"T e x t   P r o c e s s i n g  —  Merge & Print
Document"
T
(0,3),"————————————————————————————————————————————————————————————————————————"
100 C ——— INPUT OPTIONS
T (20,5),"Text File Name"
T (20,6),"Document Name"
T (20,7),"Printer/Aux/Screen   P/A/S   P"
T (20,8),"Printer Number               0"
T (20,10),"Merge File Name"
T (20,11),"Selection Criteria"
T (46,5)
RI
S1
IP
IF #A1 G 900
T (46,6)
S2
IP
IF #A2 G 10
110 C
T (47,7),"P",(46,7)
S3
IHP
IP
```

```
IF #A3 G 10
IF A3 = A G 200
IF A3 = S G 200
IF A3 # P G 110
T (46,8)
S4
IHO
IP
IF #A4 G 10
RO
HSP-ASSIGN F
A4
P
200 C ——— SELECTION
T (46,10)
S4
IP
IF #A4 G 10
T (46,11)
S5
IP
500 C ——— PROCESS
T (0,18)
RO
HSSELECT
A4
A5,200
STON
HJET-OUT TEXT*
A1
H
A2
IF A3 = P H (P
IF A3 = A H (CN
P
X
900 C ——— EXIT
(PICK.UTILITY TEXT-MENU)
```

TEXT-RUNOFF

```
PQ
10 C ——— DISPLAY SCREEN
T (-1)
```

```
T (15,0),"T e x t   P r o c e s s i n g   —  Runoff Document"
T
(0,3),"————————————————————————————————————————————————————————"
100 C ——— INPUT OPTIONS
T (20,5),"Text File Name"
T (20,6),"Document Name"
T (20,7),"Printer/Screen   P/S          P"
T (20,8),"Printer Number                0"
T (46,5)
RI
S1
IP
IF #A1 G 900
T (46,6)
S2
IP
IF #A2 G 10
110 C ———
T (47,7),"P",(46,7)
S3
IHP
IP
IF #A3 G 10
IF A3 = S G 500
IF A3 # P G 110
T (46,8)
S4
IHO
IP
IF #A4 G 10
RO
HSP-ASSIGN F
A4
P
500 C ——— PROCESS
T (0,18)
RO
HRUNOFF TEXT*
A1
A2
IF A3 = P H (P
P
X
900 C ——— EXIT
(PICK.UTILITY TEXT-MENU)
```

TEXT-RUNOFF-SEL

```
PQ
10 C ——— DISPLAY SCREEN
T (-1)
T (11,0),"T e x t   P r o c e s s i n g  —  Merge & Runoff
Document"
T
(0,3),"————————————————————————————————————————————————————————————"
100 C ——— INPUT OPTIONS
T (20,5),"Text File Name"
T (20,6),"Document Name"
T (20,7),"Printer/Aux/Screen   P/A/S   P"
T (20,8),"Printer Number               0"
T (20,10),"Merge File Name"
T (20,11),"Selection Criteria"
T (46,5)
RI
S1
IP
IF #A1 G 900
T (46,6)
S2
IP
IF #A2 G 10
110 C
T (47,7),"P",(46,7)
S3
IHP
IP
IF #A3 G 10
IF A3 = A G 200
IF A3 = S G 200
IF A3 # P G 110
T (46,8)
S4
IHO
IP
IF # A4 G 10
RO
HSP-ASSIGN F
A4
P
200 C ——— SELECTION
```

```
T (46,10)
S4
IP
IF #A4 G 10
T (46,11)
S5
IP
500 C ——— PROCESS
T (0,18)
RO
HSSELECT
A4
A5,200
STON
HRUNOFF TEXT*
A1
H
A2
H (F
IF A3 = P HP
IF A3 = A HCN
P
X
900 C ——— EXIT
(PICK.UTILITY TEXT-MENU)
```

TEXT-OUTPUT

```
PQ
HSP-LIST
P
```

TEXT-KILL

```
PQ
10 C ——— DISPLAY SCREEN
T (-1)
T (13,0),"T e x t   P r o c e s s i n g  –  Kill Printer
Output"
T
(0,3),"————————————————————————————————————————————————"
100 C ——— INPUT OPTIONS
T (20,5),"Printer Number   0"
```

```
T (35,5)
S1
IH0
IP
IF #A1 G 900
500 C —— PROCESS
T (0,18)
RO
HSP-KILL
A1
P
X
900 C —— EXIT
(PICK.UTILITY TEXT-MENU)
```

G Table of ASCII Codes

ASCII	*Decimal*	*Hexadecimal*	*EBCDIC*
NUL	0	00	00
SOH	1	01	01
STX	2	02	02
ETX	3	03	03
EOT	4	04	37
ENQ	5	05	2D
ACK	6	06	2E
BEL	7	07	2F
BS	8	08	16
HT	9	09	05
LF	10	0A	25
VT	11	0B	0B
FF	12	0C	0C
CR	13	0D	0D
SO	14	0E	0E
SI	15	0F	0F
DLE	16	10	10
DC1	17	11	11
DC2	18	12	12
DC3	19	13	3A
DC4	20	14	3C
NAK	21	15	3D
SYN	22	16	32
ETB	23	17	26
CAN	24	18	18
EM	25	19	19
SUB	26	1A	3F
ESC	27	1B	27
FS	28	1C	1C
GS	29	1D	1D
RS	30	1E	1E

ASCII	*Decimal*	*Hexadecimal*	*EBCDIC*
US	31	1F	1F
	32	20	40
!	33	21	5A
"	34	22	7F
#	35	23	7B
$	36	24	5B
%	37	25	6C
&	38	26	50
'	39	27	7D
(	40	28	4D
)	41	29	5D
*	42	2A	5C
+	43	2B	4E
,	44	2C	6B
-	45	2D	60
.	46	2E	4B
/	47	2F	61
0	48	30	F0
1	49	31	F1
2	50	32	F2
3	51	33	F3
4	52	34	F4
5	53	35	F5
6	54	36	F6
7	55	37	F7
8	56	38	F8
9	57	39	F9
:	58	3A	7A
;	59	3B	5E
<	60	3C	4C
=	61	3D	7E
>	62	3E	6E
?	63	3F	6F
@	64	40	7C
A	65	41	C1
B	66	42	C2
C	67	43	C3
D	68	44	C4
E	69	45	C5
F	70	46	C6
G	71	47	C7
H	72	48	C8
I	73	49	C9

ASCII	*Decimal*	*Hexadecimal*	*EBCDIC*
J	74	4A	D1
K	75	4B	D2
L	76	4C	D3
M	77	4D	D4
N	78	4E	D5
O	79	4F	D6
P	80	50	D7
Q	81	51	D8
R	82	52	D9
S	83	53	E2
T	84	54	E3
U	85	55	E4
V	86	56	E5
W	87	57	E6
X	88	58	E7
Y	89	59	E8
Z	90	5A	E9
[	91	5B	80
\	92	5C	E0
]	93	5D	90
^	94	5E	5F
_	95	5F	6D
'	96	60	79
a	97	61	81
b	98	62	82
c	99	63	83
d	100	64	84
e	101	65	85
f	102	66	86
g	103	67	87
h	104	68	88
i	105	69	89
j	106	6A	91
k	107	6B	92
l	108	6C	93
m	109	6D	94
n	110	6E	95
o	111	6F	96
p	112	70	97
q	113	71	98
r	114	72	99
s	115	73	A2
t	116	74	A3

ASCII	*Decimal*	*Hexadecimal*	*EBCDIC*
u	117	75	A4
v	118	76	A5
w	119	77	A6
x	120	78	A7
y	121	79	A8
z	122	7A	A9
{	123	7B	C0
|	124	7C	6A
}	125	7D	D0
~	126	7E	A1
DEL	127	7F	07
	128	80	04
	129	81	06
	130	82	08
	131	83	09
	132	84	0A
	133	85	13
	134	86	14
	135	87	15
	136	88	17
	137	89	1A
	138	8A	1B
	139	8B	20
	140	8C	21
	141	8D	22
	142	8E	23
	143	8F	24
	144	90	28
	145	91	29
	146	92	2A
	147	93	2B
	148	94	2C
	149	95	30
	150	96	31
	151	97	33
	152	98	34
	153	99	35
	154	9A	36
	155	9B	38
	156	9C	39
	157	9D	3B
	158	9E	3E
	159	9F	41

ASCII	Decimal	Hexadecimal	EBCDIC
	160	A0	42
	161	A1	43
	162	A2	44
	163	A3	45
	164	A4	46
	165	A5	47
	166	A6	48
	167	A7	49
	168	A8	4A
	169	A9	4F
	170	AA	51
	171	AB	52
	172	AC	53
	173	AD	54
	174	AE	55
	175	AF	56
	176	B0	57
	177	B1	58
	178	B2	59
	179	B3	62
	180	B4	63
	181	B5	64
	182	B6	65
	183	B7	66
	184	B8	67
	185	B9	68
	186	BA	69
	187	BB	70
	188	BC	71
	189	BD	72
	190	BE	73
	191	BF	74
@	192	C0	75
A	193	C1	76
B	194	C2	77
C	195	C3	78
D	196	C4	8A
E	197	C5	8B
F	198	C6	8C
G	199	C7	8D
H	200	C8	8E
I	201	C9	8F
J	202	CA	9A

ASCII	*Decimal*	*Hexadecimal*	*EBCDIC*
K	203	CB	9B
L	204	CC	9C
M	205	CD	9D
N	206	CE	9E
O	207	CF	9F
P	208	D0	A0
Q	209	D1	AA
R	210	D2	AB
S	211	D3	AC
T	212	D4	AD
U	213	D5	AE
V	214	D6	AF
W	215	D7	B0
X	216	D8	B1
Y	217	D9	B2
Z	218	DA	B3
[	219	DB	B4
\	220	DC	B5
]	221	DD	B6
^	222	DE	B7
_	223	DF	B8
'	224	E0	B9
a	225	E1	BA
b	226	E2	BB
c	227	E3	BC
d	228	E4	BD
e	229	E5	BE
f	230	E6	BF
g	231	E7	CA
h	232	E8	CB
i	233	E9	CC
j	234	EA	CD
k	235	EB	CE
l	236	EC	CF
m	237	ED	DA
n	238	EE	DB
o	239	EF	DC
p	240	F0	DD
q	241	F1	DE
r	242	F2	DF
s	243	F3	E1
t	244	F4	EA
u	245	F5	EB

ASCII	*Decimal*	*Hexadecimal*	*EBCDIC*	
v	246	F6	EC	
w	247	F7	ED	
x	248	F8	EE	
y	249	F9	EF	
z	250	FA	FA	
[	251	FB	FB	
\	252	FC	FC	SUBVALUE mark
]	253	FD	FD	VALUE mark
^	254	FE	FE	ATTRIBUTE mark
_	255	FF	FF	SEGMENT mark

H List of PICK Frames

Reproduced by courtesy of Pick Systems.

When an error occurs, it is very useful to know what PICK function is in progress. Indeed the output from WHAT, which lists the user activities, refers to these by frame numbers. Whilst this list will not hold true for all implementations it will mostly direct you to the correct function being processed.

Frame name	*Number*	*Function*
DB01	001	DEBUG TRAPS
TCL2	002	TCL
DISK2	003	FILE MANAGEMENT
TCL.INIT	004	TCL
TCL1	005	TCL
TERMIO	006	TERMIO
DISK1	007	FILE MANAGEMENT
SS1	008	NUMERIC
SS2	009	TERMIO
WRAPUP1	010	TCL
WRAPUP2	011	FILE MANAGEMENT
WRAPUP3	012	TCL
EDIT1	013	EDITOR
EDIT2	014	EDITOR
EDIT3	015	EDITOR
EDIT4	016	EDITOR
EDIT5	017	EDITOR
EDIT6	018	EDITOR
EDIT7	019	LIST-MANAGEMENT EDITOR
EDIT8	020	EDITOR
SYSTBL3	021	TABLES:DISK ERROR
GAF	022	ASSEMBLER

Frame name	*Number*	*Function*
PASS1	023	ASSEMBLER
ASTAT	024	ASSEMBLER
MACRO	025	ASSEMBLER
ALIGN	027	ASSEMBLER
PASS2	028	ASSEMBLER
GETOP	029	ASSEMBLER
ADDLAB	030	ASSEMBLER
LOADER	031	ASSEMBLER
MLIST	032	ASSEMBLER
OF2	033	OVERFLOW MANAGEMENT
OF1	034	OVERFLOW MANAGEMENT
TAPE1	035	TAPE
TAPE2	036	TAPE
TDUMP	037	SYSTEM UTILITY
EBCDIC	038	UTILITY
SORT	039	UTILITY
LOGON	040	TCL: ACCOUNTING
PROC1	041	PROC
PROC2	042	PROC
PROC3	043	PROC
PROC4	044	PROC
PROC5	045	PROC
PROC6	046	PROC
ABSL1	047	RESTORE
GLOCK	048	FILE MANAGEMENT
LOGOFF	050	TCL: ACCOUNTING
SS3	051	TERMIO
MSG	052	UTILITY
MD3	053	ACCESS
SETHDR	054	ACCESS
MD4/5	055	ACCESS
MD6	056	ACCESS
MD7/8/18	057	ACCESS
ECHECKSUBS	058	ACCESS
MD9/10	060	ACCESS
MD12	062	ACCESS
A.CORR	063	ACCESS
A.CORR1	064	ACCESS
BLOCK.LETTERS	065	UTILITY
DUMP1	066	UTILITY
DUMP2	067	UTILITY

Frame name	*Number*	*Function*
MD20X	068	ACCESS
MD19	069	ACCESS
MD20	070	ACCESS
MD300	071	ACCESS: LIST
MD310	072	ACCESS: LIST
MD125	073	ACCESS: LIST
MD128	074	ACCESS: LIST
MD126	075	ACCESS: LIST
MVVL	076	ACCESS: LIST
MD145	077	ACCESS: LIST
GOSORT	078	ACCESS: SELECTION
SUM/STAT	079	ACCESS: UTILITY
BATCH1	080	BATCH
BATCH2	081	BATCH
BATCH3	082	BATCH
BATCH4	083	BATCH
BATCH5	084	BATCH
BATCH6	085	BATCH
BATCH7	086	BATCH
BATCH8	087	BATCH
BATCH9	088	BATCH
DBY	089	DEBUG: SET Y: ARITHMETIC
CONV	090	ACCESS: CONVERSION
IDATE	091	ACCESS: CONVERSION
IDATEX	092	ACCESS: CONVERSION
ODATE	093	ACCESS: CONVERSION
MASKC1	095	ACCESS: CONVERSION
CHARGES	096	TCL: ACCOUNTING
CB2	097	ACCESS: LIST
CB1	098	ACCESS: LIST
FUNC2	099	ACCESS: CONVERSION
SAVE.LIST	100	LIST MANAGEMENT
FUNC1	101	ACCESS: CONVERSION
MD1011	103	ACCESS: SELECTION
MD1012	104	ACCESS: SELECTION
MD30	105	ACCESS: SELECTION
ISTAT	106	ACCESS: UTILITY
COPY.LIST	107	EDITOR: LIST MANAGEMENT
DELETE.LIST	109	LIST MANAGEMENT
MD147	111	ACCESS: LIST
UEX1	112	ACCESS: CONVERSION

Frame name	*Number*	*Function*
FUNC3	113	ACCESS: CONVERSION
UEX2	114	ACCESS: CONVERSION
TLOAD	115	TAPE LOAD
TAPEITEM	116	ACCESS
GOSELECT	118	ACCESS: SELECTION
MASKC2	120	ACCESS: CONVERSION
WHERESUBS	121	UTILITY
SLEEPERS	122	UTILITY
VARIOUS	123	ACCESS: CONVERSION
ISOS	124	ACCESS: UTILITY
MAIL.LABEL	125	ACCESS: LIST
SYSTBL2	126	FILE MANAGEMENT
STSTBL1	127	OVERFLOW TABLES
TABSUBS	128	TERMIO
CONV2	129	ACCESS: CONVERSION
DBBRK	131	DEBUG: SET BREAKS
DBPARSE	132	DEBUG: COMMAND PARSE
DBSYM	133	DEBUG: SYMBOL CHECK
DBDISP	134	DEBUG: DISPLAY
DBOUT	135	DEBUG: OUTPUT
DB06	136	DEBUG: RUNNING
DBA	137	DEBUG: UTILITY
DBADDR	138	DEBUG: ADDR GEN
DBDOY	139	DEBUG: RUNNING TRACE
COPY1	140	FILE MANAGEMENT
FILEUT1	141	FILE MANAGEMENT
COPY2	142	FILE MANAGEMENT
FILEUT2	143	FILE MANAGEMENT
WSPACES2	144	UTILITY
XREF	145	ASSEMBLER
CROSS	146	ASSEMBLER
ASEXT2	147	ASSEMBLER
OPEN	148	FILE MANAGEMENT
ASEXT3	149	ASSEMBLER
ASEXT	152	ASSEMBLER
TAPE3	153	TAPE
TAPE4	154	TAPE
PT2.PT	156	TAPE
DBOTH	157	DEBUG: UTILITY
SS5	158	UTILITY
SS4	159	UTILITY

Frame name	*Number*	*Function*
ARITH	160	UTILITY
NEW.EDIT2	161	SPOOLER: EDIT
TAPEHDLR2	162	SPOOLER: TAPE
EOJ.GNJ	163	SPOOLER: PRINTER
NEW.CLS	164	SPOOLER: TERMIO
WORKING.SET	165	SPOOLER: PRINTER
MSGS	166	SPOOLER
ASSIGN	167	SPOOLER
TAPEHDLR	168	TAPE
NEW.EDIT	169	SPOOLER: EDIT
LOCKS	170	SPOOLER: PRINTER
GENLPEQ	171	SPOOLER
WSPACES	172	UTILITY
GOSTOP	173	SPOOLER
PTRABS	174	SPOOLER
INIT	175	SPOOLER: INIT
INIT2	176	SPOOLER: INIT
INIT3	177	SPOOLER: INIT
START2	178	SPOOLER
START3	179	SPOOLER
TAPEHDLR3	180	SPOOLER: TAPE
LPEQS	181	SPOOLER
GETLIMS	182	SPOOLER
MSG2	183	SPOOLER
SERIALPTR	184	SPOOLER
SCHEDULE	186	SPOOLER
CONFIG	187	UTILITY
COM9	188	BASIC COMPILER
COMC	189	BASIC COMPILER
COMO	190	BASIC COMPILER
COM1	191	BASIC COMPILER
COM2	192	BASIC COMPILER
COM3	193	BASIC COMPILER
COM4	194	BASIC COMPILER
COM5	195	BASIC COMPILER
COM6	196	BASIC COMPILER
COM7	197	BASIC COMPILER
COM8	198	BASIC COMPILER
COMU	199	BASIC COMPILER
SAVE.GZ.1	200	SAVE
DDUMP1	201	SAVE

Frame name	*Number*	*Function*
DDUMP2	202	SAVE
DDUMP3	203	SAVE
DDUMP4	204	SAVE
DDUMP5	205	SAVE
DDUMP6	206	SAVE
ABSDBIN	207	SAVE: BINARY
ABSLBIN	209	RESTORE: BINARY
ABSL2	210	RESTORE
ABSL3	211	RESTORE
DLOAD1	212	RESTORE
DLOAD2	213	RESTORE
DLOAD3	214	RESTORE
DLOAD4	215	RESTORE
SEL.RESTORE	216	RESTORE
OLOAD1	217	RESTORE
GFE	218	FILE MANAGEMENT: GFEs
RECOVER	219	RESTORE
ACTIVATE	220	RESTORE
CAT.PVER	224	BASIC: UTILITY
BCALL	225	BASIC: RUN TIME
ERRMSG	226	BASIC: RUN TIME
DYNAMIC	228	BASIC: RUN TIME
BSTORAGE	229	BASIC: RUN TIME
BRP00	230	BASIC: RUN TIME
BRP01	231	BASIC: RUN TIME
BRP02	232	BASIC: RUN TIME
BRP03	233	BASIC: RUN TIME
BRP04	234	BASIC: RUN TIME
BRP05	235	BASIC: RUN TIME
BRP06	236	BASIC: RUN TIME
BRP07	237	BASIC: RUN TIME
BRP08	238	BASIC: RUN TIME
BRP09	239	BASIC: RUN TIME
BRP10	240	BASIC: RUN TIME
BRP11	241	BASIC: RUN TIME
BRP12	242	BASIC: RUN TIME
BRP13	243	BASIC: RUN TIME
BRP14	244	BASIC: RUN TIME
BRP15	245	BASIC: RUN TIME
BRP16	246	BASIC: RUN TIME
BRP17	247	BASIC: RUN TIME

Frame name	*Number*	*Function*
BRP18	248	BASIC: RUN TIME
BNF0	250	BASIC: BNF
BNF1	251	BASIC: BNF
BNF2	252	BASIC: BNF
BNF3	253	BASIC: BNF
BNF4	254	BASIC: BNF
BNF5	255	BASIC: BNF
BNF6	256	BASIC: BNF
BNF7	257	BASIC: BNF
BNF8	258	BASIC: BNF
BNF9	259	BASIC: BNF
BNF10	260	BASIC: BNF
BNF11	261	BASIC: BNF
BNF12	262	BASIC: BNF
BNF13	263	BASIC: BNF
BD:00	264	BASIC: DEBUGGER
BD:01	265	BASIC: DEBUGGER
BD:02	266	BASIC: DEBUGGER
BD:03	267	BASIC: DEBUGGER
BD:04	268	BASIC: DEBUGGER
BD:05	269	BASIC: DEBUGGER
BAUD	270	UTILITY
NEW.VERB	271	UTILITY
BD:06	273	BASIC: DEBUGGER
BD:07	274	BASIC: DEBUGGER
OPCODES	275	BASIC: RUN TIME
FILEUT3	277	FILE MANAGEMENT
DIAG3	282	ATP
POINTER.DMP/LD	288	UTILITY: DUMP/LOAD
CHECK.SUM	289	UTILITY
WP1	291	WORD PROCESSING
WP2	292	WORD PROCESSING
WP3	293	WORD PROCESSING
WP4	294	WORD PROCESSING
WP5	295	WORD PROCESSING
WP6	296	WORD PROCESSING
WP7	297	WORD PROCESSING
WP8	298	WORD PROCESSING
WP9	299	WORD PROCESSING
REFORMAT	300	ACCESS: UPDATE
MSG1	301	UTLITY: DB-MSG

Frame name	*Number*	*Function*
MSG2	302	UTILITY: LOAD-MSG
MSG3	303	UTILITY: EDIT-MSG
MSG4	304	UTILITY: SPOOL-MSG
MSG5	305	UTILITY
MSG6	306	UTILITY: TAPE-MSG
MSG7	307	UTILITY: MISC-MSG
MSG8	308	UTILITY: RESPONSE
MSG9	309	UTILITY: BDB-MSG
MSG11	311	UTILITY: ENG-MSG
02.EXIT	314	UTILITY
ID.TAPE.PT	315	TAPE OVERFLOW
HT.TAPE.PT	316	TAPE
ID.TAPE2.PT	317	TAPE: FORMAT-FLOPPY
XP.EXITS2	335	S/1
XP.EXITS1	337	S/1
MLIST2	338	ASSEMBLER
	340–372	(USED BY JET IF SUPPORTED)
COMPARE1	381	UTILITY
COMPARE2	382	UTILITY
MON.LOAD	394	
TST.LOADER	395	ASSEMBLER
ASM.UEX	396	ASSEMBLER USER EXITS
COLDDUMP	398	SAVE
SYSTEM.CURSOR	399	TERMIO

I Pick Licensees

Direct PICK Licensees

Altos Computer Systems	Altos 586-986 Altos 3068
Applied Digital Data Systems	ADDS Mentor
Archford Computer International	Pinnacle 68000 Pinnacle 68020
Aston Technology Ltd	Crystal Excel (68000) Crystal Excel 20 (68020) Crystal Excel 40 (68020)
CDI Information Systems Inc.	IBM Series 1
CIE Systems/Bonneco	C.Itoh 680 (68000) C.Itoh 680 (68020)
Concurrent Operating Systems Technology	Sequoia (68000)
Datamedia Corporation	Datamedia 932 ICL Clan
Electronique Serge Dassault	Dual 68000
Fujitsu Espana	128C (8086)
Fujitsu Microsystems of America	Fujitsu 2020
General Automation Inc.	GA Zebra (68000) GA Zebra (68020)
IBC Technologies Inc.	IBC MC68010
ICON Systems & Software Inc.	Sayo/Icon MPS 0202
Intertechnique (IN-2)	System 5000 System 8000 (68020)
Nixdorf Computer Corp.	Nixdorf 8890 VM Mainframe
Pertec Computer Corp.	Sabre (68000 Sabre (68020)

PICK Systems	PC-XT PC-AT
Rexon Business Machines	Systems based on the Intel 80286/ 80386 chip
Standard Telephone & Cable Pty.	STC M-68000
Systems Management Inc.	IBM CS 9000 IBM 43xx IBM 30xx
Tau Engineering Inc.	TAU M-68000
Toltec Computers Inc.	The Enmass System
The Ultimate Corp.	Honeywell Level 6 DEC LSI 11 DEC VAX IBM 4300
Wicat Computer of Australia Pty.	Wicat M-68000
Xmark Corp.	Turbo tower series

PICK Related Licensees

Cosmos Inc.	Revelation (a version of PICK under DOS, also available a networked version)
Prime Computer Inc.	INFORMATION (a version of PICK under their own proprietary operating system)
V-Mark Corp.	Uni-Verse (a version of PICK under UNIX)

Other PICK Suppliers

McDonnell Douglas Information Systems	Reality Sequoia

This version of PICK was originally written by Dick Pick and later became the property of Microdata, now known as McDonnell Douglas Information Systems. This version has been considerably enhanced and contains differences to those versions supplied by the direct licensees.

Glossary of Terms

ABS frame One of the frames within the first group of frames of the system known as the ABS section. These frames contain the object code of the PICK operating system.

ACCESS The information retrieval language of the PICK system.

AMC Abbreviation for Attribute Mark Count, the second attribute of the dictionary definition item, defining the attribute position.

ANSI An acronym for 'American National Standards Institute'.

ASCII An acronym for 'American Standard Code for Information Interchange'. Established by ANSI in 1963, it is one of the standards used to represent alphanumeric characters.

Abort The termination of a computer function in the event of a hardware or software malfunction.

Access time The time taken to reference a piece of information.

Account A group of logically related files defined by a single master dictionary. Can also define a user logon name.

Address A way of referencing a memory location or a part of a disk.

Algorithm A set of rules for solving a task.

Alphanumeric A string of characters which can contain any combination of letters, numbers and symbols.

Applications Software programs that perform specific tasks such as accounting, stock control, etc.

Array or **matrix** A whole set of variables identified by a single name.

Asynchronous A means of communication between terminals and the computer, sometimes referred to as 'async'.

Attribute A specific element of data, often referred to as a 'field' in other systems. This data element can be subdivided into values and subvalues.

Attribute Mark A reserved character used to separate attributes in an item and has the ASCII value 254 (hexadecimal FE).

BASIC An abbreviation of 'Beginners All-Purpose Symbolic Instruction Code', a popular and easy-to-learn programming language.

Background *See* Foreground.

Backup The means of copying the database to be able to recover its contents in the event of a hardware or software malfunction.

Base FID The first of a block of frames making up a file.

Batch A method of processing data in which work is grouped together in batches for processing, rather than each item being worked on individually in an interactive way.

Baud The capacity of a communications line, often synonymous with bits per second. Terminals and printers typically operate at a speed of 9600 baud.

Binary A method of representing numbers to the base of two using the numbers '0' and '1'.

Bit Contraction of the words 'binary digit'. This is the lowest level of data storage in the computer, each bit being represented as either a '0' or a '1'.

Bootstrap The process of starting a computer from powerup.

Buffer A place where information can be stored temporarily.

Bug An error of programming logic.

Byte A character of data made up of eight bits.

CPS An abbreviation of 'characters per second'.

CPU An abbreviation of 'central processing unit', the heart of the computer system, where processing is carried out.

CRT An abbreviation for Cathode Ray Tube and used to refer to terminals, the means of communicating with the computer.

Channel Another name for 'port', the connection on the computer that links to peripheral devices.

Checksum A clever means of verifying data by carrying out a calculation of its content and comparing the result to that expected, the expected value normally being held elsewhere on the disk.

Coldstart The procedures undertaken once the initial program load has taken place.

Command An instruction given to the computer to carry out a task.

Compiler A means of translating a source program into object form, the form which enables it to be used.

Concatenate Join together side by side without an intervening space.

Connect time The length of time that a user is connected to the system.

Conversion The processing of data in ACCESS and BASIC to convert data held in internal format to that known as external format or vice versa.

Correlative A processing function enabling values to be computed at run time rather than being held as a data element on the database. A derived value.

Cursor The means of indicating the position on a terminal at which the next input/output is expected.

D-pointer A dictionary record that defines a file.

Data The information stored in a computer.

Data dictionary A necessary requirement of any database system, which enables the structure and form of the database to be defined.

Data processing The input, output and processing of information.

Database A collection of data in an organized form, enabling ready storage and updating of information shared centrally.

Deadly embrace A situation where two or more processes control information needed by the other in such a way that no process can proceed.

Debug The process of removing errors of logic from a program.

Debugger A software tool to enable the corrections to program logic to be made. It allows programs to be executed step by step and information, such as the contents of variables, to be displayed.

Default An action or value presented automatically unless other instructions are explicitly given.

Degradation A slowing down in the response from a computer as it is given more work to perform.

Delimiter A character used to separate data elements. Some special characters, known as 'system delimiters' are used by PICK. These are attribute marks, value marks, subvalue marks and segment marks.

Diagnostics A series of routines designed to locate hardware or software errors.

Dictionary A file that holds records defining the structure of the next level file in the PICK hierarchy.

Disks Magnetic media shaped like circular discs which are used for storing information.

EBCDIC An acronym for 'Extended Binary Coded Decimal Interchange Code', a standard for representing alphanumeric characters.

Editor A program for editing data.

End user The person who ends up using the computer.

FID A contraction of the words 'frame id' denoting the logical address of the frame on the disk.

Field A single element of data, referred to in PICK as an 'attribute'.

File A collection of logically related items of data.

Firmware A series of operating instructions (software) fixed in ROM (Read Only Memory). ROM is a hardware 'chip' on a PCB (Printed Circuit Board).

Floppy disk A flexible single disk used for storing information.

Foreground Foreground is the task that has the highest priority in a situation where several tasks are run concurrently at a terminal. The other tasks are known as background tasks.

Frame The smallest element of data storage on a PICK disk – 512 bytes.

Function key A key that performs a special function.

GFE An abbreviation of 'Group Format Error', an error condition within a group of data frames.

Global variable A variable that is available to all users of a program.

Group The name given to a frame or series of linked frames in a file.

Handshaking A term which indicates that two processes involved in some kind of communication have a means of controlling and confirming the receipt of data sent by each other.

Hard copy Printed output from a computer.

Hardware The physical computer equipment.

Hashing The processing of an item-id by an algorithm to locate the position of data in a file.

Hexadecimal A method of representing numbers to the base of 16. Sometimes abbreviated to hex.

Holdfile A temporary file used to store a print file.

I/O An abbreviation of the term 'input/output', which relates to the way in which data can be input to or output from the computer.

Initialize To reset the system or a process to its starting point.

Interface A link between systems or processes. Can be either software or hardware.

Interpreter A software program that translates a program (in source or part compiled form) into machine code instructions which are then executed.

Interrupt A temporary suspension of computer activities caused for a variety of reasons.

Item A collection of logically related attributes; often referred to as a record on other systems.

Item-id A contraction of 'item identifier', the key of a file item. This record key is always stored in attribute 0.

Job A specific function made up of one or more programs run one after each other.

Justification The method of aligning data either to the right or left or, usually, both.

K Symbol for 'kilo' – a thousand. Using binary notation this works out to 1024.

Kbyte A kilobyte of memory – 1024 bytes.

Key The code by which a record is retrieved from the database.

Key in To use the keyboard to enter into the computer system.

Label An identifier made up of alphanumeric characters.

Language A programming code of a particular type, such as COBOL, BASIC, FORTRAN, or Pascal.

Line The connection between the computer and its peripheral devices, such as VDUs or printers.

Linkage The first 12 bytes of a frame used to define forward and backward links to other frames.

Local variable A variable that is only available to the specific user running the program.

Logoff The process of ending a working session on the computer.

Logon The process of gaining access to the computer.

Loop A series of program instructions which may be executed more than once before the program continues.

MD An abbreviation of 'master dictionary', the primary file for each account which defines all files, procs, verbs and pointers.

Machine code A programming language using 0s and 1s only and, hence, the lowest level programming language available.

Main memory *See* Memory.

Master Dictionary The primary file for each account which defines all files, procs, verbs and pointers.

Matrix *See* Array.

Mega A term meaning 'million'.

Mbyte One million bytes. Typically used to define the size of disk storage.

Memory (RAM) RAM (Random Access Memory) is the physical hardware capable of storing information.

Microcomputer A small computer, capable of handling more than one user.

Millisecond A thousandth of a second.

Minicomputer The next stage up from microcomputers, both in size and the number of users it can handle – often up to 12 or maybe 64 terminals.

Modulo The number of groups in a file.

Monitor The special software written for each implementation to control the input and output devices.

Numeric Comprising numbers only.

OEM An abbreviation for 'Original Equipment Manufacturer' and relates to someone who incorporates major components or subsystems from other manufacturers into their own systems.

Online The position of being connected to a system.

Option Characters enclosed in brackets to denote the provision of additional facilities.

Overflow The amount of available (unused) frames on the disk.

PC A computer system that handles only one user.

PCB Abbreviation for 'Primary Control Block', the working storage area allocated to each port.

PIB Abbreviation for 'Primary Input Buffer', the buffer in PROCs through which all data from the keyboard passes.

POB Abbreviation for 'Primary Output Buffer', used in PROCs.

PROC A means of storing a series of commands which can be initiated by a single command name.

PROM Abbreviation of 'Programmable Read-only Memory', typically used to store program instructions on an integrated circuit board.

Package A piece of software written to handle a specific task and made generally available with the purpose of many people being able to use the software with little or no modification.

Paging The process of transferring blocks ('pages') of information to and fro from disk.

Parameter A piece of information which can be given a specific value to suit the task in hand.

Pascal A popular programming language.

Password A series of characters which need to be input correctly before access to the system is provided.

Peripheral A device connected to the computer system. This could relate to VDUs, printers, magnetic tape units and so on.

Pointer An element of data that contains the address where other data resides.

Port The connection on the computer to which the terminals, printers and other peripheral devices are attached.

Privilege level A security code given to each user which can be used to limit access to certain facilities.

Processor *See* CPU.

Program A sequence of instructions, written in the programming language, to perform a given task.

Protocol A series of rules for defining the exchange of data.

Q-pointer A type of file pointer enabling alternative access to a file; often referred to as a synonym.

RAM Abbreviation of 'Random Access Memory', the physical memory of the computer system.

Record A collection of related information and known as an 'item' in PICK terminology.

Reset The same process as initialization.

Routine A small number of program instructions.

RUNOFF A text-formatting utility.

SIB Abbreviation for 'Secondary Input Buffer', used in PROCs.

SOB Abbreviation of 'Secondary Output Buffer', used in PROCs.

SYSPROG The System Programmer's account containing special facilities for managing the computer system.

SYSTEM The primary file of the PICK system which is at the top of the file hierarchy.

Scroll The process of displaying the next or previous screen of information.

Segment mark The special character used to separate items held on disk and whose value is ASCII 255, or FF in hexadecimal.

Select list A list of items that have been selected from ACCESS using the commands SELECT or SSELECT.

Separation The number of frames in a group in a file.

Software Computer programs.

Sort The means of placing information in a specified sequence according to the contents of particular parts of a record.

Spooling A technique for temporarily storing output on disk.

Stack A small area of memory allocated for holding data where information added to the stack pushes down the information already held.

Subroutine A series of instructions performed frequently that can be executed anywhere within a main program and, once performed, enable the main program to continue from the instruction immediately following the branch instruction.

Subvalue The subdivision of a value.

Subvalue mark The special character delimiting subvalues and whose value is 252 in ASCII or FC in hexadecimal.

Syntax The rules for the formulation of program and ACCESS statements.

System A term often used as synonymous with the computer, or the computer and its peripherals.

TCL Abbreviation of 'Terminal Control Language', the command language of PICK.

TTY Abbreviation for teletype.

Terminal *See* VDU.

Timeslice The number of milliseconds of processing given to each task during its processing cycle.

Transfer rate The rate at which information is transferred between peripheral devices, including disks and tapes, and main memory.

User-id A unique name given to a user to enable him to access the computer system.

VDU An abbreviation of 'Visual Display Unit', the terminal used to communicate with the system.

Validation The process of checking data to ensure its accuracy.

Value The first subdivisions of an attribute.

Value mark The character used to delimit values and whose ASCII value is 253 (FD hexadecimal).

Variable A data element that can be assigned a number of values.

Virtual memory A means of making available more memory for processing than the physical RAM available. It is achieved by using the spare space on disk and treating it as an extension of RAM.

WPM 'Words per minute'.

Winchester disk A form of disk technology, where the disk is contained in a sealed and non-removable unit.

Word processing The processing of text by use of an editor and a process to format and print the edited text.

Workspace An area of disk of memory set aside for work associated with a specific task or user.

Index

4GL products 297

A code correlative 106
A item 40
Aborting a process 128
ABS 41
ABS frames 41
ACC 3, 17, 268
  clearing down 270
ACCESS 1, 2, 38
  aborting 128
  accessing multivalues 142
  and BASIC programs 158, 221
  BREAK-ON 145
    option 147
  BY 137
  BY-DSCN 137
  BY-EXP 142
  BY-EXP-DSND 142
  control breaks 147
  COPY-LIST 159
  COUNT 153
  default report 134
  DELETE-LIST 159
  descending sort 137
  DET-SUPP 148
  EDIT-LIST 159
  features 99, 100
  FOOTING 150
  FORM-LIST 159
  GET-LIST 159
  HEADING 150
  introduction 99
  LIST 131
  LIST-ITEM 135, 137
  LIST-LABEL 150
  LIST ONLY 134
  lists 155
  multivalues 139
  options and modifiers 139
  QSELECT 159
  REFORMAT 154
  SAVE-LIST 158
  SELECT 155, 156
  selection criteria 144
  SORT 137
  SORT-ITEM 137
  SORT-LABEL 150
  specifying data for output 138
  SREFORMAT 154
  SSELECT 155, 156
  stages process 100
  STAT 154
  string search 144
  SUM 153
  summary report 148, 149
  throwaway connectives 143
  TOTAL 147
  totalling 147
  use of dictionaries 101
  wildcard 145
Access to the system 265
Account 7, 31, 37
  creating 21
  deletion 22
  renaming 280
  structure 9
ACCOUNT-RESTORE 280
ACCOUNT-SAVE 278
Accounting history reports 269
Adding new users 55
ALR Challenger 328

Altos 5
Application generators 297
Arithmetic expressions 168
Arnet COM4 module 326
Arnet PLUS4 extender 326
Arrays 186
Assembler 160
AST four-port/AT card 325
Attaching a device 275
Attribute 8, 34, 36
Attribute 0 38
Attribute mark 47
Audit trail 3
Available frames 496

Backup
  checking data 278
  frequency 273
  methods 273
  procedures 296
  tape rotation 273
Backward link 47
Backward link error 294
BASIC 2, 161, 170
  arithmetic 168
  arrays 186
  batch processing 218
  BEGIN CASE 201
  CALL 205, 206
  CASE 200
  cataloguing programs 163
  CHAIN 205
  CHAR 197
  COL(1) 217–18
  COL(2) 217–18
  COLOR 308
  COMMON 206
  COMMON area 181
  compiler option 163
  COUNT 197
  cursor control 172
  DCOUNT 197
  debug command summary 228, 229
  debugger 224
  decataloguing programs 164
  DELETE 185, 192
  DIM 186
  dynamic arrays 191
  END CASE 201
  ENTER 205
  ERROR() 205
  EXECUTE 205
  EXTRACT 192
  FIELD 217–18
  file control 180
  footings 177
  FOR...NEXT 202
  format mask 173, 179
  format source 165
  GOSUB 199
  headings 177
  ICONV 216
  IF 200
  input data conversion 215
  INDEX 217
  INSERT 192
  introduction 160
  literals 167
  LOCATE 194
  LOCK 190
  loops 202–204
  MATREAD 186
  matrix 186
  MATWRITE 186
  MATWRITEU 189
  MONO 308
  multiuser control 189
  new video attributes 173
  numerics 167
  OPEN 180
  optimization 229
  PAGE 179
  PRINT 308
  printers 176
  PROCREAD 221
  PROWRITE 221
  program file 161
    types 160
  program format 162
  READ 181
  READNEXT 219
  READU 189
  READV 182
  READVU 189
  RELEASE 189
  reserved words 167
  RETURN 199, 206
  SELECT 219

sounding the bell 176
statement conventions 167
SUBROUTINE 206
subroutines 199
substring 174
terminal control 169
terminal input 169
terminal output 171
UNLOCK 190
variables 167, 190
vector 186, 187
WRITE 183
WRITEU 189
WRITEV 183
Basic Time AT4 × 4 328
Batch processing 218
Baud rate 286
BEGIN CASE 201
BLOCK-CONVERT 17
BLOCK-PRINT 17
Booting the system 11
BP 16
BREAK 15, 268, 285
BREAK key 128, 268
BREAK-ON 145
BY 137
BY-DSND 137
BY-EXP 142
BY-EXP-DSND 142

C code correlative 110
CALL 205
CASE 200
CATALOG 163
Cataloguing programs 163
CHAIN 205
Change item 66
Changed items 46
Changing item-id 29
CHAR 197
CLEAR-BASIC-LOCKS 190
CLEAR-FILE 25
Clearing a file 25
CNTL 15
COBOL 34
Cold boot 285
Cold-start 11
COLD-START 78
COLOR verb 308
COMMON 181
COMMON area 81
Common dictionary 24
COMPARE 296
COMPILE 162
options 163
Compiling programs 161
Control breaks 147
Conversion codes 105, 106
D code 111
MC codes 116
MD code 117
ML code 117
MR code 117
MT code 118
MX code 119
MY code 119
U code 123
COPY 26, 52, 135
options 29
COPY-LIST 159
COPYDOS 315
Copying an item 26
COPYPICK 315
Correlative 105, 106
A code 106
special operands 109
C code 110
F code 112
G code 113
L code 116
multiple 125
P code 120
R code 120
S code 120
T code 121
Tfile 121
COUNT 18, 153, 197
CREATE-ACCOUNT 21
CREATE-FILE 23, 52
CREATE-FILE DATA 23
CREATE-FILE DICT 23
Create item 65
Creating a file 23
Creating a program file 161
Creating an account 21
Creating data items 26
Creating dictionary items 101
Creating user-ids 55

CRT 171
CT 19, 135
CTRL/C 128, 268, 285
CTRL/Q 128
CTRL/S 128
CTRL/X 128
Current buffer 62
Current line concept 60

D code conversion 111
D-item 39
Dartmouth BASIC 160
Data 32
Data dictionary 7, 9, 37
Data file 7, 32, 37
Database 1
  structure 7, 31
Datamedia 5
Date 285
  conversion codes 111
  format 40, 314
DC file type 16, 161
DC item 39
DCOUNT 197
Debug 15
DECATALOG 164
Decataloguing programs 164
Decimal conversion codes 117
Default reports 134
Defining character set 311
Defining keyboard 311
Degradation 49
DELETE 26, 185, 192
DELETE-ACCOUNT 22
DELETE-FILE 25, 52
DELETE-LIST 159
Delimiter 46
Descending sort 137
Descriptor table 191
DET-SUPP 148
Devcom Corporation 5
DICT 8, 31, 37
Dictionary 36
  attribute 1 102
  attribute 2 103
  attribute 3 103
  attribute 4 104
  attribute 7 105
  attribute 8 105
  attribute 9 125
  attribute 10 127
  attribute definition 102
  controlling/dependent attribute 104
  conversion attribute 105
  correlative attribute 105
  definition 38
  heading attribute 103
  item types 39
  items, structure 102
  justification attribute 3
  location attribute 103
  max length attribute 127
  synonyms 101
Digiboard Digicom COM8/COM4 328
Digigraphics Extend COM-8 card 327
DIM 186
Disk
  free space 289
    distribution 290
Disk map 41
Disk space allocation 34
Disk usage 289
Don Nelson 4
DOS to PICK 315
DUMP 294
DX item 39, 277
DY item 40, 278
Dynamic arrays 191

ECHO ON 289
ED 52, 65
EDIT 65
EDIT-LIST 159
Editor 2, 55
  basic commands 62–64
  buffers 60
  change item 65
  command summary 62–64
  create item 65
  introduction 60
  locate facility 71
  merging data 70
  prestored commands 73
  replacing data 68
  search facility 71
  wildcard 71
END CASE 162
ENGLISH 99

ENTER 205
ERRMSG 13, 15, 17
Evolution 4
EXCHANGE 29
EXECUTE 205
Execute LOGON PROC at debug 268
External subroutines 204
EXTRACT 192

F code correlative 112
FDISK 308
FFORMAT 274, 314
FID 41
Field 8, 34, 36
File
  allocation 40
  backup 281
  clearing 25
  create 23
  deletion 25
  resizing 52
  size 34
  sizing 49
  structure 34
File definition item 39
File dictionaries 101
File Dictionary 8, 31
File look up 121
File restore 12
FILE-RESTORE 78
FILE-SAVE 52, 276
Filesave 39
Floppy disk handling 274
FLUSH 14, 283, 285, 293
FOOTING 150, 177
FOR...NEXT loop 202
Form queue 79
FORM-LIST 159
FORMAT 314
FORMAT-DISKETTE 274
FORMAT-FLOPPY 274
Format masks 173, 179
Format source program 165
Formatting floppy disk 274, 314
Forward link 47
Forward link error 294
Fourth-generation language 297
Fragmentation 42
Frame 41, 46
Frame fault 43
Frame format 41, 42, 46, 47, 48
Frame size 41

G code correlative 113
General Automation 5
GET-LIST 159
GFE 293
GIRLS 4
GOSUB 199
Grand total heading 148
Group 46
Group extraction correlative 113
Group format 46, 49
Group format error 293

Handling multivalues in ACCESS 139
HASH-TEST 51, 154, 292
Hashing 46
HEADING 150, 177
Hierarchical data structure 7
Hierarchy of data 36, 37
Honeywell 4
Hostess Four Way Card 329

IBM 5
IBM PC 307
  defining the keyboard 311
  installing hard disks 334
  installing modems 334
  installing parallel printers 330
  installing serial printers 332
  installing slave printers 333
  redefining the function keys 313
  tape backup 337
  tape troubleshooting tips 338
IBM PC-AT 5, 321
  serial I/O 322
  system PPAs 331
IBM PC PICK 307
IBM PC-XT 5
  system PPAs 331
IBM serial/parallel adaptor 324
IF 200
INFORM 99
Information 5
Initial file size 41
INPUT 169
  format masks 173

INSERT 192
Integrity 273
Interactive debugger 224
  command summary 228
Internal subroutines 199
Intertechnique 4
IP 241
ISTAT 49, 154, 292
Item 7, 34, 36
  copy 26
  creating 26
  deleting 26
  distribution 49
  types 37
Item-id 8, 34, 38, 46
  changing 29

Key 7

L code correlative 116
L/RET 21
Large files 42
Length correlative 116
Limiting string length 174
Link errors 294
LIST 19, 155
  ACCESS 131
List available printer 80
LIST-FILE-STATS 276
List form queues 80
LIST-ITEM 135, 137
LIST-LABEL 150
LIST-LOCKS 190
LIST ONLY 134
List spooler entries 80
LISTABS 80, 83
  options 84
LISTFILES 16
LISTPEQS 80, 82
LISTPTR 80–81
LISTVERBS 18
Literals 167
Loading PICK on compatibles 318
LOCATE 194
LOCK 190
Logging off 14, 285
Logging on 14, 285
Logical operators 168
LOGOFF 14
Logon 2, 3
LOGTO 14
Looking around the system 16
LOOP ... UNTIL/WHILE ... DO ... REPEAT 203

M/DICT 18, 31
Mark 47
Mask conversions 116
Master Dictionary 7, 9, 31, 40
MATREAD 186
Matrix 186
MATWRITE 186
MATWRITEU 189
MAXFID 289, 294
MC conversion codes 116
MD 18, 31
  conversion code 117
Messages, sending 289
Microcode 4
Microdata 4
ML conversion code 117
Modifying the dictionary 36
Modulo 43, 49
MONO verb 308
MR conversion code 117
MSG 289
MT conversion code 118
Multiple correlatives 125
  Tfile 124
Multivalue mark 47
Multivalues 34
MX conversion code 119
MY conversion code 119

NEWAC 17, 22
NNCF 47
NPCF 47
Null value 55
Numerical format masks 174
Numerics 167

OFF 14, 285
OPEN 180
Open Architecture 5, 34
Optimizing file size 52
Options and modifiers, ACCESS 139
Overflow 49
  frames 41

P code correlative 120
Parallel printers 3, 78
Password 3, 21, 55, 265
  protection 266
PASSWORD 55, 266
Pattern matching correlative 120
PC compatibles 318
PC-AT floppy densities 314
PCB 41
Pertec Computer Corporation 5
Phantom process 78
PICK
  on IBM compatibles 318
  on IBM PC 307
  on PC-AT 321
  terminology 8
  to DOS 315
Pick and Associates 5
PICK BASIC 160
PICK, PC
  powering off 317
  software features 308
  tape backup 315
PICK Systems 5
POB 235
Pointer 9
POINTER-FILE 17, 156, 158
POVF 290
POWER-OFF 317
Powering off 14
Powering up 11
PQ item 40
Primary input buffer 234
Primary output buffer 235
Prime 5
Principles of lists 155
PRINT 169, 171
PRINT@ function 308
Print limiting 174
PRINT ON 176
Printer
  adding 84
  change for report 95
  directing output 90
  killing output 87
  problem solving 96
  removing entries 88
  restarting report 96
  stopping 85
PRINTER CLOSE 176
PRINTER OFF 171, 176
PRINTER ON 171, 176
Printing 77
Privilege level 55, 266
Privileges 22
PROC 233
  A command 242
  and ACCESS 150, 158
  and BASIC programs 221
  C command 235
  conditional branching 244
  cursor control 240
  GO command 244
  H command 236
  IF command 244
  IP command 241
  moving data in buffers 242
  P command 235
  passing parameter 238
  RI command 241
  RO command 241
  screen formatting 240
  STOFF command 239
  STON command 239
  storing in MD 233
  T command 240
  the stack 238
  use of STOPPTR 85
PROC 2, 40
  T 308
Proc buffers 234
Proc command summary 237
PROCLIB 18
Producing labels 150
Program Control Block 41
Program language convention 167
Programming language 160
PROMPT 170
Protecting SYSPROG 266

Q-item 40
Q-pointer 9, 40, 54, 74
  format 55
QFILE 58
QSELECT 159

R code correlative 120
R83 5

R84 5
RAM 1
Random access memory 1
Range correlative 120
READ 181
READNEXT 219
READU 189
READV 183
READVU 189
Real arrays 186
Reality 4
REBOOT 317
RECALL 99
Record 7, 8, 34, 36
Recover from backup 273
Redefining function key 311
Referencing illegal frame 294
Reflexive Q-pointer 58
REFORMAT 154
Relational operators 168
RELEASE 189
Removing a file 25
Removing an account 22
Removing data items 26
Reports from ACC 270
Reserved words 167
Response 49
Response time 42
Restore
  account 280
  file 282
  file save 278
  selective 283
  system generation 276
Restricting TCL access 268
Restricting TCL verbs 266
Retrieval lock 21, 31, 55, 265
  code 39, 267
RETURN 199
Reverse Polish notation 112
RI 241
Richard Pick 1, 4
RO 241
RUNOFF 3
  .BOX 258
  commands 253–255
  control codes 256
  .FILL 260
  .FOOTING 262
  .HEADING 262
  in operation 256
  introduction 252
  .JUSTIFY 260
  mailmerge technique 261
  .NOFILL 260
  output options 256–257
  .PARAGRAPH 258
  producing index 264
  .TP 260

S code correlative 120
SAVE-LIST 156, 158
Screen 170
Secondary input buffer 234
Secondary output buffer 235
Security 3, 265
  access 265
Segment 47
SEL-RESTORE 52, 278
SELECT 156, 261
Selection criteria, ACCESS 144
Selective restores 283
Sending messages 289
Separation 49
Serial printers 3, 78
Series 1 5
SET 274
SET-BAUD 286, 313, 323
SET-DATE 285, 314
SET-DATE-EUR 314
SET-FILE 58–59
SET-FLOPPY 274, 314
SET-FUNC 313
SET-HALF 274
SET-KBRD 311
SET-SCT 274
SET-TERM 286, 287
SET-TIME 285
Setting baud rate 313
Setting page length 286
Setting page width 286
Setting the device 274
Shutdown system 283
SIB 234
SMI 5
SOB 235
SORT 19, 137
SORT-ITEM 137

SORT-LABEL 150
SP-ASSIGN 90
  options 91
SP-EDIT 91, 94
  options 93
  redirecting reports 95
  restarting report 96
SP-KILL 87, 88
SP-STATUS 80, 83
Spooler 3, 286
  change printer assignment 95
  interactive edit of queue 94
  introduction 77
  manipulating the queue 91
  options handle 80
  problem solving 96
  removing entries 88
  restarting report 96
  status 80
    options 82–83
SREFORMAT 154
SSELECT 156
Stack 238
Start-up option F 12
Start-up option X 12
STARTPTR 84
.STARTSPOOLER 78, 97
STAT 154, 291
STAT-FILE 17, 276
STD 314
STOPPTR 85
String search 144
Structured programming 198
Subroutines 164
Substitution correlative 120
Subvalues 34
SUM 153
Summary reports 148
Suspend screen display 128
Synonym 54
SYS0 privilege 267
SYS1 privilege 267
SYS2 privilege 267
SYSPROG 14
SYSPROG-PL 17
SYSTEM 18, 31
System accounting 3, 55, 268
  clearing down 270
System Administrator, role 284
System close down 284
System Dictionary 7, 31, 55
System errors 293
System generation 276
System hangs 293
System shutdown 283
System start up 284

T code correlative 121
T-ATT 275
T-BCK 275
T-CHK 275
T-DET 275
T-DUMP 154, 156, 281
T-EOD 275
T-EOF 275
T-FWD 275
T-LOAD 154, 282
T-RDLBL 275
T-READ 275
T-STATUS 314
Tape handling 274
TCL 2
  restricting access 268
  SET-BAUD 313
  SET-FUNC 313
  SET-KBRD 311
TCL prompt 2
TDI Pinnacle 6
Temporary Q-pointer 58
TERM 286, 287, 333
Terminal
  characteristics 288
  type 287
Terminal control language 2
Text extraction correlative 121
Tfile correlative 121
  multiple 123
Throw a page, BASIC 179
Throwaway connectives 143
TIME 285
Time conversion codes 118
TOTAL 147
Totalling 145
Transferring data
  from DOS to PICK 315
  from PICK to DOS 315
TRW 4

U unconditional option 15
U code conversion 123
Ultimate 4
UNLOCK 190
Update buffer 62
Update lock 21, 31, 39, 265, 267
Update locking code 55
Use of control keys 128
User-id 22, 55, 266
Using special stationery 79

Variable length 1, 32
Variables 167, 188
Vector 187
VERIFY-SYSTEM 293
Virtual memory 1, 4

Warm boot 13
Warm-start 11
Wasted space 49
WHAT 289
WHERE 296
WHO 296
Work space 41
WRITE 183
WRITEU 189
WRITEV 183
WSX 41